Relations and Roles
in China's Internationalism

A volume in the SUNY James N. Rosenau series in Global Politics
_____
David C. Earnest, editor

Relations and Roles
in China's Internationalism

Rediscovering Confucianism
in a Pluriversal World

CHIH-YU SHIH

SUNY
PRESS

Published by State University of New York Press, Albany

For information, contact State University of New York Press, Albany, NY
www.sunypress.edu

Library of Congress Cataloging-in-Publication Data

Name: Shih, Chih-yu, author.
Title: Relations and roles in China's internationalism : rediscovering
    Confucianism in a pluriversal world / Chih-yu Shih.
Description: Albany : State University of New York Press, [2024] | A volume
    in the SUNY James N. Rosenau series in Global Politics | Includes
    bibliographical references and index.
Identifiers: ISBN 9781438498874 (hardcover : alk. paper) | ISBN 9781438498898
    (ebook) | ISBN 9781438498881 (pbk. : alk. paper)
Further information is available at the Library of Congress.

Contents

Illustrations

Tables

Figures

Preface

Why Write Yet Another China?

This book continues my career-long efforts to rewrite Chinese foreign policy. This journey began in the late 1980s with my PhD project, which was characterized by a tendency for cultural essentialism, accompanied by a belief in the power of social science to bridge cultural differences. My disillusion with the social sciences began to evolve upon my realization, in 1993, that China could not exist within any single-minded logic, nor even qualify as a category, but must follow ambiguous, therapeutic, and sometimes violent cycles.

Thereafter, an internal/domestic turn led me into fieldwork for over two decades, which enabled me to make a determined departure from the analytical framework of state-society relations adopted by mainstream studies of China. This framework had also informed the assessment of Chinese international relations in the Anglosphere since the Cold War. Thrilling de- and resocialization experiences produced a series of field reports on township factories in 1995, local people's congresses in 1999, ethnic villages in 2002, and impoverished mountain regions in 2007. In the following international fieldwork, I strove to examine the intellectual history of China scholars around the world to continue my unlearning of China. Collectively attesting to China as a strategic reification of relational dynamics, my predominantly Asian and European colleagues jointly contributed numerous personal accounts to the intellectual history project during the past twenty-two years.

Alongside these field trips, my initial experiment with critically approaching Chinese foreign policy was to engage with cultural studies, in 2000 and 2003. Ten years later, with the support of the intellectual history project, I engaged with the civilizational narratives on China as a mutually constituted identity for scholars and practitioners with diverse backgrounds. In 2015, I enlisted a postmodern thinker of the premodern period to defend the thesis of the impossibility of narrating or defining China and what this could mean for post-Western world politics. In 2019, I concluded that China, and the foreign policy in its name, could only exist as practices and processes, which can be better explained in relational terms.

At this stage, I had already come to appreciate Confucianism far more deeply, reviving a critique on social science that inspired a rereading of my past orthodox pedagogy of Confucianism. Confucianism appeared everywhere, to my eyes, including in the governmentality of the socialist autocracy. The result was a dual revelation in 2022—the articulation of post-Chineseness as an epistemological theme and a feminist claim to postcolonial Chineseness, both of which critically realign Confucianism with its time. I am simultaneously deconstructing the binary of democracy versus autocracy using the same Confucian lens alongside this book. If time permits, I also aim to challenge the colonial foundations of rule-based multilateralism along this line.

The focus of this current book is to explore the evasive, fluid, and performative characteristics that reflect the inevitable state of *all bound to be related* and coexistent in a pluriversal world. In a nutshell, my recent themes have proceeded from the balance of relationships in 2019, which strategizes identities to maintain relations; through post-Chineseness in 2022, which further dissolves identities through multi-sited relations; to *tianxia* in 2024, which surrenders Confucianism to the relation of relations—in other words, to pluriversalism.

Acknowledgments

A few chapters are revised versions of papers coauthored and presented at earlier conferences. I would like to thank Chiung-chiu Huang (chapter 2), Jason Kuo (chapter 4), Hung-Jen Wang (chapter 5), and Raoul Bunskoek (chapter 10) for consenting to the use of their coauthored papers in these chapters.

I am indebted to Stephen Hartnett, Karen Fierke, Patrick Thaddeus Jackson, Juliet Kaarbo, Chengxin Pan, and Stephen Walker in addition to three anonymous reviewers for their valuable comments on earlier drafts. Sue Casson faithfully suggested editorial changes through all the chapters to make them much more reader-friendly. Although I made significant revisions according to their feedback, I certainly remain solely responsible for the contents of the book. Encouraging and generous words also came from Simon Chang, Ching-chang Chen, Julie Chen, Young Chul Cho, Evelyn Goh, Kai He, Emilian Kavalski, Jason Kuo, Peng Lu, Reena Marwah, Honghua Men, Jungmin Seo, Giorgio Shani, Kosuke Shimizu, Shiping Tang, Cameron Thies, Tamara Trownsell, Chen-Dong Tso, Leslie Wehner, Picamon Yeophantung, and Yun Zhang. Mariko Tanigaki arranged intensive summer teaching at the University of Tokyo in 2017 and 2023, and Nele Noesselt invited me to co-teach a rigorous workshop on my topics in Berlin. Both allowed illuminating brainstorming together with younger generations. Last, but not least, the family of Raoul Bunskoek has been a constant source of inspiration, intellectually as well as socially, during the writing of this book as well as another upcoming book.

The writing of this book was supported by a National Science and Technology Council (Taiwan) grant (no. 110-2420-H-002-006-MY3).

Chapter 3 is a revised version of Chih-yu Shih, "Role and Relation in Confucian IR: Relating to Strangers in the States of Nature," *Review of International Studies* 48, no. 5 (December 2022): 910–29, https://doi.org/10.1017/S0260210521000322.

Chapter 6 is a revised version of Chih-yu Shih, "Friendship in Chinese International Relations: The Confucian Theme of Distance in Practice," *Communist and Post-Communist Studies* 53, no. 4 (2020): 177–99, https://doi.org/10.1525/j.postcomstud.2020.53.4.177.

Chapter 10 is a revised version of Raoul Bunskoek and Chih-yu Shih, "'Community of Common Destiny' as Post-Western Regionalism: Rethinking China's Belt and Road Initiative from a Confucian Perspective," *Uluslararası İlişkiler* 18, no. 70 (2021): 85–101, https://doi.org/10.33458/uidergisi.954744.

Introduction

Translating Confucianism as a Pluriversal Engagement

This book discusses the component of China's internationalism, in thought and practice, that is deeply informed by Confucian perspectives to show the (un)learning everywhere that both accommodates and revises Confucian ways of coping with differences, confrontation, and coexistence. The application of classical Chinese literature to cosmological relationality is not simply another way to achieve a reflexive explanation of China's internationalism; rather, Confucian relationality reveals and fills a lacuna in international relations (IR) theory and foreign policy analysis in general that pertains to the need of all lives to imagine and maintain mutual relations. Being a relational project, the book further aims at a fresh and more comprehensive understanding and explanation of the following four aspects:

1. Relational necessities: Confucianism reveals aspects of the relational necessities unattended to by other types of relational thinking, especially the preferences for any relationship over no relationship in the long run and for a nonsolution over a compulsory solution to preserve relationships.

2. Chinese internationalism: Confucianism frames constitutive relations into incongruent relational configurations, which are simultaneously hierarchical, performative, and reciprocal, as opposed to equal, sincere, and multilateral.

3. Confucian selves: Confucianism is ready to adapt through adopting, preaching, boycotting, or forgoing selective relational arrangements and, therefore, oblige the interacting parties to likewise unlearn and adapt.

4. Pluriversal skill: Confucianism interacts with other civilizations, but all remain distinctive as cultural trajectories while becoming increasingly hybrid on their own terms in the long run.

Background

Against the background of the perceived rise of China and the intensifying US-China rivalry, the importance of understanding the theoretical foundations of Chinese international policy has become apparent. This challenge is both philosophical and practical in nature—Does there exist a revisionist threat to the American international order or not? Simpleminded answers are consistently positive, as the balance of power between the two strongest national actors is allegedly shifting in favor of China, as is the relative influence of the two in the rest of the world.

However, before any determination to challenge the world order can be evidenced in Chinese documents anywhere, academic as well as official, intentional, albeit unconsolidated, attempts to rock the ontological and epistemological boat of the American worldview are emerging from the Global South through the claim of pluriversalism.[1] Having engaged in the provincialization of Western and American IR, such a revolutionary claim extends the quest for self-identities in post-Western, non-Western, and global IR,[2] despite the clear variety of thoughts thus incurred, and has engendered two shared themes: (1) a difference theme, which stresses how there can be no single way to engage in IR; and (2) a relational theme, which evokes the mutual constitution of all, in one way or another, to substitute for the exclusionary ontology of American IR, informed by anarchy between autonomous actors and their balance-of-power sensibilities.

Chinese revisionism, if any, is rarely narrated from the pluriversal point of view. That said, the pluriversal turn is consciously revisionist in its diverse renovative ontological configurations but does not represent the familiar or alarming kind of revisionism that defines the political correctness of the United States' China policy. After all, the turn's intellectual nature by no means inflicts any directly or immediately felt deconstruction of US-China rival relations. Even so, the hiatus in the dialogue between the Chinese and pluriversal IR is mind-boggling, given that the two characteristic claims of Chinese IR are likewise China's being different and relational.[3]

In brief, Chinese foreign policy makers are facing Washington on the latter's terms of a balance of power. They are far from thinking of any ontological revolution desired by the pluriversal turn. Moreover, their plausibly revisionist claims of difference and relationality are, puzzlingly, registered in the lukewarm interest of Chinese IR scholarship in joining an arguably friendly, nascent pluriversal lineup. In the current situation, the consensually conceived rise of China poses a power threat from the US policy perspective but might also constitute an ontological thread of revisionism that would be welcomed by pluriversalism. This leaves Chinese IR debating between serving intellectually as a potential bridge for Washington to access pluriversal IR and serving as a gap that protects the American world order from pluriversal critiques.

Purpose: The Post-Western Pluriverse

This book retrieves and develops Chinese political thought, especially Confucianism, in contemporary Chinese international relations theory and international policy analysis. Applying decolonial and denationalizing sensibilities, the book responds to the call by (1) post-Western IR[4] to re-world Global South actors in the understandings and practices of world politics that have hitherto been ostensibly dominated by the former colonizer states and (2) pluriversal IR,[5] where many coexisting relationalities embedded in differently framed justice and motivation co-constitute as well as intersect one another. Its philosophical stance is registered in the pursuit of a critical intellectual capacity that emancipates theorists and practitioners from national and, for that matter, any other epistemic binaries to reach a horizon where all relationalities cohabitate in any particular mode of thinking that is familiar and comfortable to each of them in its own terms. Through these interconnections, all can acquire a more comprehensive self-understanding and become ever more relationally conscious.

Accordingly, this book contributes to the debate on the relational turn in the social sciences in general and the pursuit of pluriversal and post-Western theories specifically, using Confucianism and China's internationalism to illustrate and apply denationalistic, decolonial, and nonbinary sensibilities. Not only does it interrogate the place of Confucianism in the pluriversal turn, but it also reinterprets the US-China rivalry away from the self/other binary. To that extent, rivalry can become a window of opportunity for unlearning ontological correctness in the long run due to the enlightenment that a self-understanding is always incomplete, insufficient, and inconsistent.

This book is distinctive in that it bridges three academic gaps. First, it establishes a dialogue between postcolonial studies and Chinese studies. Surprisingly and disappointingly, as already mentioned, the latter are largely absent from the literature of the former. Second, the book unites cosmological perspectives that are traditionally considered to be in opposition, especially liberalism and Confucianism. It shows how each attempts to include the other epistemologically, on the one hand, but mingles practically, unobstructed by much intellectual debt, on the other. Third, it traces further threads between political theory and international relations by adding Confucianism to the current literature, in which Western thought is predominantly embedded.

As such, China-in-IR is not only a name invoked by policymakers, a source of theory making, or a system of distribution but also a method of cultural translation for a specific audience on each occasion. The translation is powerful if something perceived in common can emerge to reconstitute the identities of strangers, and hence a relation, to make both mindful of the consequences of their actions for the other and reflect critically on the self/other divide. Learning and unlearning through cultural translation, an interrogator, including one who identifies as Chinese or American, can realize that they are constantly making nuanced, decentering, and relational sense of someone else, as in the case between China and the US, in the pluriversal order. Given that international policy making is increasingly divided over internally inconsistent and externally incompatible identities, and so in need of rehabilitation, a relational agenda that illustrates how, in practical life, divisions are not destined or perpetual is timely.

Significance of the Topics:
Nature, Order, and US-China Relations

THE STATES OF NATURE

Above all, the cosmological origin of modern international relations, or the state of nature and laws of nature,[6] deeply affect the theory and practice of foreign policy establishments everywhere. While the state of nature has been a foundational concept of Western political thought, there exist clear parallels in the history of political thought elsewhere, noticeably in ancient Chinese political thought,[7] although these are retrievable only through inference. One significant Western feature that appears to be widely accepted, even among historians of natural science, is that, within the Judeo-Christian tradition, the rational creator, the author of nature, is external to what He creates. The consensus is that this transcendental power is absent from the Chinese history of thought, in which heavenly reason, *Dao*, or *qi* ("vapor") informs the phenomenon of oneness that proliferates and constitutes everything, constantly changing and in different forms.[8] These two cosmological beliefs have led to two dramatically different paths of development concerning the nature of the state of nature,[9] arguably resulting in different understandings of contemporary international politics.[10]

What has escaped the literature is a relational sensibility shared by the modern European history of thought and ancient Chinese history of thought about how people in the state of nature are related. For modern European thinkers, including those most relevant to contemporary international theory such as Thomas Hobbes, John Locke, Jean-Jacques Rousseau, and Immanuel Kant, all humans are equally entitled to the rights of nature that God allows them, despite these thinkers' incongruent imaginations about the conditions of security for humans or the realistic/idealistic state of governance that provides order for them.[11] According to their formulations, God is the common lord, and his laws of nature connect all. Therefore, women and men who are strangers to one another and states that are involuntary rivals due to the lack of a common authority in the mundane world cannot be true strangers. Rather, they are God-made like strangers. They share the likeness provided by God and know each other as common subscribers to the laws of nature, even if they are not direct acquaintances. The anxiety would be intense if even a nonacquaintance should suffer the violation of their rights of nature, because that violation would allude to the breakdown of the laws of nature that constitute the identities of all humans and, for that matter, all nation-states. Rational humans—males of property and nobility, in this case—give their consent to a social contract that protects each of them from the threat of the breakdown of their rights.

In comparison, in ancient Chinese political thought, without an external authority governing the relationships between people, they are nonetheless considered related in their genesis as, cosmologically, heaven and earth combined are believed to have given birth to all phenomena.[12] In other words, a certain quality of likeness likewise constitutes both the living and nonliving in ancient Chinese thought, except that no external, omnipotent force provides the laws of nature that could oblige people of hundreds of different kinds to imagine their likeness to each other. Consequently, an unnoticeable likeness in ancient Chinese thought implies no rights of nature but a shared, amorphous origin, which can only be revealed when varieties of life are looked at collectively but which vanishes if each variety of life is viewed individually. Consequently, life, which continues in different forms, belongs to oneness, and yet belonging, while fulfilling the desire for life, must not accentuate the right to individual life. Rather, life finds security in the harmonious order that only the benevolence of the collective can guarantee. The ruler of the collective is unable to abuse their role, however, without being noticed and punished by heaven, which is composed of the hearts of the people collectively.

The Normative Order

Nevertheless, the abovementioned quest for harmony informed a variety of platforms that cherish collective life in the long run. For example, Confucianism adopted the metaphor of kinship to require benevolence in substitution for killing, Daoism equalized the haves and have-nots to neutralize the meaning of and desire for killing, Moism preached military defense on behalf of universal love to eventually deter killing, and legalism resorted to the threat of killing to establish unity and order, among others. In ancient Chinese thought, the people were bound to be related by nature but, in practice, were dependent on the guidance of the rulers and their advisers, who created differential roles for them to adopt and practice belonging accordingly. The rulers could anticipate which roles were teachable, acceptable, and practicable. Roles are thus intersubjectively evolved expectations to be fulfilled. Intersubjectivity suggests that even higher rulers had to make self-sacrifices in order to merit the submission of their populaces convincingly. Losing the people's hearts would grant all the legitimacy to slay the ruler. Therefore, that bad autocrats necessarily fall is the Confucian law of nature.

Deeply rooted in these discourses lies the same anxiety registered in Western thought about anarchy and the threat to life. Such anxiety about the loss of the relational order, to which the people are capable of subscribing in both intellectual and practical terms, is not distinctive of either the Chinese or the European history of thought. That said, none of these ancient Chinese schools were preoccupied with God-bestowed ontology. No Christian kind of individual transcendence made sense. Instead, this thought consisted primarily of relationships, each undergirding a particular art of governance. The art was consistently about teaching the rulers and people how to remain related rather than contriving durable rules for the rulers or the populace to observe. Given the European ontological sensibilities' abhorrence of the absence of the rights of nature in Chinese thought, together with the contrasting Chinese preoccupation with the metaphoric art of belonging to collective circles, which is not essential to the European state of nature, these might provoke mutual anxiety.

In practice, however, becoming related through marriage, gift giving, ritualized brotherhood, or belonging to a greater encompassing group or site of living and thus transcending genetic relations is not only common but also ethical. This is why and how the Confucian role relations, embedded in metaphoric kinship, strive to create ever-expanding relations until all become nominally or compulsorily related. Improvising extended kinship is the ultimate resort of Confucianism: to obligate the fulfillment of the expectations to establish common points of identity, cut across binaries, prevent estrangement, and reconcile strangeness in a consensual order that does not depend on any universal laws and rights that are suitable only for like people. Belonging, as necessity, cannot but practice pluriversalism. In an ultimate sense, international relations involve a transient yet secular transcendence of the self through the making of sacrifices that accredit the role in context and bind the specific other to honor peaceful coexistence in their collective.

US-China Relations

The charge against China of revisionism in the Anglosphere targets both the growth of national power and the wielding of it by the authoritarian Communist Party in its practices related to domestic control and international expansion.[13] This charge is justified by the perceived despotism of the ruling Chinese Communist Party (CCP), its revisionist foreign policy, and, ultimately, American IR's lenses of liberal rights and realist power. In contrast, the political thought preparation of the CCP leaders seems to have relied on relational rather than rival strategies—to preempt in the more remote regions, such as Latin America, by contriving a partnership through gift giving; to mitigate the alarm of the West by cyclically complying with liberal governance, as in anti-proliferation; and to impose punishment in the neighborhood to avoid appearing vulnerable, such as over the South China Sea. None of these stances appears to follow the pure logic of power, with China yielding when in a relatively strong position but confronting others when weak.[14] While these responses can be explained by using the conventions of Chinese political thought, such an inward-looking rationality would simply reproduce the political correctness of the American self versus the Chinese other and thus fail to reveal the pluriversal coexistence or widespread cultural translation already occurring in practical life.

In other words, Chinese relationality contributes to pluriversal IR only when it shows how the binary thinking in the United States' China policy along either territorial or ideological divides fails to bind and subdue the agency of the actors at various levels, including that of the nation-state, because the actors can facilitate mutual roles to be learned and practiced and create relational intersections. In the Confucian context, this means that sophisticated gift giving, for example, is a plausible method of role making and self-unlearning to enable transcendence over different divides. Likewise, the relational strategies of the American liberal system can be plausible, too—for example, using the skill of marketing or the appeal to stability. Post-identities—in our case, post-Chineseness as well as, by extension, post-Americanness—would be the empirical testimony to pluriversal IR. The chance is always there that, at some point, actors will cease to exclusively reference their self-understanding to appraise others in the world. This is why a theoretical consciousness that reveals these practices and agencies is critical for the rise of pluriversal IR and

Confucian IR, which has coached such a significant populace to engage in coexistence and which empirically reifies this theoretical consciousness.

Theme: Relations and Roles

Past kings in European history resorted to dividing territories through religious war to attain emancipation from the Church. For them, dividing sovereign territories is the origin and the methodology of international relations. Defying the methodology would give the impression of being medieval, backward, and evil. However, sovereignty is a Christian norm, after all. Regardless, the principle of sovereignty guided subsequent colonial wars and decolonization to create ostensibly mutually exclusionary borders in the colonizers' own image in the postcolonial age and reproduce the myth of anarchy.

This book contrarily relies on the classical thought of Confucianism to infer and develop a general argument about relationality that is applicable to contemporary IR regarding why and how international policy necessarily involves a relational rather than a dividing logic. It advances the theme that relations constitute power. Specifically, policymakers assess one another against the imagined points of their resemblance, as opposed to relative power, as having a particular disposition. The selected point of resemblance connects them and informs their relational lenses. According to the resulting disposition, they further create and adopt roles to establish stable relationships. Through the relational lens, no one is a complete stranger. Even a seeming stranger lives with a role expectation by becoming related as some kind of alien. Culture and identity make a difference to the arrangement of the relations and roles of those belonging to a different relational configuration. They make no difference in inevitably relying on a certain relational lens to understand each other. Inventing room for strangers is ultimately how an actor remains ontologically secure.

In both the Christian and Confucian tradition, therefore, strangeness is the common indicator of political incorrectness. However, the ways in which they each overcome strangeness do not correspond well. In the European tradition, the social contract, embedded in the laws of nature, reconciles strangeness except for those deficient in Christianity. Christianity, consent to rule, equality, and the rights of nature together ensure solidarity between like individuals. Such likeness facilitates the system analysis of international politics, according to Kenneth Waltz,[15] who relied on the imagined likeness of units to transcend their separateness. Although there is no central authority that coordinates states or allocates the values among them, they all think that they know with whom they are dealing in terms of aspirations and patterns of behavior that are shared by all. They differ only in terms of their capability, skill, and priority of preference, none of which is ontological in nature. In contrast, Samuel Huntington's theory of the clash of civilizations connotes a qualitatively different threat,[16] which is intellectual as well as ontological, because the laws of nature are not consensual across his civilizational divides, nor a relevant reference to inspire solidarity. It is in this very kind of context of civilizational discourse that critical reflections on the state of nature have become pertinent and timely again in the twenty-first century.

In a pluriversal world, however, neither the Huntingtonian clash of civilizations nor the Waltzian systemic likeness of all actors, both of which necessitate surveillance over and rivalry with ontological strangers, is apparent.[17] After all, it is merely the philosophical technicality of managing strangeness that differentiates them from Confucianism. In fact, other imagined states of nature and humanity than Christianity and Confucianism are by all means present.[18] Ubuntu, as a significant example most evident in southern Africa, provides a distinguishable lens relative to Christianity and Confucianism.[19] According to this cosmology, humans are owned by their shared nature, which is not external to humanity as is the Christian God. Therefore, humans are who they are only if they sustain and nurture one another to reflect the necessity of life, each in their own consciousness of forgiveness and hospitality. The Ubuntu sense of solidarity arises from the self-dignity of individuals as the reification of the spirit within all beings. Ubuntu contrasts with the Confucian drive for a self-disciplining, little self to submerge (or transcend) individuality into benevolent kin relations.

For all three cosmologies, individual interests are subdued to the extent that relational solidarity is emphasized. Anxiety about strangers or aliens characterizes all relations, including Confucian ethical relations. The philosophical technicality of Confucian IR pertains to how nations constantly seek to camouflage strangeness and negotiate their extended kinship roles. Leading actors in the circle of former colonizer states mistrust China's role taking in the current international regimes, as Chinese representatives usually side with the majority of Global

South post-colonies, whose roles in the existing rule-based governance are neither voluntary nor stable. China typically relies on improvising specially arranged partnerships qua role relations in context with specific others, aggravating the image of a revisionist power that is undermining the multilateral order that was initially honed in the former colonizer states. Seemingly unfulfilled, expectations that China's rules and values be tuned into liberalism have reduced China to an estranging force.

Nevertheless, the quest for role relations, regardless of the leaders' styles or preferences, continues, so even rivalry must develop mutuality in order to proceed meaningfully. Thus, roles and role structures are not automatic. It takes intersubjective effort to improvise, preach, and practice. Role enactment requires the casting of other actors into certain *alter* roles and counter-roles, in addition to self-restraint. To be understood and pragmatic, altercasting relies on the prior relations between the self and the *alter*, from which the roles evolve. This is why the comparative state of nature and concomitant conceptualizations of the stranger, which inform the prior relations, are essential to the subsequent theorization of international relations.

Altercasting under the conditions of unspecified role expectations between strangers can be either spontaneous, where prior rights or kinships are perceived to exist, or contrived from ground zero, through mutual preaching and adjustment, obliged to by goodwill or sacrifice. Confucians use the metaphoric kin relations to naturalize benevolent relations between the peoples of the world. Metaphors invoke role making and role taking. Obliging and performing roles are thus essential to Confucian internationalism. European international relations are not qualitatively apart, to the extent that the state of nature is likewise a metaphor,[20] and the laws of nature that substantiate the social contract are by all means a role scheme, calling for socialization through role making and role taking.

One of the aims of this book is to explain how Chinese (or, more specifically, Confucian) thought has coped with the anxiety about strangeness that gives rise to the contemporary Chinese as well as East Asian international policy and alludes to the theorizing of the post-Western IR. For convenience, the notion of relations is used in this book as an antonym for strangeness and refers to *the imagined (points of) resemblance*, which is intended to convey a condition of mutual constitution, informed by common kinship, natural rights, religion, desires, ideology, history, experience, ritual, mission, neighborhood, identity, affiliation, career, and so on, whereby the actors are discursively or socially acquainted or intellectually comfortable with the presence of each other.

Structure: Cosmology, Relation, and Identity

This book follows the flow of (1) cosmology, i.e., the Confucian idea of *tianxia*; (2) relation and role in comparative perspectives; and (3) identities in China's internationalism (see figure I.1). Cosmology tackles the myth of totality and interprets the phenomena of existence. Cosmological views anywhere can testify to the widespread belief in the naturalness of all—the natural and the social, on one hand, and the past and future,

Figure I.1. Structure of the chapters. Created by the author.

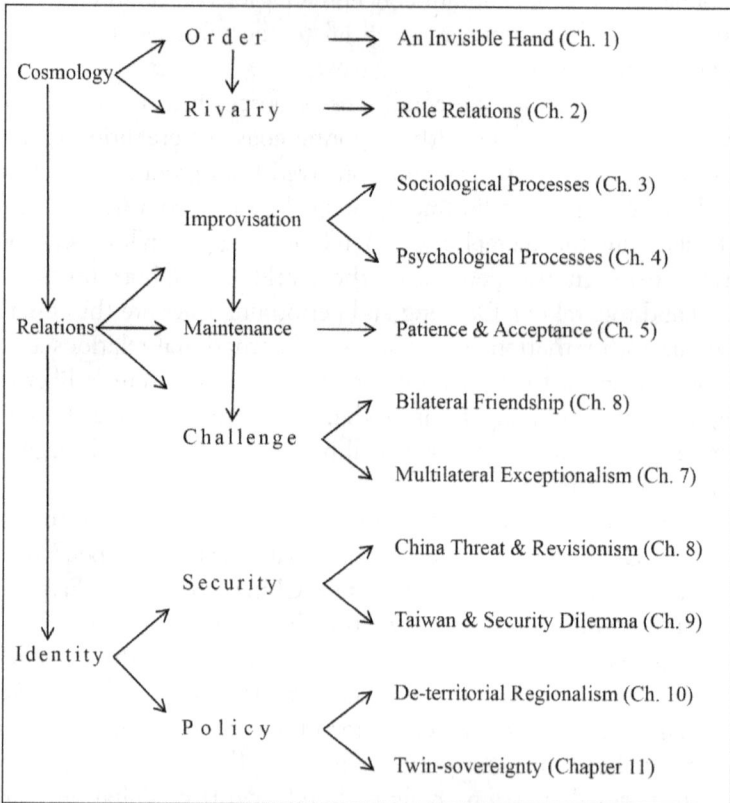

on the other, being related—although the question of what relates them and how they are related varies across different cultures and religions, evolving into different relational configurations.[21] Apparently, relationalities anchored in God(s), the universe, ancestry, destiny, a spirit, a path, historiography, and so on inevitably define the points of resemblance between people in different and sometimes contradictory terms and further socialize their respective populaces through roles to reproduce resemblance. In practice, roles are relatively easy for strangers coming from another relational configuration to learn and adopt, compared to a cosmological belief. Mutual expansion and coexistence that enable people to move beyond cosmological divides are macro consequences that are often ignored by role theorists, who conceive roles as merely a position, policy, or socialization mechanism. Encountering relational strangers through intersubjective role processes can cause the identity cycles of confusion, estrangement, restoration, and emancipation.

The first section of this book recognizes that no self-awareness can sustain nuances or complexities in the void of a collective cosmological root evolving from an ancient time, which attests to the ultimate power of relationality that transcends material capacity. The elusiveness of a cosmologically inspired order engenders a trajectory of contemporary values and institutions. Each considering their institutions and values normal and universal, cultural clusters easily regard one another as strangers. Strategic decisions are inevitable for all actors wishing to position, stabilize, and adapt such a self-in-relation, leading to what Anthony Giddens calls structuration.[22]

The first section interprets the Chinese cosmology of *tianxia* ("all under heaven") as if it were not an exclusively Confucian concept. I attempt an ontological-level translation—that *tianxia* is *a system in which all are bound to be related.*[23] Such a culturally indifferent translation creates an intersection through which the IR scholarship emerging from different communities can access each other's cosmological sites and travel back and forth. Once discursively connected, *tianxia* expands the ontological horizon of the current IR through the addition of a relational dimension that the literature has hitherto neglected. Relationally, for example, *tianxia* enables any ready nations to simultaneously engage in hierarchy, mutuality, and governability by improvising reciprocal roles and equality, sovereignty, and governmentality by prescribing universal rules. The different kinds of international order and strategic style that *tianxia* accommodates can inspire and emancipate students of IR from a fixation on power and the interests of nation-states to achieve a deeper self-understanding and explanation of the roots of the (mis)perceptions between rivals.

The second section recognizes, however, that, in a pluriversal world, many cosmologies coexist in parallel as well as co-constitutively. Self-identity is challenged by strangers who subscribe to different cosmological beliefs. Role making and role taking to accommodate the "other" and emotional mobilization to affirm the self together yield two processual aspects of relational policy. Consensual mutual acceptance is never guaranteed or long-lasting, however, so patience becomes intrinsic to relational maintenance. In typical dialectics, tolerance toward indulgence and measured control of dispute inform the minimal level of friendship, on the one hand, while self-righteous disengagement or intervention commits to an allegedly prior order, on the other.

The second section illustrates the theoretical potential, pertaining especially to the reciprocation between relational theory and role theory, two presumable allies that oblige nations to relate. In contrast to the Christian notions of the state of nature, relationships spawned by *tianxia* rely on their subscribers to improvise roles for each other. By empowering the weak parties involved in a situation of power asymmetry, mutually agreeable roles either neutralize or camouflage the strangeness between the related actors, regardless of their relative power status. Three strategic options arise to avoid strangeness affecting their interaction: (1) Role making and role taking require patience, which marks a Confucian feature of IR and accepts nonsolutions as a plausible prescription for any emerging symptoms of estrangement. On the other hand, (2) a readiness to sanction upon betrayal and perform anger is less emotional than pedagogical, its sole purpose being to deter others from terminating a perceived role relation. In these processes, (3) gift giving, or ritualized sacrifice, a Confucian technique designed to cast others in role relations, appears essential to international policy at all levels, in pursuit of maintaining and restoring norms to which others have already committed.

Abandoning the existing literature's point of view by unlearning its assumptions about international politics, the last section focuses on ontological identities. The discussion recognizes that observing deviance in values and institutions as a threat nevertheless reveals incongruent interpretations of relational identity caused by a cosmological fixation. The nationalist quest for unity can appear suppressive from a liberal values and institutions point of view. The socialist quest for emancipation from imperialist legacies can likewise appear as an antagonistic gesture. When a self-concept is examined with suspicion from the perspective of unfamiliar liberalism, defense against its perceived ideological attack can easily incur the charge of revisionism. Consequently, a quest for coexistence of identities strikes the nerves of power competition.

The last section interrogates such politics of identity. This force occasionally alludes to involuted relations, which arise when roles are unilaterally improvised and imposed by self-centric policies without a minimum of negotiation or concomitant self-restraint. Such self-centrism appears most serious where others are deemed members under the leadership of the same group, belonging to which is conveniently considered a privilege as well as a duty. Given that multiple belongings, such as socialism, Confucianism, and liberalism, are common for every relational self, strategizing the priority among belongings, especially when belongings cut across national boundaries, is dangerous politics. The politics of separatism is thus more about ontological than physical security; belongings are invented and denied, leading to the political elite's apprehension of lost legitimacy, considering that the past colonialism, ethnic diaspora, provincialism, and Cold War legacies likewise generate multiple sources, rendering integrative nationalism practically implausible. Even where the imagined boundaries tentatively converge, the Right/Left, modernity/tradition, and central/local dichotomies are familiar divisions that plague the national identity, not to mention the constant realignments between these forces. Maintaining a balance between these different relations and broadening their horizons may provide a solution to involution, but they call for creatively improvising roles. Historically, a cycle of boundary spinning and closure has resulted, testifying to the unstable processes of expansion and coexistence.

A Note on Methodology

The research undertaken for this book was based on three traditional methods: metaphors, case studies, and interpretation. Part One begins with the metaphors of the "state of nature" and the game of *weiqi* to position the cosmology of *tianxia* on a comparative platform. That said, the role and its reification through gift giving are the most frequent metaphors throughout the book, assuming prior scripts, *alters*, and imagined audiences in all actions. Thus, relations are role relations, emotions are role emotions, and identities are role identities. Case studies are heavily applied in every chapter. North Korea and the US are the two corporate actors most prominent in the book, whose relations with China are reviewed and deconstructed in several chapters. Other notable topics include relations with South Korea, Taiwan, Japan, Russia, India, and Vietnam, all involving the US-China rivalry to varying extents. Finally, the book borrows the interpretative heuristic to attend to the historical background, context, and social and psychological necessity when analyzing classical literature, policy documents and statements, and interviews. The binary of the empirical and the normative is inappropriate for this book, as a selected cosmology evolving into norms and institutions to create observable patterns of behavior is the foundation of both the empirical and the normative.

PART ONE

Cosmology

Denationalizing *Tianxia*

Part One provides arguments about how a Chinese cosmological meta-phor, *tianxia*, makes sense of and copes with the world, gradually adapts, and reconstitutes contemporary international relations. As a relational ontology, *tianxia* is concerned with maintaining an equilibrium between freedom, on one hand, and control and order, on the other, and there-fore readily connects with many other ideas that similarly interrogate the dynamics of order. As a strategy, *tianxia* approaches these dynamics as if it were impossible for any actor or object to be unrelated to each other; it therefore competes with the liberal idea of autonomous actors while at the same time unlearning its own naturalness.

1

De-Sinicizing *Tianxia*

The Invisible Hand of International Relations

The discussion on the Chinese world order and soft power seems to have missed the relational aspect; instead, it emphasizes the "charm offensive":[1] practical relevance or irrelevance of Chinese cultural values.[2] It is fully recognized that China's international policy is unpopular among both China's neighbors and the major powers[3] for allegedly being unilateral, uncooperative, unstable, trivial, and arrogant, and hence negative soft power.[4] Nevertheless, China can still set agendas, primarily in terms of excluding those issues involving the Dalai Lama, Taiwan, Hong Kong, Uyghurs, territorial disputes, intervention, and multilateral regimes. These agendas do not always correspond to the usual realist calculi of power and interests. Rather, an obsession with nomenclatural propriety continues to direct China's preference for long-term relationships and politically correct rituals to reiterate them.[5] Therefore, China's soft power is not a result of China's charm but of a desire to foster mutual acceptance by sensitizing each other's agenda, pertaining especially to the sensibilities of ontological security. As such, the international order can manage without shared values, norms, or institutions!

In the following discussion, soft power is defined as reifying relations by adopting each other's agendas. Specifically, other nations reluctantly adhere to China's agenda because China can always retreat from its ostensibly nonnegotiable requests following a display of anger, boycott, or denouncement, hence providing room for the other parties to restore the relationship. Intrinsically, this capacity for agenda setting is linked to the Confucian practice of *tianxia*. In a nutshell, *tianxia* offers an analytical frame for studying how a national agenda becomes mutual and manages the differences in the positions adopted by national actors. In practice, *tianxia*, denoting these differences, achieves order by either reconciling them or, if this fails, tentatively marginalizing, relativizing, or camouflaging them. Thus, *tianxia* incurs a universal logic that all may adopt, albeit the second approach of avoiding differences has an intuitive appeal within Confucianism.

The literature generally confirms that Confucian *tianxia* embraces hierarchy,[6] which may take the form of leader-follower relations in the modern world. Nations familiar with the derivative discourses of *tianxia* are potentially subject to Chinese soft power. However, I argue that *tianxia* provides soft power for both sides. Whenever Chinese leaders take ritual respect for granted, they lose reciprocity, commit unilateralism and egocentrism, and corrupt *tianxia*. If their counterpart likewise subscribes to a similarly hierarchical *tianxia*, this party can name and shame China, despite possible sanctions, and still expect that a stronger China will eventually exert knowingly insincere self-restraint[7] to win their heart again. While the cultural readiness of the weaker party to shame China constitutes the soft power of the weak, the cultural willingness of China to ease up after a period, resume denationalistic *tianxia*, and rebind the other party to China's agenda constitutes the soft power of the strong.

In the short run, a dispute causes the uncomfortable revelation that all seem self-centered. In the long run, adopting a nonsolution to a dispute until it eventually becomes insignificant maintains a minimum level of mutuality. Although it is impossible for actors to always be consistent and credible role players in these cycles, *tianxia* remains a romantic yet credible cosmological source of power that supports all who appeal to its timeless relational capacity.[8] This chapter distills an analytical lens of contemporary international relations (IR) from Confucianism's advice to rulers. Norms and prescriptions reveal explanatory heuristics, for Confucius and Hobbes alike in this regard.

Denationalizing *Tianxia*: A Definition

The nascent revisiting of the notion of *tianxia* in the IR literature has encountered an incongruence, mainly caused by the irresolvable discrepancy between the two forms of interpretation.[9] One lauds *tianxia*'s potential to transcend the obsession with autonomous national actors that perpetuates the imagined characteristics of the anarchy of the modern state system,[10] while the other reduces it to simply another discursive device of hegemonic control.[11] Given the rising popularity of the *tianxia* discourse that is accompanying China's rise, various groups of people (e.g., neighbors, power competitors, liberals, and racists) have allied themselves with an impossible epistemic community that orients the dominant understanding of *tianxia* toward being alarmist in nature.[12]

For hegemonic control anywhere and at any time, a discourse that justifies this hegemonic order seems inevitable.[13] Presumably, this hegemonic discourse distinguishes the normal from the abnormal and detects the latter as a target to be converted or eliminated.[14] Given that *tianxia* is allegedly an all-compassing ontological order, it automatically creates the impression that it is a discursive tool of hegemonic control. However, in my subsequent theorization, I will rely primarily on pre-Qin Confucianism (during the Zhou dynasty before 221 BCE) and, to a lesser extent, Daoism to attain a meaning of *tianxia* that is exempt from both modern nationhood considerations and their concomitant understandings of Chineseness, to avoid the "rise of China" bias. Such classical Confucianism anticipates drives toward harmonious relations between all who adopt different but coupling roles that transcend their otherwise differing identities and practices.[15]

For the sake of de-sinicizing *tianxia*, I translate *tianxia* as a lawlike, inevitable system whereby all actors are bound to be related. According to this definition, *tianxia* is neither culturally distinctive nor consensually understood because all of the actors differently strategize the balance between freedom and control in their relations. I further define *tianxia*'s order as patterned practices of interaction. Order is the practice of relating. Factors such as rules, norms, power, or consensus (which may cause the rise and fall of order) do not form part of my definition of *order*. Multiple partnerships, for example, establish parallel orders without synchronic rules. Dominance establishes order without norms. Customs establish order without consensual meanings. Self-restraints in asymmetry establish order without the use of power. To summarize, the *tianxia* approach interrogates how actors who seek order to cope with inevitable relations negotiate with one another to create a balance between freedom and control.

Culture certainly influences practices. What is culturally distinctive about pre-Qin *tianxia* is its preference for the metaphor of a kindred hierarchy and dyadic reciprocity, together with its ironic stress on the formless, similar, and equal constituent of every actor before the metaphor links them through hierarchical yet reciprocal role taking. Such metaphorical *tianxia* could be conceived of as constituted by Euclidian points, Democritean atoms, or Freudian id, in the cosmological sense that all things are essentially the same before assuming their existential and heterogenic forms. Immediately, such lenses of classical *tianxia* defy the function of hegemonic control that is typically informed by some standard of normalcy to guide identification, intervention, and conversion. In short, cosmologically, *tianxia* approaches differences as if they were ultimately irrelevant to order. An ontological pursuit that clarifies the meanings and forms of existence would disrupt *tianxia*. *Tianxia* thus escapes ontological pursuits and calls for mechanisms to desensitize differences through ritual and symbolic reciprocity. Empirically, these interactive mechanisms have been enacting the metaphor of kindred, typically hierarchical roles that have been improvised or incurred for the context, usually bilaterally.

Contrary to pre-Qin *tianxia*'s escape from substantive ontology, an ontological pursuit is an investigation of the relations between actors all belonging to the same, usually prior ontology, such as individuals surviving the state of nature, as well as an interrogation of the existential identity of each actor in such terms, as an entitlement to life and property. Dissimilar ontologies necessarily clash because they relate actors in different ways to make them appear to be constituted by entitlements and obligations that cannot be related or coexistent. Encountering that recalls no noticeable existential entitlement would allude to exclusion or conquest for strangers. Pre-Qin *tianxia* appears to be exactly this strange kind of hegemonic ontology to contemporary nation-states, embedded in the laws of nature, that relates not through prior rights but through negotiation for patterned reciprocity in kindred role relations.

From pre-Qin *tianxia*'s perspective, actors satisfy their need for relationality through engaging in hierarchical rituals and role-play that desensitize their cosmological differences. To the extent that pre-Qin *tianxia* evades ontology, it is spontaneously counterhegemonic. Hegemonic control that produces order advances through arbitrary intervention, thus depriving conforming strangers of discretional privileges, the integrity of selfhood, and freedom from political correctness. Pre-Qin *tianxia* romanticizes the hierarchical order by discouraging substantive control.[16] Its order, which presumably rests upon the promise of nonintervention, is composed of ritualized role-playing, such as ancestor or heavenly worship, gift giving, sworn kinship, regular summits, and even words of politeness,[17] which symbolizes a selfless center that reconfirms nonintervention.

To illustrate the above, the "invisible hand" analogy can be drawn. The invisible hand that Adam Smith famously used to describe "the perfect market" can illustrate *tianxia*, too. While the market rarely remains in equilibrium, the forces of adaptation constantly push it toward some degree of equilibrium. Likewise, *tianxia* is inclined toward an equilibrium that is rarely achieved in actuality but sufficiently powerful to orient the actors toward it. Hence, *tianxia* is the international reification of the invisible hand. Echoing the characteristic mix of freedom and order, I would label idealistic *tianxia* as "spontaneous" (or "public") and rule-based governance as "governed" (or "hegemonic") *tianxia*.

The supply and demand of the market parallel spontaneous *tianxia* and governed *tianxia*. In spontaneous *tianxia* freedom and order are positively associated, but under governed *tianxia* they are negatively associated. *Freedom* is defined as the ability and legitimacy to continue what one conventionally does within one's conventional scope. This is tantamount to a guarantee of ontological security for each actor to continue the way they are. When all are allowed to remain as they are, *tianxia* is spontaneous and perfect. Equilibrium arises when the ruler, or hegemonic actor, exerts self-restraint from exceeding the maximum level of intervention, taxation, or belittlement that the subjects or weaker actors will accept. They reciprocate with role-playing that supports the minimum level of deference and order that the ruler or hegemonic actor expects (see figure 1.1).

Figure 1.1. Spontaneous *tianxia* and governed *tianxia*. In the case of spontaneous *tianxia*, control and order are negatively associated, whereas they are positively associated under governed *tianxia*. Equilibrium is achieved where the ruler, or hegemonic actor in the case of IR, exerts self-restraint by taking care to avoid exceeding the maximum level of intervening, taxation, or belittling that is acceptable to the subjects, or the more minor actors in the case of IR, who reciprocate with role-playing that supports the minimum level of order that is acceptable to the hegemonic actor. Created by the author.

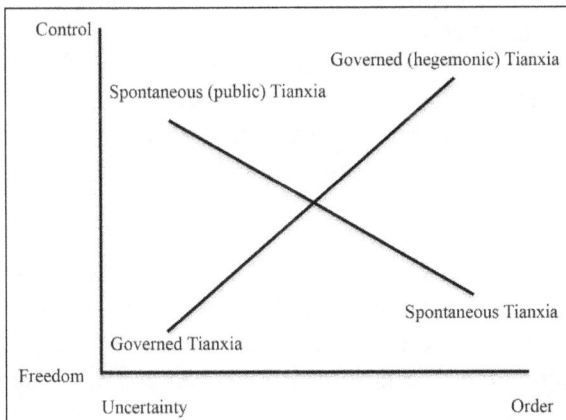

Classical Sources for Spontaneous *Tianxia*

The nascent literature on Chinese *tianxia* mainly elaborates spontaneous *tianxia*.[18] Arguably, it possesses Confucian as well as Daoist dimensions. The *Analects* of Confucius portrays *tianxia* as a manifestation of the Great Way, which is so imaginatively broad that all find room to prosper within it.[19] How does the Great Way come about? According to the *Analects*, a ruler who does not slaughter their subjects can unite all forces in *tianxia*. Confucius (551 to 479 BCE) particularly stressed low taxes to enable the population to enjoy ample crops. This demonstrates the self-restraint of the ruler, and *tianxia* earns the credit of belonging to the public. According to Confucian logic, people living in poverty elsewhere will join this ruler. Even aliens in barren lands will accept them. Additionally, if they have a sizable population, the ruler should train efficient troops to defend their territory so that their people will feel secure. Eventually, the logic continues, all of those situated far away will join the domain, which will ultimately encompass all. The land spontaneously exemplifies *tianxia* because the population follows the ruler of its own accord. These principles offered by Confucius indicate that *tianxia* constitutes not only the virtuousness of the ruler but also an essential art of governance, territorially soft borders, and rational dependence. It evades all engagement with ontological questions.

Spontaneous *tianxia* involves a lawlike principle. The ruler, who abides by Confucianism, could presumably avoid becoming a target of revolt and enjoy submission to discretional power and tributes from those who similarly wish to avoid becoming a target of the conquering forces. Such a principle is not based upon a social contract or agreement of the ruled because the beneficiaries of harmony, symbolized by gift giving, marriage, or relief from conquest, can remain alien. It is not a prior agreement necessarily evolving from the state of nature. Rather, spontaneous *tianxia* concerns how to leave the people to continue living under their own conventions. If the ruler claims to own the mandate of heaven, this could amount to an analogy of a natural contract between the ruler and heaven that, according to Mencius, is composed of the whole people.

The *Analects*' encouragement of rulers to refrain from extraction for all and continuously imagine that "all are bound to be related" harmoniously is logical. This attitude reproduces a relational world in which no consent of the governed is necessary. The beneficiaries can remain uninformed. Both a social contract and hegemony are irrelevant. Therefore, *tianxia* cannot impose a collective, shared order or norm.[20] If a ruler insists that all beneficiaries show deference, *tianxia* will be reduced to self-centralizing hegemony. For order to emerge, deference is only meaningful for the sake of rituals that indicate mutual acceptance. It is easier for both the ruler and all other actors to believe that, metaphysically, they are eventually returning to the same *Dao*, albeit each with different appearances or roles, so the higher roles are by no means more desirable or worth fighting for.

In short, spontaneous *tianxia* is rationally consensual in nature due to its promise of order without intervention. However, given the internal drive of spontaneous *tianxia* to keep the equilibrium from tilting toward control as opposed to freedom, it is too thin to guide actual interactions in reality. People must figure out their relationships intersubjectively. As such, the confirmation of a ritual hierarchy with the ruler is more important than the contents of the relationship. Accordingly, relying on the ruler's recognition to gain legitimacy in the domestic political competition manifests the ruler's soft power.[21] Nominal recognition is essential to order in spontaneous *tianxia*, where order and freedom coexist, but a convergence of values, religion, or institutions is counterproductive.

Spontaneous *tianxia* could pose a threat to the system of Westphalia in the same way that market forces threaten political regimes. Even so, the market can never replace the government. These are two different, coexisting, and yet mutually constituting systems. For example, the market economy bypasses the nation-state to some extent. While the company cannot run the government directly, its interests constitute the government's agenda. In comparison, the bilaterally negotiated Belt and Road Initiative corridors, which have been popular since the 2010s and cross sovereign borders, likewise make the system of Westphalia dependent on, and therefore vulnerable to, the influence of the corridor provider.[22]

The system of Westphalia contrarily depicts governed *tianxia*, in which the desire for ungoverned freedom remains unfulfilled. Rather, control is the standard solution because differences in values, religion, or institutions become threats to the rights of nature.[23] The typical advocacy by Beijing for nonintervention in so-called rogue states, for example, indicates that China is acting in its self-interest rather than fulfilling its responsibilities under global governance. However, nonintervention, which pre-Qin Confucianism would recommend during times of extreme chaos, reproduces the virtue of self-restraint, making the difficult practical relationships with rogue states seem more like a family feud. Actors subscribing to spontaneous *tianxia* do not expect a family feud to continue forever, as they would an irreconcilable ideological rivalry, such as between socialism and capitalism or secularism and fundamentalism. Patience instead of conversion is considered more practical here.

Differences in Westphalia's relational configurations explain why liberal regimes struggle to understand the strengths and weaknesses of the stranger *tianxia*. Specifically, this concerns the irony that the ontology of spontaneous *tianxia* rejects the idea of global governance and, therefore, espouses counterhegemonic sensibilities. In practice, spontaneous *tianxia* relies on engagements in context to ritualize mutual acceptance, making it unlikely that the realist balance of power, neoliberal regime, or constructivist pursuit of peace will serve as a consistent guide. Note that Westphalia is territorial (i.e., multi-sited), while spontaneous *tianxia* encompasses all (i.e., it is holistic). This contrast reinforces the impression that a Chinese leader stands at the center or top of a hierarchy to rule the world. Chinese *tianxia* cannot help but imply revisionism from the perspective of equality and the mutually exclusive characteristic of sovereign states under Westphalia.[24]

However, spontaneous *tianxia* does not govern through hierarchy or the deference that the emperor receives. Deference is not for the emperor to enjoy, either. A display of deference toward a morally higher actor, at best, symbolizes a relationship of mutual acceptance. Such a lofty image is designed to calm the population, not inspire in them a fear of exploitation or interventionism. However, deference may involute when a leader abuses their higher role.[25] Nonetheless, just as it is impossible in the case of a capitalist market to predict how long it will take for each macrorecession or micromonopoly to return to equilibrium, it is also impossible to guarantee how long it will take for an abusive leader to return to the practice of self-restraint. In any case, *tianxia*'s evasion of an ontological order and its corrupt cycles merely reminds the members of Westphalia, new and old, of its seeming tendency for conquest.

For proponents of Westphalia, the liberal remedy to anarchy embraces identity, value consistency, and duty of global governance. Liberalism informs the moral judgments on the conditions and the performance of those national actors involved in events. In contrast, integrity defined by role obligations and metaphors of kinship under Confucian *tianxia* unavoidably breeds suspicion regarding the indiscriminate application of norms and disregard for mutuality under liberal governance.

After all, *tianxia* espouses less the prior consent of the population that justifies ruling than the art of role making. In the absence of a social contract in world politics, spontaneous *tianxia* appears even more dreadful, as its pledger improvises various partnerships, kinships, communities of shared future, "one country, two systems," and so on that assume neither anarchy nor consent.

For Westphalia, along with liberal governance, rule-embedded universalisms are useful methods for transcending the concerns for power or national interests. The remedy of universalism serves to overcome both self-interests and fear of great powers—mainly former colonizers, in other words—constituting a relational practice that allegedly connects all national actors to form governing regimes.[26] For the *tianxia* kind of order, rituals composed of improvised roles camouflage the discrepancy between identities and practices everywhere to make room for all to contrive relationships in their distinctive contexts while simultaneously symbolically connecting all who give the pretense of honoring the same moral center. As a result, insincerity is a prominent psychological feature in balancing order and freedom in *tianxia*. Shallowness is, arguably, the strength that enables coexistence via rituals (as opposed to intervention/long-armed jurisdiction and conversion/jailing) and the weakness that shuns governing. It is no wonder that subscribers to Westphalia, which is Christian in nature, are wary that *tianxia* claims to relate all yet ignores their rights and duties, which inform rules-based governance and the ensuing self-restraint.

Tianxia as Mutual Soft Power

Tianxia is a system of soft power that every nation can access, regardless of its level of power. Whereas some nations can provide order, others rely on this order and provide checks and balances. The extent to which order rests upon intervention or nonintervention reflects the dynamics of the balance between contending providers, shifting subscribers, and their internal forces.[27] The provider's reputation immediately impacts how its prescribed order is received. For instance, the interventionist image of a provider such as Washington, DC, may attract and alienate potential subscribers. Similarly, the noninterventionist image of Beijing's leaders can simultaneously attract and alienate. The fact that subscribers to order can choose to be alienated from the providers of an order indicates that the level of power is not the determining factor. Rather, it is also the kind of order (i.e., spontaneous or governed) that constitutes the subscribers' identities that, combined with their level of power, affect the preferred balance between order and freedom. Subscribers facing particular conditions can always rebalance between freedom and order.

The order exemplifies spontaneous *tianxia* wherever it prescribes no specific norm of governance for its subscribers to follow. Instead, it is the result of rituals and gift giving. Nonetheless, global governance can also be a form of spontaneous *tianxia*, provided that the subscribers can still resist intervention and withdraw from prescribed practices or are exempt from supporting intervention elsewhere. Spontaneous *tianxia* acknowledges that no solution can be permanent and, instead, tolerates nonsolutions to keep the parties to a conflict coexisting in peace. Nonsolutions certainly violate the rules, so they are allegedly exceptions. Exceptions transform the violation of rules into the benevolence of the system. Rules appear to be universally applicable in theory while they are undermined in practice.

Concerning Westphalia, the order that Washington asserts and provides to cope with global issues is usually multilateral, so it applies to all. Since it is unlikely that Washington will constantly monitor and convert or jail all who abort the US-led neoliberal order, resistance is potentially ubiquitous. In other words, the US order is an implicitly governed *tianxia*. The soft power of the subscribers to the US-led neoliberal order is their ability to discredit US leadership. Conversely, however, the greater soft power that Washington nonetheless wields is based on subscribers' continuing desire that opportunities and ways of life are asserted in the world that is prescribed by the neoliberal order.[28] Although subscribers may dislike an arbitrary US president or their interventionist platform, the subscribers' quest for the freedom to act or not will eventually yield once they judge that freedom from rules may ultimately jeopardize order. Washington can take advantage of the resulting self-restraint of subscribers to continue to entrench its neoliberal order.

The soft power of the United States lies ultimately in subscribers accepting those neoliberal rules and agendas as their own, which will promote the coexistence of order and freedom and therefore transform an initially governed *tianxia* into a voluntarily spontaneous *tianxia*. Such a transformation reminds one of Richard Neustadt's stress on the presidential power to persuade instead of giving orders.[29] According to Neustadt, the power to rule is the power to convince each potential ally that it is in their own interest to act in ways that are in line with the president's wishes. The essence of spontaneous *tianxia* lies precisely in branding the president's agenda without invoking the president's power or interest, rather than in Confucian benevolence. At this stage, interventionism evolves into everyone's governmentality to protect the hegemonic interests as everyone else's own. This is certainly a remote destiny.

Alternatively, in Confucianism's historical practice, order may form through a relationship whereby the actors enter into reciprocal arrangements. Different combinations of relational hierarchies constitute the identities of both actors in a bilateral relationship. A Confucian leader's order is usually bilateral in nature,[30] so it is a relational order that is exclusively arranged for the other party. Presumably, no party has any cause to worry about intervention provided that both perform their ritual roles and exchange the appropriate favors periodically. Confucianism's preferred order has explicitly been *tianxia* throughout the twenty-first century, with or without the label, allowing other parties to shame China by withdrawing from a ritual (e.g., a newly inaugurated leader not first visiting Beijing), performing the deferential ritual to another great power (e.g., inviting the US Navy to visit), appealing to an indiscriminate rule to deal with Beijing as a stranger (e.g., treating Chinese citizens as merely international visitors, especially in Taiwan), or even acting in an explicitly destructive manner toward the ritual (e.g., defying the "One China" principle). Beijing's punishment would discredit *tianxia* as freedom, but restraint from sanctions would likewise create the impression that *tianxia*, as reciprocal order, aborts reciprocity. This almost guarantees that Beijing must punish and then yield. (See chapter 4 for a discussion of the acted anger.) The soft power of the other party lies in the ease of shaming Beijing.[31] It also embraces the anticipation that Beijing could not afford a permanent severance of a reciprocal relationship. In turn, Beijing's greater soft power arises from the calculation of the other party to take advantage of Beijing's eventual settling and, therefore, in the long run, habitually and willingly return to Beijing's bilateral agenda that is already familiar to them all.[32]

In fact, in its contemporary diplomacy, the longest expression of anger that Beijing has consistently imposed on the other party was its seven-year boycott of a bilateral summit with Norway. This was related to the awarding of the Nobel Peace Prize to Chinese dissident Liu Xiaobo (1955 to 2017). The shortest expression of anger was the implicit threat to end economic aid in response to the Dalai Lama's visit to Mongolia.

This lasted a fortnight. In between these incidents, there was anger at the Philippines for its bidding for justice through international arbitration over what China believes to be a bilateral dispute. There was also staged anger at Seoul over Washington's deployment of the THAAD (Terminal High Altitude Area Defense) missile defense system in South Korea. Among these examples, only the Philippines specifically backed down from the initial practice that angered China, but it is still ready to resume its position at a future point. The performed anger at Vietnam was the least sincere, as mixed messages of punishment and reward were sent continuously. The anger at Tokyo's nationalization of the Senkaku Islands simultaneously claimed by Beijing was probably stronger but insincere, too, as no real sanctions have been imposed and the Chinese prescription is to delay the settlement rather than solve it permanently. Note that Beijing's ontological security has never considered the values or institutions of the other side.

If Beijing's soft power is to couple with the other party of interaction,[33] it deals with Washington in the same way. Given Washington's insistence on rule binding, Beijing's coupling policy presumably performs rules explicitly at moments that are perceived to be critical to Washington, such as during the war on terror, but relaxes at other times or when associated with other actors. Even where Beijing complies, it still complies in particular contextual terms so that Beijing benefits, to the extent that Beijing enforced an associated anti-terrorist campaign in Xinjiang. In other words, Beijing's rule binding embraces a different kind of self-restraint, one that can befriend Washington rather than remaining faithful to the norms.[34] For Beijing, there is no inevitable contradiction between the US-undergirded order and Beijing's preoccupation with role relations. For the sake of its working relationship with Washington, Beijing can be a part-time regime subscriber.

Furthermore, Beijing provides no alternative norms to replace the liberal norms.[35] Spontaneous *tianxia* offers far more practical freedom to the other party and equalizes actors with different power levels. Each is entitled to an evaluative position and the legitimacy to expose the stronger side's infidelity. As such, the weaker power could expose Beijing's practice of control that is incompatible with spontaneous *tianxia* and shame Beijing into reconsidering its policies. This occurs frequently. Beijing has periodically but continuously annoyed significant neighbors, including Hanoi, Ulaanbaatar, New Delhi, Manila, Tokyo, Pyongyang, Taipei, and Hong Kong, creating the impression that Beijing owns no soft power. All of these neighbors seem to have resorted to shaming each other in their customary manner.

Compared with *tianxia* under the tributary system, Beijing's balance between providing order and imposing rituals is more complicated in the twenty-first century.[36] First of all, nominally, there are no more vassal states. All states are sovereign today. Any unilateral request or imposition from Beijing would appear as sheer bullying instead of preaching, rectifying, or caring, as dynastic emperors used to claim. Second, China's rise has dramatically expanded its influence, engendering simultaneously a great deal of conflict, where there have been few prior references to guide relationships. Resorting to historical analogies, documents, and discourses to ritualize the evolving coupling relationships immediately incurs suspicion of conquest. *Tianxia* is one such analogy. The Middle Kingdom is another. Both concepts are annoying to the system of Westphalia, as the latter maps the world in terms of sovereign nations or globalization and values' indigeneity and localization.

Nevertheless, the neighbors are all too familiar with their relationships in the past. They come from a shared historical habitus and appreciate the bifurcation of the two provided routes of *tianxia*. In contemporary IR, there is historical and cultural relationality that prepares Beijing and its neighbors to conceive each other in certain ways.[37] Specifically, this is linked to the Middle Kingdom imagination of China as lying at the center, with her neighbors at the periphery. Despite the conscious attempt by both sides to transcend such tributary imagination, these bilateral relationships continue to foreground an implicit hierarchical consciousness.

Consequently, neighbors struggle to move these relationships but strongly suspect that neither Beijing's nor their own consciousness has succeeded. The hierarchical pretension of Confucian *tianxia* breeds confrontational sensibilities in each actor, whose anger makes little sense to a Westphalian, where the weak "suffer what they must."[38] In other words, the parties feel that their self-conceptions of their roles are threatened qua ontological security rather than physical security. Hence, a nominal event, such as a visit by the Dalai Lama, can trigger their mutual estrangement more than an intended, tangible harm, such as anti-Chinese campaigning, and yet be far briefer in duration.

After becoming sovereign, following benevolent leaders elsewhere is politically incorrect. Neighbors, due to the colonialized history, are generally sensitive to sovereign equality and thus alert to transnational influences as control symbols. Specifically, the hierarchical subconsciousness embedded in *tianxia* results in cycles of role deserting and role repairing. The invisible hand of *tianxia* urges the two actors to find ways to oblige each other so that some mutually reciprocal relationship can emerge.[39] The interplay between spontaneous and governed *tianxia* suggests the existence of a ceiling on the intensity or duration of any confrontation. If a neighbor tries to shame China for failing the test of *tianxia*, it could risk colluding in reproducing *tianxia* as its a priori lens, and China ostentatiously occupies the central position;[40] if a neighbor abandons the use of *tianxia* when coping with Beijing, it could then suffer as either a victim of confrontation or a chess piece of the United States in its quest for allies. In sum, the ability of China's Asian neighbors to shame Beijing by revealing how Chinese behavior collides with *tianxia* ironically reproduces China's discursive order.

Nowadays, Beijing's soft-power elements are not welcome in Asia, nor is deference expressed by other Asian nations. Instead, Beijing continues to act as a role model by evading the synchronization of rules and practicing noninterventionism in bilateral engagements. *Tianxia*, informed by Beijing's bilateral agenda, transcends the regimes and rules policed by Washington and attracts audiences everywhere, be they subscribers to liberal governmentality or not. Beijing's soft power, embedded in coupling national freedom with order, is sequential:

1. A practice that turns from universal, liberal prescriptions (which often opt to speak of "the China model," to the alarm of the Chinese authorities,[41] who deny any universal route of governance) and a plausible role model of economic growth everywhere that justifies the freedom to adopt or continue illiberal governance

2. An appreciation of indigenously contrived solutions to problems so that intervention yields to support in kind, mainly in terms of necessities and infrastructures (which incurs the charge of bribing dictators in exchange for energy and ports), which creates the freedom to adopt or continue illiberal governance

3. The dispensing with an interventionist duty, and hence less control, which makes minding China's own business the only solution that can strengthen Beijing's position to

protect the extant relationship from interference by the other major powers (which closely echoes Barack Obama's overtone on strategic patience toward North Korea, even though Washington hardly substantiated this until Donald Trump's term; more on this topic can be found in chapter 3)

4. The expectations of the other side, based upon the familiarity with *tianxia*'s cycles and "the invisible hand" of freedom and order, that China will not display anger and that hegemonic *tianxia* will not continue forever (because China could likewise be harmed as a simultaneous subscriber) mean that there is always room for reconciliation, which is usually accompanied by carefully crafted, symbolic concessions or gifts from China

China's capacity and the spilling of her population over her borders into her neighbors' territory illustrate China's rise. These Chinese immigrants exploit mineral resources, invest in the infrastructure, marry locals, bribe politicians, purchase goods through tourism, burden the local ecology, and cause conflicts. The national consciousness attached to borders prevents the Confucian treatment of all people in the world as distant kin. Consequently, Beijing's conscious pursuit of a positive image, qua soft power, is nearly disastrous in practice, and yet the abovementioned soft power that Beijing unknowingly possesses continues to keep others adhering hopefully to Chinese agendas. Such agendas parallel rather than replace the US-led agendas, since the Chinese agendas are not about rules.

Conclusion

Once conceived of as the force of equilibrium between freedom and order, *tianxia* allows for a comparative study of the styles of international order and their behavioral consequences. Such *tianxia* provides a scheme that is broader than the current IR theorizing to accommodate those (Confucian and liberal) practices that initially appeared to be mutually estranged. The task of spontaneous *tianxia* is to allow all varieties to coexist harmoniously. Westphalia becomes a period in a cycle in which spontaneous and governed *tianxia* alternate, depending on the soft power of the hegemonic actor to shape the preferences of the other actors.

Accordingly, rule-based interventionism and ritual-oriented noninterventionism are parallel modes of *tianxia*, each with its own cycles while together in a pluriversal relation.

Unaware of the driving force toward an equilibrium between order and freedom, current subscribers to Westphalia feel anxious about the estranging paradigm of *tianxia*, which to them seems revisionist. In practice, however, Westphalia and *tianxia* are similarly questing for the ideal of spontaneous *tianxia*, which embraces freedom. However, the rules and regimes of Westphalia may differ dramatically as time passes, therefore making enforcement more typical than freedom. Spontaneous *tianxia* differs in that it does not change over time—an amorphous and timeless sameness embedded in pre-Qin Daoism perseveres in all actors and nonactors. This leads to a situation whereby the lingering lens of a reciprocal hierarchy between the actors, together with the imagined non-existential Daoism, hinders the Chinese leaders from learning about multilateral regimes that require a rules-based self-identity. Despite the fact that the system of Westphalia assimilates Beijing as an adherent to national interest and power, from time to time, spontaneous *tianxia* continues to inspire Beijing to resort to self-restraint as opposed to expansionism.

Beijing usually pays more attention to ritualized reciprocity with actors historically unfamiliar to *tianxia* through gift giving designed to exempt both sides from the need to control. This is one of the reasons why China's image is better in Latin America and Africa than in Asia,[42] where neighbors perceive insincerity, complain about arbitrariness, display annoyance or contempt, and await appeasement.[43] As such, the power level of an actor does not determine their preference between governed and spontaneous *tianxia*. Conversely, the choices of all actors affect the strategy of how to relate with others. This has nothing to do with being Western or not. In practice, governed *tianxia* under Westphalia can evolve into spontaneous *tianxia* through assimilation. This is the process of internalizing rules and norms. On the contrary, spontaneous *tianxia*, informed by Confucianism, can be reduced to governed *tianxia*. This is the process of losing self-restraint and abusing deference.

Tianxia is also the practical wisdom to shun ontological pursuits. It is an art of reconciling differences and a lawlike principle for the ruling elite to maintain harmony. Spontaneous *tianxia* gives Beijing greater soft power because the other actors stay with China's relational agenda regarding bilateral role making despite simultaneous compliance with the regimes led and guarded by the United States. With their intellectual capacity to reveal Beijing's ulterior self-centered calculation and express their contempt for such calculative behavior, the relational others in China's neighborhood can take ownership of the weapon of the weak to compel Beijing to retreat from a dispute eventually. Consequently, anxiety emerges regarding the uncertain timing and manner of when and how Beijing will surely, somehow, embark on the next cycle of self-restraint. The focused anxiety reproduces China's status as the Middle Kingdom. *Tianxia* portrays the inescapable dilemma between order and freedom at all levels. All, who are bound to be related, remain obliged to improvise a mutual ritual every once in a while.

2

Rivalry in *Tianxia*

Hegemony as Role Relations

Introduction

The cosmology of *tianxia*, in which all are bound to be related, is so evasive that it compels all to negotiate agreeable mutual roles and predicts that all will. This open-ended order alludes to the process of role making that is exempt from prior consensual duties. This chapter explores the Sino-US rivalry in terms of the two parties' role cultures. It reflects on the cosmology of the Chinese game *weiqi* (literally, "encircling stones"; *go* in the Japanese jargon) to deepen the theory of rivals in international politics and analyze contemporary Chinese internationalism. Such a metaphor enables Henry Kissinger to comfortably formulate a narrative that explains the strategic intent behind China's rise.[1] However, scholars and practitioners have not taken up Kissinger's reflections according to *weiqi*. Foreign policy studies rarely theorize the role of rivals in international politics beyond a rudimentary, undifferentiated understanding of rivals as simply bodies who oppose each other.[2] Kissinger is arguably the only influential strategic practitioner in the Anglosphere who has displayed an appreciation of the differences between the philosophical orientations of the United States and China toward their roles in world politics.

This chapter derives a Confucian lesson of Chinese international policy from the cosmology of *weiqi* and argues for an alternative explanation of the processes of international relations (IR) under the circumstance of US-China rivalry. It will first defend the utility of *weiqi* in theorizing

IR and China's internationalism. A comparison with chess will follow. A striking contrast is that every chess piece abides by rules that are specifically written for it. Identities inform behavior regardless of the context. In contrast, all of the stones in *weiqi* are identical, although, contingent on the context, their functions and influences differ sharply and evolve over time. Such an indistinctive identity provides no clue to behavioral tendencies without a context.

Cast into the role of power rivals, neither Beijing nor Washington, DC, seriously expects the other to honor any role duties, meaning that the two countries are not mutually obliged to any significant extent.[3] Therefore, on the one hand, Beijing is ready to both engage in and suffer ethical harassment, as if no role obligation existed between itself and its rival. They cannot practice mutual acceptance. On the other hand, Beijing's obligation as a rival is to enhance the recognition of China as always being more beneficial to the world than the United States is—in other words, to balance its role relations with others more effectively.[4] This benefactor role necessitates Beijing's pursuit of strategic partnerships all over the world, which subdues Washington's influence. Finally, this chapter suggests how Washington's expectations of Beijing as a chess player misconceive the latter's competition style.

Chinese Internationalism as *Weiqi*

In *weiqi*, competitive relations between rivals do not determine how they interact. A prior relation between rivals is that the board of *weiqi* constitutes both players ontologically, with the result that the expansion of one's opponent restricts one's potential. Still, one can also manage to survive inside the other. This resonates with the Chinese philosophy of yin-yang. Yin and yang are configured as existing inside each other, and their colors are the same as the stones of *weiqi*—black and white. Yin-yang informs a worldly IR, where the actors are mutually constituted and their relationships fluid, making it unlikely that one will act unilaterally without simultaneously reconstituting the entire world and also their own identities.[5] Therefore, one party's present gain is not equal to the other's future loss. These factors suggest that a player's existential security relies more on their position on the board than on their relationship with the other player.

Weiqi incorporates Chinese cosmology and cultural wisdom.[6] Some IR scholars have framed *weiqi* as illustrative of contemporary Chinese strategic culture.[7] This metaphor is plausible. On the one hand, *weiqi* is an elitist tradition that all scholar-officials had to learn and practice.[8] On the other hand, several studies have noted the parallels between the strategy of *weiqi* and Chinese strategic patterns in areas such as Chinese guerrilla warfare,[9] operations in the South China Sea,[10] and the partnerships in China's Belt and Road Initiative (BRI).[11] Noticeably, among other Chinese philosophical clichés, the game of *weiqi* reproduces the practical philosophy of *guanxi*, the proclivity for long-term thinking, the culture of yin-yang, and the peculiar stress on *shi* (勢, or the macrotrend affirmed by individual events taking place either consecutively or simultaneously).[12]

However, if we consider *guanxi* as the mutually obliged relationship embedded in the metaphor of kin, the notion that interactions between rivals or opponents can make any sense of *guanxi* within Chinese culture is problematic. When it comes to rivalry, nations seeking harmonious role relations rarely behave harmoniously. To discover harmonious *guanxi* between rivals defeats the purpose of the game, which is to outperform the opponent. It also misrepresents the process of the game, which easily incurs fierce competition. Such competition defies the ethical, often hierarchical in some sense, relationships that exist outside the game. To the extent that *weiqi* cannot be sufficiently informed by the value of harmony or *guanxi*, it is an extended metaphor for Chinese strategic competition.[13]

Winning a game settles the final role positions of both players; the winner is the symbolic cosmological leader, and the loser accepts the subordinate role. Before the end, they have no agreeable relation, let alone *guanxi*, although, separately, each imagines a role relation with the board as *tianxia*. Specifically, as *weiqi* compels rivals to outperform each other, the rivalry relationship is distinctly unlike other types of *guanxi* in Chinese society, including those between rulers and officials, teachers and students, and various family members. While artificially constructed *guanxi* can emerge between strangers, through gift giving to oblige both sides to take certain roles,[14] none of these dyadic roles can guide interactions with rivals.

In a nutshell, *weiqi* provides the metaphoric lesson for how players engage in rivalry without a consensual role conception. The players in *weiqi* compete over their capacity to gain acceptance in the rest of the world, giving an American observer reason to misperceive that they are no different from chess players.

Tianxia as the Stone Board of Weiqi

The board of *weiqi*, a metaphor for the earth, symbolizes the mothering force that enables the stones to procreate. The black and white colors of the two troops symbolize yin and yang—the philosophized genesis of living forces, which the stones represent. All players of *weiqi*, regardless of who they are and where or when they are playing, owe their role to the board. Modern players achieve rankings even though some have never participated in the same games as rivals. These rankings do not reflect who the player's opponents are. Ultimately, one's role performance on the board comprises one's own record;[15] the other player's moves on the board in each game are not conclusive. As it is impossible for a player to eliminate or disqualify their opponent, the board guarantees the coexistence of both players. To that extent, the board could reflect a degree of the Confucian state of nature and the configuration that nothing is unrelated even before the game starts.

Given that the board encompasses the whole space, each player must enhance their role relations with the board. One's *role relation* refers to *the state of one's role being accepted*, regardless of the contents of the role's conception, and one's *role* refers to *the functions one is expected to fulfill*, which is substantive. In *weiqi*, a role relation on the board comprises primarily the sum of the imagined relationships that each gradually establishes throughout the game. *Weiqi* stresses the summation of role relations rather than the promotion of specific role conceptions. In other words, agreeing on a role is more important than the role's contents. Between the players, the role relations are, by their nature, thin. Therefore, as there are only two players, the proper role duty of each is to encircle more space on the board in order to win, since more space indicates a broader scope of acceptance of one's contextually differential roles by the people of *tianxia*, or in other words, the *guanxi* of *tianxia*.

Accordingly, *weiqi* is no cultural anomaly. It still pertains to role relations, although *guanxi* culture evades rivalry. As the board compels both coexistence and rivalry, success depends on a player's skill in outperforming their rival with regard to winning acceptance. Despite the absence of any threat to their survival, the players block each other's efforts to encircle further space as they compete for the attention of *tianxia*; they are bound to be related in the sense of waiting for the same population to follow one of them.

A culture of harmony cannot theorize this rival relationship into certain normative role expectations as it does in the case of the other social qua ethical dyads. Accordingly, *weiqi* illustrates the nonethical, thus discursively inexpressible, aspect of Confucian culture concerning rivalry. Exactly because the rival is not an expressible role in the culture of harmony and yet rivalry is common in daily life, *weiqi* distinctively reveals how rivals explain away the ultimate relevance of rivalry by cultivating their relationships with the board rather than each other. Their rivalry, therefore, becomes technical rather than existential in nature. Rivals do not obligate each other with expectation, duty, or entitlement. Space, greater and lesser, is of the same quality, after all. Epistemologically, their lens is ultimately through the board's perspective, although technically they must at times prevent each other from commandeering space.

As such, *weiqi* distinguishes roles from role relations. A role made for oneself that is rejected by others does not have role relations. Role relations are thin for the rivals, who at times sabotage each other. The game, therefore, evades the necessity to specify the rival role. The opponent is not even an inevitable enemy, as rivals in *weiqi* do not necessarily engage with each other. Essentially, *weiqi* demonstrates how a nation can practice coexistence and rivalry simultaneously, without needing to create a clear role for the rival.[16] Indeed, one grants the rival a role only after winning or losing, at which point, paradoxically, the rival ceases to be a rival, as the game has finished.

The importance of role relations suggests that the pressure of harmony between the actor and the entire population is far stronger than that between rivals. One enhances one's overall harmony by performing one's self-role faithfully, thereby winning the trust of all others. Therefore, the highest level of self-actualization is achieved through continuous self-rectification, which exempts one from any lingering egocentric desire. This has the effect of being recognized as being harmoniously related everywhere, which is called "internal transcendence."[17] One's role relations are, therefore, ultimately a matter of one's goodness rather than compliance with any all-encompassing prior rule or norm. This state contrasts with the external transcendence that is familiar from the Christian tradition, in which compliance with external truth and goodness is essential for overcoming original sin or deficiencies. Nevertheless, both the Christian compliance to truth and goodness and Confucian selflessness are practices of self-restraint, despite their apparently different cosmologies.

Instead of destroying devils who abort the previously given imperative of goodness, *weiqi* requires a player to establish connections everywhere on the board. In Confucianism, role relations can remain in place for long periods and cover great distances only after self-rectification has successfully cleansed one's desires. Confucian humanism assumes that restored selflessness reflects humanity's original goodness, as opposed to faith in an external God. Therefore, a Confucian actor with greater integrity presumably achieves better role relations than their rival. Goodness is unconnected with seeking the kingdom of God or servicing his righteousness, and success is ultimately an internal process of self-rectification.

However, the roles created for rivals are straightforward in the IR literature,[18] as seen in the case of chess. For example, in Alexander Wendt's constructivist formulation, rivals are a prior, collective representation that supervenes their nation-states.[19] There are expectations regarding how the other player will and must continue to act as a rival and a need to predict how they will do so. Rivalry forms part of world order in the English-school tradition[20] as well as "the liberal international order."[21] Wendt's use of role, which explains the rivalry embedded in the European tradition of natural law,[22] sometimes makes no sense to a *weiqi* rival, who can contrarily make moves that neither comply with the prior consensual norms nor make any apparent contribution to their position in said rivalry. According to its context, a *weiqi* rival focuses on being accepted by the entire world, particularly the part of the world that is not involved in the current rivalry. Once accepted, one simultaneously restricts one's rival's options according to how they are received. The lessons of *weiqi* add to the role-theory sensibilities of role relations that echo the relevance of "role location" but marginalize "role sources" or "role contents."

Winning the Game of *Weiqi*

A *weiqi* player needs to encircle more space than their opponent in order to win the game. Engagement is usually inevitable because, sooner or later, the two players encroach upon each other's territory and the disadvantaged party has no alternative but to launch an invasion.

Despite being a significant step toward taking more space, capturing the other side's troops does not guarantee victory, nor is it the goal of the engagement. The tactics of taking space and engagement require different abilities.[23] A player must usually anticipate how different moves may alter their opponent's range of options. One's strength of engagement is determined by how many steps in advance one can maximally preempt the opponent. The intense, comprehensive engagement thus resembles chess. Consequently, players demonstrate no benevolent characteristics to each other during the fierce engagement.

In contrast to engagement, taking space, which is the game's purpose, is not entirely concerned with logical reasoning. There is a good deal of uncertainty because it takes a troop of many stones to encircle an area of space, and thus the impacts of placing one stone in an open space are usually unclear. At this initial stage, almost all of the stones on the board appear disconnected. Strategic planning is heuristic, and engagement is not usually part of the game plan at this stage. Instead, the aim is to develop one's holding to prepare for strategic opportunities in the making. Disconnected stones can come under threat at any time, as the game evolves. At the same time, they can also play a critical role in encircling space in the future. In short, it is impossible and unnecessary to be certain which stones will connect with each other when first placed in the open spaces.[24]

As the game proceeds, several disparate aspects of playing converge into one real-world lesson about taking space. If we consider the open spaces as being analogous to unallied third parties, taking space is like strategically investing in networking to (1) keep third parties from supporting the rival, (2) prepare them for defection in a time of need, and (3) mobilize their minor support. These strategies toward third parties are not about regulating their policies, synchronizing their governance, or converting their values.

Accordingly, losing space constitutes a definitive threat. The best way to win is not by directly attacking one's rivals but instead by taking space that could be used by one's opponent later. The second strategy for winning is based on invasion, which becomes necessary when the rival's ample space can be anticipated, if not invaded. At this moment, the previously disconnected stones can become vital by providing links. Accordingly, the strategic wisdom of *weiqi* suggests that any relationship can become helpful in a way that cannot be anticipated in advance. The third strategy for winning concerns squeezing, which entails forcing one's rival to squander some space in order to protect the space they have already taken. If the two competitors are almost equivalent in terms of the amount of space they have each taken toward the end, squeezing is their only resort.

Moreover, the strategy of abduction is occasionally applied. A player can bluff with no chance of succeeding if their opponent defends immediately, but bluffing can push their opponent to choose between a minor loss or a more significant one. The bluff of the ostensible stake reveals the negotiable characteristic of *weiqi*.

The stones on the board reflect a familiar cosmological belief that is embedded in various schools of thought. Specifically, all of the stones and space points on the board are of equal value. There is no distinction, as there is in chess between the king, queen, bishop, rook, knight, and pawn. The value of a particular stone depends on how it contributes to a guarding or invading troop and can change as the game goes on. In short, a stone must be used in association with a troop in order to be helpful, yet a small troop can be sacrificed for more significant gains elsewhere. Since all stones are of equal quality, it makes little difference which stone is lost during engagement with the opponent. Removing a rival's stone is valuable if it enables a player to exert a stronger hold on their own space. Therefore, the game's result does not depend on which stone or even how many stones one can save or remove.

Last but not least, *weiqi* allows a player to accept defeat and resign at any time without counting the amount of space each player has taken. In practice, players save time and energy this way. More importantly, the rivalry ends without further battle, which would be unavoidable if the losing side were to insist that the game continue. Players primarily care about their relative place on the board. The early end of rivalry avoids further battles, squeezing, or simply the scene of winning and losing. Given that the game's ultimate purpose is to take space rather than destroy the opponent, an early ending makes sense if one side has already claimed sufficient space. Equally important is the social gesture of the loser—conceding is considered more graceful and civilized than unnecessarily sacrificing more troops on both sides.

China and the US in their Rival Roles

Weiqi had not been straightforwardly applicable to the Sino-US rivalry after World War II.[25] Even so, its setting was analogous to the beginning of *weiqi*, in which engagement is not apparent. From Beijing's perspective, no prior norms, such as human rights, peace, or capitalism, constituted their role relations. The US was either an imperialist, exploitative capitalist or a hegemonic actor. Each of these roles had a different meaning according to how Beijing interpreted the primary contradiction of the world in Marxist and Maoist terms. This scenario first changed following the rapprochement in the early 1970s because at this time it was possible to place the US in the role of a friend. In the twenty-first century, the role of the US as a partner emerged, indicating that the two could cooperate on certain world agendas.[26] However, these roles have no substance that is agreeable to both sides, as a typical social role might. *Weiqi* is, therefore, an appropriate metaphor.

The rise of China has sensitized the possibility of Beijing enlarging its sphere of influence in areas that its future rival would not consider critical. With regard to *weiqi*'s stress on peripheral and open spaces of equal potential value,[27] Chinese investments in Africa, South Asia, central Asia, and Latin America are classic examples. Although these investments may appear insignificant at the global level, Washington became alarmed at the emerging connections between these investments and Beijing's global influence. The idiosyncratic arrangements of these investments could potentially harm Washington's global leadership and the liberal order that constitutes the American identity.[28] From Washington's perspective, Beijing is invading its neighborhood and America's backyard, requiring Washington to perform an act of rebalancing. Such an eye-for-an-eye response reflects the chess player's perception of a *weiqi* player's rationale.[29]

A *weiqi* player would not engage in such escalation, as it contributes little to the overall role relations in the world. Washington may have wished that its military presence at various Indo-Pacific sites would deter Beijing from expanding. Still, Beijing's intention in the South China Sea, for example, may never be one of forced settlement. Beijing is also culturally well prepared to transfer its rivalry elsewhere. This is how Beijing's early investments have become points of connection.

The contribution of *weiqi* to this metaphor is its exemplification of a strategic perspective that is unfamiliar to Washington, in which coexistence and rivalry are symbiotic for Beijing. The pivot to Asia was Washington's initial way of balancing China, and Beijing has replied through neither counterbalancing nor appeasement. A *weiqi* metaphor would point to the hope that some of those points where Beijing establishes relationships separately will connect into a comprehensive sphere of mutual acceptance. The long-term hope is that, eventually, this network will cushion rule-based governance.

Washington's rebalance seeks to line up allies for a demonstrated edge over China in power and technology to contain this development. As Washington boycotts Beijing's quest for role relations, Beijing could avoid engagement and continue to seek ties. Beijing devoted what Washington would regard as useless, if not meaningless, efforts to recruit oral support worldwide. The image of having good role relations is especially crucial to a Beijing that competes to receive recognition.[30] Beijing's rival who has no role to play in Beijing's pursuit of role relations in the world cannot be Beijing's direct target unless the country takes offense in the face of it. A sensible strategy for Beijing is to outperform its rival elsewhere on local terms. This would mean actively showing goodwill to the rest of the world and coming close to a strategy of role diversification.[31] Regarding Sino-US relations, Beijing contrarily envisions no specific role for the US. According to a review of the internal debates, a trial attempt at a "new type of great power relations" was ambivalent and lukewarm.[32]

It is difficult for Washington to appreciate the *weiqi* strategy, in which Beijing finds no necessity to battle the US, nor does this concern harmony. With no clear, established, prior role relations due to a lack of intensive encountering, such as between China and Africa, a *weiqi* player would be nonconfrontational. Where there exist good (yet unstable) role relations with Washington, such as in central Europe, the *weiqi* player would plan an invasion. If there exist established, stable role relations that undergird Washington's leadership, such as in Japan, the *weiqi* player would attempt only occasional bluffing. Where role relations exist for both parties, such as in central Asia, a *weiqi* player would squeeze. The strategic lesson from *weiqi* is to improve role relations wherever possible so that "you cannot use them against me." In the eyes of Washington, however, Beijing's rationale must be that "I can use them against you." This is analogous to a chess player who cannot help but perceive an existential threat.[33]

The Sino-US rivalry, therefore, bears thin role relations, which means that the two parties are unstably related. Neither is there a kind of prior, thick relation embedded in the prior consensual rules and norms among the world of nations, nor any mutual expectation that has been successfully improvised through intersubjective role making. Without clear role expectations, a rivalry is a half-rivalry at best. Half-rivalry is necessarily incomplete, discretionary, and intermittent. It is incomplete because moves comprise concessions, albeit inconsistent ones, in addition to invasion, squeezing, or bluffing. Taking space can also represent a unilateral, disengaged strategy. It is discretionary because disengagement, strategically arranging investment, and concessions regarding global governance issues are all meaningful alternatives. It is intermittent because the winner is yet to emerge to discourage the strategies of bluffing or squeezing.

These imagined and practiced role relations between actors and the world explain Beijing's pattern of rivalry more effectively than specific role duties informed by rules. Nevertheless, rule enforcement has suffered discredit due to Washington's unilateral, arbitrary actions in the "America First" campaign, which harmed allies under the Trump administration, and the withdrawal from Afghanistan under the Biden administration, which reminded the world of America's losing of the Vietnam War. Whenever Washington competes for better role relations, be it with Pyongyang, Hanoi, or Riyadh, it likewise relaxes its imposition and enforcement of the rules.

Weiqi versus Chess Players

No two *weiqi* players share the same characteristics and capabilities, and, correspondingly, no two chess players in Washington are the same. Even the same player will not maintain the same style throughout their career. The binary of these two strategic orientations does not exist between Beijing and Washington as it does between the *weiqi* and chess considerations of the rival's role. Although people cannot play both games simultaneously, they can learn to play both games well. In practice, however, chess appears to be an appropriate metaphor for twenty-first-century Washington. The following explores chess players' responses to Beijing's overall orientation with regard to competing in the realm of role relations. Three examples are used for illustration—the South China Sea, Africa and Latin America, and the Belt and Road Initiative.

A chess rival has a clear opponent, the specific purpose of achieving checkmate, and the belief that their opponent will think and act in the same way. With all resources already displayed on the chessboard at the start of the game, the strategic skill required to destroy the opposing king's troops is crucial to achieving victory. An imagined physical showdown is the ultimate event. Such an undifferentiated understanding of the rival role conceives of all of the competition primarily for a better role relation, each in its context, as steps toward building a grand alliance for the showdown.[34] In contrast, Beijing's construction of a potential role relation is never precise at the beginning and could even be considered backward, if not completely irrelevant. This is because the area that receives Beijing's investment could be a failing state and one that is incapable of competing alongside Beijing at the same systemic level. This leads to the perception of a surprise attack, where a perceived link emerges later between these seemingly irrelevant areas and those already under contest.

For example, Beijing's BRI uses earlier investments in South Asia, Africa, and central Asia, which have no connection either conceptually or physically. In hindsight, these initially unlinked areas appear to have been registered as part of a grand strategy to undermine the rules of global governance. On the other hand, Beijing is now de-escalating after this ostensibly intense pushing and squeezing, particularly in areas where confrontation risks escalation. This creates the impression of Beijing's vulnerability. Good rivals in a chess context never blink first. Washington's China policy represents how a chess player perceives and reacts to a rival. Chas Freeman sees this in Washington's use of all means to "cripple" China's industrial policies and prevent its rise as a technological power and military competitor.[35]

A chess player would easily conceive of playing *weiqi* as a geopolitical competition. Given that the board in *weiqi* is a metaphor for the entire world (a spontaneous *tianxia* that no one owns), the act of taking space revolves around making connections between the stones, hence representing a struggle for broader role relations in the world. Contrary to the control and influences within geopolitical thinking, role relations aim to promote acceptance. Once accepted, a stone is safe. A stone can be considered safe on the board in three different degrees. First, it is safe if it is one of the encircling stones that guard a space that has already been taken. An example of this would be the Chinese practice of constructing reefs and shoals in the South China Sea. The second scenario is squeezing stones that crowd space that neither rival will take. This is exemplified by the postcolonial lands of Latin America and Africa. The third scenario reflects the connecting stones that explore new role relations in spaces where the rival is unprepared, as with the BRI.

The differentiation and sophistication of these role relations make little sense if the ultimate goal is monotonous geopolitical control. However, role relations must vary according to the conditions. For example, an encircling stone may pursue a right of veto to deny the rival's entry, a squeezing stone may constitute a parallel presence in an untaken market, and a connecting stone may reflect hospitality in a strategically innocent neighborhood. Furthermore, the question of whether an act constitutes an invasion, squeezing, or abduction is contingent upon the perceived balance of relations and is, therefore, theoretically undecidable in advance.

In the first example of the South China Sea, Beijing perceives a risk of US "invasion," which may reduce the space that has already been taken by China to a state of being unowned. Washington is the only player capable of closing in quickly, as China has already established many connected bases in the area. Even Washington, with its base in the Philippines, can only pass through, usually with Chinese destroyers monitoring the passage of its ships. Note that a critical strategy of *weiqi* is to deprive the rival of sufficient space to qualify for ownership. Being logistically able to endure longer than anyone else, Beijing merely needs to wait for the US ships to leave each time. Each encounter simply allows Beijing to reiterate its claim.[36] Nevertheless, there has been no systematic attempt to compel others to renounce their claims or harass others' passage. Rather, the aim is to have other claimants recognize China's de facto veto rights.

For the chess player, who sees all moves made by the other side as motivated by a desire to ultimately capture their opponent, Beijing cannot have any innocent alternatives to balancing the US presence. Evidence of Beijing's balancing could include the uttering of Asia for Asians, the alleged reinstallation of the tribute system, or simply military expansion and domination.[37] In fact, domination and capture are the chess player's goals. Accordingly, Beijing cannot be engaged in "peaceful rise" activities.[38] Beijing's emerging power has thus given rise to a perception of the inevitability of the country undermining the rules of international order in Asia, which undergird Washington's world leadership.[39] Given the militarization of the South China Sea shoals, the only solution to the threat of checkmate must be countermilitary moves—"if the US does not keep pace, PACOM will struggle to compete with the People's Liberation Army on future battlefields."[40] There is the war-prone inclination to reinstate a military base in Taiwan to counter China's presence in these international waters.[41]

If the South China Sea shoals can be viewed as bases that have been specifically built to outlast the rival, Beijing's actions in Africa and Latin America may not reveal such a clear purpose. Given that role relations are the competition point, a grand strategy may be too rigid to adapt, especially for a vast space of relational uncertainties. For a *weiqi* strategist, since both continents are postcolonial societies with profound European legacies, the tasks are mainly to win hearts and accrue relationship assets to gain future benefits. The other rivals and their past connections form no target. Therefore, Beijing squeezes rather than encircling the space. However, with the amount of investments and number of migrants gradually growing on both continents, this could constitute a potentially lethal threat in the eyes of a chess rival. Former secretary of state Hillary Clinton was the first statesperson to raise the charge of new colonialism relating to China's presence in Africa.[42] She contrasted Washington's style with that of Beijing and blasted the latter's irresponsible rule breaking.[43]

The same perspective emerges in the criticism of China's presence in Latin America, which, according to former secretary of state Rex Tillerson, "does not need new imperial powers that seek only to benefit their own people."[44] The media immediately noted the lingering Monroe Doctrine in his remark. Based on a think tank report,[45] a subsequent comment raised alarm about "the Chinese regime's ulterior motives" that appear to unmistakably target the US, saying the motives of Chinese investments are "thinly veiled and evident both in the structure and locational choices of such enterprises. The ventures reward ideological, anti-U.S. friends, strengthen geopolitical alliances, and serve as a platform for espionage."[46]

The real global challenge to Washington appears to be the BRI. The BRI is almost a perfect metaphor for the middle stages of *weiqi*, in which the rivals are prepared to connect their earlier stones, which have already been spread separately across the board. In the eyes of the chess player, the rival's focus cannot be the BRI per se but rather the US. This understanding perceives an offensive. Indeed, the BRI does not square with the extant rules of global governance that undergird Washington's leadership. For example, the bilateral sensibilities of each project, lauded by Beijing as mutual respect, undermine the multilateral spirit required for global governance. Consequently, Washington perceives that the "Xi administration is engaged in a concerted imperialist policy towards its developing neighbor states" to break through the US encirclement.[47] Accordingly, Washington needs to protect its primacy, together with New Delhi.[48]

Granted that the BRI may have emerged from a few previous, unconnected projects, a chess player could still contend that the *weiqi* player can learn how to play chess and aim to achieve checkmate. For example, Beijing could secure a treaty port from the local authorities if they fail to exercise their repayment schedule and, as a result, strengthen China's position vis-à-vis the US. In short, the desire for control naturally accompanies the capacity to control. However, a chess player, new or old, can conversely (re)learn *weiqi*, too. For example, Washington has attempted to create something of a "balance of corridors" and "balance of vaccines." The former balance proceeds primarily with the cooperation of New Delhi, Tokyo, Canberra, and, in the 2020s, the EU and NATO to compete with or offset Beijing's rising influences through the BRI, while the latter balance proceeds in the name of humanitarianism. None of these rivaling policies are aimed at confrontation. Instead, they mimic the *weiqi* players' anxiety about their goodwill being recognized in the open space, as either a security provider or benign investor, depending on the perceived need of the local actors. This metaphor can explain the quest for role relations to balance China's image. In other words, a chess player can learn not to view a rivalry as necessarily an eye-for-an-eye battle to achieve checkmate.

Conclusion

In practice, the chess player has role relations in mind, even though their learned responses are confrontational and containing and even include military preparation for escalation. Consider, for example, the delight of Washington to see more minor South China Sea claimants looking to the US for security support. This attests to a pursuit of good role relations. Equally noticeable has been the warning that China's foot in Africa and Latin America is exploitative and neocolonialist in nature. This warning is designed to sabotage Beijing's role relations. Instead of confronting US power directly, *weiqi* advises that Beijing should move into areas where Washington does not have any investment. For a *weiqi* player, these seemingly marginal spaces on the board may become valuable in the future, even though IR analysts would not recognize such areas as having any natural appeal.

Beijing's behavior in its role as a rival contradicts the assumption of mainstream IR—namely, that rivals will oppose each other. Instead,

Beijing will focus on its own bidding for an enhanced role relation on the world stage. The metaphor of *weiqi* is a handy heuristic device because simultaneous engagements and mutual invasion are typical characteristics of the second stage of *weiqi*. This is true for Washington, too, as its China policy stresses the simultaneity of competition and cooperation. The second stage begins roughly at a point when the alternative ways in which the board will be divided begin to surface after the earlier arranged stones show their potential for further connection. The players at this stage will begin to plan where and how to defend and invade in more detail. During such an invasion, it is more challenging to decide where else and how to start another event such that subsequent events can later merge into a macroforce that will either consolidate one's initial advantage or reverse a disadvantage.

The first two decades of the twenty-first century closely resemble the second stage of *weiqi* in the following sense. Washington's rebalance to Asia, arrangement of military presence in Taiwan, or accusation of genocide in Xinjiang is an invasion from the *weiqi* perspective. Two *weiqi* strategies ensue. First, in typical *weiqi* fashion, Beijing cycles through phases of role making, squeezing, and disengagement in the South China Sea, when neither side aims at confrontation. The timing of each strategy, however, is contingent on how Beijing evaluates the space that it considers to have been taken already. Second, disengagement becomes Beijing's main theme once rivalry prevails over friendship. Disengagement allows Beijing to focus on competing for acceptance elsewhere. An increasingly popular quotation by Mao—"you advance in your way and I advance in mine"—reflects this lack of mutual expectations, or what one might term a "thin" role relation, between Beijing and Washington. The same applies to Washington's presence in Taiwan. The principle is to squeeze the opponent and crowd the space just enough to leave no room for them to build ownership.

Washington's expectation of a rival is that this rival will square with its rules and try to reduce the rivalry through a shared commitment to global governance. The China threat is intuitively plausible because Beijing reluctantly cooperates and even sabotages many global governance issues through its bilateral efforts. These include collaboration with different failing states and Beijing's uncompromising military activities, which allegedly bully its neighbors. Washington will continue to stress the importance of military strength, even though this only forms part of what is called the all-society approach: a *weiqi* player does not try to force a solution where none is apparent. On the one hand, and somewhat ironically, Beijing does not aim to replace Washington, even as the latter anticipates an upcoming, vehement competition. On the other hand, Beijing is not unprepared militarily, even though it avoids escalation. Washington may misperceive such reluctance as weakness.

A final note on the notion of space is in order here. Space in the current literature is exclusively territorial. In practice, however, it is open to influence and can be both constructed and reconstructed. Therefore, in the same territory, there may exist multiple orders, such that politics and security do not dominate the agenda of a seemingly fixed population. Schools, families, and companies thus provide access points that allow the actors to make nuanced future connections in the fields of academia, society, and finance, thereby allowing them to influence governmentality in those spheres sporadically. The same dynamic can arise in other fields, like culture, religion, transportation, migration, technology, law, and so on. Stylistically, the quest for influence can be achieved through either sophisticated maneuvering or awkward interference.

Consequently, all actors have direct and indirect stakes in all matters that concern Beijing, which compensates for Beijing's initial disadvantages with a few abovementioned fields. The liberal order, based upon individualized rationality and revealed preference, parallels these multiple fields of governmentality that were once considered to require no further management. In practice, Beijing may continue to participate in this liberal order, apart from the fact that Beijing's encircling of previously uncontended areas has already reconstituted this rationality and the population's preferences everywhere.

Relation

Practicing Confucian IR

Part Two analyzes the coexistence of *tianxia* with other cosmological ideas, especially the neoliberal metaphor of the state of nature. Its first two chapters study the practices of relations that construct roles and perform role emotions to oblige others' reciprocal feedback. The third chapter then demonstrates why and how patience is inevitable when obliging fails and calls for nonsolutions to substitute for conflict resolution, which usually reproduces the conflict. The last two chapters trace the restoration attempts of *tianxia*, along with patience, as Confucianism falls into its minimum state of bad friendship or a certain unilateral claim to exception.

3

Role and Relation in Confucian IR

Relating to Strangers in the States of Nature

Introduction

This chapter uses role theory to bridge the gap between Confucian and Western conceptions of international relations (IR). Its comparative analysis of pluriversal IR mainly focuses on two different types of relations: prior rule-based relations and improvised relations. The diverging cultural preparations for these two relations partially explain the existence of multiple IR universes. The chapter demonstrates that both Confucian and Western IR have prior and improvised relations, similarly dealing with the estrangement between the actors. According to these types of relations, role making and role taking can reveal how these two seemingly irreconcilable IR cosmologies interact and coexist.

Western IR and Confucian IR represent two styles of prior relations—the state of nature and *tianxia*—and two styles of improvised relations—an interactive process that socializes *alters* into like members and establishes the parameters of mutual acceptance regardless of the differences between the actors. Based on the introduction and first part of this volume, chapter 3 first discusses the Confucian "state of nature" and its sensibilities toward strangers, compares them with the social contract tradition, and introduces the Confucian style of relations and roles. To illustrate the value of a composite agenda of relations and roles, the chapter uses Kim Jong-un of North Korea (NK) as an example to demonstrate how a presumably weak actor can rely on both shared prior relations and improvisation within role making to obligate reciprocal responses from strong actors—the US and China—even if the US is unfamiliar with Confucianism.

The Confucian State of Nature

Due to the evasiveness of Confucian relationality, while heavenly reason constitutes all, it belongs to an unlimited variety of people and objects. However, from the perspective of these ten thousand phenomena, they are easily mutually misperceived as strangers because of the absence of a transcendent divinity to remind them of their prior resemblance, embedded in a common but undecidable form of existence. Misperceived strangeness would curtail their natural relation, so ways of interacting must be improvised to neutralize the mutually perceived strangeness caused by the unlimited, albeit superficial and transient, variation. On the one hand, variety is a heavenly phenomenon and, therefore, natural. On the other hand, it makes no sense to attempt to draft universal rules or norms in light of the apparent variety qua strangeness. Investigating strangeness against a standard out of curiosity or converting an *alter* life accordingly is strongly discouraged.[1] Such an attitude leads to a policy preference for relationship management over governance.[2] Gift giving is, arguably, the most common (self-)socializing mechanism within Confucianism's dyadic relationship management style.[3]

Confucianism preaches the wisdom of "keeping the aliens governable by not governing them." This evasion of any ontological settlement suggests that, to Confucius, aliens are not equivalent to strangers. He praised the true benevolent persons as those who presumably bring with them gifts and lofty postures that are appreciated by aliens and whom aliens have no difficulty accepting; however, unfaithful rulers can become estranged, even in their own neighborhood, because they levy rather than give.[4] In other words, distance does not define strangeness, which is internally untamed.[5] Strangeness is thus politically incorrect but revealing wherever the audience rejects self-roles. It is the heavenly mandate—a kind of natural contract between each ruler and heaven—that obliges rulers to win acceptance from the existing members of the population through their benevolence, which further enables those who accept them to accept one another. Mutual acceptance is called face culture. Face, as the vernacular side of the role, pertains to *concealing the stranger inside everyone.*

The notion of a stranger derived from Confucianism echoes the recent call for a critical reflection on the literature on the stranger. The critical approach discovers "ahistorical, orientalist, racialised, colonialist, and historicist fault lines" in the literature.[6] It justifies a parallel call for a relational analysis of the stranger. It foregrounds the revisiting of Confucianism.[7] The Confucian stranger is simultaneously an internal object, shameful, unrelated, threatening, and an external object to appease, and so neither an orientalized outsider nor an autonomous entity. This stranger appears only where mutually congruent expectations fail to emerge, for they lose a role relationship. Such a conception of the stranger contrasts with the other kind of stranger in the social contract tradition. In the latter version, the stranger can and should be socialized into a prudent citizen, constituted by their prior right of nature.[8] Once socialized, prudent citizens are entitled to individualized preferences and opinions that inform their identities distinctively. In comparison, Confucianism regards strangers as misperceived self-identities caused by their inherent diversity, which can and should be avoided by all who acquiesce to mutual benevolence.

Relational strangers, who are related through their likeness according to the European traditions of the state of nature, would suffer under dreadful anarchy were it not for the security provided by the social contract. At the state level, diplomacy offers a way to cope with the imagined anarchy between these like strangers.[9] The difference between the Confucian and Western cosmologies in formulating the state of nature alludes to the subsequent bifurcation of the relation conception. Let us take Thomas Hobbes as an example, since his narrative on anarchy inspired modern IR. Hobbes "ascribes to each person in the state of nature a liberty right to preserve herself, which he terms 'the right of nature.'"[10] Humans will recognize as imperative the injunction to seek peace and do everything necessary to secure it, when this can be done safely. Hobbes calls these practical imperatives the "Lawes of Nature,"[11] a rule-prone relation that binds all to the absolutist Leviathan, who may compromise this right in exchange for providing security.

Social contract theorists generally embrace "natural rights," with or without Hobbes's Leviathan, as the prior relation that constitutes all individual and national actors. Alexander Wendt, for example, shows how anarchy is about collective qua social figuration. English-school scholars, especially "solidarists," tend to agree.[12] Such prior relations, informed by the law of nature, postulate an a priori humanist ontological semblance. A noticeable component of the Hobbesian state of nature speaks to "the primitive units," such as families, ordered by "internal obligations"—affection, sexual affinity, friendship, clan membership, and a shared religious belief.[13] This latter line of thinking echoes the core of Confucianism—kindred love. However, in general, the natural law in the West transcends primitive relations. Instead, it privileges autonomy, rationality, and equality, where all are entitled to possess identities and desires as a natural right. Such shared entitlement offers a guarantee of security, which breeds social tolerance, solidarity, and communitarianism.[14]

Confucianism, likewise, adopts an implicit stance on the state of nature. Confucius stated clearly that the ethical order was built upon humans' natural love for their kin. He used the family—the Hobbesian primitive "unit"—as a metaphor to guide rulers so that all living beings may be metaphorical brothers under the reign of the son of heaven. Confucius inspired later generations in their quest to adopt the "kingly way," embedded in the patriarchal virtue of benevolence toward kin. Regardless of its different interpretations, benevolence is pragmatically about the ruler prioritizing either moral exemplification to calm self-centering calculation or the provision of affluence to reduce concerns about scarcity.[15] A couple of complementary concepts, *Yi* (oneness, which connotes being accepted anywhere) and *Dao* (the Way, which connotes accepting or carrying all),[16] that ontologically constitute both humans and nature could be in line with the moral or affluent style of benevolence.[17]

This familial and patriarchal metaphor is spontaneously hierarchical, ritualistic, and moral. The metaphor is composed of familial roles, not specific human actors. Familial roles define proper benevolence; benevolence indicates love; love camouflages strangeness otherwise. Note, however, that metaphorical love is ritualistic rather than affective. Benevolence is practical gift giving promising affluence or sacrifice in the ritual to exemplify a common origin in heaven and earth. Benevolence as role-playing inevitably produces contradictory relations.

On the one hand, roles replace identities, which incorrectly connote strangeness, so individual differences are silenced. Once having taken a kindred role, one cannot be a stranger. Without it, one cannot belong. Benevolence, as role-playing to win acceptance by the existing members of the anarchical relations, ostensibly alludes to rule-based governance. However, such benevolence is exclusively for maintaining a relationship with a specific audience—for example, Washington, DC. On the other hand, benevolence camouflages who we are, thereby shielding individual differences and tolerating rule evasion as exception, but there might be numerous exceptions.[18] In short, Confucianism's predisposition to avert strangeness can be a mixed blessing for those who subscribe to rule-based governance.

Confucianism relies on the seasonal rituals of heavenly and ancestor worship to socialize all into their familial obligations to demonstrate benevolence toward each other. The mysterious and yet commonsensical notion that heaven and humans constitute each other continues to be widely quoted today,[19] testifying to this desired symbiosis between nature and society. Confucian education, aimed at the learned class's malleability to mingle with but not be inquisitive about nature, the family, the regime, the population, and encountered aliens, contrasts with the humanist tradition, embedded in truth, ethics, and aesthetics, in Western education. Preferably for Western IR, consensual rules and norms will cast newcomers in liberal roles and establish an ontological likeness to enable the appreciation of each other's entitlement to rights. The presence of strangers represents role failure. The problem for Western relations lies in *alters'* solidarity being insufficiently embedded in rights consciousness, whereas for Confucian relations it lies in the self's insufficient benevolence. Their respective prescriptions are intervention and socialization for the former and gift giving and ritual education for the latter.

Given the aversion to hidden strangeness in the Confucian self, the right of nature that recognizes autonomous selves can, in contrast, appear threatening. Hence, a plausible relational proposition under Confucianism is that *the need to have a role is more vital than which specific role exists.* Confucianism's relational base for role theory leaves both values and institutional guidance blank, for the self and the *alter* to improvise according to their bilateral trafficking. The relational inevitability of all being kindred and friends does not determine which kindred or friendly roles to enlist or how. All are obliged to do so, presumably through appropriate, at times competitive, gift giving. Kindred and friendly relationships evolve accordingly through inconsistent, cyclical, and contradictory role making. Thus, Confucian relationality breeds anxiety about revealing the self as an incorrect stranger and the absolute need for self-discipline.

In sum, role making to connect actors with no apparent prior resemblance shows how (mis)perceived strangers cope with each other's otherness and strategize relationally.[20] By imposing and facing socializing pressure, both parties are intrinsically concerned with interrogating how the self and the *alter* (un)learn through role-playing. Confucianism is conscious of this and mindful of how a stranger-*alter* exposes a stranger-self. As in Confucianism, the processes whereby a strategic agent casts a target stranger in the role of accepting the former's self-role conception contrast with those that socialize the stranger to follow rules and norms, as in the social contract tradition.[21] These two kinds of prior relations constitute and yet divide states beforehand, and roles subsequently socialize each other.[22]

Defining Relation and Role for Confucianism

Contemporary Confucian IR interrogates the place of Western IR in *tianxia*.[23] Confucian relations are intellectually accessible to Western nations through Confucian role theory because it is directly comparable with Western role theory's symbolic interactionism tradition. As no stranger is cosmologically possible in a social environment, presumably strangers can only be internal to each self. Confucian role theory proceeds to tame inner strangeness. By reversing the typical processes in the Western role theory of socializing role takers each to their respective positions,[24] gift giving in Confucianism abides by the *alters'* benefits instead and attends to winning acceptance of the self-roles by as many *alters* as possible.[25]

Given that *strangeness* and *resemblance* are antonyms, I will use *relations* to indicate how actors imagine their symbolic *resemblance to one another* (in terms of their genesis, kinship, nationality, race, residence, religion, culture, ideology, alliance, interests, alma mater, work, etc.) and therefore should, through self-restraint, act in solidarity to a minimal degree,[26] taking "roles" to fulfill *specific expectations that one must fulfill*.[27] These definitions arise from readings of symbolic interactionism.[28] The significant component of the readings is a *social* construction, as relationalism attends to *prior* patterns, processes, social interactions, discourses, cultures, practices, and so on that constitute the identities of the interacting actors,[29] on the one hand, and a foreign policy role points to a salient position in social situations as well as socially recognized categories of actors, on the other.[30] In comparison, the abovementioned definitions further consider those aspects of relations and roles that are not socially or practically prior either between strangers or actors estranged from the past association. This de-emphasis on constructing a prior social consensus is epistemologically intrinsic to Confucianism.

However, symbolic interactionism attends primarily to how to socialize *the alter* according to the perceived prior consensus.[31] For example, this was the essence of Westernization when Russia joined Europe or China left the Sinic order.[32] Confucian relations focus instead on how the self can prove to the *alter* that the self can be socialized. This leads to attempts mainly to preempt the *alter*'s perception and wording instead of behavior. In addition to the interpretation of the self concerning the self's role,[33] which is important to symbolic interactionism, the interpretation adopted by the *alter* is an equally (if not more) stressful target of the Confucian self's role enactment, leading to self-socializing to satisfy the perceived *alters*' expectations.

Accordingly, the prior construction for international politics occurs in three kinds of role locations—prior rules and norms applied to all interacting parties, prior conventions viable only for the interacting couple, and a prior history of the national self-role conception shared by a domestic audience. The most relevant Confucian role location, reciprocal rituals, constitutes a procedural continuum; those acting on behalf of the national self select a role judged to be both acceptable to the *alter* and legitimate to their audience and, then, provide gifts that are deemed appropriate for the presentation of the selected role to convey the socializability of the bilateral self to the *alter*. For the Confucian ritual, legitimacy and gifts are the two major points to consider.

Legitimacy, the former concern that is contested domestically, reflects the self's interpretation of a prior (metaphorically extended familial) relation that is perceived to be shared among the domestic audience of the national self as well as the members of the international community to which the national self, bilateral self, and *alter* commonly belong.[34] Gifts, the latter concern, are improvisations to lure the *alter*, introduce the national self-role, and cast the *alter* in a counterbilateral role. Gift giving is a particular style of symbolic interactionism. An improvised gift is embedded in social meaning, although rarely intended to reproduce the prior social (i.e., multilateral) norms. Rather, the gift giver will do so if it is essential to bypass the norms to achieve a mutually acceptable relationship, specifically with the *alter*. In sum, a gift should make the *alter* feel accepted. It can be welfare, honor, or help when in need but never interventional for the *alter* or implicating third parties.

Striving for domestic legitimacy nonetheless alludes to caring for a distinctive self-interest only on the part of the nation, implying ulterior, incorrect strangeness and embarrassing relationality.[35] The self-interest sensibilities reveal strangeness that discredits the role relations. As a result, Confucian relations must balance between the self and mutual interests.[36] Wherever a mutually agreeable role relation between two strangers emerges successfully, it can evolve into a bilateralized prior relation and dominate one's multilateral duties elsewhere because being accepted by a seeming stranger necessarily indicates a salient role. On the contrary, the repeated role failure or mutual estrangement caused by domestic interests or legitimacy concerns threatens solidarity.

Following symbolic interactionism, however, the multiplicity of the social environment determines that each actor is involved in more than one relation, which makes the aggregate of communities of practice necessarily dissimilar for different people.[37] A role that can ensure a minimal level of acceptance can camouflage the incongruence caused by multiplicity, and hence a nominal, abstract, and metaphorical set of role conceptions, for as many occasions as possible. For a nominally selfless, practically inconsistent, and politically bribing actor, the prime motivation is to win acceptance. Specifically, the gift lures the *alter* to not stress its distinctive preferences and interests or values and identities to acquiesce to those likewise incongruent components of the self.

Further, if we consider the strategic implications of the definitions above—that roles are about actor-centered expectations, but relations are about collective resemblance—then relations that align the members belonging to *tianxia* concern resemblance and, thus, are *symmetric* in their epistemological relevance and importance in determining the level of relatedness to their *alters*. However, mutual roles are often expressed through socially higher and lower statuses in a hierarchy (see chapter 1), which exemplify the *asymmetric* norms of interaction. For weaker nations to compel a stronger counterpart to comply, they must rely on the skill of evoking a co-constituted, or symmetric, resemblance. Altercasting the stronger party into accepting the self's role conception through gift giving becomes essential for triggering the reciprocal relation. A resulting order of *tianxia* immediately ties the self-integrity qua ontological security of the stronger party to acceptance and deference by the weaker party.

Preoccupied with the quest for mutual acceptance, Confucian IR can make an additional contribution to relational IR in the following three ways. First, when a strong nation seeks approval from a weak *alter* to indicate the socializability of the former, even a weak nation's relational identity can be privileged. Second, governments can temporarily prioritize acceptance over rule setting when the rules and norms fail to prevail because all must have roles "regardless of the variation in their regional environments, political systems, and political culture."[38] Third, enacting rules in a particular context may convey less about successful socialization to the prior social norms than the strategized expedience of the self to win acceptance by those who strive to socialize the self. The two relationalities intersect in a pragmatically undecidable hub of coexistence, and whichever better controls the mutual estrangement prevails.

Figure 3.1. Relations and roles of the two states of nature. Created by the author.

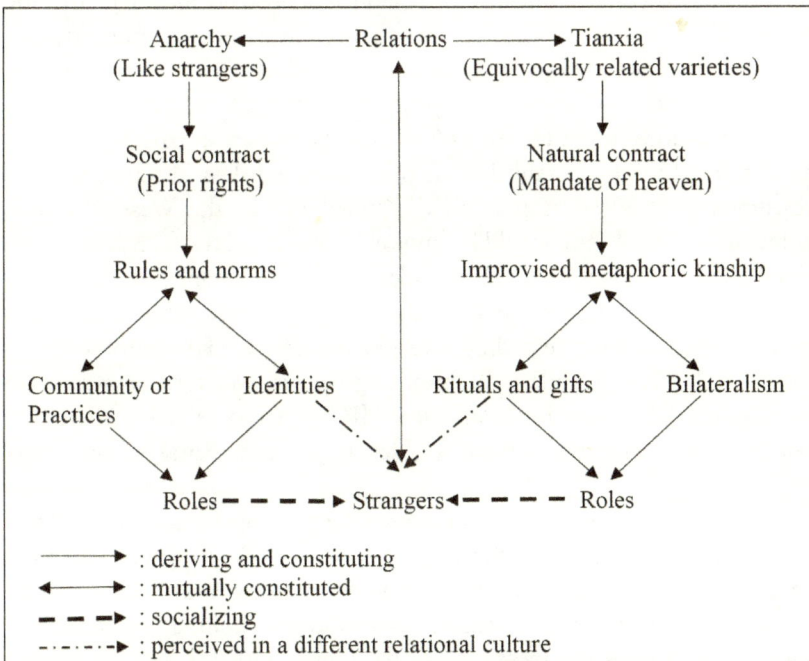

Confucian IR and Chinese Relational Policy

Socializing self and stranger is the primary agenda of Confucian relations. Confucian foreign policy is the improvisation of self-socializing through role making. If we take the People's Republic of China (PRC) as an example, its roles can include comrade, friend, neighbor, brother, partner (with many different versions),[39] and so on. These roles are not internationally consensual but historically familiar and should be appropriate internally and bilaterally. Gift giving is presumably oriented toward the benefit of the *alter*. Gifts are improvised for others in their contexts to encourage them to accept the PRC as it is. Beijing has, historically, had multilateral self-role conceptions of the PRC—for example, a responsible major power, a world revolutionary, a socialist nation—which neither are constituted by any consensual rules nor constitute any bilateral interactions. The aim of having such multilateral roles is to calm others' alarm about the PRC being self-centered and to demonstrate its socializability.[40] At most, a multilateral role can justify boycotting the West's imposition of rules in the developing world on the grounds that no one should be left out or singled out as punishment if multilateralism is meant to include all equally. Rarely does Chinese internationalism involve rule setting.

Even so, as the right of nature has evolved into a Western relational habitus to oblige *all nations* to care for human rights, regardless of their specific relationships or identities,[41] Beijing cannot escape the expectation that it should enforce multilateral rules to establish a minimal level of resemblance to Western countries.[42] Acceptance by the West of a newcomer as a normal state would be unlikely without successful role taking.[43] Beijing is caught between taking sides to win acceptance and avoiding taking sides to remain related to all, albeit separately achieved. This is particularly poignant regarding the global agenda of nonproliferation, for example. This agenda is illuminating because Western countries are more potent than the PRC, and the PRC more so than North Korea, but North Korea has not easily yielded to the socializing pressure that trickles down.

Given that nonproliferation is a regime encompassing allegedly "normal" states, Beijing must weigh the priority between Washington, a seeming stranger with whom Beijing seeks a role relationship, and Pyongyang, an acquaintance determined to pursue nuclearization. Beijing has vacillated, showing both sides its sincere desire to comply with the expectations of each. In particular, Beijing shows how much sacrifice it has made in order to protect Pyongyang. After the first-generation leader Kim Il-sung passed away, the new leadership under Kim Jong-il decided to preempt Beijing's further estrangement due to its abortion of role duty (such as supporting NK's nuclearization). It took Beijing over a decade to establish the internal legitimacy to decide that the relational value for the PRC to be accepted by the West is too high a stake to renounce, while the long acquaintance with Pyongyang could be restored, albeit being in disarray currently. After all, in this reckoning, Beijing would be far better placed to protect Pyongyang having created a good relationship with Washington and its Western allies,[44] which Pyongyang would understand in due course. From this perspective, Beijing balanced internal legitimacy regarding Pyongyang's long-term comradeship and gift giving toward Washington.

The power asymmetry between the two allies does not silence the relatively weak Pyongyang,[45] whom Beijing could not convince or restrain because Beijing would betray the prior socialist relations that bind Beijing's own identity to Pyongyang's interests.[46] They are epistemologically equal actors in terms of their readiness to assess each other's role performance. In any case, Beijing's self-casting in joining the sanctioning of Pyongyang is unconnected with the value of nonproliferation that undergirds the solidarity between the members of the nonproliferation regime. A strategic partnership with the US was a priority due to the need to control the risk that China, on the rise, would become increasingly less acceptable to a growing number of countries. Given China's stranger identity in the eyes of Washington, a mutually congruent expectation with Washington would create a salient role for Beijing, through which Beijing may assess all of its other future relationships, including the request to Pyongyang to abandon nuclearization.

Pyongyang's act of shaming Beijing for its betrayal led to the perception that the Sino-NK relationship was beyond repair.[47] Pyongyang's strong sanctions testify to the strength of the bilateral relationship in defining Beijing's ontological security.[48] Hindsight confirms that Beijing was constantly on the alert to resupply necessities to North Korea at the first glimpse of a forthcoming NK-US rapprochement, without conditioning such supplies on Pyongyang's continuity or even effective denuclearization. In other words, Beijing's compliance with nonproliferation is intended to satisfy the expectation of estranged Washington. Its tolerance of being reduced to a betrayer of Pyongyang, despite Pyongyang's rejection of Beijing's advice regarding denuclearization, was already at the maximum possible level.

Confucian relations are biased toward the restoration, reinforcement, and enhancement of reciprocal role relations. At the same time, Western

IR expects to see a newcomer socialized into becoming a subscriber to the consensual rules. With Washington again resorting to competitive relations in general and economic sanctions in particular, Beijing's quest for acceptance is failing badly. According to *weiqi* tactics, Beijing appeals to a "shared future for humankind" in its public diplomacy to tame the potential anxiety in the rest of the world toward its rivalry with Washington. Ensuing Chinese foreign policy consistently attempts to create bilateral partnerships elsewhere to insinuate that (1) the responsibility of the nascent US-China rivalry does not lie with China and (2) Washington's window of opportunity to embark on a partnership role remains open. Thinking *tianxia* while acting bilaterally in this way, Beijing can explain away its strangeness from liberal international relations and wait for Washington to reverse its estranging behavior.

Case Study: Pyongyang's Improvisation

Pyongyang is a good case because it has been an incorrect stranger to Western and Confucian relations for almost two decades. The notion of a stranger can explain Pyongyang's quest for acceptance—acknowledging North Korea's nuclear status in the nonproliferation regime, removing all sanctions, and seeking permanent peace and security for the Korean Peninsula and the world.[49]

The case will illustrate the processes that led to the breakthrough in June 2018 in the relations between Kim Jong-un and Donald Trump. They were seemingly permanent rivals but succeeded in attending a historic summit.[50] In a nutshell, Pyongyang evoked nostalgia for nationalism and kin metaphors in Seoul and Beijing. It took advantage of the existing role relationships between Washington and Seoul to explore a new role relationship with Washington. All three reverted quickly, indicating that the drive away from strangeness can override the incongruent role conceptions that appeared to be deeply rooted in their earlier interactions. The overnight reversal of the bitter exchanges between Pyongyang and Beijing attests to the irrelevance of realist power.

PYONGYANG'S FIVE PRIOR RELATIONS

A nation usually has many prior relations that restrain its agency for relating to strangers. A review of the literature yields five relations inductively. These are generally prior multilateral relations that are amenable to neither Pyongyang nor its *alter*.[51] The dominant ones since the end of the Cold War have been the hegemonic relations led by Washington, aimed at synchronizing all nations according to, in our case, the nonproliferation agenda. Pyongyang tried to take small steps of concession as a gift to cast Washington into the role of security provider but failed due to a perceived insufficient conformity to nonproliferation.[52] In response, it adopts a "powerful state role"[53] that in hegemonic relations is equivalent to an utterly estranging role of a "rogue state."[54]

Related but distinctive are the postcolonial relations arising from the Japanese colonial legacy.[55] Tokyo's dual role as a former colonial master and a US ally makes Pyongyang's aversion toward Tokyo almost irresolvable. Pyongyang asserts its independence and power by denouncing Tokyo's dependence on Washington. A break would have to originate from Tokyo's economic aid qua gift giving to Pyongyang.[56]

The *Juche* idea ("thought of subjectivity") has been the most crucial role source that has given the North Korean people the morale, reason, and determination to strive together to attain all-around autonomy.[57] Kim Jong-un would have been particularly vulnerable to inheriting the *Juche* spirit as a third-generation leader who contributed very little to the spirit if not because he was determined to resist the legacies of his father, Beijing, and Washington. This triadic revulsion provides him with a desired independent mark on the *Juche* identity and the image of a ruthless leader in Washington's eyes—an ontological stranger to the right of nature. A change occurs only after the *Juche* identity, originally enacted by the powerful-state role, is extended to include a development-state role.[58] This role opens a window of opportunity for Tokyo, Beijing, and Seoul to arrange economic gifts.

Pyongyang has more room for choosing between entry and exit in two other prior bilateral relations. One involves Korean national relations, as the Cold War split Korea into two regimes.[59] Of the entire world, only Pyongyang and Seoul directly subscribe to Korean national relations, which obliges both sides to enforce either an integrating or a conquering platform toward the other.

Pyongyang inherited the fifth prior relation from historical relations with tributary China, which later continued in the shape of the allegedly comradely, kindred relationship with socialist China.[60] Consequently, Pyongyang automatically anticipates Beijing's support during times of need and resorts to defiance if dissatisfied. Embarrassingly for

Pyongyang, Washington may blame Beijing instead of Pyongyang for the latter's nonconformity. Because Beijing likewise relies on the bilateral relations to fulfill its reciprocal self-identity, shaming, such as purging the pro-China forces in North Korea, can be Pyongyang's threat to estrange Beijing while at the same time representing a brinkmanship-motivated request for compensation and restoration.[61] Pyongyang has the leverage to oblige Beijing to remain silent regarding its recalcitrant acts or boycott interventionism on its behalf.[62]

Pyongyang's repeated missile tests to deter Washington and distancing from Beijing testify to a powerful-state role,[63] in Pyongyang's quest for the ultimate status as an equal party to the Treaty on the Non-proliferation of Nuclear Weapons. While the estranging role conception of a rogue state is, in all senses, transient, improvising a resemblance in terms of Pyongyang either committing to nonproliferation or being accepted into the nuclear club is unrealistic. Instead, improvising a resemblance through gift giving can provide an alternative path. In reality, Seoul substitutes for Beijing as the site for Washington and Pyongyang to improvise a shared network.

INTER-KOREAN RELATIONS

Moon Jae-in, the former South Korean president, invited Pyongyang to form a joint Olympic team in South Korea in February 2018. Kim Jong-un accepted and sent Kim Yo-jong, his sister, to lead the delegation. A summit was arranged for Kim to meet Moon in April. Kim's agreement to a Korean national role obliges Moon to act on his behalf. Thereby, a total stranger, if not an enemy, suddenly gained access to the Washington-Seoul alliance through a gift to Kim from Moon. Before Kim arrived in Seoul, he forwarded a gift-like message to the two most influential players—Washington and Beijing, both of whom the powerful-state-role player had fearlessly antagonized in 2017.

Initially, Kim himself paid a secret but later highly publicized visit to the Chinese president, Xi Jinping, to honor Beijing's socialist and strategic leader's role. Consequently, Beijing not only reversed its estrangement from Pyongyang but even gained a higher position in the hierarchy. What a gift for Beijing!

On the other hand, Pyongyang did not trust Washington's guarantee. While a stranger to rules, Pyongyang demanded that Washington's guarantee of its security and equal status was the appropriate first step toward ending their mutual strangeness. For Washington, the correct first step toward reducing strangeness was, in contrast, for Pyongyang to comply with the nonproliferation rule rather than any bilateral agreement. Moon took advantage of his dual role as an inter-Korean patriot and Washington's faithful ally. Kim cast Moon in a Korean national role; Moon cast Trump in an ally role. Thus, there was no risk of Kim being rejected by Trump. Moreover, Moon brought a significant gift from Kim—forgoing the cliché of the "reduction and withdrawal of US forces in South Korea."[64]

The first encounter was sensational. Kim Jong-un was the first North Korean leader to set foot in South Korea. After crossing the line, Kim improvised an on-site invitation to Moon to step back into North Korea. Chung-in Moon, who had attended all three summits held since 2000,[65] pointed to such ritual symbolism as a crucial step toward the success of the "audacious" third summit in Panmunjom. He highlighted a statement in an NK report that "it was an act that demolished the artificially drawn demarcation line. That impromptu gesture by Kim moved all Koreans." The twelve-hour gathering succeeded in "restoring normal inter-Korean relations," enacting a shared one-nation role by agreeing on a joint liaison office, a spirit of national reconciliation and unity, the reunion of separated families, the modernization of the eastern transportation corridor, and the building of roads between Seoul and Sinuiju.[66] The consensual reference to "the nation" in the Panmunjom Declaration for Peace, Prosperity, and Reunification of the Korean Peninsula was regarded "as a starting point for putting an end to the history of division" and "inheriting and further fostering the unification plans" of 1989 and 1994.[67]

National relations trickle down to constitute interpersonal relations, too. In Chung-in Moon's words, Kim's "charm offensive was taken seriously by many" and even became a "sort of rediscovery of Kim." Furthermore, the personal trust and amity between the two leaders and their spouses were visible. The "endless exchanges of toasts among them cemented human networks, signaling a bright future for inter-Korean relations." All of this was attributable to Kim's reliance on Moon Jae-in's willingness to play "the role of honest broker," including making numerous clandestine contacts between officials to persuade Pyongyang to proceed.[68]

THE HISTORICAL RELATIONS

Beijing's compliance with Washington's expectation that Beijing would support denuclearization alienated Pyongyang.[69] Comparing the role analysis that combines relational analysis with that which does not,[70] the latter is far more pessimistic. Beijing expected Pyongyang to remain acquiescent for a short time at least. This, for Beijing, was to overcome its estrangement from Washington through a gift of compliance with the nonproliferation rule for the time being. From Beijing's perspective, eventually, Pyongyang would understand that being an acquaintance in the major power relationship would enable Beijing to protect Pyongyang from US intervention.[71] There was also speculation that Beijing felt anxious about its own sidelining regarding the issues of inter-Korean relations and Pyongyang-Washington summitry.[72] Beijing could have done little about this, had this speculation proved true.[73] Although annoyed by the high profile of Pyongyang's resistance based upon the *Juche* idea, Beijing displayed enormous pleasure and honor in celebrating Kim's March visit, as if Pyongyang's pique in the recent past had never happened.

Contemporary sovereignty and historical vassal are currently parallel roles for almost all East Asian neighbors of China.[74] Such a trajectory contextualizes the contrivance of the *Juche* idea, but the sovereign relation here does not incorporate a prior resemblance of the right of nature as it does between EU nations. Being sovereign actors entails mutual estrangement and requires improvisation and constant negotiation, at times inspired by the historical tributary relations, between two long-term acquaintances. In the tributary relations, Pyongyang could afford to be recalcitrant without suffering any security anxiety and even take advantage of the embarrassment created for Beijing, which would appear to be failing in its benevolent role.

In the same vein, Beijing's siding with the international sanctions against Pyongyang's nuclearization is more a double play of showing displeasure to the acquaintance, Pyongyang, and placating the seeming stranger, Washington, than compliance with the nonproliferation regime.[75] As such, Beijing's commitment to sanctions could not be wholehearted because they circularly estranged Beijing from an acquaintance. In reality, Seoul has been so dependent on Washington that, from Pyongyang's perspective, Seoul's goodwill could not effectively serve Pyongyang's quest for equality and respect. To earn respect from Washington, Pyongyang needed to act in the name of a far greater relational entity, which includes China. Ironically, when they both faced pressure from Washington, they were unable to cooperate. In preparing for contact with Washington, Pyongyang had relieved Beijing of the pressure to comply with nonproliferation.

It has been a relational prophecy that China and North Korea are bound to be related. That is why Pyongyang could feel fairly certain that Beijing would be willingly cast as a helping hand and delighted about this.[76] In fact, Kim appeared in the media to be busy taking notes while Xi spoke. This dramatic humility constituted a ritual metaphor for the tributary relationship. Xi recollected how past leaders resembled "close relatives"; Kim reiterated that his trip was precisely based on "this passionate relationship and the moral propriety."[77] China's soft power lies in its patience with role incongruence, and Kim's in knowing that China can merely await his return. Despite a considerable difference in size, they are both relationally equal and socially hierarchical within their historical relationship.

The first visit took place after a US secret envoy visited Pyongyang to confirm Washington's readiness to attend a summit prior to Kim's first summit with Moon. Kim's successful role altercasting of Xi, his senior, solidified his confidence about meeting with Trump as an equal.[78] Most importantly, Beijing had no intention to take advantage of Pyongyang when it was vulnerable or retaliate against its recalcitrance. Rather, Beijing was ready to support Pyongyang's desire eventually to become a developmental state. In fact, between controlling and supporting Pyongyang, the stronger actor's choice was strictly in line with the weaker actor's expectations.[79]

HEGEMONIC RELATIONS

Through Seoul, Pyongyang is no longer a stranger to Washington, nor is it an acquaintance who would comply with the role duty of denuclearization. To begin with, the Panmunjom Declaration deliberately adopts a textual structure in the order of inter-Korean relations, a peace settlement, and denuclearization to indicate the desired sequence and synchronous approach that binds the security of Pyongyang to the speed of denuclearization.[80] This is a strategic road map for targeting Washington's earlier insistence on unconditional, complete denuclearization. Washington was able to listen to Seoul, however, and receive an indirect promise from Pyongyang regarding initiation of unilateral, full denuclearization.

In addition, the issue of a peace treaty to end the Korean War, which was an unlikely message to be delivered directly from Pyongyang to Washington, was then presented to Washington. The treaty insinuated that Pyongyang was becoming a normal state that would not require nuclear weapons. Premised upon the Washington-Seoul alliance, the inter-Korean détente could merely implicate Seoul's role-making effort to oblige Washington to support its ally by joining in the peace treaty process. Even by the time of the Winter Olympics, the expectation regarding Seoul was already that collegiality at the Games would be "inducing inter-Korean dialogue to act as a driving force for U.S.-North Korean dialogue."[81] Without Seoul's role as an ally in the hegemonic relations, Kim would have lacked any channel by which to cast Washington into recognizing North Korea as a nuclear power before proceeding with complete denuclearization.[82]

Moon Jae-in enacted his junior ally role by praising Trump for the "maximum pressure" approach, expecting that the stoked "ego of the impulsive American leader" would support his effort.[83] Moon reassured Pyongyang that it was unnecessary to worry about regime replacement. Both sides understood that the inter-Korean relations were "designed to provide a more secure environment in which North Korea could maintain its denuclearization commitment and continue negotiations with the US."[84] Moon also facilitated an opportunity for Washington to review "the level and the scope of denuclearization for the first time" by arranging for Kim to identify them in their joint declaration.[85] No risk that Washington might lose face was possible through such a medium.[86] If Washington had rejected Pyongyang's indirect denuclearization offer by Seoul, it would have risked witnessing an inter-Korean détente without denuclearization. This was not a familiar rule-based consideration. Washington was still obliged to respond positively, even if the junior ally seemed to act incompatibly with what the alliance was supposed to achieve—namely, containing, if not overthrowing, Pyongyang. Once Pyongyang and Washington were able to develop a direct relationship, Seoul would, by contrast, be obliged to pace the inter-Korean relationship in accordance with Washington's North Korea policy.

Conclusion

Both relations and roles are intersubjective, but relations constitute the actors prior to their interaction, while roles require the actors to improvise according to their conditions. These two theories share significant epistemological common ground in substituting the mutuality of actors for their autonomy and neutralizing the analytical relevance of power by introducing culture and identity.

To avoid the mutual estrangement caused by differences in culture and identity, the flexible style of Confucian relations obliges the actors to establish and maintain relations through improvising roles that are agreeable to each other. This contrasts with rule-based relations, the stronger ontological sensibilities that enable the actors to feel a level of solidarity prior to exploring their differences. Confucian relationality evades solidarity. Under Confucianism, humankind neither is shaped in the same image as the Christian God nor has the same capacity to relate to him. As a result, the amorphous heavenly reason is embodied by an unlimited variety of dissimilar lives. Therefore, universal rules and norms to equally constitute people who are alike or generate the community of practice in the Christian and liberal traditions are implausible.

Western IR is rooted in the imagined state of nature where strangers become prudent citizens by subscribing to an indiscriminate social contract. Given *tianxia*'s aversion to universal rules, gift givers are reduced to unruly strangers in the social contract perspective. On the other hand, whenever gift givers fail to enlist an appreciation of the Western *alters*, they see the latter threaten to expose their internal strangers. Western IR finds a place in Confucian IR when (1) gift givers strategically follow a professed universal rule in an event as a gift to win temporary acceptance by the parties to a social contract or (2) the parties to a social contract relinquish their demand on the rule in an event as a gift to ensure that nonsubscribers feel accepted and gradually consent to conversion in the future.

Wherever role relations have been practiced with a bilateral consensus, these already improvised relations, such as the NK-China relationship, create a bilaterally specific prior relation—they become acquaintances. A breach of Confucian prior relations calls for further gift giving to reconfirm or restore and rebuild it. Sanctions are justified only if their purpose is to restore reciprocal role-play. Another significant point of comparison is how to cope with strangers' relations. Given the ontological vagueness under the *tianxia* circumstance, politically incorrect strangers inside are simply exposed by those without a record of reciprocity, such as North Korea and the US, or China and the US. However, since all are bound to be related, *tianxia* relations oblige all to explore and cultivate a resemblance in order to camouflage any strangeness. These processes will continue despite their failure at a particular time.

The case study shows that intervention is required to ensure the socialization into followers of those not following rules. Still, gift giving appears an equally effective socializing mechanism that evades the rules and yet reconnects perceived strangers to the extent that expediently abiding by rules can constitute a gift for the time being. Therefore, two relationalities exist simultaneously on different agendas, between different actors, at different times. Roles are improvised to socialize the actors of different relationalities and connect them at the intersection. All nations can access both relationalities. Western and Confucian relations are not in an either/or relationship.

4

Performing Anger

The Ethics of Foreign Policy Role Emotion

Given role's socialization function and that all are bound to be related through improvised roles, mechanisms for signaling a mutual assessment of each other's role-playing are essential for the reproduction of agreed-upon relations. Anger at the perceived abandonment of a role, for example, can vent anxiety or frustration. At the corporate level, expressed anger fulfills the function of reminding others of their role obligations and stopping their deviant role-play on behalf of their nations. It conveys a warning of an emerging cessation or a deterrence to continuous abandonment. In contrast, suppressed anger indicates a willingness to bypass the deviance for the sake of maintaining relationships. The latter concerns patience, which is the topic of the next chapter. The present chapter deals with strategic anger that concerns the self- and *alter* socialization of nations.

As Andrew Ross puts it, "affect is not a property of an individual but a capacity of a body that brings it into some specific social relation, such as a nation or political movement."[1] Anger as a kind of affect is no exception. Note that actors have increasingly expressed anger that shapes international politics. Yet the question of why and how actors affect international political outcomes through the expression of anger has attracted scant research attention. This is probably because the definitions of anger vary widely within the field of politics and international relations,[2] and the analytical references to it hardly attend to its relational nature. The notion of relation indicates a certain perceived prior consensus between the relevant international actors regarding their respective duties. Anger is meaningful only for those other national actors who shared a prior relationship. This is in addition to the major concern in the literature on emotion in international relationality, primarily for the identity function of a national actor.[3]

To the extent that anger and relation are mutually constituted, (1) different relational consensuses produce different types of anger, and (2) anger reproduces relations via different mechanisms. Accordingly, in the four sections that follow, this chapter proposes two research agendas. The first section defines anger relationally. Anger must be conceptualized as a relational rather than an individual concept. After all, as observers, we do not know whether leaders are sincerely angry and so need to neutralize the level of sincerity in our analysis. In addition, we can distinguish the anger that everyone else can presumably understand from the anger that is intended mainly for the audience of a specific cultural cluster to handle. The coexistence of parallel clusters provides a clue to the pluriversal relationalities of international politics, and pluriversality complicates the practice of anger.

The second section elaborates on the first agenda regarding leaders' anger as constituted by relations. Specifically, the differentiation between four separate types of anger corresponds to the leaders' choice of how to socialize with national role conceptions—the audience role, self role, *alter* role, and collective role—depending on the judgment of the leaders regarding the audiences' and leaders' conditions. The third section pertains to the second agenda and infers four causal mechanisms through which relational anger affects international political outcomes—emotional deterrence, emotional performance, emotional cultivation, and emotional mobilization. The fourth section discusses the implications of both agendas, while the fifth section offers a tentative conclusion.

Defining Anger

Relation and Anger

The word *anger* is widely used in the field of social sciences but often invested with differing meanings. This chapter adopts a simple definition while recognizing that there exists no universally accepted set of terms for describing any type of emotion:[4] anger is *an oppositional disposition to fix a relationship*.[5] To reiterate, the book defines the relationship as *the process of practicing imagined resemblance that obliges reciprocity or recognition,*[6] whereas points of resemblance can exist in endless forms, such as value, rule, religion, place, position, race, ethnicity, profession, hobby, partnership, hometown, generation, ownership, citizenship, partisanship, and so on. As such, anger is a response to the abortion of the entitlement to status, treatment, or ownership that presumably accompanies a perceived consensual obligation, informed by a certain point of resemblance. It is not, in other words, a disposition that favors those individuals who are gifted with strength or attractiveness[7] but, rather, an aspect of a kind of emotional community.[8]

Unlike the conventional definition of anger employed in the field of psychology, the following discussion does not treat it as inevitably an inner state of mind felt by an *individual* actor.[9] This analytical distinction is crucial. Social scientists cannot assume any particular actor's internal state of mind in advance, as an actor may express an emotion before they feel it. This is particularly true when actors are plurally connected for functional or historical reasons. As a result, even if an individual actor intentionally expresses anger toward another in a given relational setting, social scientists who follow the conventional definition in order to conceptualize anger would mistakenly assume that the strategic expression of anger was sincere qua internally determined. At the same time, natural science is already familiar with "acted anger."[10] The analytical omission of the relational component from the conventional understanding of anger can create systematic errors during the interpretation of behavior.

The individualist definition of anger makes it difficult for social scientists to analyze the politics of anger within international relations, where most individual or corporate actors necessarily express anger toward one another *strategically*, irrespective of whether this is sincere or not. As Alexander Wendt wrote, "in both academic and lay discourse we often refer casually to states 'as if' they have emotions and are therefore conscious. States are routinely characterized as angry, greedy, guilty, humiliated, and so on."[11] Nevertheless, attributing an emotional reaction—anger—to a state, as Janice Stein warned over a decade later, would be a complex argument because "it attributes to the collective what is an embodied individual experience."[12]

By defining anger relationally, we overcome the analytical difficulty regarding the emotional aspect of treating the state as a person. Therefore, it is not a question of whether leaders are sincerely angry or not but rather how leaders rely on anger to socialize their nation into a role conception to meet the expectations of the international *alters* and domestic audiences. Their judgment of the anger level of the domestic audience is likewise pertinent to their adoption of anger.

Relational anger is a kind of anger that leaders can multiply via ethical argumentation in public. Recent research extends emotion from psychological to sociological agendas.[13] Robert Solomon claims that anger is "a way of being-in-the-world, a relationship between oneself and one's situation."[14] Following the earlier definition, anger is the emotion of lost entitlement. Ethical relations justify the sense of entitlement, order, or justice, which a national actor claims, among other perceived subscribers. The anger frames "the conflict as a wrongdoing requiring rectification, for which the target bears responsibility."[15] When national leaders appeal to anger, the assumption is usually that the angered nation, itself already constituted by the relationship, should understand and even expect it.

Anger represents an indirect, convenient statement of ethical justification for the angry nation to rectify and take retaliatory actions. It prompts those sharing the collective identity to ensure rectification or compensation. Therefore, in the relational state of anger, some prior ethical understanding between the subject and object of the anger must be perceived as given and yet violated.[16] Relational anger makes a difference in international relations and foreign policy analysis. It indicates the ethical positions that the leaders choose from a domestic repertoire and is a harbinger for ensuing policy consequences.

Finally, a few inferences may be helpful here, given the relational definition of anger. First, the domestic audience's psychological state of anger can be either sincere or insincere.[17] The target of anger can be consensual norms, values, and rules aborted in either the role-playing of the target states, the entirety of the target states, or both.[18] What causes the performance of anger can be bad role-play, bad states, or both. The causes suggest the direction of the solution, on the one hand, while the degree of sincerity in the leader's and audience's anger implies its respective strength and duration, on the other. Together, they imply consequences among members of the audience, and stakeholders in particular,[19] who learn to appreciate, adjust, avoid, or mimic certain behavior if they wish to repair the relationship, or simply observe with concern.

RELATIONAL ANGER AS A CULTURAL SIGNAL

States, as the primary actors in international relations, express anger as they indirectly convey prior relationships in order to send their counterpart a *cultural signal* of the perceived ethically damaged relations between them by using universally recognizable expressions,[20] such as the strong words, intense tones of voice, reddened faces, and clenched fists of presidents, prime ministers, cabinet members, spokespeople, and other governmental officials. Anger must be interpreted in relational settings because the message that something is very wrong must refer to a perceived obligation to reciprocate or give recognition according to a perceived consensual relationship. To that extent, anger is constituted by "a network of interlocking judgments concerning one's status and relationship with the offending party."[21] In the same vein, concealing sincere anger to preserve or restore a prior relationship is another aspect of relational anger.[22]

Nevertheless, the fundamental problem is that states may be unable to understand or appreciate each other's expressions of anger in international as well as cross-cultural settings.[23] This is due to the absence of a "prior consensus" that is mistakenly assumed to have already been established among the players. In other words, the lack of shared cultural memories among the actors prevents comprehension based on the same point of resemblance. This ineffective communication or understanding of relational anger has a direct international political outcome: states are unable to appreciate the root cause of an expression of anger when the ethical relations between them are damaged from the perspective of only one party to the interaction; as a result, it is difficult to identify a viable diplomatic approach to repairing the damaged ethical relations. In short, diplomatic friction arises and control diminishes when the relational anger is incommunicable, incomprehensible, or unacceptable to others in international relations.[24]

Since relational anger is a cultural signal, states that are culturally bound together or share common knowledge about interpreting the signal can effectively communicate or comprehend expressed anger in relational settings.[25] This suggests that the expression of anger as a response to damaged ethical relations is better understood between states within the same cultural clusters than between those that exist outside these, as is the cause of anger for renovating or restoring the damaged ethical relations. Following this logic, relational anger is a socializing mechanism for states belonging to a distant cultural cluster but can spread to multiple issue areas for states in the same cluster due to the relatively high level of sympathy expected of the target nation and the strong sense of deprivation thus inflicted on the angry nation.

There are several cultural clusters in the world. Historically, Confucian East Asia is a particularly distinct cultural cluster, where states are culturally encouraged to be sensitive to the specification, management, and maintenance of ethical relations. This pattern is well documented by such diplomacy historians as John Fairbank, in his description of the Chinese tributary system,[26] and such political scientists as David Kang, in his alternate account of the endurance of peace despite the absence of a balance of power in East Asia.[27] As a result of long-term cultural practices, states are more inclined to communicate with one another through relational anger within East Asia rather than outside it, as are states of any other cultural cluster or regime with a certain consensual point of resemblance.

Distinct and Universal Relations

In a pluriversal world, the pragmatic task of international relations is for national leaders to improvise points of resemblance, upon which they arrange mutually acceptable methods of interaction. In contrast, if such a collective identity is attempted in the name of universal as opposed to pluriversal value, the national actors are expected to subscribe to the same rules and norms to reproduce the collective identity. Accordingly, defiance of the imagined prior resemblance can be placed on a continuum where distinct and universal types of resemblance lie at the two extremes. Through invoking relational anger, deviance from distinct resemblance emerges when the agreeable way to know and relate to one another within the cluster—neighbors, partners, treaty signatories, Commonwealth countries, and so on—is aborted. Relational anger, embedded in terminated distinct relationships, aims to restore the angry state's recognized difference, exemption, respect, and conventions and is perceived to be consensual in a prior historical or cultural trajectory.

For distinct resemblance, the aborted relationship that causes anger creates a role expectation for the leaders in the eyes of the domestic audience, who are familiar to the other party. They perform anger in response to an affront to their nation to reproduce the imagined resemblance that restores the coexistence with the angered nation. The anger can stay within the scope of the disputed policy agenda if it is judged that the violation is merely an innocent mistake. However, if an intended offense is perceived, anger can become contagious and spread to involve the entirety of the angered nation, igniting a relational crisis.[28]

In contrast to this distinct relationship, the termination of perceived universal resemblance can spark collective anger among individual political leaders worldwide because the collective norms, such as natural rights, equality, peace, human security, and global governance duties, that constitute their identities arguably transcend national distinctions and interests.[29] Political leaders personify their nations through role taking. Different leaders share the same role duty to protect their shared collective values for universal resemblance. To the extent that individual political leaders are cognizant of the collective nature of the violation, they must act on these violations as a personal insult in order to be accepted by an imagined universal audience. In this sense, collective anger is fungible because it pushes for a universal approach to the offender, individual or nation.

Relationally Constituted Anger—The First Agenda

Given that the state cannot feel, individual political leaders must practice and perform anger on behalf of the state through role-play. The leaders' anger supports the socialization component of role theory that conceives role-play as intrinsic to actors who are learning and internalizing social expectations.[30] This role-play explains how relations constitute anger and how anger mobilizes or reproduces relations. On the one hand, nations rescue a perceived role relationship partly by showing their seriousness about their expectations that are now in jeopardy, thus calling for anger. Leaders' anger at the perceived deviation from the role validates the role expectation of their international and domestic audiences. In the process, leaders socialize their nation into a specific self-role. They personify their nation.[31] Leaders judge the type of violation and perform anger accordingly. This process creates the first agenda of relational anger.

On the other hand, leaders' nationalized anger is a mechanism for molding the domestic and international audiences into restoring the prior points of resemblance that are now in jeopardy. With their anger nationalized, leaders act as the socializers of other nations. This is the second agenda, which studies how leaders' anger reaffirms, reproduces, or renovates the points of prior resemblance.

In the first agenda, consider four types of anger with role-play: strategic audience-role anger, assertive self-role anger, contagious *alter-role* anger, and collective universal-role anger (see figure 4.1). These categories give harbingers for ensuing policy orientations. They do not fix the actors, however. Both leaders and the masses may shift as the site, time, and issues change.

Figure 4.1. The two agendas of relational anger. Created by the author.

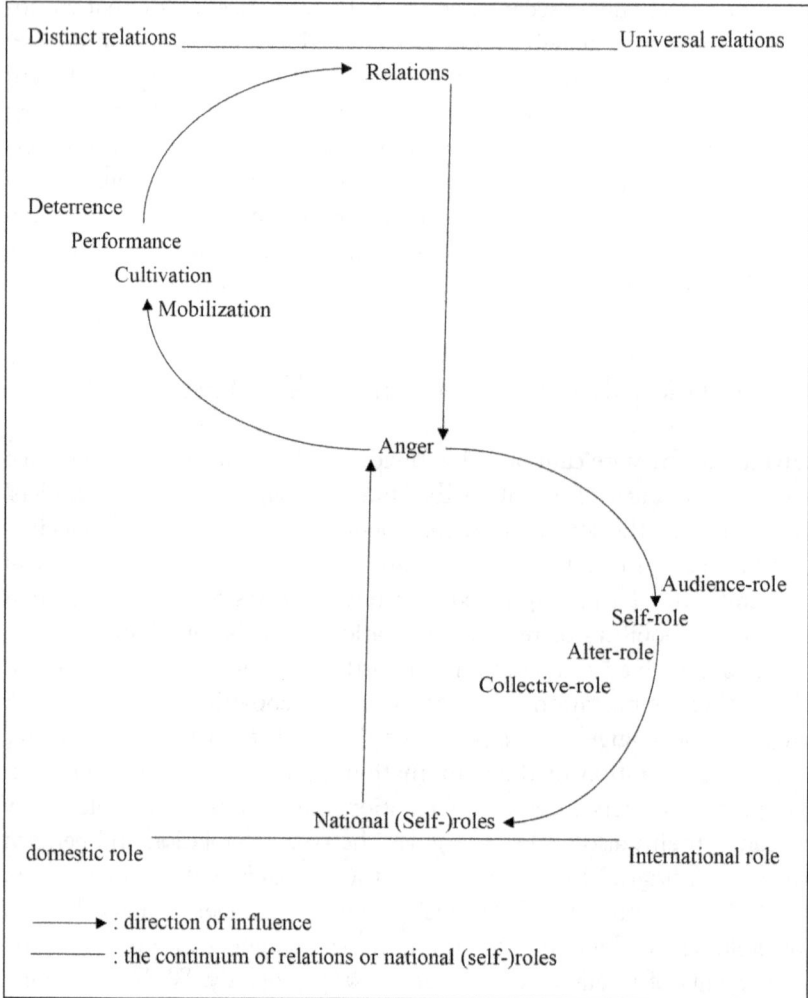

Distinct relations _____ Universal relations

Relations

Deterrence
  Performance
    Cultivation
      Mobilization

Anger

Audience-role
Self-role
Alter-role
Collective-role

National (Self-)roles

domestic role   International role

——→ : direction of influence
—— : the continuum of relations or national (self-)roles

STRATEGIC AUDIENCE-ROLE ANGER

To prevent the domestic audience's anger at a familiar violation from escalating, the leaders represent their state in performing anger toward another state as a lasting ritual for the domestic audiences of both the angry nation and its angered target at a specific role location. We call this strategic audience-role anger. Such an acted anger is a way for the political leaders of a state to affirm the role expected of their state in response to, plausibly, a likewise-acted provocation of the angered party for the latter's domestic audience. Anger soothes the domestic audience's anxiety about the denial of the national self-role. It avoids escalation that would interfere with an ongoing relationship. In addition, a failure to perform anger may damage the credibility of the leadership. Moreover, it reminds the other party to cease pushing any further. As such, audience-role anger alludes to strategic patience and the readiness to adopt a nonsolution for an indefinite future. Strategic anger as a quick political posture need not last long. It applies to both distinct and universal resemblances.

Possible examples include Beijing's "One China" issue regarding Washington's arms sales to Taiwan since 1979 and Pyongyang's lack of a summit with Beijing under Kim Jong-il (1994 to 2011) due to Beijing's objection to the former's nuclear development, since audience-role anger causes no real sanctions, as Beijing's and Pyongyang's aim in performing audience-role anger toward Washington and Beijing, respectively, was to fulfill the domestic role expectations that each of the nations would act independently and fearlessly.

Assertive Self-Role Anger

When leaders represent their state as showing anger toward another state followed by measured sanctions at a specific role location to demand the repair of an unfulfilled expectation, possibly due to negligence, this is assertive self-role anger. The deviation from the expectation of a perceived prior resemblance by the target nation, which arguably meant no harm, challenges the self-image of the angry nation. Judging the audience's genuine feelings,[32] the angry nation displays assertive anger to confirm the national self-role that has been neglected by the other party, which necessitates the other party recognizing the angry nation's expectations. Given the relevance of the other party's recognition, the angry nation needs to prevent the anger from becoming contagious. Sanctions are thus restricted to the location of the violation and proceed cyclically, in the case of slow improvement. Self-role anger is more likely to be applicable to the violation of distinct rather than universal points of resemblance. In the latter case, the collective role would be unambiguous, and the angry nation would not be alone; hence, there would be no focused challenge to its national self-role.

To extend this example, an unexpected rise in US arms sales to Taiwan might incur Beijing's self-role anger. Beijing's anger disrupts the bilateral military exchanges from time to time to compel the US to reiterate its One China policy. Other examples include the case of Hanoi toward Beijing's maritime patrolling of the disputed water of the South China Sea as well as that of Beijing toward Tokyo officials' visit to the Yasukuni Shrine, where the military leaders who invaded China during World War II are worshipped. Hanoi nevertheless continues friendly relations with Beijing with regard to other agendas, especially in the capacity of communist comradeship, despite the heated demonstrations on the streets demanding that the Chinese ships leave. Similarly, Beijing's daily business transactions with Tokyo in the economic and not-for-profit sectors continue, regardless.

Contagious Alter-Role Anger

When leaders represent their state by *extending their anger to another nation in its entirety as an object of the anger*,[33] the process amounts to contagious *alter*-role anger. The angry nation blames the violation of the perceived prior consensus on the angered target nation, either because the target nation is a recidivist or because the mood of the domestic audience of the angry nation is judged to be explosive. The anger extends beyond the role location, being simultaneously applied to other agendas of the same target state. It is the entire state that is the target. Leaders' credit is in jeopardy if their state fails to exact revenge of some form. This is tantamount to taking things "personally" at the state level. The complete denial of the *alter* as a legitimate role player can hardly reflect a universal role expectation. *Alter*-role anger tends to occur between historical rivals.

The *alter*-role anger lasts for a long time. Concerning the issue of US arms sales to Taiwan, the rise of China can increase the Chinese audience's expectations, escalate the blame for the violation to the level of the entire US in the future, and shift toward *alter*-role anger. In the case of Seoul, the issue of comfort women jeopardizes the overall relations with Japan, thereby damaging the economic, social, and educational exchanges. The contagious anger toward Japan constitutes the national identity of Korea.[34] However, the competitive domestic identity as a liberal democratic nation or postcolonial ally can socialize other Korean leaders into the insincere audience-role anger to restore overall relations with Japan. For an example of a universal relation converted to a distinct relation, consider the US sanctioning of Iran by blocking the entire nation politically, economically, socially, and academically. These sanctions together indicate the turn of the nonproliferation agenda to an issue of a personal kind of anger. Therefore, other subscribers to the nonproliferation regime do not necessarily follow.

COLLECTIVE UNIVERSAL-ROLE ANGER

When leaders represent their state by *extending their anger, along with other nations, to another state for violating a universal norm*, their nation exemplifies collective universal-role anger. Once socialized through universal role relations, leaders can prioritize anger over geopolitical considerations on behalf of their nation. Collective anger characterizes the internal condition of those actors who are culturally prepared to believe in integrity, universal humanity, and solidarity.[35] Nations benefit from socialization in terms of the collegiality experienced at an international organization,[36] the collective identity of which arguably constitutes the national identity of every member. A violation committed by the target nation with the intention of depriving a victim of its worth simultaneously threatens all other parties.[37] The collective anger cannot easily dissolve upon the correction of the violation committed by the wrongdoer, whose credit is lost, and a thorough transformation or constant monitoring is required. Unavoidably, some members of the collective group can always act through spurious audience-role anger, at best.

US arms sales to Taiwan could shift into prompting collective-role anger if the UN members were able to feel collective anger at US interventionism and accept socialization into the collective role embedded in China's claim. The opposite might also occur, wherein the members could line up with the US to support arms sales to Taiwan through collective anger at Beijing's territorial claim over Taiwan. Such a case of balance of anger, as the emotional aspect of balance of relationships, is more frequent in the 2020s—with the ongoing battles between Russia and Ukraine, Israel and Hamas, and, economically as well as technologically, the US and China, for a few noticeable examples—and reflects the ambiguity in the claims of universal order in the contemporary world. Having a sense of universal order seems more urgent than which specific order to have. Collective anger engulfs and divides the world through its incapacity to sustain any sense of universal order (see table 4.1).

Table 4.1. Traits of the Four Types of Relational Anger

Type	Strategic	Target	Scope	Duration
Audience role	Yes	Issue area	Mixed	Transient
Self-role	No	Issue area	Distinctive	Cyclical
Alter role	No	Angered party	Clustered	Perpetual
Collective role	Possible	Regime change	Universal	Event-based

Created by the author.

Anger-to-Mode Relation—The Second Agenda

The theory of relational anger creates a complete circle through the addition of the second agenda, which interrogates anger as a causal mechanism to socialize the audience into roles that reproduce relations. At least four causal mechanisms in the politics of relational anger emerge from the two common assumptions on which they are based. The first assumption is that individual or corporate actors are connected through prior social norms, which differ from one cluster of actors to another.[38] No actor can behave without taking into account their relations with other parties. Second, individual or corporate actors react to anger in order to remain relational.[39] Since such emotions as anger spread through enacted public roles, one actor's expression of anger toward another can reinforce or reconstruct the prior social norms that are shared by the interconnected actors.[40]

Combined in a given relational setting, one of the four anger mechanisms can incur potential causal processes. The first mechanism is *emotional deterrence*, which is a causal process in which leaders represent their nation to express anger toward another state to *change the course of action of the latter and bring it into compliance with some imagined prior social norm*. On this causal path, relational anger is a protective belt of distinct prior resemblances that the angry state values but from which the targeted state wishes to deviate.[41] It is a particular norm for protecting against deviance by either a stakeholder state or an unspecified watching state that likewise shares the norm. In this way, the angry state can remind the target and clustered third parties how seriously the state values the prior social norm that is under threat or simply the act of complying in general. However, if overdone, deterrence may backfire.[42]

The second mechanism is *emotional performance*, which refers to the causal process whereby leaders perform anger toward another state to *make a political statement about their relationship*. Unlike emotional deterrence, emotional performance lacks the clear purpose of shaping another state's course of action. Instead, emotional performance arises from a nation's stress, through its leaders' anger, on some prior social norm, which is tantamount to a ritual, despite others' failure to comply with that norm.[43] Audience-role anger aims at such reaffirmation with the domestic audience. Self-role anger to clarify one's expectations of the other party serves the same function, as making a statement. Emotional performance may cause inconvenience but not harm to the target party. The angry actor may have no explicit expectation of what others ought to do in order to comply with the violated social norm.

The third mechanism is *emotional cultivation*. This is a causal process whereby leaders, on behalf of their nation, *cultivate the affective dispositions of other actors, domestically and internationally, so that the latter can cooperate in performing anger on a future occasion*. When cultivating the affective dispositions of certain individual actors,[44] leaders can appeal to ideological, historical, and cultural narratives to encourage potential allies and citizens to consider either a certain consensus as having already been established or a specific enemy as having emerged. Accordingly, emotional cultivation contributes to enhancing soft power. Cultivation enables the activation of an affective clue when the cultivated norm comes under threat again, on some future occasion.[45] This helps to explain why states or spontaneous relational groups invest in patriotic education or propaganda.[46]

The fourth causal mechanism is *emotional mobilization*,[47] which occurs when an actor *uses verbal or visual stimuli to activate the affective dispositions of other actors to take angry collective action on behalf of a presumed common cause*.[48] Emotional cultivation prepares these affective dispositions in the long term, before a potential ally is ready for emotional mobilization. Emotional mobilization is short-term, in comparison. It fits *alter*-role and collective-role anger well because these types of anger prompt actions that seek to hurt or change the target states.

By rescuing, affirming, reproducing, or reinforcing imagined points of prior resemblance between the related actors, various types of relational anger enact consequences and reify relations. Leaders reiterate the relational norms by making self-righteous claims during emotional performance, preempt the violation of the relations by the targeted actor through emotional deterrence, affirm and reproduce a prior resemblance through emotional cultivation, and rectify the challenged relations through emotional mobilization.

Discussion

Pluriversal Relational Anger

Role and relations constitute anger. This is how anger acquires socializing functions to enact national roles. If there existed only one kind of spontaneous, individualized anger, all would be able to empathize with one another's anger and appreciate the moral position involved.[49] In other words, all moral positions are universal. In practice, a global emotional community does not exist under pluriversal circumstances. Anger is not always communicable, comprehensible, or acceptable to the audience because the cause of the anger, embedded in different prior relations, is misperceived.[50] In other words, anger differs in kind, too. The literature already tackles the difference in the degree of anger but less so its relationality, apart from racial and feminist concerns.[51]

While the difference in degree may help to explain the strength of the actors' disposition, the coexistence of pluriversal relations can take advantage of anger's performance either to socialize unfamiliar others into recognizing them or to testify to the leader's successful adoption of the national self-role that is expected by other relational cluster members. The coexistence of pluriversal, ethical relations encourages the improvisation of points of resemblance.[52] When the nation is pluriversal domestically, self-role anger is destined to be performed inconsistently, with contending relations agitating each other. Incompatible *alter*-role anger will also confuse the other party.[53] Relational anger is the most appropriate approach to such seeming irony, which explains the cycles in self-role anger that are typically observed in the Global South, where the contesting national roles were cultivated by the former colonial powers.

Moreover, the types of anger associated with the same angry nation, issue area, or target nation may change as the national conditions of both parties evolve. Role anger directed at Washington's arms sales to Taipei, for example, can develop alongside China's relative strength, the United States' China policy, and Taiwan's national goals. Audience-role anger performed by Beijing may cause Taipei's *alter*-role anger toward entire China, that is not engrossed in Beijing's Chinese reunification sensibilities or Washington's universal-role anger registered in the democratic peace. The universal-role anger claimed by the US would echo the view that anger, apart from the universal kind, is ethically problematic.[54] As a result, Beijing's audience-role anger escalates into assertive self-role anger, for example, during a military exercise in the Taiwan Strait, where emotional mobilization ensues to reify the commitment to reunification.

The vicious circle continues with Washington's intensified universal-role anger, designed to serve as an emotional deterrence toward Beijing, which mobilizes Taipei's *alter*-role anger toward entire China, leading to Beijing's self-role anger aimed likewise at emotional deterrence and further aggravating Washington's universal-role anger, with the result that all other emerging points of resemblance between China and the US are shelved.[55] Chapter 9 further elaborates on the US-China-Taiwan ontological security dilemma.

CHINESE RELATIONAL ANGER

Instead of Xi Jinping's personal anger,[56] "wolf diplomacy" has become a popular yet negative portrayal of a belligerent China in its entirety in the 2020s.[57] Likewise, Vietnam, Korea (South as well as North), and Japan rarely observe their leaders expressing personal anger. In other words, statespersons,[58] as opposed to angry leaders, are not perceived as angry because their leaders act in an angry manner. In contrast to "China's anger," which is designed to represent the entire nation as angry in collective terms,[59] the leaders of the Anglosphere rarely emerge in collectivity. One generally hears more about US leaders' personal anger than nations' collective anger. Without the relational context of a cultural cluster, sincerity would belong exclusively to universal-role anger. Under authoritarian circumstances, the masses would appear incapable of expressing anger without mobilization.[60] Orientalism lies between these lines of analysis.

In the Anglosphere, leaders do not need to represent their citizens' collective emotions physically nor investigate whether their citizens are indeed angry since leaders are like individuals in their universal humanity. All individuals are presumably capable of sympathizing with their anger. Anger is not destructive for a leader in the Anglosphere, because it displays humanity, passion, and even integrity.[61] Even so, collective anger can likewise shift toward strategic anger. The occasional audience-role anger, aimed merely at making a statement, helps to explain Washington's patience toward Havana, Pyongyang, and Beijing over the years.

In the Confucian configuration of East Asian international relations, leaders' passion is unappreciated, since they are supposed to be selfless. A universal style of anger likewise exists to arouse individual members of a national actor. With *Dao* conceived of as the *genesis of everything known* and determining the ultimate resemblance between all, everyone is cosmologically bound to be related.[62] Any rejection of the attempts to improve, establish, and reproduce the proper relationships immediately violates the relationality, denies the other party's role, and incurs anger and fear of its individual members. Thus, relational anger in general at the rejection of gift giving, concessions, a ritualized hierarchy, royal marriage, and so on, improvised to make mutual roles, has a universal underpinning, since the all-around role relations are universally expected of all, regardless of their contents. In short, under Confucianism, *the first-order (universal-)role obligation is to have roles.*

Under Confucianism, anger empowers small nations. Given its flexible nature, role making manifests a Confucian community of practice of bilateral relationships.[63] Such bilateralism is conducive to pluriversalism rather than universalism. Both parties can perform role anger in the face of a perceived betrayal, so anger is always potentially contagious.[64] Anger is the soft power of all to all in these multiple bilateral relationships because anger can deny or insist on the ontological security of the other, alongside the watching third party. Even the most powerful cannot live without their role relations being vulnerable to denial. Pluriversality is practical as well natural under these complicated circumstances. In contrast, collective universal-role anger is most likely to be contingent on the hegemonic actor to enforce the allegedly universal norms.

Conclusion

Relational anger creates an agenda of socialization that can categorize the various types of anger and implicate the different tendencies within each to take a national self-role. Relational anger creates an additional agenda to study the mechanisms that trace the processes leading to international socializing outcomes. This chapter has articulated, with the inspiration of Confucianism, why anger must be conceptualized for relational expression rather than individual existence for most analytical purposes.

5

Patience with Nonsolutions

Emotion and Trust in Role Creation

Introduction

Patience is an inherent feature of foreign policy making, designed to preserve state relations; leaders choose patience over specific solutions that are likely to harm existing relationships. However, the international relations (IR) discipline has tended to ignore this topic.[1] The prevailing belief is that nations automatically subscribe to self-help logic and, therefore, have little patience with or trust in protracted, unsettling processes.[2] While David Edelstein emphasizes that foreign policy makers occasionally express patience indirectly by moderating their long-term rivalry in the interest of short-term gains,[3] such patience is a calculated delay in enforcing the ultimate conversion of estranged others and not intended to last indefinitely. To that extent, while patience usually brings benefits, it also reproduces self-centeredness, which is incompatible with mutual coexistence in the long run.

However, patience can be necessary for adopting a perpetual nonsolution, which is critical for controlling mutual estrangement. Patience oriented toward a nonsolution thus disputes the same conception geared toward a delayed victory. A relational analysis that is informed by Chinese Confucianism and the concept of trust can reveal the inevitability of patience in international relations in general. Patience might appear conniving because competitive behavior or violations of norms on the part of a relational stranger might discredit the consensual norm that constitutes the self-understanding of the subscribing nations. Therefore, relational IR has generally not attended to nonsolutions as normal, nor does it view patience as a credible foreign policy attitude, especially between nations that lack religious, historical, geo-cultural, and colonial connections. In contrast, improvised role relations emphasize context- and actor-specific arrangements to facilitate continuous interaction,[4] while nonsolutions and patience serve as rational options to ensure mutual acceptance.

For a definition, consider patience as *the readiness to refrain from enforcing a solution to a dispute*. Bringing forth Confucian rationality and relationality contributes to an understanding of patience as something that is aimed at maintaining stable relationships and overall reciprocity in the long run regardless of the incongruence between the norms of relational strangers. This chapter cites relational and affective reasons to infer that, for the most part, nation-states prefer nonsolutions to adversarial tactics when confronted with the emergence of mutual estrangement. It illustrates four states of patience by tracing the policy cycles embedded in Beijing's changing relationships with Washington and Pyongyang, which the Confucian style of patience inform.

Patience as Relational Emotion

The relationship between patience and international policy relies on the former as an affective disposition that tilts international policy away from anger, depression, or impulsivity toward the direction of self-control.[5] That said, patience does not directly lead to a specific foreign policy. That is why improvisation is an inevitable process of policy reification. Given patience's affective characteristic, patience necessarily prompts improvisation to seek mutual acceptance between the parties to a dispute. If improvisation requires the actors to go beyond routines and conventions, the evidence already suggests that patience and cognitive flexibility predict each other.[6] Therefore, patience is cognitively conducive to improvisation.

The literature on emotion considers patience a mechanism for emotional regulation, indicating the propensity of an actor to wait calmly in the face of frustration and adversity.[7] However, it is more than simply a capacity to delay gratification, which embraces an individualist calculus and defeats the purpose of maintaining relationships in the long run.

Patience enables individuals to explore alternative beliefs, practices, and experiences and encourages self-cultivation.[8] It almost always leads to inhibitory self-control.[9] At best, patience exemplifies how the collective life in the individualist self feels like taking pleasure in pain,[10] but the collective consideration is implicitly registered in the disposition to restore unity to a disordered system.[11] The religious aspect of patience encourages "substitution strategy," displays "compassion and lovingkindness," and even seeks the elimination of "suffering for all living beings."[12]

In short, the emotion literature confirms that, rather than a rationalist trait that fixes one to one's self-interests, patience is a moral affect. Actors with patience exert ego-control, as opposed to dispositional impulsivity and narcissism, and bring forth relational sensibility and responsiveness to socially desirable behavior.[13] Patience is consistently accompanied by a successful sense of belonging, manifested by secure attachment,[14] social monitoring as well as support,[15] and religiosity or spirituality.[16] Equally importantly, research shows that patience that comes to terms with a collective relationship does not mediate self-differentiation.[17] Conceding that self-differentiating actors are ordinary, including in IR, relational sensibilities are not incompatible, nor are they uncommon in any real-world setting.

Patience as a relational necessity and disposition connects foreign policy in a similar vein. It predicts the tendencies to either preserve a relational setting of mutual acceptance or breed such an atmosphere rather than producing specific platforms, which are forced to rely on the agency of the actors to improvise. That said, it is relevant to know how a readily patient foreign policy maker judges their present environment, as either relationally conducive or estranging, before understanding how they will orient self-control over impulsivity for confrontation. This is why their degree of trust in their counterparty's readiness to enter into a mutually acceptable relationship must make a research agenda of the international relations of patience.

Relationality and Patience

Accordingly, to distinguish between patience and stalemate, patience goes beyond risk-taking or an actor's restraint in making demands or concessions, even when they occupy a position of strength.[18] Whereas a stalemate indicates a dual lack of willingness to accept the status quo and inability to change a situation, patience indicates a willingness to accept circumstances in order to transcend disputes, which partly explains why it is considered uncommon from a logic-of-power perspective.[19] Given the relational necessity for nations to secure their acceptance by others, relational patience offers a deeper explanation of the deliberate use of nonsolutions as a bilateral policy tool. To that extent, patience is not about awaiting the right time to achieve a goal that has been temporarily blocked. Rather, the policy of patience is to avoid being trapped in a goal consciousness at the expense of an overall relationship. As such, patience implies a recognition that, after all, no solution will last forever in a volatile world and, therefore, forcing a specific solution is unnecessary in the long run. Moreover, a nonsolution that stabilizes a long-term relationship may be rewarded by cooperation dividends elsewhere and, in some cases, even a satisfying solution.

This explains the utility of relational sensibilities for analyzing patience through the lens of Confucian internationalism, in which patience is a deliberate, established orientation; thus, there is no such adherence to consensual notions of anarchical society,[20] practice communities,[21] organized hypocrisy,[22] and normative power,[23] among others, as in realist and liberalist IR theory. Patience may be considered unwise when violations by individual nations are perceived as threats that must be handled. A seeming act out of determination may still unintentionally reproduce a nonsolution in the long run, either when a stalemate becomes normalcy or when solutions no longer appear worth attempting, as demonstrated by the United States' respective withdrawals from Vietnam in early 1975 and Afghanistan in 2021. This calculated tolerance of nonsolutions alludes to the inevitability of improvised relations between nations that lack a collective identity and must, therefore, rely on nonsolutions rather than enforcement to mitigate or avoid further estrangement.[24]

Since patience is a relational practice and relations are always intersubjective, only the actors themselves can determine whether or not they are patient. Accordingly, this chapter analyzes patience from the actors' point of view and categorizes patience and relation by giving the actors the benefit of the doubt. This relational interpretation enables us to see international relations, even during apparent conflict, as a more ready, long-term platform for engaging than rivalry.

In line with the previous chapters, the notion of *relation* is defined here as a perceived point of resemblance that inspires mutual acceptance and solidarity, where resemblance indicates the degree of acquaintance and collective identity anchored by consensual practices and values. From the right-of-nature perspective, realists believe that all nations perceive a need to prevent others from gaining dominance or upsetting power balances[25] but caution against making attempts to "right the world" contingent on capability. As such, the realist principles reflect qualified understandings of relations embedded in natural rights, while liberalist responses to rights violations are prone to interventionism. This explains why subscribing to the idea of a prior resemblance in terms of rights can result in the undervaluing of patience, since it involves the understanding of a "correct order" among nonsubscribing strangers.

Failures that trigger intervention include civil war, terrorism, ethnic cleansing, human rights violations, nuclear proliferation, the infringement of free passage, intellectual piracy, internet hacking, and so on. In this regard, patience can be interpreted as collusion when it is extended to rogue states. Nonetheless, in those contexts where natural-law traditions and derived rule-based governance styles are not considered the norm, as in the relations between two strangers, patience is more plausible than intervention as the principle of interaction. Alexander Wendt uses an example involving space aliens and humans when describing a scenario with no prior relations: "The mechanism here is reinforcement; interaction rewards actors for holding certain ideas about each other and discourages them from holding others. If repeated long enough, these "reciprocal typifications" will create relatively stable concepts of self and other."[26]

In this example, Wendt emphasizes the value of the interaction process over the effects of prior relations that presumably determine identities or interests. He continues, "We do not *begin* our relationship with the aliens in a security dilemma; security dilemmas are not given by anarchy or nature . . . but the point remains: identities and interests are constituted by collective meanings that are always in process" (emphasis in original).[27] However, when discussing how collective identities emerge between nations in situations where no prior relations exist, Wendt only offers three simple categories—friends, rivals, and enemies—to serve as identities or institutions. In this manner, he limits the collective identities of nations without considering improvised relations based on interactive processes involving a limited number of states.

This limitation has critical systemic implications. First, the absence of a system-wide collective identity frees nations from an obligation to monitor and discipline deviant behaviors. Second, the improvisation of multiple collective identities, each within an increasingly narrow scope, substitutes pluriversalism for universalism, in which any system ignoring plural relationalities is unstable. Third, there is a tendency among states to practice patience in anticipation of all nations eventually acknowledging a need to coexist with one another. Compared to relations based on natural law, weak prior relations necessitate a bilateral sensibility. Wendt's curiosity about aliens is preempted by Confucianism, according to which all are obliged to improvise mutually accepted roles, even before they acknowledge each other's existence.[28]

A Confucian understanding of relationality entails a collective identity based on the romanticizing idea of a greater self, defined as *a social body of those sharing imagined resemblances*.[29] Given that the greater self pertains to their ontological security of being who they are, lesser (relational) selves are obliged to act in harmony through adopting consensually improvised roles. Being always dynamic in context, the practical characteristics of improvised role taking necessitate patience for the greater self to claim unity and remain ontologically existential. To endure, the greater self must be selfless and pluriversal in nature. Thus, bilateralism reduces the importance of prior consensual rules when addressing the specific idiosyncrasies of the relations between any two members. Even between rivals, an approach that acknowledges the identities of both sides can achieve an improvised relationship status with peculiar consensual rules, reciprocity obligations, and degrees of patience.

Between strangers, the greater-self formation requires that they honor improvised points of resemblance, even shallow ones, such as shared acquaintances, travel experiences, or simply being together. Otherwise, the absence of mutual obligations to act benevolently means that the greater self fails to connect and the relational selves automatically perish. This explains why incongruences in small circles can trigger anxiety,[30] and why actors are prepared for nonsolutions to preserve the greater self and keep the relational selves feeling mutually accepted. When breaches occur, patience provides time for improvisation, perhaps in the form of different kinds of gifts or engagements that suggest tolerance or disapproval. A lack of depth in actors' prior relations explains the necessity for ongoing gift giving, perhaps to the degree that it becomes a periodic ritual that supports the reproduction of the greater-self romanticism. Confucianism is implicit in any policy that treats nonsolutions seriously—not because the delayed gratification is guaranteed but because intangible relational security concerns moderate the need for such calculations.

Trust and Patience

In cases where two actors share specific historical trajectories, contextually and historically crafted prior relations differ from resemblances in terms of their commitment to commonly accepted rules or norms. Deviation from these relations prompts a need for focused relationship restoration. Punishment may enforce role expectations that are still perceived as valid and proper, and compromise may lure a defecting party to resume relations. Since neither one guarantees a satisfactory solution, many examples of a mixed approach and unresolved incongruences resurface and escalate.[31] In these mainly bilateral processes, the patience of one party is obliged by the willingness of the other to abide by the role expectations. The perceived trustworthiness of the other party is, accordingly, a critical factor.

IR scholars analyze trust in terms of intentions conditioned by interests, capacities, values,[32] and obligations,[33] among other factors, with perceptions of nonharming intentions suggesting control over uncertainties and thus the ability to block rapid conflict escalation. Mutual role expectations, strengthened by a shared ideology, strategic interests, religion, race, history, language, institutions, and the like, arguably represent the most important trust-assessment factor. The parties are obliged to reciprocate in certain areas and refrain from unilaterally asserting their position without considering each other's needs. When perceived obligations to reciprocate are illusory in content, trusting relationships can turn into romanticizing, with the potential for frustration.[34] Any sense of patience in response to frustration assumes that the other party will resist unilateralism and self-centeredness. In relationships characterized by periodic aggravation, alienation, or disrespect, a nonsolution is almost the only alternative to punishment or retaliation. The choice between these two measures is always politically challenging and transitory.

Given the relational necessity of establishing a sense of mutual acceptance when no prior relationship exists, the trust-building process entails mutual role-making factors involving evaluations of capabilities and intentions to honor role expectations. In short, a willingness to create mutually acknowledged roles is more important than an agreement on specific role content. An absence of prior relations exempts actors from obligations to enforce existing norms. Although consensus formation stands as a long-term goal, expressions and acknowledgments of goodwill represent important steps in the trust-building process. Trust in another party's policies, values, and identities is built on confidence in its willingness to create and participate in a greater-self identity. Such trust reflects some of the following five beliefs:

1. In the uniqueness of the potential relationship[35]—for example, Beijing's assertion of a special connection with Pyongyang and the assumed reciprocation.

2. That the other party understands its obligations[36]—for example, Beijing's belief that Tokyo will refrain from escalation if it observes Chinese patrol boats in disputed waters.

3. That one (usually the stronger) party in an asymmetrical relationship will respect the other's inability to respond in a congruent manner, at least for the time being.[37] For example, Beijing views Taipei as understanding that its periodic unification pressure is designed to reconfirm the transient nature of Taipei's alienation from the "One China" principle and that any nominal acknowledgment of that principle will be rewarded with economic concessions.

4. That access exists to the other party's policymaking processes.[38] In Vietnam, this involves using cross-Communist Party channels to communicate Hanoi's intentions whenever a maritime dispute with the Chinese government arises.

5. That compensation will be offered for any harm caused by incongruences within opposing agendas.[39] For example, whenever Washington, DC, approves an arms sale to Taiwan, China expects a reconfirmation of US support for the One China policy.

Patience that accompanies trustworthy intentions is conducive to establishing agreeable role relations, regardless of whether or not a short-term solution to a dispute is present. In such situations, the ability to honor loosely defined role expectations is more important than specificity. Consider two scenarios: in one, mutual role expectations have yet to be formed, but the two parties view each other as trustworthy; in the other, mutual role expectations are well understood, but a sense of trustworthiness is lacking. Presumably, patience will be greater in the first, regardless of the level of ambiguity within the role expectations. Ambiguity can lessen the potential frustration over altered mutual expectations, while the potentially escalating tensions become arguably more manageable due to the perceived confidence in the eventual formation of relationality.

Table 5.1 presents a summary of the ways in which patience can produce nonsolutions according to conditions defined by the trust and relationship status. In scenarios where a certain degree of bilateral consensus exists (row 1), nonsolution aims to prevent further estrangement or alienation and encourage patience to await restoration opportunities. Otherwise, the motivation is to reduce the degree of unfamiliarity when prior relations are lacking (row 2).

Regarding trust in existing mutual role expectations, the "engagement" policy aims to reduce the potential for a perceived win-lose scenario. In practice, this means circumventing disputes and developing a sense of cooperation as if a greater-self identity were still intact. A "boycott" policy aims to prevent the other side, which is perceived as untrustworthy, from achieving the goal that it is currently pursuing. Both approaches leave room for the restoration or substantiation of a greater-self relationship in the presence or absence of trust. A "reciprocation" policy entails a belief in the potential for future relationship development. This belief encourages gift-giving behaviors aimed at reciprocity, resulting in expectations of a greater-self identity. In cases where both greater-self relationship potential and trust level are low, there is a tendency to follow a "push" policy until opportunities arise to gain a better position, without making concessions in terms of political principles.

Table 5.1. Four Types of Patient Nonsolutions in Foreign Policy

	Trust in role making: Problem-solving	Mistrust in role making: Tit-for-tat
Relationship to be reproduced	Engagement	Boycott
Relationship to be improvised	Reciprocation	Push

Created by the author.

Two Nonsolution Policy Examples

Continuing chapter 3's case, Beijing's interactions with Pyongyang and Washington, as respective symmetric and asymmetric examples, provide a good illustration of evolving relations and applications of patience. The Sino–North Korean and Sino-US cases represent two Chinese approaches to bilateral relations. One reflects a perception that concurring role expectations already exist; the other, that a relationship based on mutual national interests is progressing. A central factor in both cases is whether Beijing believes that the other party is willing to explore new or additional role-based relations. According to the aforementioned relational view of patience, Beijing's (dis)trust in Pyongyang affects its preference for a boycott or engagement policy. In the Sino-US case, Beijing is waiting for signs of trust to emerge before choosing between a reciprocation or push strategy. All four orientations are conducive to nonsolutions, thus underscoring the assertion that Beijing perceives improvisation as more important than specific solutions to individual problems without substantive prior relations.

China–North Korea

Beijing and Pyongyang's bilateral relationship is a composite of trust and the lack thereof.[40] At times, Beijing is unsure whether Pyongyang is serious about participating in a reciprocal relationship according to what it perceives as mutually agreeable role expectations. Depending on the actions and rhetoric that Pyongyang is expressing at any particular moment, the Chinese leadership has fluctuated between boycott and engagement policies.

The two countries have created hierarchical roles for each other according to historical contexts, as chapter 3 notes. Regardless of which specific relationship was being emphasized—as Confucian disciples, tributary brothers, war allies, ideological comrades, security partners, or geo-cultural neighbors—they adhered to roles based on reciprocal goodwill when abiding by obligations to consult on major issues, such as economic development, national unification, and responses to the perceived US threat. This partnership gives Pyongyang leverage over Beijing because the latter needs to acquiesce to the former's recalcitrance to maintain minimal role relations.

Disagreements and a sense of estrangement have emerged from the changes in Sino-US relations and the question of Korean Peninsula denuclearization. Beijing's dual approach consists of engagement that is aimed at maintaining Pyongyang's international relationships while experimenting with various boycott-oriented strategies in response to recalcitrant behavior. For example, Beijing insists that any resolution to the denuclearization issue requires multiparty negotiations with no specific deadline—an instance of patience. Another example is the 2014 joint statement issued by Xi Jinping and former South Korean president Park Geun-hye, which emphasized their "firm opposition to the development of nuclear weapons on the Korean Peninsula,"[41] which was noteworthy for its lack of reference to both North Korea and any specific details on the actions that China planned to take in order to achieve that goal.[42] The statement's limited references reflect Chinese concerns about engaging with North Korea.

There are multiple examples of Kim Jong-un pursuing his aggressive strategy outside the mutual Chinese–North Korean role expectations: the December 2013 execution of Jang Song-taek, Kim Jong-un's uncle and adviser, who had personal ties with negotiators in Beijing; the nuclear tests in February 2013 and January 2016; a hydrogen bomb test in March and September 2017; several long-range missile tests in 2016 and 2017; and the delay of an official visit to China by Kim until 2018.[43]

In early 2013, the official Chinese media outlets warned Pyongyang to "cherish" its friendship with China based on past acts of support and hinted at stronger reactions to further nuclear tests.[44] Pyongyang's third underground test in 2013 showed that this warning had no effect. Beijing's measured boycott actions also included a March 7 announcement by Chinese Ministry of Foreign Affairs spokesman Qin Gang that China would support any UN Security Council response provided that it constituted "necessary and proper methods."[45]

In 2016, the Chinese Xinhua News Agency explained that the country's support for UN sanctions was designed to stop North Korea from straying too far from a denuclearization path and encourage a return to a "dialogue track"[46]—in other words, to pay more attention to relationship management. In the same year, Beijing responded to the hydrogen bomb test with a strongly worded statement on the trade in North Korean mineral products, which included a contraband list. The new rules came into force immediately.[47] In April 2017, the day before a China-US summit meeting, an editorial in the state-run *Global Times* commented on the firing by Pyongyang of a ballistic missile off its eastern coast, saying, "there is little strategic trust between the two sides because of serious communication problems."[48]

Given the deeply rooted bilateral relations, Beijing was unwilling to enact or support sanctions that might go beyond boycotting. The Chinese leadership appeared reluctant to make any specific response that carried a clear message. In July 2017, the UN Security Council voted unanimously to restrict oil exports and ban textile exports to North Korea. The US accused China of supplying North Korea with most of its oil, possibly influencing China's September 2017 decision to discontinue both refined oil exports and textile imports from its neighbor.[49] Washington's accusation spotlighted Beijing's caution in taking any action or making any comment that might be perceived as an attempt to destabilize the Kim regime.

After confirming a breakthrough meeting with Donald Trump and South Korean president Moon Jae-in, Kim Jong-un visited Beijing on March 27, 2018. In sharp contrast to the preceding two decades of mutual resentment, engagement has become the central theme for Beijing-Pyongyang relations in early 2022.[50] Kim visited China again in May and June 2018 and January 2019 to consult with Xi Jinping about his meetings with Donald Trump, followed by a visit to Pyongyang by Xi in June 2019. According to the Xinhua News Agency, Xi asked Kim to remain in personal contact "via exchanges of visits, of special envoys, and letters," referred to "the two parties' glorious tradition to exchange views on important issues," and pledged to "adequately bring the two political parties' engagement into full play" as well as "enhance engagement between the people in both countries."[51]

Both sides tried to act as though no problems existed. North Korean television showed Kim diligently taking notes while listening to Xi, who expressed support for Kim without referring to any specific shared goals or expectations. In April 2019, China's UN representative Wu Haitao asserted that "sanction measures toward the DPRK should not affect humanitarian aid."[52] Note that China has consistently pushed for reconsideration of the sanctions on North Korea since the June 2018 Kim-Trump summit.[53]

Sino-US Relations

Despite their World War II alliance, Chinese scholar Yan Xuetong argues that the US today is best viewed as a "fake friend" of China, as opposed to the "real friend" that existed between 1978 and 1988.[54] Yan argues that China has always expressed high expectations for American support on core Chinese interests, such as the One China principle. Yan's "real friend" has no emotional substance (see chapter 6). It refers to someone reciprocating mutual support as opposed to liking. Therefore, real friendship is contingent on behavior. Beijing has improvised while exploring a "major power relationship"—defined as the mutual acknowledgment of core interests on both sides, with Washington contrarily adhering to the obligations embedded in what it views as the responsibility of all nations to abide by liberalist principles.[55]

Following his first official visit to the US as Chinese president in 2013, Xi Jinping perceived Barack Obama's agreement with Xi's belief that they "should *follow a new path*" (emphasis mine) and "work together on building a new type of great power relations based on mutual respect and win-win cooperation for the benefits of people in the two countries as well as the world." Obama appeared to reciprocate by improvising the "future relationship to develop means for frank and constructive communication."[56]

During the Obama administration, China sought opportunities to create an atmosphere of reciprocity to establish mutual trust and a cooperative intent,[57] despite the lack of any official American endorsement of the idea of "a new type of great power relationship."[58] Thus, during the September 2016 G20 summit held in Hangzhou, Obama described the US and China as agreeing to expand cooperation in economic and trade relations, investment, international crime fighting, scientific research, education, energy and environmental protection, and global security. Regarding Taiwan, Obama used the occasion to proclaim that the US maintained its support for the One China policy and opposed any means to pursue Taiwan's "independence." Immediately following the summit, China announced the cancellation of a long-standing ban on imported American beef, ascribing the decision to "risk assessment" results.[59]

There are other examples of Chinese efforts to generate a sense of Sino-US reciprocity. When Xi and Obama met in Beijing in November 2014, in his official welcoming remarks, Xi used a well-known Chinese metaphor, "A pool begins with many drops of water"[60]—a statement emphasizing a reciprocal relationship process rather than a specific role arrangement. Xi made a rare appearance at a joint news conference, even taking questions from reporters. The two sides agreed on a breakthrough involving information technology tariffs, which American officials described as "open[ing] the door to expanding a World Trade Organization agreement on these products, assuming other countries can be persuaded to accept the same terms."[61]

Beijing's role expectations for Washington are less about specific programs than a willingness to explore different ways in which a bilateral relationship might develop. Beijing cites at least three trust-building references: Taiwan, trade, and the United States' China-containment strategy in Asia. Regarding the Taiwan issue, Beijing views Washington's position—including the nonsolution of always withstanding support for Taiwan's independence—as an essential indicator of America's willingness to engage in relationship building. Taiwan has proved a sticking point ever since the relations between the two countries were normalized in 1979.[62] Instead of attempting to agree on a solution to the unification issue, Beijing has focused on the propriety of Washington's actions. China's demonstrated desire was to explore a new relationship that would be sufficient for ensuring its continued patience. The purpose is to convey trust in Washington's willingness to avoid abandoning its efforts to identify a workable relationship.

Immediately following the November 2016 election, President-elect Trump accepted a congratulatory phone call from Taiwanese president Tsai Ing-wen, which triggered a strong protest from Beijing. Since then, China has consistently shown ambivalence about yielding on any topic while occasionally giving signals that it is willing to discuss issues involving trade, military exchanges, and climate change, among others. In December of that year, Xi Jinping reportedly approved the flight of a nuclear-capable bomber over the South China Sea to "send a message to the incoming administration."[63] The official Chinese press was particularly alert to Trump's linking of China's "agreements on trade and other issues" to his puzzlement over "why the United States has to be constrained by the One China policy."[64]

Trump signed off on two congressional bills: the March 2018 Taiwan Travel Act (which encourages visits between US and Taiwanese officials at all levels) and the John S. McCain National Defense Authorization Act for Fiscal Year 2019 (NDAA),[65] which requires the US government to support and enhance Taiwan's security, to promote exchanges between senior Taiwanese and American defense officials, and to assess all existing threats in the interest of maintaining Taiwan's deterrence capability. The Chinese navy conducted live-fire drills in the Taiwan Strait on April 13, 2018, five days after the congressional debate on the NDAA began.[66] The wording of the Chinese announcement was straightforward in presenting a warning to both Washington and Taipei. One week before President Trump signed the bill, the Chinese media reported naval maneuvers in

the Yellow, East, and South China Seas.[67] On August 8 of the following year, the US State Department approved a $2.2 billion arms sale
to Taiwan. The Chinese foreign ministry demanded, on August 9, that
the US "immediately cancel the planned arms sale and stop military
relations with Taipei to avoid damaging Sino-US relations and harming
peace and stability in the Taiwan Strait."[68] On August 14, the Chinese
government announced that routine air and naval exercises in the area
would resume.[69]

   While expressing a stake in resisting any changes to its One China
policy, Beijing has not alluded to any specific solution to the Taiwan
issue. Its efforts do not appear to be contingent on the past successes
or failures of its reciprocating and pushing actions but rather on a willingness to patiently await a new form of relationship. However, Beijing
consistently pushes back whenever Washington takes action or makes
an announcement that it perceives as offensive. The climax thus far of
such a pushback in the twenty-first century that attracted global attention was the military exercise in August 2022 designed to implement
an unprecedented seventy-two-hour blockade of Taiwan following the
failure of repeated warnings that the speaker of the US House of Representatives should not visit Taiwan. Note, though, that the blockade's
risk of escalation remained well regulated throughout. Other tools of the
push policy include investment in the so-called rogue states, intercepts
of the US military in the air or at sea, the countermobilization of votes
in international organizations, and long-armed sanctions on individual
policymakers.

Conclusion

Embracing the nonsolution to dispute, patience acknowledges the volatile
nature of foreign policy conditions that entail changes. In this view, a
permanent solution is implausible for any agenda. To the extent that the
dispute does not cause further aggravation, a nonsolution is a practical
solution. Even when such a volatile nature is not acknowledged, as often
occurs if the historical lens adopted by policymakers is relatively short-
term, the striving for a solution, successful or not, will probably not last
forever. For a general theorist, given that any policy platform or goal is
eventually transient in nature, patience deserves acknowledgment as a
more rational approach to a relationship than goal hunting and a better

foundation for another round of patience in the future. Accordingly, the choice is simultaneously about the historical horizon between patience and goal consciousness. Those used to being goal-driven typically conceive of patience merely as a strategy for delayed gratification. They could be surprised by their own flexibility in reverting a particular trajectory of policy in due course to favor a nonsolution.

For facing US-China rivalry, even a US Secretary of State would realize that their shared responsibility, obliged by the entire world, is exactly to work through their differences. Patience is a relational emotion that explains the tendency to use nonsolutions but does not explain which specific policy outcome will emerge. There is no fixed form for willingly expressing patience in the name of relationship maintenance, thus making improvisation a challenging task whenever national leaders perceive the existing relations as having been harmed or the negotiating parties as untrustworthy. However, in the cases discussed in this chapter, pushing is preferable to punitive or disciplinary actions to maintain or restore relations.

Prior relations that generally constitute national identities are considered weak if they impose no specific rules or norms on the participating actors. Relationalities that are short on behavioral specifics may require improvisation by the negotiating parties. Weak prior relations may necessitate a willingness to develop congruent role expectations in order to reduce the mutual distance. This rationale for patience has produced four policy styles that can be used to analyze the foreign policy scenarios beyond China. Further scrutiny is required to understand how different improvised- and prior-relations combinations might explain the links between trust and patience.

Chinese leaders seem prepared to convey an appearance of patience to establish an external image of stability, provided that their negotiating partners indicate a willingness to go along with a perceived prior relationship. Their gift-giving practices are illustrations of relationship building. However, in practical terms, the focus on mutual acceptance can distance China from other parties' internal institutions or values due to the strong expectation that the other party will always maintain a distance from China's internal affairs. Consequently, straightforward solutions to disputes are rarely, if ever, the primary objective. Chinese internationalism involves setting aside contested issues, maintaining limited relationships with adversaries, and improvising in response to evolving situations. Based on past examples of nonsolutions, the Chinese style of patience indicates an inclination to use them in all disputes, with individual cases reflecting the relational cultures of the parties in question and their concomitant constraints.

6

Corrupting Friendship

Distance Sensibilities in International Gift Giving

Introduction

Friendship is an ordinary diplomatic discourse, describing the relations between two countries, especially socialist ones. A friendship between two people involves positive affection,[1] which nations, as actors, do not practically possess, so the friendship between nations is, strictly speaking, a metaphor or role making. A reference to friendship suggests that two nations would be fond of each other if they were capable of feeling. Nations are incapable of feeling,[2] although the role conception embedded in friendship can constitute the identities and emotions of the leaders;[3] thus, diplomatic references to friendship compose an intentional rather than spontaneous statement. Although signing a treaty of friendship has been common practice in history and contemporary international relations (IR), war can still break out between the parties to a friendship treaty; thus, diplomatic friendship treaties do not guarantee friendship.[4] They camouflage the opposite. Internally, this irony indicates the plausibility that friendly relations and discourses suppress certain incompatible differences while boasting friendship.[5] Externally, such references to friendship may emphasize the friend/enemy dichotomy and the dichotomy between the self and the other, which is familiar to contemporary IR.[6] Therefore, the IR literature on self-interest and security is not intensively engaged in exploring friendship.

The literature on friendship in IR consists of two seemingly incompatible agendas. On the one hand, friendship reflects the collective identity of similar states[7]—for example, democratic, socialist, or Commonwealth states. The theory of democratic peace illustrates how analytical friendship can be a dependent variable, as explained by a shared democratic culture. On the other hand, friendship facilitates transcendence over differences in religion, ideology, race, colonialism, or power level.[8] In the second agenda, friendship creates an independent variable[9] that reconciles differences as observed, for instance, between the US and Saudi Arabia.[10] These two agendas coincide with the Confucian consideration of friendship being both a virtue and a danger.

In accordance with Confucianism, this chapter nonintuitively considers positive emotions as a potential *danger*. Compared with the hierarchical ethics of Confucianism, which are supported by the metaphor of kinship, friendship is neither hierarchical nor kin-related in nature. The conceived danger of friendship implies that unethical friendship is attractive and assumes a peculiar kind of otherness in society. It is neither marginal nor subordinate; rather, another side of society's (socially desirable and yet ethically undesirable) humanity prevails. The anxiety about friendship is thus an inherent recognition of the variety of needs in society and the estranging tendency within the self.

This chapter introduces the thoughts of Confucius and his disciples on friendship. In the following discussion, *friendship* refers to *the practice of expected support between equal actors*; thus, friendship is actional and intersubjective. However, this practice differs from Western social science, wherein positive affection is almost always constitutive of friendship.[11] The study of Confucian friendship contributes to IR in two aspects: (1) ethical friendship that reflects a particular prior relation and imposes norms and expectations on friendly parties, and (2) improvised friendship that reflects no such perceived prior consensus and lures friendly parties away from their other relations to satisfy their own internal needs. Finally, the chapter attempts to adopt a broader scope of engagement to demonstrate the analytical contribution of Confucian friendship to the study of China-US international policy.

A note on the practice of gift giving seems appropriate here.[12] Gift giving is a ritual for reconfirming relationships, whether hierarchical in nature or not. In the past, gift giving was what denoted the tributary system and heavenly worship. It remains a widespread practice in modern times.[13] In IR, gift giving by presumably friendly parties takes various forms—for example, arranging a zero-interest loan, lowering a tariff, building or maintaining local infrastructure, supplying a vaccine during a pandemic, calling off a military exercise, casting a favorable vote, abstaining from boycotting, sending an ambassador of goodwill, extending an invitation to a gathering, awarding a medal, conceding in a dispute, praising an action, and even giving priority regarding seating, among many other improvised offerings, which can be symbolic or material in nature.

The Confucian Principles of Friendship

The fundamental norm that governs Confucian friendship is trustworthiness. Zengzi, a student of Confucius, and Mencius, the legendary successor to Confucius, bequeathed to future generations the notion that "trustworthiness" is the essence of Confucian friendship.[14] *Trustworthiness*, in Chinese, connotes keeping one's word and faithfully playing one's roles. In the Confucian ethical order, people are friends only because they enact the role of a friend, not because they like each other. Accordingly, strangers make friends and protect their relationships from discord. Still, trustworthiness and gift giving can degenerate quickly to the negligence of other, higher ethical duties. Confucius was alert to the corruptive potential of friendship. Thus, he focused on taming this concept.

The earliest reference to friendship as one of the five ethics appears in the *Doctrine of the Golden Mean* of the *Classic of Rites*. Confucius's own discussion of friendship in the *Analects* conceives of it as a necessary evil. Confucian friendship implies an irony of filling the lacuna of non-kin relations versus preempting it from indulgence. Friendship in the latter tendency can lose the proper distance and evolve into partisanship. All of the codes of propriety contrived for performing the roles of hierarchical dyads will immediately face the challenge of such partisanship.

Confucianism is essentially a belief in kinship. Besides friendship, all other hierarchical dyads assume spontaneous benevolence due to the natural care and love for one's kin. However, friends are not kin, nor a hierarchy. Intimate friendship challenges the enforceability of any code of propriety and indicates why Confucius was consistently wary of the potential abuse of friendship. However, he could not avoid discussing friendship because relationships outside kinship would otherwise be built between irresponsible strangers.

FRIENDSHIP AS VIRTUE

Confucianism implicitly states a lawlike principle that unrestrained friendship would cause society to lose order. This prediction leads to the teaching of propriety that preempts this harm. The key theme, which one infers from the *Analects*, is proper distance. For example, Confucianism warns that officials must not develop their own private relationships[15] lest these interfere with their loyalty to the emperors. Normatively, a virtuous actor should not indulge in friendship lest intimacy compromise friends' moral duty to the order of greater or higher scope. Empirically, the degree of distance predicts what would happen if distance were not maintained correctly. Intimacy traps one in the wrongdoing of a friend, whereas distance enables one to provide early warnings before the wrongdoing escalates.

Confucius advised that friends should refrain from engaging in conflicts of interest and maintain the group's harmony by avoiding partisanship (*Analects*, Weilinggong). Due to this concern about distance, Confucius refused to show gratitude to those friends who would bring him valuable wagons or horses; however, if they arrived with meat exclusively for making sacrifices to ancestors, he would express his appreciation (*Analects*, Xiangdang). Friendship is trustworthy if it contributes to the other four ethics. Even so, Confucius could be emotional about friendship. He was spontaneously pleased when friends traveled a long distance to visit him (*Analects*, Xueer). These remote friends were unlikely to pose a risk of committing partisanship. Therefore, the only reason for them to meet, regardless of the journey's inconvenience, was to show respect to each other. Such reunions reproduced the ethical order.

Confucians of later generations followed his distance sensibilities. They believe that only where distance is properly kept can friends be trustworthy to each other. Yan Yuan (521 to 481 BC), for example, indicated that gentlemen would make friends by reading one another's narratives and maintained that friendship, embedded in these ethical narratives, can contribute to the practices of benevolence (*Analects*, Yanyuan), presumably because these narratives are ethical lessons reminding one to display benevolence. Therefore, Yan Yuan believed that physical interaction is insignificant to friendship among the elite. To allow friends to be mutually trustworthy, Mencius suggested that people should consciously adhere to friendship proper exclusively for friends, such that they would not rely on their seniority, nobility, or kinship (e.g., brotherly) networking; these practices might reduce friendship to calculations of usefulness; other than the attraction of friends' virtue, no further rationale is proper for friendship (*Mencius*, Wanzhang). For example, Zi You (506 to 443 BC), another student of Confucius, believed that one would lose friends if they murmured and gossiped; seeming proximity and intimacy could ultimately lead to estrangement (*Analects*, Liren).

Confucius offers a few specific clues about making friends properly. He wished to make friends only with those who were superior to him (*Analects*, Xueer). This concept of superiority did not refer to more wealth or a higher status but to self-cultivation to keep the ethical order. Note Confucius' advice that one should befriend only the learned gentleman wherever one travels, who will display benevolence and ethics. Therefore, distance did not connote estrangement. Confucius was delighted to make many virtuous friends (*Analects*, Jishi). He would not hide his reservation without feeling ashamed about a friend who gave him a reason to complain (*Analects*, Gongyechang). For Confucius, friends are obliged to learn constantly from each other (*Analects*, Zilu). That said, Confucius cautioned against interference with friends who do not listen and recommended addressing an issue of concern with a friend, and abandoning the friendship as a last resort, because one would shame oneself by having a friend who does not listen (*Analects*, Yanyuan). Proper rituals were prioritized such that Confucius would voluntarily make the funeral arrangements for a deceased friend, whomever they were, if no one else would (*Analects*, Xiangdang).

FRIENDSHIP AS A DANGER

Everyone naturally indulges in friendship to some extent. Indulgence exposes the ethical otherness or strangeness inside each self. The best approach to governing inevitable otherness, for Confucians, is to disguise it through rituals and role-play within the four hierarchical relationships. Generations of Confucians have dreaded the loss of hierarchical relations. Contemporary IR adopts the norm of sovereign equality, inspiring the other side of virtuous friendship: dangerous friendship. Accordingly, dangerous friendship is the root of unethical collusion between friendly nations.

According to Confucius, one's mistake in exceeding propriety anywhere *always* arises from the abuse of friendship and results in an overly partisan position (*Analects*, Liren). By attributing mistakes to improper friendship alone, Confucius implied that more benevolence from the other actor in the hierarchical dyad could restrain the wrongdoer. An act of wrongdoing is not contaminating unless the wrongdoer's friends emulate their practices of insufficiency. Partisan mercy can cause a deficiency in benevolence proper for the other four hierarchical relationships. This notion explains why Confucius followed the Daoist advice that a proper friendship for the elite would have to be as tasteless as water (*Zhuangzi*, Shanmu). The awareness and incapacity of Confucianism in the presence of personal friendship set the parameters of friendship as the ability to either support or undermine the other ethical relations.

The most widely cited Confucian dictum on friendship is his criteria for distinguishing decent from corrupt friendship—the three criteria for decent friendship being to be "straightforward," "understanding," and "well informed," and those for corrupt friendship being to be "circumventive," "toadyish," and "specious" (*Analects*, Jishi). Confucius probably intended to wish for friends who were blunt about his ethical impropriety, understanding about his dedication to ethical duties that constrained him from devoting much time to supporting friends, and well informed about remarkable ethical practices elsewhere. He avoided people who were circumventive of their ethical duties, toadyish toward others who violated ethical relationships, or specious in twisting norms to encompass ethical misconduct.

The Confucian Approach to International Friendship

EQUAL FRIENDSHIP VERSUS HIERARCHICAL SOCIALISM

Two principles of IR were apparent at the birth of the PRC: sovereign equality and socialism. Friendship is a means of connecting sovereign states because it implies equality and peace.[16] Socialism further incurred two second-order norms: proletarian internationalism and anti-(capitalist) imperialism.[17] Sovereign equality adopted the expression of friendship in European diplomatic history; thus, the first normative narrative that Chinese leaders had to learn was created. Proletarian internationalism under the leadership of the Soviet Union appeared in those narratives of socialist brotherhood and friendship.[18] These norms helped Beijing display the departure of the new state from the inferior past.

Mao's decision to lean to one side, which obliged Moscow to give up the Kuomintang, was a means of substituting a new ethical relation for the previous ones. Beijing's entry into the socialist camp enabled several bilateral treaty relationships to develop with other socialist countries.[19] This relationship was brotherly, friendly, and hierarchical in nature, meeting the sovereign and socialist criteria simultaneously. According to Yan Li,[20] the friendship rhetoric attributed "the Soviet people's happy life" to the leadership of the communist party and "the superior socialist system." However, the "friendship rhetoric" was simultaneously an entitlement statement that obliged the Soviet Union to share its experiences with its new friend.[21]

For the PRC leaders, the friendship rhetoric eased the hierarchical sensibilities that existed in the role of "little brother" and "follower" of the Soviet leadership. That said, friendship obliges Beijing to learn from well-informed friends.[22] Therefore, learning intensively is in itself a demonstration of trustworthiness qua friendship.[23] The resulting intimacy espouses the role expectation of selfless support by the other party, thus contradicting the hierarchical relationships, which require one's deference and obedience. Eventually, intimate friendship easily infringes prerogatives that belong exclusively to the superior party. Once the sense of friendship has been damaged, hierarchical duties will be aborted simultaneously.

FRIENDSHIP TO ABORT UNWANTED RELATIONS

Intimate friendship is, ironically, a harbinger of unstable relationships.[24] Friendship that is exempt from prior relations can entice the other party to adopt Beijing's ethical position, such as during the Cultural Revolution. This friendship would encourage the other party to abandon its ethical order[25] and hence be a bad friend, according to the Confucian criteria. Without hierarchical sensibilities, the incurrence of friendship in Beijing's diplomacy aimed at renouncing unwanted relationships. Five unwanted prior relations have been renounced since the establishment of the PRC.

First, friendship signals the ending of both superiority and inferiority. Hierarchy used to be the order of nature in the past tributary system.[26] The succeeding republican China has consistently appeared in the self-image of an inferior, which continued throughout the suffering during World War II and the survival needs of the PRC during the Cold War. The discourse of friendship that implicates equality is particularly appropriate in these contexts.[27] In reality, this friendly role contradicted realism's survival instinct, hence the policy priority on equal status over diplomatic recognition, as expressed in Mao's famous quotation, "Put the house in order before inviting guests." He hoped to acquire equality of respect for China from imperialist countries *after* China was able successfully to cleanse the domestic imperialist legacies.[28]

Second, friendship symbolizes the ending of a war.[29] The PRC was actually at war with almost all of its major neighbors, such as the Korean War (1950 to 1953), the offshore island crises (1954 to 1958), the Sino-Indian border clashes (1962), the Sino-Soviet border clashes (1969), the Sino-Vietnamese War (1979), and so on. The friendly role reified by gift giving can redefine China's international image, detached from the cause of the war.

Third, friendship transcends intergovernmental confrontation.[30] Carefully contrived programs that facilitate people-to-people diplomacy were intended to show the absurdity of containment at the state level.[31] The rhetoric of friendship also offsets the hierarchical order based on the level of power or seniority of the national leaders, which was disadvantageous to Beijing's sense of equality during the same period. Undoubtedly, citizens who enacted people's diplomacy acted on behalf of the state,[32] albeit indirectly. Practices of friendship between two peoples are neither realist nor liberal in nature. Their interaction reconciles the binaries, which allows mutual acceptance to take root.[33]

Fourth, friendship can bypass socialist identity.[34] Since the Sino-Soviet rift developed, the ideological resemblance has become irrelevant to relationships with a third socialist country. Especially after the Soviet Bloc's collapse in the 1990s, no relationships other than friendship have been appropriate. Consider Sino-Vietnamese relationships. Each time, their quarrels prompt a reunion between the two top leaderships in their party capacity rather than their governmental capacity.[35] Hanoi calls Beijing a "good brother," whereas Beijing calls Hanoi a good friend, neighbor, comrade, and partner. For Beijing, the four goods avoided making any direct reference to the socialist brotherhood and Beijing's duties as a presumably older brother. The brotherly relationship has reappeared in Beijing's Vietnam narrative only after Hanoi and Washington began to treat each other as partners and friends that are relationally less intimate than brothers.

Finally, friendship dissuades suspicious others from worrying about the return of hierarchy. In fact, the rise of China has invited fear of the China threat and the impression of arrogance,[36] rooted in the past tributary system. Adhering to the rhetoric of friendship represents Beijing's promise to avoid enacting the role of a superior.[37] Thus, the partnership concept is prevalent in Chinese international relations in the twenty-first century. The term is almost interchangeable with *friendship*, except that *partnership* alludes to the existence of a joint project, resulting in a materialist friendship.

In all of these practices, the Chinese diplomatic rhetoric of friendship connotes the prevention or conversion of improper relations.[38] Hence, friendship is indeterminate and yet attests to distance sensibilities: China is neither a (1) subordinate, (2) belligerent, (3) rival, (4) obligated brother, or (5) superior. The purpose of all of these activities is to keep the other side at a proper distance: to (1) keep the strong party at a distance, (2) create distance from a previous rival, (3) avoid contagious engagement, (4) discontinue the socialist brotherhood, or (5) remain at a distance from the internal affairs of the weak party. Friendship offers no clue to a hierarchical order rather than alleged sovereign equality.

In addition, no other Confucian ethic but friendship offers the proper basis for a new relationship. These new friends could include South Asia, African states, and Latin America.[39] Obliging a friend is no more than a request to trust a China that is no longer feudal, dependent, inimical, revolutionary, or expansionary but equal and peaceful. Consequently, the corrupt Confucian friendship that entices or even corrupts the other party may easily emerge. Krishna Prakash Gupta sounds an anxious Confucian when he comments on China's friendship as a relationship emerging from "China's internal need."[40] According to his description, China is blatantly a corrupt friend: "It is only in enemy-territories that China clamours most to secure socio-economic justice. Among friends, she is completely oblivious to the people's misery, oppression and exploitation."

Examples Illustrative of China's Practices of Friendship

Two Relational Types of Friendship

The Confucian point of view implies that friends may be either decent or corrupt; the former supports the friend's fulfillment of a prior duty, and the latter is detrimental to it. Friendship is neither value- nor power-oriented. In a nutshell, the friend category is always convenient for nations with an inadequate acquaintance or unpleasant past. In these cases, some gift giving, instead of a threat, bargained exchange, or shared belief, is usually the proper mode of interaction. The rationale is to establish a long-term relationship that can be of future use, regardless of past grievances. This scenario is the mode of corrupt friendship.

Contrary to gift-oriented friendships, duty-oriented friendships, in which both parties perceive a prior mutual commitment that brings expectations of selfless support, also exist. The other side of the duty-oriented friendship would be sanctions on the abortion of duty. This scenario is the mode of decent friendship.

Two propositions derived from this discussion that may develop a way to move beyond realism and its derivatives based upon national interest, systemic structure, or democratic peace are as follows:

1. The more one perceives that the other party shares one's ethical pursuit, the more one engages in decent Confucian friendship. This action is attributed to the inference that shared ethics allows one to anticipate the other party's appreciation for one's bluntness, understanding, and experience sharing.

   1.1. The less the other party is perceived as sharing one's ethical pursuit, the less one engages in decent friendship (because one is indifferent to the duties of the other party, embedded in the other's ethical order).

2. The more one perceives that the other party possesses equivalent material strength, the less one engages in corrupt Confucian friendship. This incentive is attributed to the inference that one cannot easily corrupt the other party capable of its affairs, and vice versa, dispense with either party's duties through fudging, gift giving, and sheltering.

   2.1 The less the other party is perceived as possessing equivalent material strength, the more one engages in corrupt friendship (because one can provide material incentives to the other party or receive them from it and corrupt the weaker side's ethical duties elsewhere).

Based on these two propositions, an actor may engage in four stylistic types of friendship (see table 6.1): (1) Corrective friendship involves facing an actor of equivalent power who is perceived as sharing the prior

Table 6.1. Confucian Friendship in International Relations

	Major power (little to lure)	Minor power (much to lure)
Prior cultural relations (much to preach)	Good (corrective) e.g., Japan, Russia	Both (dialectical) e.g., Vietnam, North Korea
Prior cultural alterity (little to preach)	Neither (illustrative) e.g., United States, India	Bad (indulgent) e.g., Pakistan, Myanmar

Created by the author.

ethical order of either socialism or the tributary system. Thus, one cannot provide these friends with material benefits that are consequential to their welfare but can be critical of their perceived ethical misconduct. (2) Illustrative friendship refers to facing an actor of equivalent power who is perceived as having no shared prior ethical order. One cannot provide pivotal benefits or straightforward advice but merely pose as a model to be emulated. (3) Dialectical friendship means facing an actor of relatively minor power who is perceived to share the prior ethical order, both socialist and cultural. One can make material offerings to entice them away from their duties elsewhere and criticize their perceived ethical misconduct simultaneously or in cycles. (4) Indulgent friendship indicates facing an actor of relatively minor power who is perceived as having no shared prior ethical order. One's most convenient friendship method is to indulge in offering material benefits and shielding them from their duties elsewhere.

THE FOUR POLICY TYPES OF FRIENDSHIP

Corrective Friendship

Realism failed to make sense when a vulnerable Beijing accused Moscow of revisionism in 1956. Following the establishment of the PRC in 1949, Beijing relied on a friendship treaty to oblige Moscow to show support.[41] In the aftermath of the Korean War, Beijing struggled for its survival in the face of containment by Washington. However, after Moscow adopted what Beijing perceived as revisionism—the peaceful coexistence of socialism and capitalism—Mao Zedong listed Moscow with Washington as a target of the world revolution. The rhetoric of friendship resumed during Deng Xiaoping's and Mikhail Gorbachev's reigns to signal the end of anti-hegemonism (i.e., the social imperialism of the USSR). China formally signed a friendship treaty with the Russian Federation in 2001, which denoted friendship, partnership, and neighborhood to replace comradeship.[42] Given that the shared ethical order has become obscure,[43] corrective friendship has evolved into a unilaterally illustrative friendship. In 2013, Xi Jinping declared that the two parties best illustrated the "major-power relationship."[44] The friendship, from then on, has been enhanced through various kinds of gift giving. Alliance has explicitly been avoided throughout the 2020s, despite the mounting security pressure from NATO that both parties face.

Despite their geo-cultural differences, Japan and China share a Confucian legacy of over a thousand years. The rhetoric of friendship frequently composes bilateral diplomacy. However, they criticize each other from time to time.[45] Beijing criticized Tokyo for failing to refute the pre–World War II order entirely,[46] whereas Tokyo criticized Beijing for failing to fit into the liberal and equal IR. These mutual corrective roles proceed amid their power parity. Beijing retaliated against Tokyo's spiritual pursuit of national continuity by making cutbacks to material exchanges.[47] This corrective policy makes no neoliberal sense, since their intensive economic and social connections fail to shorten the distance from the wrongdoer. Japan's friendship with China is increasingly illustrative, however, given Japan's adherence to liberal IR, which China does not share.

Illustrative Friendship

The perception that China and the US belong to different ethical orders is illustrated by Beijing's continuing practice of sovereign noninterventionism,[48] instead of Washington's preference for liberal interventionism. The rhetoric of friendship is only available in nonofficial relationships.[49] In the Shanghai Communiqué, the Normalization Communiqué, and the August 17th Communiqué, friendship is not a relevant word. Even so, Beijing's criticism of American interventionism is incomparable to the high degree of emotion observed in the finger-pointing criticism of Moscow or Tokyo. Although there are numerous Chinese migrants in the

United States, many sister cities and schools, and friendship associations between the two countries, no state-level solidarity between China and the US is observable within the international organizations. This type of friendship is insincere and preoccupied with unilaterally illustrating how Washington should practice a "major power relationship."[50]

China's relationship with India likewise proceeded with Beijing's use of illustrative friendship. Their partnership in the nonalignment movement of the 1950s collapsed during the clashes over the colonial borders in 1962. Given their common aversion to the past Western imperialism,[51] a duty to reconcile their dispute exists. While they are endowed with differing national sensibilities registered in their respective encounters with colonialism, the balance of power cannot prevail between them. Emotionally, it centers on which side has won greater international recognition. The two sides perceive the other as on an independent civilizational trajectory, not subject to transformation.[52] Thus, the rhetoric of friendship continues. China's best option is to show how the superior Chinese approaches can improve the welfare of other actors in South Asia. In this regard, China facilitates the establishment of the Asian Infrastructure Investment Bank, even contributing to India's development.

Dialectical Friendship

China can easily entice a weaker party to default on its duties elsewhere, where it has much to offer due to its developmental strength and experience. If the other party shares the same prior order, Beijing is obliged to offer corrective advice. Vietnam and North Korea are perceived as sharing the majority of China's worldview—namely, Confucianism, socialism, an Asian perspective, and anti-imperialism. However, Beijing's support could turn into a corrupt friendship. For example, Beijing wished to entice Hanoi and Pyongyang to soften their rivalry with Washington when Beijing decided to reconcile with Washington. Beijing is ready to correct Hanoi during the latter's intervention in Cambodia and Laos or Pyongyang during its nuclear testing at the expense of regional stability. With their shared prior relations, Hanoi and Pyongyang have, in reverse, extended corrective friendship toward Beijing,[53] to the effect of Beijing sometimes conceding first.

Beijing's alternation between decent and corrupt friendship results from its indetermination regarding the maintenance of certain prior relations. Beijing hopes that its internal reform and rapprochement with Washington will enlighten its friends, but this idea threatens their sovereign equality qua national dignity. Hanoi's and Pyongyang's China policies are likewise dialectical in nature.[54] For Pyongyang, for example, the cycles proceed between taking advantage of Beijing's economic gifts and opposing Washington. Beijing is, at best, an annoying friend to them. From Beijing's point of view, the continuation of a corrective relationship testifies to a decent friendship. Beijing believes that it knows what is best for its two friends, but the weaker friends can be acquiescing or resistant on their own terms, considering that Beijing also needs recognition by its weaker friends.

Indulgent Friendship

Weak actors who do not share China's ethical order can expect only corrupt friendship from Beijing, as Beijing is uninterested in correcting their policy toward any ethical order. Beijing resorts to political and economic aid to ensure that these countries attend to Beijing's needs even if their ethical duties elsewhere may require them to take a different route.[55] Both Islamabad and Naypyidaw enjoy indulgent friendships. Therefore, Islamabad can develop nuclear weapons, hold onto its opposition to India in the territorial dispute over Kashmir, and benefit from Beijing's unreserved investment. Naypyidaw enjoys Beijing's support in shielding itself from UN and US intervention, acquiescence over the ethnic conflict along the Chinese borders, and economic aid and investment.[56] Islamabad and Naypyidaw benefit from China at the expense of their other ethical roles.

Islamabad and Naypyidaw differ emotionally regarding the tracks of their relationships with China. Islamabad and Beijing support each other almost without reservation. The former is ready to defend Beijing's Xinjiang policy in the face of Muslim countries.[57] Beijing's corrupt friendship, evidenced by its heavy investment in those areas, incurs a kind of criticism that is familiar to Myanmar. The international concern is that they will forgo their duties on human rights or terrorism. According to Confucian standards, their alienation from international norms makes Beijing a corrupt friend. In the case of Islamabad, however, the metaphor of fraternity has emerged in the eyes of Beijing. Undoubtedly, Confucius would be anxious about such a transition from emotional friendship to ethical brotherhood.

US PRACTICES OF CONFUCIAN FRIENDSHIP

The theoretical implication is that Confucianism provides a conceptually general rather than a culturally specific framework that is not restricted to the analysis of Chinese internationalism. For realism, national interests determine who is or is not a friend. Conversely, the Confucian friendship frame argues that the decision on the friendly role—friend or not and what type—sequentially establishes the national interest conceptions.

As an obvious case, Washington can resort to a corrective policy toward a friend of equivalent capacity such as Beijing. To criticize Beijing's wrongdoing envisions a rising China as a good friend, whereas an alien identity encourages its containment or defeat. If China does not belong to the friend category at all, as former secretary of state Mike Pompeo declared[58]—"The free nations of the world are starting to understand that China doesn't share those democratic values that we hold dear"—then a whole-of-society approach is essential to cope with the existential threat that Beijing poses.[59] This differs from the alternative judgment that Beijing is at least a friend, albeit sharing few prior relations. This is the perspective of Henry Paulson Jr.,[60] former secretary of the treasury, who illustrated how China can learn to (1) develop rules of engagement in the South China Sea, (2) work constructively with America's allies and partners, (3) open up its economy, (4) be proactive in protecting proprietary foreign know-how and end policies that directly or indirectly compel technology transfer, and (5) work with the US on its top strategic priorities.

The same is true regarding Washington's policy toward Pyongyang, except that Pyongyang is not comparable in terms of capacity. Pyongyang represented a rogue state that needed to be converted before its current leader, Kim Jong-un, became a friend of Donald Trump. Washington has been able to apply a dialectical friendship by using both corrective and gift-giving policies toward Pyongyang. Such friendship emerges in a context that defies the realist expectation of the stronger Washington continuing to impose sanctions on the weaker Pyongyang. Nor can realism explain Pyongyang's refusal to jump on the bandwagon with Washington or Beijing. Nevertheless, the sudden resorting to the friendly role by Kim and Trump reflects the Confucian advice that all are bound to be related. Washington shifted toward a dialectical policy and Pyongyang toward an illustrative policy through a peace pact with Seoul, which obliged the latter to mediate (see chapter 3).

Conclusion

This chapter shows how Confucian friendship may be applied wherever intimacy becomes a factor in policy orientation and a relational norm informs the expectation of being a friend. Friendship is functional to Beijing's renouncement of a wrong prior order, such as imperialism, war, a tributary hierarchy, or social-imperialism, from a distance. If the other party is historically prepared to appreciate one's ethical order in one's judgment, duty-oriented (good) friendship ensures that it does not harm the order. Suppose that one perceives that the other party is ethically unrelated. In that case, one's gift-oriented (corrupt) friendship exercises little restraint in alluring it to meet one's internal need even at the cost of the recipient's duty elsewhere. This pursuit of friendship is not necessarily accompanied by positive emotion. Rather, cultural and historical intimacy contributes to intense friendship. In contrast, unfamiliarity releases friends from ethical apprehension.

Confucius predicted that friendship without ethical concern would indulge in material gift giving that would hinder the fulfillment of the friend's duties everywhere. The normative advice of Confucius on distancing friends continues to have an impact, whereby an ethical order continues to constitute the friendly relationship to the extent that the friendship is ironically full of mutual criticism. In these friendly moments, Beijing may act in defiance of power asymmetry. It is expected that the same will apply to Washington's relational practices.

7

Doomed to Expand

Exception and Exceptionalism
as the Mechanisms of Relating

Introduction

During my first year as a graduate student at the University of Denver, in 1984, a high-tech drilling company invited me to attend a consultation meeting to ask me about the most appropriate way to express condolences to its Chinese partner, whose mother had passed away. I never usually wore a suit; I made an exception and bought a one-dollar orange suit from a local thrift store, hoping that this would generate some degree of professional respect. Usually, I would refuse to answer such questions, but I thought that I was the only hope if the company were to avoid misbehaving. This was a completely unconventional engagement for the company. On the other hand, the company confidently paid me seventy-five dollars, according to the market rate. An international student entered a professional role in a foreign market. A liberal-society company was able to fulfill a social role in a collectivist culture. Both were exceptions from our respective perspectives.

An exception—*the negative of normalcy, consensus, or routine*—is a matter of degree and a widespread daily phenomenon. To strategize for adaptation to unfamiliar relational systems, people improvise exceptions for each other.[1] On the other hand, exceptionalism—*a claim to the prerogative of oneself being an exception* and often a justification to refuse adaptation to each other—is linked to a distinctive self-identity vis-à-vis a prior system in terms of collective identity, rules, and norms.[2] Making exceptions indulges deviant others, while claiming exceptionalism indulges oneself. Both the making of exceptions and claiming of exceptionalism contradict multilateral relations.[3] However, this chapter argues that exceptionalism is likewise a relational practice, a phase of a cycle, and a prelude to (un)learning, as another phase in the cycle that will invoke the improvisation of mutual exceptions, sooner or later. During the (un)learning phase, nations engage in the expansion and coexistence of divergent multilateral relations.

The following discussion offers a critique of the literature on exceptionalism, in which the idea about exceptionalism is preoccupied with how actors claim their own exceptions from multilateral processes, often allegedly as a way to defend multilateralism. This literature omits a parallel practice, in a Confucian condition, that seeks to maintain multilateral processes by acknowledging the need for others to each be qualified for certain exceptions. Both kinds of multilateralism rely on the politics of exception—asserting self-exception (i.e., we are not together) versus conceding alter-exception (i.e., we are together)—to engage strangers or betrayers. I detect two threads of exceptionalism—self- and alter-exceptionalism. Confucianism embraces the latter category, which aims to exempt an alter, rather than the self, from role obligations. Such a method of categorization attests to the need to bring the notion of relationality back into the analysis. Both threads are likewise relational, with self-exceptionalism imagining the claimants to be outside their relational circle but alter-exceptionalism imagining them to be inside it.

Encounters with strangers can nevertheless prepare nations to (un)learn in order for divergent multilateral relations to simultaneously improvise expansion and coexistence. In this regard, the study of Confucian relational culture, which makes familiar the improvisation of exception but shuns exceptionalism, contributes to an inclusive understanding of exceptionalism by situating it in pluriversal relationalities. However, the alleged "Chinese exceptionalism" in the literature that is informed by Chinese internal and national sources, especially Confucianism, while analytically plausible, is insufficiently IR theory, to the extent that Confucian exceptionalism is not a recognized style of multilateralism in the liberal tradition. Only when acting against liberal and realist internationalism does the literature's version of exceptionalism become appreciable.[4] In contrast, this chapter invokes Confucian multilateralism to interrogate how and why exceptionalism is intrinsically a relational and emotional practice rather than the individualistic and rational practice that is embedded in liberalism and realism.

I define multilateralism as *several nations practicing mutually agreeable patterns of togetherness.* Accordingly, I will show that Confucianism embraces an insider's exceptionalism while liberalism embraces that of an outsider. Despite their differences, both inevitably seek to expand until ways to coexist with strangers belonging to different relations reconstitute the identities of all sides. Exceptionalism, as a cause of anxiety for multilateral members about relational fragmentation,[5] is rarely perpetual, because exceptionalism would mean nothing without ultimately belonging to its multilateral circle. The vicissitude of exceptionalism contrarily affirms its prior relation, composed of liberalism and realism. In an evolving pluriverse, the revival of Confucianism gives rise to anxiety about a stranger's exceptionalism, thereby making role emotion an intrinsic dimension of exceptionalism.

Since analysts fail to recognize that exceptionalism involves a relational process, they frequently mistake it for an identity claim.[6] According to this view, China is inevitably a practitioner of exceptionalism in order to have an identity as a normal state. The recognition of alter-exceptionalism enables comparative analysts to avoid projecting the familiar liberal understanding of exceptionalism onto the Confucian practice of exceptionalism. The following discussion introduces how Confucianism understands and justifies exceptionalism and compares it with liberalism. The chapter traces how Confucianism diverges from liberalism with regard to what accounts for multilateralism—inclusiveness versus rule-based governance and benevolent exceptions versus universal enforcement of rights—and the resulting exceptionalist orientations.

Exceptionalism as a Relational Claim

Exceptionalism can mean a variety of things in international relations. One common thread in the literature is the emphasis on internal and national difference, which justifies certain exemptionalist prerogatives.[7] Exemptionalism presumes certain prior engagements with an entire system or assemblage of actors,[8] to which the claim to the exception is addressed. In other words, exemptionalism is made plausible by a prior relational

configuration. Exceptionalism ties its claimant to the fate of prior relations. Without the relational analysis, a claim to exceptionalism would
appear to be no more than a binary discourse, invoked to romanticize a
political project of an allegedly autonomous actor.[9] Against this relational
background, an exceptionalist is only ostensibly self-centered, either
by asserting their freedom to exit the relation or assuming a consensus
within the relational circle on their exclusionary status.

To ensure a focused discussion, further consider *exceptionalism*
as *unilaterally claiming a distinction to justify the claimant's prerogative to
renovate the relational conditions*. It is therefore the prerogative to adopt
extraordinary means with the purpose of revising, defending, or restoring
the consensual norms and rules that have become endangered due to
corruption, invasion, or defection. For example, a version of American
exceptionalism might be the duty to maintain liberal institutions through
an interventional, long-armed jurisdiction.[10] A version of Confucian
exceptionalism might be to maintain the imperial family's benevolent
leadership of the encountered world.[11] As a long-armed jurisdiction contradicts the consensual principle of sovereignty, America simultaneously
claims an outsider's position. On the other hand, providing benevolent
leadership reifies a built-in relational role for the emperor's exceptional
role. For an example of the outsider's theme, consider principled realism.[12] It enforces liberal rules of international relations through measured
sanctions incompatible with these rules. In contrast, consider moral
realism.[13] It relies on benevolent leadership through granting exemptions
and privileges to maintain an existing role relation, hence exceptionalism
in an insider's capacity.

In addition, according to this definition, *distinction* usually indicates
*a certain quality of being divine or selected, informed by an exclusionary
consciousness* (of the inevitability to assume or concede a duty). Examples include an imagined mandate of God; a mission of civilizational
awakening; a one-of-a-kind, geo-cultural identity; an innate capacity for
leadership; an unparalleled history; or an alert to racial extinction.[14] Also,
according to this definition, *relational conditions* refer to the qualities of
consensual rules and norms and are (1) constitutive of the identities of
its members, (2) conducive to their solidarity, (3) alert to the impacts
of nonmembers, and yet simultaneously (4) adjustable and sustainable.
As such, exceptionalism advances two implications—an exceptionalist
claim casts all relational *alters* to the collective identity, to which the
exceptionalist similarly belongs, and an exceptionalist claim alludes to

the existence and paralleling of different relationalities that recall either the alienness of strangers or the distinctiveness of the exceptionalist themselves.

The resulting platforms of the exclusionary prerogative are aimed either at correcting, enhancing, or uniting strangers and failing members to renovate the relevant relations, if this appears possible, or decoupling from them temporarily, in a contrary hope for opportunities to renovate the relations, if this appears unachievable at present.[15] Logically, when two relational strangers meet (see the bottom circle of figure 7.1, between C

Figure 7.1. The relational logic of exceptionalism. Created by the author.

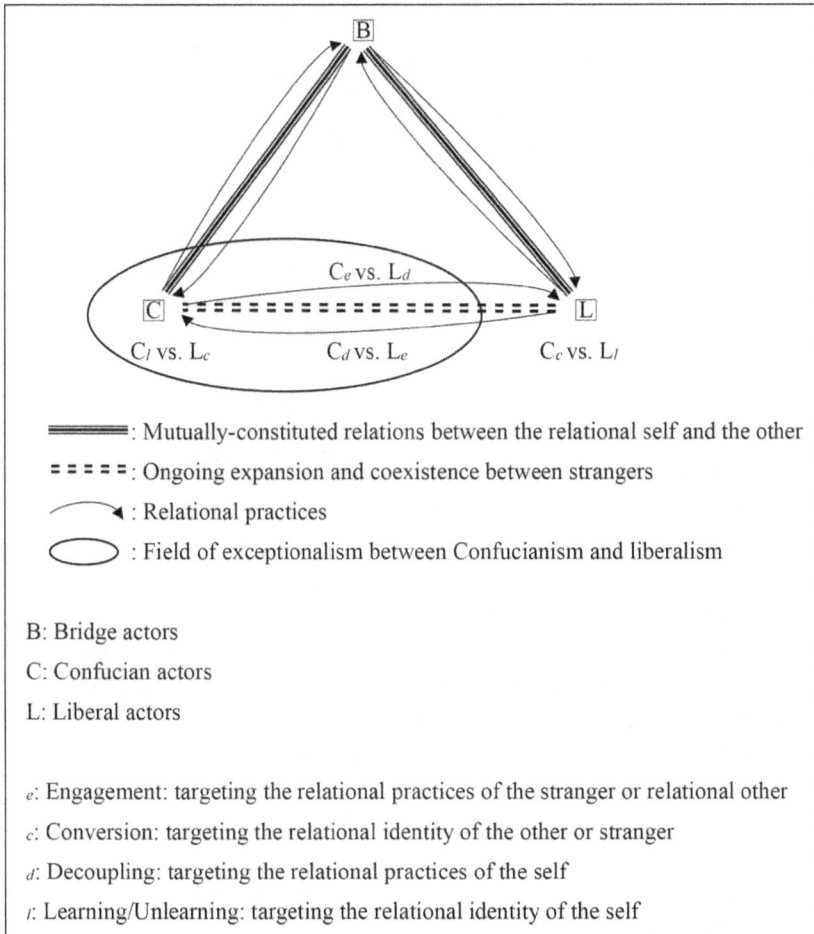

: Mutually-constituted relations between the relational self and the other

: Ongoing expansion and coexistence between strangers

: Relational practices

: Field of exceptionalism between Confucianism and liberalism

B: Bridge actors

C: Confucian actors

L: Liberal actors

e: Engagement: targeting the relational practices of the stranger or relational other

c: Conversion: targeting the relational identity of the other or stranger

d: Decoupling: targeting the relational practices of the self

l: Learning/Unlearning: targeting the relational identity of the self

and L), they can adapt by targeting either "the stranger" or "the self" and, when enforcing the expected changes, changing either "the existential identity" or "the practices." Four possibilities emerge here:

1. Engage the stranger's relational practices through exemplification, role making and taking, a long-armed jurisdiction, punitive sanctions, and other measures that echo the superiority consciousness of the self's exceptionalism

2. Convert the stranger's relational identity through intervention, execution, revolution, conquest, subversion, or brainwashing, and possibly be forced to make an exception to the self's relational norms by accepting arbitrary violence

3. Decouple the self's relational practices from the stranger or defector through quarantine, isolation, containment, decoupling, disengagement, and the like

4. Learn and revise the self's relational identity away from exceptionalism through (un)learning, moving beyond missionary or superiority consciousness and achieving expansion toward and coexistence with the stranger

Relational Expansion as a Necessity

The literature on comparative exceptionalism typically attends to the internal and national sources of allegedly exceptionalist nations and compares their claimed natural differences.[16] Even so, exceptionalism affirms multilateralism since a legitimate claim of exemption must be an exception rather than a constant. For example, while Washington has yet to approve the Law of the Sea, it continues to enforce it upon the other national actors. In this particular case, exceptionalism not only affirms its multilateral identity but also insinuates the presence of a stranger or a defector from the Law of the Sea who should be corrected. These strangers either embrace their own versions of exceptionalism/exemptionalism or belong to a different multilateral order. To that extent, exceptionalism that aims to enforce its multilateral order reflects an impulse to expand at the cost of the other multilateral order, which is to be corrected.

This book argues that the converting kind of exceptionalism is doomed to be self-defeating. On the one hand, if one thread of multilateralism could manage without another, for an IR agenda, ultimately, a balance-of-power analysis would suffice—relations would merely tag onto the power matrix between autonomous selves, and autonomous selves would not trust any multilateralism. However, engagement is far more typical than rivalry in international relations, even for the advocates of exceptionalism. Engagement becomes particularly apparent for migrant or border populations who are unnoticeable in IR theorizing. On the other hand, the expansion that aims to substitute one multilateral order for another would defy the imagined naturalness of all relational identities,[17] such as anarchy, Heaven, human rights, and so on, as if the order were only able to expand through conquest and suppression.

A relational analysis would attend to how exceptionalist practices instead seek to strategize the acceptance of norms in some minimal or nominal way by strangers belonging to differing multilateral relationalities. To that extent, what can inspire "nationalized" exceptionalism to revise the existing parameters and accommodate the encountered strangers is to naturalize coexistence, or the comparative "extra-local,"[18] rather than forcefully substituting other factors for these.

Accordingly, all relational systems expand, regardless of their power level, and exceptionalism is an ironic practice that foregrounds the simultaneous processes of expansion and coexistence. Consider, as shown repeatedly in previous chapters, a relational system in which the *members collectively reify certain consensual points of resemblance to constitute their acquaintance and solidarity.*[19] With consensual resemblance embedded in their shared ecology, genes, insecurity (imaginative as well as experiential), and living conventions, among other aspects—being immediate and bestowed at birth—the relation is foundational to humanity, although the points of resemblance emphasized vary across the groups to enmesh each one in certain characteristic identities. As being related pertains to ontological security, the danger of losing relations is most threatening. On the one hand, relations refused or guarded against by strangers will appear to lack legitimacy and ultimately allude to dispensability. On the other hand, relations that are professedly fungible will appear definitively threatening to strangers. This necessarily makes expansion and coexistence the twin missions if a relational system is to survive.[20]

First, a relation cannot be limited within its own circles, lest this harm its romanticized naturalness—as in, for example, the rights of nature, heavenly kinship, God's blessing, or the continental divide—and the associated vested relationality. An exceptionalist consciousness can evoke a missionary purpose at times.[21] For those (included in B in figure 7.1) lacking an imagined coherent relation, as in the case of bilingual children, migrants, or colonies, their purpose may be merely to reconcile the differences with patience, which makes them a peculiar sort of civilizational bridge or "trialectical" or "non-aligned" platform.[22] This can be achieved in many creative ways, as subaltern, postcolonial, and feminist studies have repeatedly demonstrated.[23] On the other hand, exceptionalism can embrace a hierarchical sensibility that turns the self into a "civilizer state."[24] Unilateral expansion to civilize or colonize strangers into a particular relation easily appears egocentric in the eyes of the latter and backfires, despite at times being well intended or spontaneous.[25]

Even a civilizer state cannot help but (un)learn. (Un)learning moves theorization beyond a specific, presumably liberal, type of international relations.[26] (Un)learning occurs when exceptionalist actors relinquish civilizing, intervention, or isolation and begin to reflect critically on the very existence of their relational selves. No one is bounded, in their own terms, by their present relationality nor subjugated by the encountered relation. Eventually, all would have to adopt, albeit inconsistently, a pluriversal practice that is not so similar to each other and yet simultaneously not so estranging,[27] either. The simultaneity attests to a kind of "fuzziness."[28] All proceed in a cycle between various degrees of (un) learning and exceptionalism.

Liberal and Confucian exceptionalisms differ in terms of the cosmological assumptions upon which the two multilateral cultures evolved. In a nutshell, liberal multilateralism originated in everyone's equal entitlement to the same rights of nature, so contriving universal rules for those like ones offers a plausible, appropriate style of governance.[29] Encountering strangers calls for the use of an extrarelational intervention to convert them, as strangers know of no humanity that is informed by such rights.[30] American exceptionalism answers the call for such an interventionist leadership role. Contrary to America's transcendent status outside, everyone is already an insider under Confucianism, regardless of their differences. Universal rules are implausible unless all share the same identity. Confucian relationality conceals differences through mutual benevolence, exemplified by the metaphorical father. Those who fail to show benevolence threaten everyone else's relationality and reduce all to strangers. Accordingly, what constitutes Confucian power is relational and supposedly spontaneous—through everyone else voluntarily joining forces with the metaphorical father.[31] Chinese exceptionalism lies in the self-image of China as the most benevolent site in the world. Transcendence is self-sacrifice, or selflessness, under Confucianism rather than self-fulfillment under liberalism. Exceptionalism that galvanizes the distinctive self is anathema to Confucians.

The Absence of Exceptionalism in Confucian Multilateralism

The literature on American exceptionalism, which is intrinsically religious in nature, studies why and how American liberalism has its roots in the internal conditions in the United States,[32] accounting for an original state that sets the US as the destiny of human history.[33] The American elite generally understands, even if it disagrees with, the exceptionalist claim and the mission it inspires.[34] Despite the rule-based governmentality informed by liberalism, exceptionalist America is unrestricted by the liberal measures to either enforce the rules or ensure its superiority.[35] Exceptionalist America and those incapable others are like nations, so America's triumph is ultimately also their own. Its superpower, which ensures no peer competitor,[36] solidifies this exceptional status in enforcing rule-based governance. In short, this transcendent quality invokes, metaphorically, God's role.[37]

Contemporary Confucian exceptionalism has also been associated with the People's Republic of China (PRC) as a nation-state concept.[38] The most frequently stressed points include civilizational longevity, national humiliation, and socialism with Chinese characteristics, alongside the more recent, faddish China model. Combined, they have transformed China into an exceptionalist nation in terms of its history and mission in the world.[39] Except for the Cultural Revolution, however, which represents a lacuna in the literature on exceptionalism and a contradiction of other exceptionalist claims, the others have seemed insignificant anyway, if not entirely irrelevant, regarding the PRC's diplomatic platforms. In rhetoric, the exceptionalism of this internal sort consistently yields to the claim of normalcy regarding the PRC's role in the world.

Normal statehood, which is best indicated by the world's, especially former colonizer states', acceptance of China's equality and integrity, connotes a willingness to comply with the consensual rules of the time and, therefore, a multilateral commitment.[40] Ironically, if the core of the PRC's multilateral commitment has been its acceptance by the rest of the world as a normal country, its leaders must attend to many other countries' unique, non-Western conditions that make them exceptions to the Western rules or norms, such as Pyongyang or Islamabad, accused of nuclearization; Naypyidaw or Juba, accused of ethnic cleansing; and Ankara, Bucharest, or Caracas, accused of illiberalism. This irony leads to an ostensibly self-contradictory style of multilateralism that simultaneously observes the consensual rules to attain points of resemblance with their Western subscribers and grants exceptions from some of these rules to unwilling, unready countries.[41]

To reconcile these self-contradictory commitments, a materialist emphasis on tangible contributions is considered essential to achieve acceptance and intimacy in each dyad.[42] A materialistic gift can neutralize the rhetoric of value, meet the needs of different others separately, and adapt to the changing context on each occasion.[43] Note that materialism coincides with the common propensity of Marxism and Confucianism to care about the living conditions of the lower classes.[44] The Confucian justification for an exception from peace and harmony in ancient times rests unfailingly on materialistic concepts, such as famine and unequal distribution.[45] The exceptional measures under Confucianism aim mainly to foreground the spontaneous support of the populace to ensure the removal of oppressors rather than establish or enforce consensual rules.

As a result, the PRC's multilateralism is hesitant to discover how we are all minimally related as a result of being like-humans but is oriented to providing benevolence to influence how we accept an alter, despite our apparent differences. These acceptance or belonging sensibilities amount to China's (1) equal membership in international organizations; (2) advocacy for peace, harmony, and development;[46] and (3) role-play in context,[47] all of which concern mutual acceptance, reified through the paying of fees, qualifying sanctions against violators, the boycotting of US unilateralism, the mediating of local conflicts, abstention rather than taking sides, connecting the so-called failing states, and arranging zero-interest loans, for a few examples. The PRC's international multi-lateralism reverberates with the spirit of two PRC domestic institutions.[48] One concerns political consultation and its mobilization institutions, through which as broad a spectrum of sectors and strata as possible is invited to be articulate on their own behalf.[49] In the case of multilateralism, this particular spirit denotes inclusivity. The other spirit is decentralized implementation,[50] whereby the local actors determine how to execute a policy orientation. Such multilateralism embraces the ideal of the absence of war, intervention, and poverty.

Without referring to any of those abovementioned internal sources of exceptionalism, Xi Jinping believes that nations can become united through adversity in a shared development-oriented humanity.[51] Foreign Minister Wang Yi elaborates on "genuine multilateralism" accordingly, that "should adhere to respect for national sovereignty as well as equality of all countries, big or small; adhere to the diversity of the world, and respect for legitimate development rights of all countries and development paths of their own choice."[52]

Exception and Exemptionalism under Confucianism

These concerns regarding inclusiveness, decentralization, peace, harmony, development, and role-play were compliant with and registered in the Confucian world order long before the nation-state emerged.[53] The Confucian theme of world order refers specifically to the "mandate of heaven" (MoH). However, Confucius advised that a public career should be rejected when the polity is too morally corrupt to be governable.[54] Such self-quarantine from public affairs entails abandoning benevolence toward others and contradicts the MoH. More significant is Confucius's judgment that the oppressor's "tyranny is fiercer than tigers" and, for Xunzi, that the oppressor should be overthrown.[55] Mencius further suggested that slaying is the proper way to cope with a dictator.[56] To that extent, the MoH is a license to choose between Confucius's isolation and Mencius's slaying when it appears that the mandate is no longer being followed.[57]

Killing, as well as conquest, were culpable actions under Confucianism. Confucius was reluctant to welcome even justified killing. Justified killing might sound more acceptable but hardly seemed better practice to him.[58] For Confucius, the best situation would be to end corrupt governance and revive good governance through exemplification, which is, in every sense, preferable to slaying.[59] Even so, he refused to advise his students to avoid princes who had killed unethically as long as their subsequent reign displayed benevolence toward their people.[60] According to the historical record, Confucius once executed an eloquent opponent—Mao—while serving Duke Lu. This engendered continuous debate about Confucius's prudence for millennia to come. Whichever side is taken, the justification for killing points to the Confucian alienation from such exceptionalism. After all, killing would institutionalize negativity to normalcy, which, in Mencius's words, indicates the teaching that "he who takes no pleasure in killing men can be accepted anywhere."[61] For Confucianism, these incidents of execution mentioned above by no means indicate exceptionalism, although they are certainly examples of exception when the occasion demands.

It is useful to infer a conceptual distinction between exceptionalism and exception to expound further on the unspoken exceptionalism of Confucianism. The notion of exception refers to a practice that would only be followed in unusual circumstances. Therefore, it is followed not to attain the actor's own self-role but to demonstrate *benevolence toward someone else*. In comparison, exceptionalism is pursued to *attain the actor's own self-role*. In this regard, Confucianism is not disposed toward embracing exceptionalism.[62] On the other hand, Confucianism is ready to recommend exceptions to relate to a stranger or reproduce and restore role propriety.[63] To the extent that making exceptions for an alter is inconvenient, it is an act of self-sacrifice and benevolence. In short, instead of appreciating the agency of the self to fulfill the like identity of the group members, Confucianism pits the self against the group. In actuality, Confucian exceptionalism preaches self-disciplining for anyone disposed to assume the MoH, as indicated by the spontaneous joining of forces with others. By making exceptions for all separately, the selected sacrifice, each according to their need, maintains peace and harmony by promoting continuous relational renovation.[64]

In the same vein, civilizing, another platform of modern exceptionalism, is of little interest to Confucianism. Confucius was conscious of the difference between the civilized ways of his life and that of an alien, which included "untied hair" and "left-tied clothes,"[65] but unenthusiastic about actively converting the latter. This was left to the alien to decide. Confucius was also confident that the remote, alien land would accept him as long as he acted with sincerity and in good faith.[66] Civilizing was not a significant issue, only that he was sufficiently virtuous himself to be worthy of respect. Therefore, in line with the Confucian sensibilities about peace and harmony, civilizing referred mainly to performing rituals to honor familial piety and its application to rulers.[67] Such a focus on formality likewise alludes to the propriety of anyone in an official capacity resisting showing an interest in or curiosity toward an alter's way of life.

A derived intellectual proclivity under Confucianism is the control of curiosity concerning how strangers behave. After all, the key to maintaining peace and harmony is to educate people to care about the acceptance of others by acting benevolently toward them. Knowledge vis-à-vis a stranger is considered proper only if it can provide a clue regarding what role and benevolence to improvise for the stranger.[68] This epistemological disinterest, in general, contrasts sharply with the Western intellectual traditions, in which curiosity is a vehicle for reproducing the consensual likeness (of God) and designing comparative studies effectively to convert aliens. The contrast also explains the lack of interventionist ethics in Confucianism. Identity sensibilities, which reveal the differences between people, would destabilize the Confucian ethic order embedded in the metaphorical fatherhood.[69] For liberal multilateralism, however, it is essential to make an informed judgment about how far a stranger is disposed toward rule-based governance, qualified for solidarity, and excused from intervention.

As repeatedly mentioned in the previous chapters, heavenly reason imbues everyone—everyone is bound to be related.[70] Being unrelated causes anxiety.[71] The MoH envisages the inevitability of mutual role making. The heavenly way produces many thousands of varieties of living things (wanwu) that cannot share any point of resemblance on a grand scale.[72] Confucius was disposed to employ the kinship metaphor to generate rituals and roles for these things.[73] To make parental roles credible, parents' acts of material or reproductive benevolence toward children are essential, pointing to the romanticized naturalness of hierarchical and yet selfless relationships. With everyone's security needs presumably being met, all will accept these ritualized kin roles. Rituals not only remind individuals of their roles periodically but also oblige the display of benevolence through these roles.[74]

The controversy consists of two levels. First, it lies in who can claim possession of the MoH and, second, the irony of engaging in slaying to prevent oppression. Confucianism generally posits that, ultimately, only those who display the most benevolence can enjoy the support of the people to win the MoH[75] (see chapter 1's discussion on the invisible hand) and hence are justified by the result. Accordingly, Confucian power involves moral power that a ruler does not automatically possess.[76] Its recipients are the ultimate owners of the moral power, through which they determine whom to follow.[77] Ultimately, all bad autocrats fall. In short, restricted by a limited capacity for war, the ruler of the MoH must have already anticipated the support needed to eliminate the oppressor. This cosmology is still embraced by the Chinese Communist Party (CCP) today.[78] Being better related testifies to possessing the MoH and exceptionalist quality qua self-sacrifice as benevolence to rule.

In comparison, liberal exceptionalism concerns self-defense on the part of an autonomous state. Possessing sufficient power to be an exceptionalist nation—in other words, a hegemonic nation—is considered the ultimate guarantee of universal, rule-based governance. While the US follows consensual rules, it simultaneously transcends these rules in its capacity as the guardian of the rules.[79] Liberal governmentality thus alienates Confucian multilateralism, which treats every other actor differently; this obliges all of them, in return, to accept the fact that China is different from them; this recognition but camouflage of difference keeps the rules to a minimum, perhaps reduced solely to the principle of no killing, and also rejects intervention. Therefore, Confucian multilateralism can be regarded as revisionism from the perspective of rule-based governance. Rather, its ideal stage is akin to laissez-faire.

Chinese leaders can experiment with different styles of coexistence between the Confucian and liberal relationalities.[80] In comparison, learning could pose a challenge for American exceptionalism unless its adherents first unlearn the concomitant belief that rule-based governance embedded in rights sensibilities fits all.[81] Once the CCP can perform well in the market and enhance its capacity for providing benevolence to others while simultaneously neutralizing the consensual norms between liberal countries, the perception of an existential threat is doomed to emerge periodically,[82] despite the fact that the CCP may celebrate the inclusion of the market under a socialist system.

Previous chapters continually point to a peculiar kind of benevolence that arises to suit the occasion—namely, learning and performing a liberal norm that seems of the utmost importance to the liberal stranger for the occasion.[83] This can occur at the societal level, too, through mingling, which allows populaces to adapt according to the context without being compelled to adhere consistently to one particular norm. Through this varied mixture, liberals and liberalism are no longer strangers to Confucian societies.[84] A field of interaction emerges between the Confucian and liberal relationalities (see figure 7.1). The field hosts the dialectics of decoupling and engagement of both liberal and Confucian states. In addition, it involves the interventionist agenda of the liberal state and the (un)learning of the Confucian state to enhance inclusiveness. Amid the tendency of both to expand, they are destined to undergo fuzzy cycles of coexistence, confrontation, and alienation.[85]

Conclusion

Multilateralism concerns how to coordinate coexistence or togetherness. It inevitably expands through every encounter to prevent strangers from causing disorder. Confucian multilateralism dispenses with crafting any consensual rules and instead arranges exceptional treatments to meet, symbolically or substantively, the other party's material needs. In short, Confucianism approves a mutual kind of exceptionalism that is reciprocal and bilateral, albeit in multiplicity. In addition, Confucian exceptionalism reveals, in contrast, how an exceptionalist claim to exempt the US from liberal rules-based multilateralism is ultimately relational and thus being liberal is ultimately relational. To that extent, US exceptionalism connects the stranger and liberal multilateralism. It is through this lens that the study of Chinese exceptionalism contributes to our understanding of American exceptionalism.

The literature heeds an equivalence, sometimes disapprovingly, between difference, specialty, and uniqueness on the one hand and exceptionalism on the other, as if the latter mainly connotes the local agency, nuance sensibilities, and genealogy of a site. Such equivalence alludes to exceptionalism as an identity rather than a relation. While this clarifies why exceptionalism is claimed in the eyes of exceptionalist leaders, it reproduces the self/other binary to the neglect of the encompassing relations. A relational analysis points to exceptionalism that is always cyclical, adaptive through learning and unlearning, contingent upon its prior multilateral engagement, and intended toward becoming or remaining related.

In Chinese internationalism and practical living, exceptions to the rules and norms abound but hardly amount to the familiar kind of American exceptionalism.[86] This is linked to the Confucian style of multilateralism, informed by the cosmological MoH, which considers everything heaven-bred and mutually constituted. To survive, mutual acceptance is imperative, so differences should be de-securitized. Accordingly, universal rules, which assume a substantive collective identity and suspect absolute differences between strangers, should be avoided, too. Chinese exceptionalism answers the call of the MoH to assume the duty of displaying benevolence to each according to their need if they are to attain belonging. However, all can display benevolence and make reciprocal exceptions for strangers to establish mutual acceptance. In the same vein, all, including the head of state and an overseas student, are ready to assume the name and role of China. Confucian exceptionalism is for anyone who demonstrates a remarkable capacity to display the broadest, greatest benevolence and so attract the spontaneous joining of forces.

Having no alternative to remaining inside, China engages in exceptions rather than exceptionalism, including slaying the oppressor. Otherwise, food and sacrifices—namely, food for Gods, which tended to be the most common forms of benevolence in ancient times—were designed to express goodwill and symbolize reciprocal role taking. Confucianism cherishes learning to perform rituals, such as a Denver drilling company learning the death ritual in China; making exceptions to practice more inclusiveness; and exemplifying benevolence. To this extent, Confucian exceptionalism, unuttered, never assumes transcendence or even difference. The contemporary predicament of Confucian exceptionalism in terms of relating to strangers is twofold: being a rule breaker or the protector of a rule breaker regarding a prior relation, defined by substantive consensual rules, such as liberal governmentality,[87] and being ignorant of how alters differ in their terms, or, from their perspective, how Confucianism differs in Confucianism's terms.[88]

PART THREE

Identity

(De)securitizing Chineseness

Part Three presents the engagement of *tianxia* with the neoliberal order, which boils down to the question of how neoliberalism relates to the intensively disputed notion of Chineseness. This is an ontological puzzle in which defining China is simultaneously self-defining for liberals. Beneath the policy agenda of the US-China rivalry lies the relationship between Chineseness and liberalism, be it coexistence, conversion, cycle, or hegemonic war. The first two chapters discuss how ambivalent liberalism characterizes the approaches to China's socialist market reform and unification with Taiwan. In the next chapter, China's internationalism explores an intersection with the neoliberal order. Attesting to pluriversal internationalism, the last chapter fantasizes a step outside the ontology of sovereignty and that of security community.

8

Western Belonging Aborted

The Ideological Background of the US-China Rivalry

A Long Route of Constructing Chinese Revisionism

The Cultural Revolution was, in every sense, an anti-relational gesture internationally and internally.[1] Nevertheless, there was not even a discussion of the Chinese revisionist threat during the 1960s and '70s, although the rhetoric of world revolution, which was revisionist in nature, to say the least, was unambiguous. China was not regarded as an ally or friend of the United States by any standard during the Cold War. However, China's military and economic capacity was insufficient to substantiate such a challenge. Designing a revisionist role for China would have been strategically redundant, if not irrelevant.

Less than a decade later, the CR (Cultural Revolution) had ended. Having been the main targets of the CR, both the Chinese Communist Party (CCP) leadership and China's cultural heritage had been rehabilitated. Washington was ready to embrace a China that was reverting to normalcy. Having anticipated an increasingly participatory China in the liberal world economy, the liberal narratives accommodated China in a pupil role, coined first by Beijing in its alleged determination to "make up the missed capitalist lesson."

Ironically, the demoralized CCP and Chinese cultural traditions—the two previous rivals—have evolved into a realignment in the twenty-first century in terms of their common aversion toward liberalism and, hence, defiance of the pupil role. This same China has begun to grow in strength, resulting in it becoming a revisionist power in world politics forty years later, in the eyes of the American leaders. Post-CR normalcy, represented by the same authoritarian party and the same Chinese traditional culture, primarily Confucianism, now indicates revisionism in the new era, despite having been the target of the consciously revisionist CR. The bestseller *The Hundred-Year Marathon*, by Michael Pillsbury,[2] even reads continuity into the pre-CR, CR, and post-CR stages, as if revisionism has been a consistent theme in China's approach to the world.

In brief, the Cultural Revolution composes the prior relation that connects seemingly separate developments inside and outside the People's Republic of China (PRC). These developments ultimately lead to the image of Chinese revisionism. The ending of the CR allowed friendly relations to develop between the PRC and the US, informed by the ideological opening up to liberalism. The subsequent emergence of the alert to the Western (mainly neoliberal) thought invasion prepared the realignment of the socialist CCP with neo-Confucianism. The change of role expectations toward China would have been much milder without the sharp contrast between the pupil role and friendly role in the prior romanticization of the bilateral relationship. This chapter argues that the ideological realignment in China is linked to the US's liberal identity and ontological security. Contemporary Chinese politics fails the role expectation of becoming liberal, thereby inflaming the perception of a revisionist threat that far exceeds the level of a shift in the balance of power. The policy discourses are oriented toward the China threat and revisionism thereafter.

The US Perception of Chinese Revisionist Power

Revisionist power is the designation for those nations that challenge the status quo. In short, they are *the actors who seek to change the status quo—the rule, balance of power, and challenger's status, place, or role*. The contrast between revisionist and status quo powers is a classic concept of realism.[3] It has been transformed by John Mearsheimer's offensive realism through the assertion that "all states are revisionists."[4] His illustrative references are consistently former colonizer states, though.

Nevertheless, the term "revolutionary diplomacy" completely disappeared from the Chinese media after 1978.[5] Engaging China was the dominant theme in Washington's China policy for three decades. A role identity of China as a stakeholder qua status quo power and "responsible major power," respectively, emerged in the American and Chinese narratives,[6] despite several interruptions, such as the June 4th crackdown on the pro-democracy movement (1989), the Taiwan Strait Missile Crisis (1996), the US shelling of the Chinese embassy in Belgrade (1999), and the South China Sea plane-crash incident (2001). It was claimed by many China watchers that, in 2008, the world simultaneously experienced a global financial crisis and the emergence of an assertive, arrogant China, which eventually changed the course of US-China relations.[7] Was the pupil no longer a pupil?

This question was particularly relevant to the subsequent rise of a sense of loss among China watchers, especially in light of liberals' judgment of China as "increasingly working within, rather than outside of, the Western order."[8] In other words, despite the abovementioned incidents, among liberals, a rather optimistic view exists on China coming to terms with the "Western order." According to John Ikenberry's representative analysis, "the most farsighted Chinese leaders understand that globalization has changed the game and that China accordingly needs strong, prosperous partners around the world," and "as Beijing's growing commitment to economic liberalization has increased the foreign investment and trade China has enjoyed, so has Beijing increasingly embraced global trade rules. It is possible that as China comes to champion the WTO, the support of the more mature Western economies for the WTO will wane. But it is more likely that both the rising and the declining countries will find value in the quasi-legal mechanisms that allow conflicts to be settled or at least diffused."[9]

While some early warnings against false expectations could not invoke policy change,[10] the sense of loss finally burst out at the start of the Donald Trump administration in 2016, security experts and China experts debated among themselves about whether or not the rise of China posed an existential threat to the US.[11] While they disagreed with each other about the best way to cope with China's rise, the consensus of these experts was nonetheless that Beijing has been violating the rules of global governance. According to the national security report of 2017, "China and Russia want to shape a world antithetical to U.S. values and interests. China seeks to displace the United States in the Indo-Pacific region, expand the reaches of its state-driven economic model, and reorder the region in its favor."[12] In 2018, the national defense report confirmed this by summarizing that "China and Russia want to shape a world consistent with their authoritarian model."[13] According to the report released in February 2019 by the Asia Society Center on US-China Relations, "the current leadership has sought to use China's new wealth and power in ways that are inimical to the very global order that fostered China's rise." One of the three areas that the report identifies where the rise of China is most harmful is "China's hardening authoritarianism."[14] Even a dissenting assessment likewise includes references to authoritarian politics that are in violation of civil liberty and protectionist encroachment on free, fair trade.[15]

During the first decade of the twenty-first century, prominent China experts still agreed that China was coming to terms with the international order. China's learning capacity within the international organizations was noticeable to the extent that it acquired an image of being a "social state," ready to conform to the rules of international relations.[16] If the designation of revisionism requires an intention to change the rules, in addition to the rise of national power,[17] China's readiness to adopt the role of a responsible power would not guide its rising power into revisionism. However, by 2010, only a small number of China experts disputed the alleged Chinese revisionism.[18]

The disagreement between experts is more technical than fundamental because the two major points of difference are (1) whether or not China adopts full or selective revisionism[19] and (2) whether or not China is already enforcing, or will potentially enforce, revisionism.[20] The two contending sides resemble each other in considering liberalism to be increasingly unlikely to make the list of possibilities for China's future. During the first decade of the twenty-first century, indeed, liberalism as a threat substituted for liberalism as a technique of reform and prompted the CCP to give serious consideration to how to cope with it.[21] It was also during this decade that the question of how China rose to the status of a major power in world politics became a deliberately crafted agenda in both the Sinosphere and Anglosphere.[22]

The Return of Chinese Liberal Critics and Dissidents

There was no such alarm among China experts at the beginning of the reform. This was when a restored order with the CCP leadership seemed to fit the liberal international economy, if not ideological values. In addition, the CCP has been consistently agreeable to the revival of

Confucianism since the end of the Cultural Revolution. Indicating a romanticized post-CR China, research on the contribution of Confucianism to economic development created a trendy agenda in the 1980s regarding China and other East Asian economies.[23]

Alongside economism, a debate on neo-authoritarianism in the late 1980s reflects the unpreparedness for ideological guidance. Inspired by Samuel Huntington's argument of authoritarian necessity during the initial period of modernization, neo-authoritarianism was ideologically open to both centralization and civil society to prevent extremism, right or left, from inflicting the economic reform.[24] Such an instrumental proclivity reinforced the quest for some ideological guidance to justify or orient the practice of authoritarianism or the resistance to it. Amid the same instrumental atmosphere, the realignment of Confucianism and liberalism seemed genuine to external observers during the 1980s. Purged in the 1950s, they were successfully blended in Taiwan, whose economic growth immediately attracted Chinese reformers following the CR.

The institutionalist turn in the discipline of political economy inspired China watchers. Steven Cheung, whose writing on property rights enthused even the CCP leaders, was among the first to apply the Coase Theorem to property rights reform in China.[25] Victor Nee straightforwardly explored the role of the market in the reform.[26] Inspired by fascination with the newly discovered state-and-society relations in China that were not totalitarian in nature, the institutionalist passion dominated China studies for the next three decades. Andrew Walder and Jean Oi attended to the calculative workers and peasants, respectively, the revelation of whose choices opened up the previously monotonous image of central (read "totalitarian") planning.[27] Others, who stress local agencies[28] or adaptive firms[29] rather than individuals, similarly expose rationalities that were unknown before and during the CR. Even a discussion of democracy made the academic agenda.[30] The statist sensibilities lingered on in the literature to qualify romanticized marketization,[31] implicitly continuing to echo hope for civil society.

Traces of liberalism inside China emerged within (or returned to) the CCP's state apparatus. Most notable were the late Li Shenzhi (1923 to 2003), during the Jiang Zemin period, and Yu Keping (1959 to present), during the Hu Jintao period. The leadership highly respected both. Li became vocal after retiring from the Chinese Academy of Social Sciences (CASS), while Yu was the adviser to Hu. Li inherited a legacy from the early republican liberalism of the 1910s.[32] Both were explicitly in favor of democracy, but Yu was not clearly in favor of liberalism. Yu's "Democracy Is a Good Thing,"[33] published in 2006, caused a sensation. Initially, he was the chief of the Central Compilation and Translation Bureau, a top CCP think tank, which proved to be one of the most active promoters of democratic governance.[34] On the other hand, those most critical of and troublesome to the CCP were likewise affiliated with the apparatus. Liu Junning (1961 to present) and Xu Youyu (1947 to present), both officially warned by the CCP in 2009 for signing a petition in favor of a liberal constitution, were previously affiliated with the CASS, too. Liu had been purged in 2002.

Xu was a dedicated Red Guard during the Cultural Revolution. He was converted after the CR through the belief that the entire generation had to learn how to overcome ignorance.[35] A similar case was Zhang Rong (1952 to present), a famous novelist from an orthodox CCP family, who was similarly a hard-liner during the CR but converted later. Both Xu and Zhang were critically reflexive of their Red Guard career. It was a time of Maoist faith, which they were both, since the immediate aftermath of the CR, determined to avert. They exemplify a link between today's devotion to liberalism and an abhorred self-memory inflicted by their CR experiences.[36]

Realignment occurred during the 1990s. Internally, contrary to the romantic association of Confucianism and liberalism outside China, *River Elegy* (1988) marked the first comprehensive attack on Confucianism and was also a harbinger of the rise of liberal critics during the 1990s. In this popular film, the arrival of (oceanic) "blue civilization" is allegedly about to terminate the "yellow (read 'Chinese') civilization" symbolized by the Yellow River, the (yellow) Loess Plateau, and yellow skin.[37] Due to the alert to political liberalism after the June 4th crackdown on the pro-democracy movement, liberal critics achieved significance primarily in support of the argument for property rights and market reform, since many others who made these arguments were not liberals. Western China scholars, for example, likewise found their concerns for Chinese civil society intertwined with the major themes of the reform—decentralization and privatization.[38] Some boldly discussed human rights in jurisprudence journals even during the politically intense years following the crackdown.[39]

In contrast to the rights sensibilities, these uncertain, chaotic years bred nostalgia for the security and equality that had been familiar during the previous central planning system. New Left critics emerged to counter the rampant platform of liberalization. They particularly stressed the well-being of peasants and workers and the state's capacity to ensure balanced development.[40] The New Left's appeal to socialism amounted to a legitimacy challenge to the CCP. Moreover, the joint force of the New Left and neo-Confucianism to oppose further liberalization was under formation. The ensuing product that pleased both was the unprecedented advocacy of "the harmonious society," signaling Hu's shift in priority to those disadvantaged strata following a quarter of a century of rampant growth.[41]

Chinese liberals have been involved in foreign affairs in two main ways. Their more apparent involvement has been the support they have consistently received from Western countries. Liberals could pay academic visits to the West, seek political asylum in the United States or Western Europe, or receive international NGOs' research grants and human rights awards. Liu Xiaobo (1955 to 2017), the leading drafter of *Chapter 08*, was a dissident writer, a visiting scholar at several Western institutes, and a Nobel Peace Prize laureate. He was prosecuted for treason. Many of his co-drafters, including Su Xiaokang (the author of *River Elegy*), have resided overseas under arranged asylum.[42] Beijing considers these interactions interference in China's internal affairs and responds with legal means from time to time.

The second method of involvement is to engage in foreign policy debates. A notable example was China's "major power diplomacy" debate.[43] Liberal critics are consistently critical of the confrontational policy, which they believe to have a victim consciousness embedded in it. Such victim consciousness arises from modern historiography that is obsessed with the invasion of China by the Western imperial powers. For the liberals, China is entitled to occupy the status of a major power only if the Chinese people can move beyond their sense of having been victimized.[44] The timing of this debate coincided with the promotion of a harmonious society. Albeit unsuccessful, the debate constituted a de facto attempt by the liberals to reappropriate the latter away from their intellectual rivals. The purges, suppression, and criticism of the liberals by their intellectual rivals and government authorities unavoidably led to the impression in Western countries of an unfriendly, ruthless regime on the rise.

A Revisionist Power Composite of Confucianism and Socialism

Those groups that first realized how serious revisionism could become an issue included the CCP's think tanks. At the 15th National Congress of the

CCP, held in 1997, the notion of "relations with major powers" appeared in the official party document for the first time. This was the first indication that a self-image of China becoming a real major power was emerging in the policy papers. Such a connotation contrasted with Deng Xiaoping's diplomatic wisdom, which is best summarized by the idiom "to conceal one's strengths and bide one's time." Deng intended to transcend the isolation externally and the internal slackening off since the June 4th crackdown.

In 2003, a tentative intellectual solution to the growth spurt of China was the notion of a "peaceful rise."[45] Coined by the head of the Central Party School, Zheng Bijian (1932 to present), this expression was a statement of intended peace but was jettisoned because the term 'rise' might still trigger alarm. Nevertheless, the anxiety about China being treated antagonistically was registered in Zheng's attempt to soothe the Western nations. In 2005, President Hu Jintao devised a theme—a harmonious world—to guide China's path to attaining the status of a major power. Again, the opposite of a harmonious world may have been exactly what the CCP feared. Namely, China on the rise was becoming a less trustworthy target in the eyes of the other major powers. For Hu's foreign policy, the guiding principle of "peace and development" was linked to the major diplomatic theme in the mid-1980s—"peaceful development." Ultimately, Hu's successor, Xi Jinping, decided to stress "striving for achievement" in 2013, which evolved into a longing for "the shared future for humankind" in 2015. Both Hu and Xi attempted to reassure the world that China's rise threatened no one.[46]

Hu's promotion of "the harmonious world" was the wedge that opened up the way for Chinese culture to contribute to the subsequent discussion. The widely read and cited book by Zhao Tingyang (1961 to present)—*Tianxia Tixi*, also published in 2005—defined the cultural agenda of Chinese international relations throughout the early 2020s. Zhao came from a Daoist tradition but inspired and incurred Confucianism in subsequent debates. The differences between Daoism and Confucianism notwithstanding, both traditions agree that *tianxia* is a complete contrast to the Western world order. In this regard, Zhao's Confucian ally Qin Yaqing (1953 to present) has been triumphant in achieving worldwide attention by publishing his Chinese international relations through the lens of Confucian relationality.[47] Qin's Confucian sensibilities continue to resonate well with Xi's call to build a "community of shared future for humankind," in which China will achieve "the great rejuvenation of the Chinese nation." Alongside Qin's study of relationality has been his curious inquiries into Chinese diplomatic history, especially the references to the tributary system and concept of *tianxia*.

However, it is not only Confucianism that has been at play. The reform that arose from the aftermath of the CR has been primarily a materialistically oriented platform, the core aim of which was, according to Deng, to emancipate the productive force. In fact, in 1987, the "primary stage of socialism" was the officially sanctioned Chinese characteristics, which determined the necessity of developing the productive force. During the entire Jiang Zeming era (1989 to 2002), the CCP applied Deng Xiaoping's advice to concentrate on economic production. According to Deng, this sole focus was undergirded by two cardinal principles. They concerned the CCP leadership under the guidance of socialism and the policy of openness to the outside world. Note that both Confucius and Marx sought to promote the material welfare of the populace. Given that socialism lost its ruling credit during the CR, Confucius's key advice on governance—that the people had to be left affluent and secure in their lives—was the best source of legitimacy on which the demoralized CCP could rely. As the economy recovered during the 1980s and continued to grow impressively in the 1990s, Hu Jintao raised the slogan of "scientific development" to incorporate "sustainable development" and environmental concerns. Within this discursive trajectory, socialism's encouragement to mingle with the capitalist world and participate in international regimes appears friendly and even enthusiastic toward a liberal, multilateral political economy. China experts were generally ambivalent regarding the future role of China on the rise.[48]

To the extent that production and welfare are the shared values of Confucianism and socialism, both strands of thought can be compatible with the international liberal institutions in practice. Logically, not only do they each comprise a certain anti-Western or anti-capitalist consciousness, but they also contradict each other in terms of their orientations toward modernity. Rehabilitation after the CR realigned these past ideological rivals into seeming supporters of China's compliance with the international regimes. This is unconvincing in theory, however. With the rise of China looming significant during Hu's reign, the arguments about China eventually making a different dominant force in the world emerged in various assessments. The literature differed regarding China experts' views of the expected changes that China's rise would produce. However, a vague consensus seemed to be that the status quo would alter, becoming a version of "neo-socialism."[49]

Contrary to the optimism of both the Chinese authorities and the Confucian scholarship, which promise that China's rise will fit into the existing multilateral regimes, the Anglophone literature conceives a rise embedded in Confucianism as a guarantee of change. For a prominent example, William Callahan selects Zhao Tingyang's *tianxia* to show how it is conducive to China's expansion of hegemonic control over its neighbors.[50] Callahan is uninterested in Zhao's romantic portrayal of a world system with no center or Zhao's apparent distinction from Confucian belief in the hierarchy or China's centralizing role. For Callahan, the Chinese nation-state will take advantage of the *tianxia* discourse, regardless of whether this is Confucian or Daoist in nature. In his understanding, China is essentially a territorial entity, so *tianxia* cannot escape from the reduction to a legitimating discourse for the foreign policy of a sovereign state that pursues hegemonic control. Such criticism reproduces the same hegemonic culture as practiced by the Western imperialist powers. With *tianxia* being reduced to a pseudo-discourse, Chinese revisionism constitutes little more than a power challenge to the dominance of the US in East Asia.

Contrary to Callahan, David Kang sees a real difference, in which Chinese history testifies.[51] Kang argues that East Asia, which centered around a strong China, tended to be peaceful, while a weakened China led to disorder. He explains this apparent anomaly by focusing on the hierarchy that undergirds the relationships between Confucian societies. For Kang, the Confucian order explains the history of East Asian international relations more effectively than do realism, liberalism, or socialism. Kang's interpretation nevertheless connotes a revision of the current international order.

Alongside Kang, but ironically also in line with Pillsbury in a peculiar way, Martin Jacques perceives that the rise of China will lead to the adoption of entirely different rules to maintain the international order. Echoing Lucian Pye,[52] Jacques argues that China is a civilizational state, a civilization pretending to be a state.[53] He pays particular attention to Confucianism, which requires the CCP to assume the moral responsibility to act selflessly. This leads to his judgment that, although engrossed in a hierarchical consciousness, China's rise may lead to democracy between national societies, whereby states of varying sizes will participate more equally in global affairs. Neither Kang nor Jacques is an alarmist. Their view of the Confucian hierarchy promises a plausible alternative to the Western international relations that have become so familiar, albeit unsatisfactory, to the world. However, Jacques almost confirms that China will be a revisionist power in the eyes of the West, observing that "the West is going to feel extremely disoriented by the world that is in the process of now being made."[54]

While, historically, Confucianism and socialism have followed an incongruent, if not entirely confrontational, trajectory, they both seem to contribute to the revisionist image of China on the rise. Criticism of the Chinese Communist Party and praise of Confucianism had easily existed hand in hand for experts watching China through to the end of the CR. Therefore, Confucianism was once a nostalgic phenomenon for China experts everywhere. Pye was one of the few exceptions; he delved deeply into the psychology of the symbiosis of the two ideologies in the ironic juxtaposition of "the Mandarin and the Cadre."[55] Richard Madsen notes a similar phenomenon with his sarcastic term "the communist gentry."[56] Their treatments tended to place a stronger emphasis on cultural practice than on socialist ideology. Wang Gungwu concurs regarding the expectation of a different order in his in-depth reflections on China's history and discourse.[57] For him, the revival of Confucianism inspired and echoed the CCP's two-legged platform, with the other being socialism.

The New Left and Political Neo-Confucianism

An absolute message of revisionism in the formation of the CCP-socialism-Confucianism collusion sticks out most sharply in Wang Fei-Ling's (1959 to present) tracing of an alleged ulterior China order.[58] For Wang, the Left and Confucians are almost the same agents of such a China order. He criticizes China's inner drive for dominance and suppression. He views the combination of socialism and Confucianism as having been consciously contrived by Xi Jinping since he came to power in 2012. This combination has allowed Xi to add much-needed activism to Confucianism and transformed a cyclical Confucianism worldview into an ambiguous teleology in the name of "destiny" for humankind. Xi may be the first top leader to attempt such a philosophical improvisation. Mao, widely considered a Confucian, at least strove to cleanse his past through the CR. However, Xi, who grew up during the CR, is becoming an ironic Confucian plus Communist.

In the intellectual history of post-CR China, these two past rivals and the two victims of the CR were able to unite due to their shared aversion to liberalism. Liberalism is an intellectual resource for Chinese scholars and Communist cadres who have lost trust and confidence in the CCP. Liberalism would have been an impossible legacy to retrieve without the demoralization of the regime by the CR. Pragmatically, a joint mission of all Chinese intellectuals is to revitalize China through the global liberal institutions, but socialism and Confucianism are commonly on guard against the ideology of liberalism.[59] Once allied, despite their other differences, the two ideologies unintentionally lay the foundation for China to ultimately loom revisionist.

In reality, the intensity of polemics between the Right and Left was revived only during the 1990s. Marxists of all varieties were largely silent at the start of the reform. There was a brief campaign warning of "spiritual pollution" during the early 1980s, which reemerged after the 1989 crackdown on the pro-democracy movement and gathered momentum in the nonideology of national security.[60] The New Left's nostalgia for Mao and the CR was initially unrelated to these political campaigns but useful to them due to the sensibilities to the Chinese characteristics in the nostalgia. The New Left critics, a label contrived and imposed by their liberal rivals, were never purely academic or philosophical in nature. Political implications are apparent in the New Left's mindfulness of the macronational historiography, state (financial) capacity, and mass-line perspectives, while the Right was mindful of individual freedom, limited government, and marketization.[61] Chinese bestsellers of the time recorded their contending positions,[62] now known as the New Left versus the liberals. The polemics continued into the 2020s.[63] In the age of the Internet, mutual denouncement is pervasive on almost every issue. Between them, international sympathy consistently goes to the Right as the New Left critics can conveniently act as apologists for the CCP authorities, despite their unconcealed displeasure at the displacement of workers and peasants during the reform.[64] The authorities likewise place considerable pressure on the Right, to the effect that the party cadres are being phased out. Journalists and professors, especially those specializing in economics and law, are the major components of the liberal side.

Confucianism revived along with the "cultural heat" that rescued society from a loss of faith in the aftermath of the CR. Some Confucian scholars were well-known cultural revolutionaries; for example, Xie Xialing (1945 to present) is among the most notable of these.[65] These figures represent the hybrid of Confucianism and the Left in person. The factionalism that developed during the CR reflected a thread of previously purged Confucian traditions, taking revenge against the Party in the name of the CR. As a result, the love/hate relationship between Confucian circles and the Left is always complex and ironic. Alongside the rise of the New Left, the authorities began to support the revival of Confucianism as a moral discipline for individuals.

With the input of Taiwanese Confucian scholars who were eager to help with their romantic desire to enhance respect for Taiwan, the Chinese Academy of Social Sciences coordinated a series of large conferences to promote research on Confucianism. The realignment of Confucian scholars between China and Taiwan occurred amid the intense atmosphere bred by the debates between the New Left and the liberals. The further realignment between Confucianism and the New Left was not on the radar of Taiwanese Confucianists, who were sympathetic to liberalism in the contemporary neo-Confucian traditions that began after the PRC was established in 1949.[66] These traditions were notably anti-Communist in nature.

However, the liberal romanticism of Taiwanese neo-Confucianism was an unheeded harbinger of the future estrangement between Chinese and Taiwanese Confucian scholars that occurred over a decade later.[67] In fact, the emergence of Confucian socialism in the New Left circle indicated an opposite potential for a realignment between socialism and Confucianism. Gan Yang (1952 to present), a prolific New Left critic, specifically advocates "The Republic of Confucian Socialism" to support Hu Jintao's harmonious society.[68] According to Gan, the two substantive rationalities of Maoist equality and Confucian harmony, together with Deng Xiaoping's instrumental rationality, constitute the three cornerstones of his desired republic. According to Gan, the Confucian ideals of great harmony, a moral personality, and an ethical orientation directly motivated the early-twentieth-century activists to adopt socialism. Confucius was a socialist to the extent that he prioritized the equal distribution of wealth over the release from poverty. Confucianism contributes to contemporary socialism, particularly in the Chineseness embedded in the China-centric historiography and caution about liberalism and capitalism.[69]

Whether deliberately or not, the importance of the harmonious-world theme is apparent.[70] It testifies to Confucianism's concerns over substantive rationality in addition to a moral personality. One focus of neo-Confucianism's development in China throughout the 1990s was the move away from instrumental rationality in terms of the Anglophone and Taiwanese narratives on Confucianism's contribution to economic modernization. Only at the level of substantive value can neo-Confucianism enhance the legitimacy of the CCP and socialism. Meritocracy is of particular relevance in this regard.[71] In short, with Confucianism, socialism represents more than simply the Western learning of modernity. Instead, its concerns for collective welfare and suspicion toward individual and instrumental rationality resonate well in the Chinese cultural tradition, so socialism is legitimately Chinese, and Confucianism, socialist. To some extent, Marx is "the Confucian sage."[72] In the same vein, the rights orientation embedded in liberalism and capitalism is an increasingly common target of neo-Confucianism and the New Left.

Nevertheless, it is in the international arena where their shared aversion to the liberal and capitalist influences is most easily discernible. Such aversion inevitably breeds nationalist sensibilities. For the New Left, China's integral and capable national sovereignty, which is rarely available elsewhere in the formerly colonized world, indicates the success of the CCP. For example, one notable New Left scholar, Han Yuhai (1965 to present), maintains that Chinese historiography's mission is to establish a China-centric interpretation and develop a China consciousness.[73] For Chinese neo-Confucians, it is the revival of Chinese values in the name of a sovereign China that inspires their endeavors. Their shared historical sensibilities point to the quest for China-centric worldviews.

Nevertheless, the social relationships between the New Left and neo-Confucians are never clear or direct. Even less apparent is whether the references to *tianxia* or the tributary system in their writings are compatible at all. For example, the first contemporary *tianxia* philosopher, Zhao Tingyang, specifically denies that his *tianxia* writings have any connection with either Confucianism or socialism.[74] For him, the philosophy of *tianxia* has no political standpoint, nor should it. Zhao has been an intellectual liaison. His connection with the ideal of *tianxia* and Qin's work on Chinese relationality resonates with Confucianism. On the other hand, he is otherwise very much in line with the New Left orientation as he urges the study of the mutual constitution of Chinese classics and Marxism.[75] He attends New Left gatherings and publishes in those forums; for example, *Du Shu* ("Reading"), where New Left critics appear most often.

Therefore, in the eyes of the liberals, the national and historical sensibilities, from which they all likewise originate when disputing liberalism and Western political thought, form the genuine foundations of their alignment. Almost a conspiracy, these sensibilities appear alarming as resources that will enable the CCP to take on the entire world. In the alarmist words of Wang Fei-Ling, the advocacy of the China Dream and great rejuvenation of the Chinese nation by Xi, which amounts to a Chinese totalitarian pursuit, benefits significantly from Sino-centrism and Han-Chinese nationalism between the lines of these seemingly uncoordinated, incompatible scholarships.[76]

In practice, Xi has been himself a conscious Marxist and Confucian. In the past, both the first-generation leader Liu Shaoqi (1898 to 1969) and the contemporary leader Jiang Zemin (e.g., on rule by virtue) have promoted Confucian ethics at the individual level.[77] However, Xi's reliance on Confucianism conveys an extension of Confucian values to guide international relations. According to the Confucian teachings, he developed the notion of "strive for achievement" to reconstitute neighboring relationships and international relations at large.[78] His many references to this include "neighbors nearby closer than distant kin," "all men are brothers," "*tianxia* is for the public," "benevolence leads to love for people," "harmony transcends differences," "the cultivated virtue sustains the heavy world," and so on.[79]

He proceeds to elaborate on the four implications for diplomatic principles: (1) protect the multiple and mutual constitution of world civilizations from attack or conversion, (2) respect all national cultures without discrimination, (3) learn from one another, and (4) creatively and scientifically develop cultures for the use of all. The camp of political Confucianism strongly supports the idea of "a community of a shared future for humankind."[80] As the Belt and Road Initiative has emerged strongly, the PRC appears to have combined materialist socialism with Confucian *tianxia* to reconfigure the political space and revise the whole world order in due course.[81]

Becoming "Revisionist"

All the charges of Chinese threat and revisionism consistently refer to China's authoritarian or autocratic style of governance, suggesting that revisionism is more than the rise of China's economic and military power. Initially, the authoritarian style alerts the China watchers and policymakers because China's successful economic growth under authoritarianism provides a plausible substitute for liberal democracy for postcolonial regimes. According to a prevailing impression, the process seemed to begin in 2008, a year of global financial crisis, in which China stood firm.[82] It gained pace throughout 2017, when the two-term limitation imposed on the presidency was removed from the Chinese constitution and the anxiety about Chinese revisionism and autocracy was simultaneously officialized in American China policy for the first time.[83] The felt threat is ontological, as it challenges the inevitability of liberal democracy that characterizes the "Western order." Thereafter, China's military capability escalated into an urgent issue and fed the expectation of a hegemonic war through an almost unified lens of otherwise intensely divided American politics.[84]

However, authoritarian governance has continued since the Chinese Communist Party came to power in 1949, while the serious perception of threat and revisionism arose only in the recent decade. This sudden emergence of a threat perception calls for an intellectual process, in China as well as the United States. If what makes the assessment of a threat and revisionism convincing is China's authoritarian style of governance, we need an explanation of how this became an issue. The chapter argues that authoritarianism does not make economic success a threat. Rather, the aborted expectation at the end of the Cultural Revolution that China would become a liberal democracy was the major cause. This chapter is a brief intellectual history of contemporary Chinese political thought that constitutes contemporary US self-identity, albeit negatively. It traces the realignment between Confucianism, socialism, and liberalism during the past three decades. Only when embedded in this background could a disappointed US policy circle collectively change its mind within the short span of a few years.

Retrieving Confucianism and reforming socialism have been the CCP's two approaches for reestablishing the post-CR identity in the face of rising liberalism. The two former rivals became allies. Together, they refused liberalism that once loomed promising to the outside world. Given that the vision of harmony was intended to directly address China's role as a "responsible stakeholder," neither ideological identity is intended to shelf international liberal institutions. As such, China's rise poses an epistemological and ontological threat as the coexistence of liberalism with Confucianism and socialism in the arena of domestic thought falls into rivalry.

The Cultural Revolution and its ending have been the shared habitus of almost all subsequent political thought, the return and realignment of which bifurcate into incongruent role expectations in China and the image of a revisionist China among China experts. This prior relation has evolved around the treatment of liberalism. Initially, liberalism seemed compatible with the transition to the world economy for the pupil China, but the change backfired on liberalism. Against the background of ideological realignment in China, experts who once romanticized an emerging liberal China have instead perceived an assertive, estranged China on the rise, resulting in their refocus on Chinese authoritarianism, which has remained unchanged in Chinese politics throughout all these years.

9

Neither Balance nor Deterrence

Relational Security across the Taiwan Strait

Scholars agree that a major focus of the rivalry between Washington, DC, and Beijing is Taiwan—a backer of Washington—because Beijing's vital interest lies in China's unification with Taiwan.[1] Beijing's immediate interest is to prevent Taipei from declaring Taiwan's official independence from China. To protect its vital interest, Beijing repeatedly pledges that it will not preclude the use of military force.[2] On the other hand, the vital interest of Washington is to prevent Chinese revisionism. According to the leading US think tank reports,[3] the two indicators that exemplify Chinese revisionism are China's material power overtaking that of the United States and the rising popularity of China's authoritarian, as opposed to liberal, model of governance. For Washington, Taiwan joining China would represent defeat according to both indicators. Taiwan's remaining outside Beijing's rule constitutes one of Washington's highest stakes.[4] The situation may appear to be a classic security dilemma in alliance politics,[5] wherein Washington is trapped too deeply in Taipei's quest for independence. Still, it is not typical, because two security dilemmas exist simultaneously between (1) Washington and Beijing and (2) Taipei and Beijing.

Taipei has not declared independence officially, despite Taiwan possessing every other attribute of independent statehood apart from diplomatic recognition. Taipei has launched anti-Chinese campaigns to the effect that most voters would support independence.[6] Given Beijing's demonstrated determination to deter Taiwan from declaring independence, Taipei has not taken such a final step. Between Taipei and Beijing, the understanding used to be that both would refrain from forcing a solution. Note that Beijing's anxiety is directed toward Taiwan's independence rather than US dominance in the world, as Taiwan's independence would destroy Beijing's regime legitimacy.[7] However, if Washington could ensure its absolute superiority over Beijing, there would be no reason for Taipei to comply with the existing understanding.[8] Accordingly, Washington's dominance has direct implications for Beijing's vital interests.

With the US-China rivalry escalating, many commentators regard the potential of Beijing abandoning the China-Taiwan understanding and unilaterally resorting to military unification with Taiwan as part of the hegemonic competition.[9] Washington's urgency contributes to the overall deterrence, with a stress on military power.[10] Taipei's security guarantee offsets Beijing's deterrence, leading to Beijing's further investment in the military capacity to deter Taipei from declaring official independence. In the past, when China was not a competitor, Washington could restrain Taipei's independence and keep Beijing's anxiety at bay. With China on the rise,[11] Washington can no longer afford to control Taipei's independence, lest this might create the impression that Washington fears competition with China. Given that Taiwan's independence is less about military rebalancing than a quest for self-identity for China and Taiwan, the stronger Washington's commitment to Taiwan's security, the more likely China's invasion appears.

This chapter critically revises the classic theory of security dilemmas by incorporating the notion of ontological security. The literature on security dilemmas considers the anarchical structure as the cause of security dilemmas. It argues that the anarchical structure does not necessarily cause security dilemmas, even if there is a change in the (a)symmetry of power, unless the change poses an existential threat to both sides. The chapter relies on relational analysis to explain how an existential identity always requires other parties to confirm it, while mutual confirmation does not directly concern the balance of power. Therefore, a security dilemma that rests upon the existential identity is a relational dilemma, and confirmation of one defies the other. Attaining or restoring ontological security may follow efforts to rebalance the power (a)symmetry. In short, the ontological security dilemma is the cause of the security dilemma, as the latter is conventionally understood.

Relational Ontology and the Security Dilemma

THE REVISIONISM-INFORMED SECURITY DILEMMA

Given that Washington's goal is to deter Beijing from taking military action against Taiwan, the security dilemma in the region differs slightly from the conventional security dilemma. The conventionally understood security dilemma is a popular topic among East Asian international relations scholars.[12] The literature generally describes how rational actors, uncertain about each other's intentions in a metaphorically anarchical state of nature, set out to pursue a comparative security advantage unilaterally but contrarily exacerbate the mutual fear, resulting in a spiraling military build-up that breeds mutual insecurity.[13] It is recognized in the literature that for a security dilemma that stresses deterrence to cause the fear of the other involves more than a belief that is rooted in the anarchic nature of international relations.[14] The discussion further entails an assessment of the revisionist intention of the parties to the security dilemma.[15]

Both revisionists and anti-revisionists can initiate a security dilemma, with the former perceiving irrevocably aggravating mistreatment, such as Beijing fearing the closing of the window of opportunity for unification due to Washington's or Taipei's continuous encroaching, and the latter preempting a perceived future violation, such as Washington blocking Beijing from pushing for armed unification. Deterrence mitigates the revisionist threat by reducing the targeted power's desire for a new order. Through deterrence, the targeted power can likewise dissuade the anti-revisionist power from suppressing the alleged reform qua revision of the current order. A security dilemma ensues when the two parties provoke anxiety in each other about losing their respective visions of the collective order. A deterrence-induced security dilemma thus reflects a conflict over the relational order that constitutes the identities of the relevant parties,[16] even from a distance.[17] A relational tragedy is induced not by the anarchical structure but by the actors enforcing contending collective identities.[18]

For constructivists, deterring (anti-)revisionism always involves a prior pattern of practices and relations that make sense of the parties' threat image of each other.[19] Accordingly, anarchy is simply another collective identity that provides a prior lens to enable the subscribing national actors to assess the other party.[20] In contrast, alternative versions of collective identity lack such a dilemma, as scholars of hierarchical East Asian relations argue.[21] Therefore, even for anarchy, which honors no particular value or rule, a perception of revisionism can still exist under the circumstances of offensive power, dominance, or empire building. Acts of deterrence against an expanding power can cause a security dilemma only if the perceived expanding power conceives of an imperial intention, camouflaged by the anti-revisionist pose. Otherwise, every nation would be committing (anti-)revisionism all the time because all strive for greater power.[22] Revisionism as an analytical term would lose relevance. Nevertheless, every actor may feel a threat in how others treat them,[23] as long as a denial of entitlement or identity by another actor is perceived. Indeed, a sensitive or vulnerable actor may perceive all potential sorts of ontological threats.[24]

ONTOLOGICAL THREATS AND SECURITY

According to R. D. Laing,[25] an ontological threat is an existential threat, being more a threat to the self than to the body.[26] Specifically, in the current chapter, it refers to *being denied a relation that constitutes what one believes one is*. According to this definition, ontological security in international relations cannot be denied to a national actor directly.[27] The threat is only real when the relation of belonging that constitutes a nation's being faces denial, which is a particularly acute point in the separatist movement.[28] A separatist may make no physical threat but an ontological one, because they cannot be categorized by belonging to an already-agreed-upon relation.[29] To the extent that ontological security is primarily relational in nature, scholars simultaneously locate it internationally and internally.[30] Combined, it is what the domestic constituency collectively believes about what the nation is entitled to in the world. Denying the relations composes an ontological threat and a powerful motivation per se for all parties subscribing to the relations to take action, not necessarily contingent upon the balance-of-power calculus.[31] This means that deterrence must be mutual in nature.[32] A weak power can sometimes challenge a stronger one, and the latter can make compromises. Both protect a specific relation that constitutes the national identities of the disputing parties.[33] The force of ontological security is registered in the domestic determination to protect an international relational order that is threatened by (anti-)revisionism.[34]

Scholars note that ontological security is necessarily discursive and interpretive in nature,[35] expressed through narratives on values and history. Being intrinsic to the regimes' and leaders' legitimacy, the notions of natural rights and democracy are the components of onto-logical security for liberal democratic countries, including the US. In contrast, national unification is the paramount ontological issue in the Chinese discursive environment. Instead of being the major indicator of the ontological security condition, military capability can support or revise, but not determine, an ontological relation. Such an ontological relation is prior and continuous.[36] It simultaneously defines the national identities of actors subscribing to the same prior relation.[37] Preparing for war can pose an ontological threat, for war could disrupt long-established, peaceful coexistence. Therefore, China's preparation for armed unification disrupts four decades of comprehensive exchanges with Taiwan. How-ever, the literature notes that stabilizing peace, which assumes mutual recognition, can likewise constitute an ontological threat,[38] for peace could disrupt a long-established rival relationship. Accordingly, signing a long-term peace pact with China could jeopardize Taipei's pursuit of an un-Chinese identity.

From the ontological security perspective, in which all can inflict a relational breach on the other, Beijing and Washington are more than asymmetric players in terms of military power, and so are Taipei and Beijing. The alliance security dilemma between Washington and Beijing over Taipei would be misleading without modification. If it were a typical alliance dilemma, caught between abandonment and overcom-mitment,[39] an overcommitment to Taiwan would jeopardize the peace prospect between Washington and Beijing, but abandonment would destroy the credit of Washington as an ally. The current discussions on commitment always begin with Beijing's military initiative to take over Taiwan, regardless of their often-incongruent theoretical perspectives,[40] as if the moral hazard of Washington instigating Taipei into vicarious deterrence—in other words, preparing to win an independence war with Beijing—were irrelevant. Think-tank-run military simulations unanimously adopt a leader/follower formula without exception, with Washington replying to Beijing's choice between armed unification and peace.[41] Neither Washington's nor Taipei's ontological security is pres-ent, and, as for Beijing, only the military calculus applies. The security dilemma lies between the deterrer Washington and revisionist Beijing in these simulations.[42]

In reality, however, parallel security dilemmas of different ontological kinds incur parallel moral hazards of different relational agendas. The following section introduces a model to restore the relational equivalence of all three actors. It complicates the typical two-actor frame and clarifies the ontological security in the security dilemma (see figure 9.1).

Figure 9.1. The two versions of the security dilemma. Created by the author.

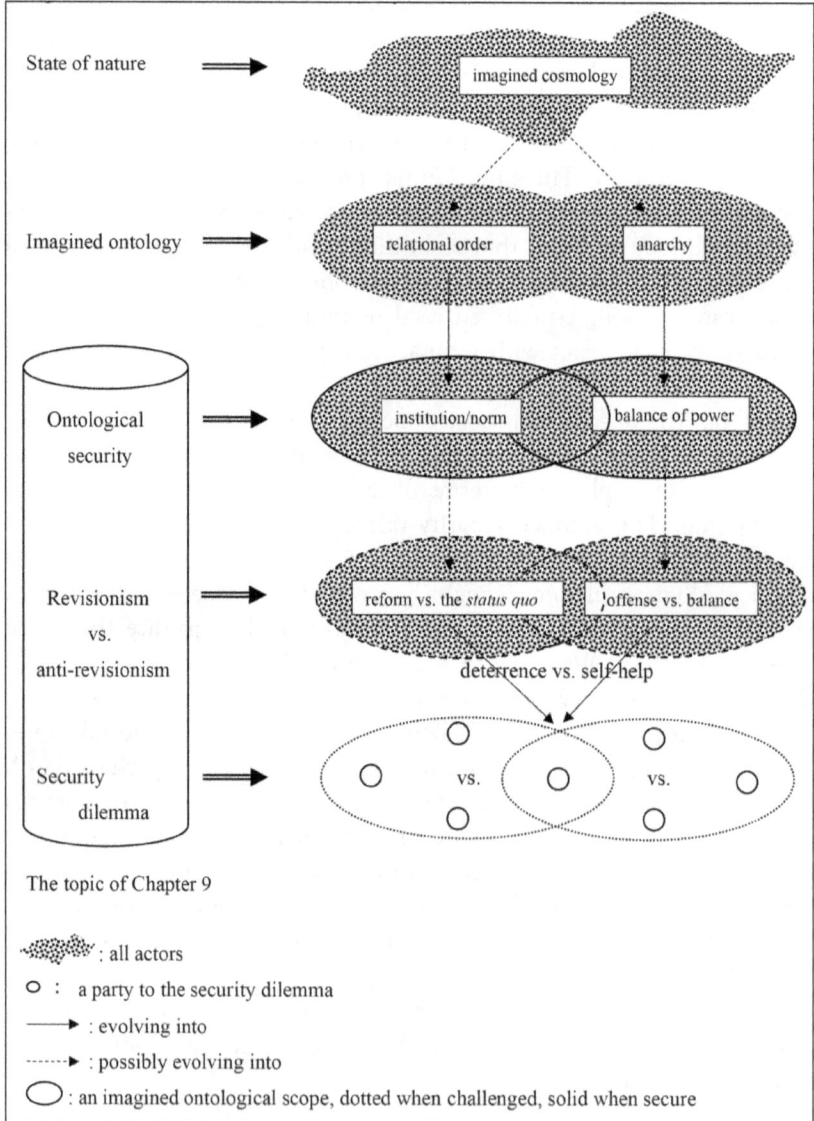

Relational Threat as Deterrence

RELATIONAL SETTINGS

Ontological sensibilities constitute all three actors, whether they know it or not. As Viktoria Akchurina and Vincent Della Sala state,[43] an ontological security dilemma arises when "enhancing confidence in the identity and continuity of a political community threatens the ontological security of other actors." Relational deterrence targets ontological security. It proceeds with "denial," which forces the deterrees to recognize, according to Paul Cornish,[44] that "a mutually acceptable outcome—a tolerable status quo—is both available and desirable." To that extent, a deterree has to be "a would-be enemy [who] chooses to be deterred."[45] Yielding to deterrence by the deterrer assumes that they care about maintaining the ongoing interaction pattern as a component of their ontological security.[46]

For Washington, ontological security anchors its leadership in the hegemonic (neoliberal) rule-based order. To deny a perceived revisionist actor's entitled recognition of either a sovereign or democratic identity constitutes Washington's relational deterrence.[47] For Beijing, the peaceful coexistence of China's equal sovereignty with others, achieved through cleansing the imperialist legacies and reclaiming the lost territories, including Taiwan,[48] defines its ontological security. The withdrawal of goodwill to destabilize coexistence constitutes Beijing's relational deterrence. Finally, Taipei's ontological security is Taiwan's political autonomy and cultural superiority over China. Taipei's relational deterrence is to estrange Beijing by reiterating colonial modernity and stressing international identity.

Taiwan

The Qing dynasty conceded Taiwan to Japan in 1895. Under Japanese colonialism, Taiwan acquired a civilizational identity of belonging to Japan and surpassing China.[49] Japan returned Taiwan to China at the end of World War II. Taiwan became the rare postcolonial society, ruled not by the formerly colonized population but by a migrant Chinese regime, which arrived with the expectation that Taiwan would re-sinicize. Ruled by a presumably inferior government claiming superiority,[50] the deprived postcolonial population simultaneously suffered silencing by the continuous Chinese Civil War and Cold War.[51] When both receded, the postcolonial population transcended the Chinese consciousness by retrieving a colonial modernity consciousness,[52] which fits the American neoliberal order well. Colonial modernity informs contemporary Taiwan's ontological security. It reverses the colonial inferiority and distinguishes Taiwan from China. Such a consciousness contributes to the indifference to the territories and waters that the former Chinese migrant regime used to claim but failed to obtain through US or Japanese consent.[53] Having felt increasingly intimate with "superior" Americans and Japanese, the postcolonial population can regain self-respect.[54]

Taipei's separatist sensibilities indicate revisionism to Beijing, whereas Beijing's appeal to unification poses revisionism to Taipei and Washington, and Tokyo.[55] Taipei thus holds the strongest relational deterrence against unification: a readiness to declare official independence. Derived from Taipei's relational deterrence, the second-order relational deterrence lies in Washington's hands—the determination to protect Taiwan from unification with China. Taipei also faces Beijing's relational deterrence—the plausibility of armed unification, which nullifies Taiwan's colonial modernity and Washington's neoliberal order. A double ontological security dilemma—Washington versus Beijing and Beijing versus Taipei—constitutes Taiwan's identities.

The United States

Alexander Wendt traces different versions of collective identity among Western nations to the evolution of political thought in the European tradition.[56] These collective identities inform Washington's security sensibilities toward a realist balance of power and neoliberal institutionalism. In his discussion on the hegemonic transition from the US to China via war, Graham Allison's reference to the "Thucydides Trap" attests explicitly to the construction of contemporary American ontological security thinking.[57] The collective identity and hegemonic competition enable many think tank analysts to position Beijing under revisionism, embedded in the symbiosis of resilient authoritarianism and mounting military capability.[58] The symbiosis challenges the hegemonic rule-based order.

While the Thucydides Trap discourse divides the literature,[59] engagement and containment, as two resulting policy platforms, share the goal of protecting the liberal order and, eventually, neoliberalism, converting

China.[60] At times, well-noted American exceptionalism intervenes to justify the use of extrainstitutional means through the American destiny within world leadership, testifying to the belief in the imperative of US dominance to protect the hegemonic rule-based order.[61] Exceptionalism deters revisionists by threatening to deny their belonging to the collective identity.[62] Challenges to this order, in terms of the military and the value, risk the revisionists' relational coexistence because actors subscribing to the order will side with the exceptionalist.

China

Arising out of the memory of imperialist invasion,[63] territorial integrity and issues concerning historical correctness are intrinsic to the identity of China becoming equal sovereign.[64] Given that almost all borders carry colonial legacies, claiming lost territories is essential to Beijing's ontological security.[65] Exempt from an overall order, Beijing is used to a state-by-state relational arrangement.[66] On the one hand, making concessions to secure mutual acceptance and smooth decolonization is a relational practice of redrawing borders. Refusing to compromise is equally vital, on the other hand, in order to both reject the colonial legacies and assert China's revival. The former applies to relatively smaller neighbors;[67] the latter, to Russia, India, and Japan,[68] as well as anyone insisting on legalizing the colonial borders and even inviting intervention from the US or Europe over the South China Sea.[69]

Colonial borders were given at the point of independence for smaller neighbors, so redrawing them would shake their sovereign dignity. Taipei's increasing separatist sensibilities are direct result of the Japanese occupation, the Chinese Civil War, and the Cold War. Peaceful coexistence with China affirms neighbors' equality and dignity. The situation leads to an ontological security dilemma. Mutually deterring relationally, neighbors are vulnerable to China's denial of respect but ready to ruin China's anti-imperialist identity through an escalated outcry. Along with Hong Kong, Taiwan causes Beijing's strongest anxiety because both were not considered disputed territories until less than a decade ago. While armed unification can ruin the image of "One China" or a peaceful rise, Beijing's solution is to enhance the credit of anti-independence instead. Washington's military support for Taipei challenges such credit. Reiterating the possibility of armed unification maintains Beijing's credit.

Figure 9.2. The three-party ontological dilemma. Created by the author.

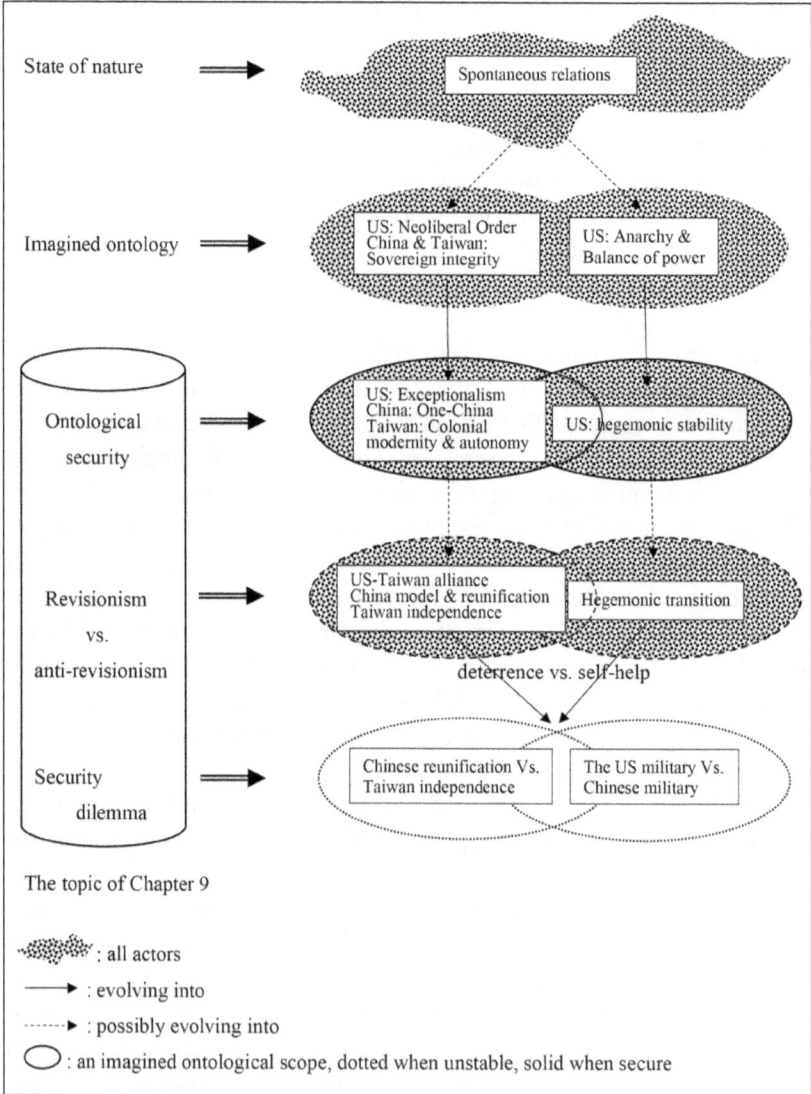

State of nature ⟹ Spontaneous relations

Imagined ontology ⟹ US: Neoliberal Order China & Taiwan: Sovereign integrity | US: Anarchy & Balance of power

Ontological security ⟹ US: Exceptionalism China: One-China Taiwan: Colonial modernity & autonomy | US: hegemonic stability

Revisionism vs. anti-revisionism ⟹ US-Taiwan alliance China model & reunification Taiwan independence | Hegemonic transition

deterrence vs. self-help

Security dilemma ⟹ Chinese reunification Vs. Taiwan independence | The US military Vs. Chinese military

The topic of Chapter 9

: all actors
⟶ : evolving into
-----▶ : possibly evolving into
◯ : an imagined ontological scope, dotted when unstable, solid when secure

A Practical Model

Given the ontological security nature of the interaction, the interaction is neither directly interactive nor spiral as a typical military security dilemma would have predicted. Such a kind of interaction shows how the general model of security dilemma fails to understand the policy rationales of different actors in specific cases. The following model is practical in the sense that it shows case-sensitive relational concerns and that the rise and fall of a spiral is primarily based upon the perceived threat to relation instead of an objectively measurable, but not necessarily signaled, physical threat.

To protect its ontological security, embedded in the neoliberal order, as well as its exceptionalist identity, Washington seeks to protect Taiwan from armed unification by Beijing. Washington resorts to relational deterrence at the systemic level by naming Beijing an autocracy, decoupling China from the neoliberal order, and coordinating the Indo-Pacific alliance to face China. At the local level, Washington provides Taipei with advanced weapons, arranges visits by top congressional leaders, proposes Taiwan's membership in UN organizations, softens the stance on One China, and engages in military drills and patrols in the nearby waters. All of these measures and related activities arguably aim to enhance the credit of the United States' protection of Taiwan and lower the probability of Beijing resorting to armed unification. Let the perceived likelihood of armed unification from Washington's perspective be

$$p_w = f(M)$$

and

$$f(M) = 1 - l \left[(m_w - m_b) / m_w \right]$$

where m represents the military capability,
p represents likelihood, or probability,
M represents the use of arms,
w represents Washington,
b represents Beijing, and
l is the coefficient denoting the level of anti-revisionism determination.

As such, the US military advantage over China is negatively associated with the perceived probability of armed unification. Under these formulae, the military advantage reflects Washington's ontological security and the anti-revisionism coefficient, the qualifying force of relational deterrence.

Next, given that Taipei's ontological security is registered in the superiority of colonial modernity but threatened by the prospect of unification with China, let q be the probability of Taiwan's independence becoming official:

$$q = k / (1 + p_w)$$

where k represents the pro-independence coefficient.

Thus, the probability of Taipei officially declaring independence is negatively associated with Washington's assessment of the probability of Beijing resorting to armed unification. The negative association denotes that Taipei's ontological security of being autonomous from China is contingent upon Washington's protection and judgment of Beijing's tendency to use force. As for the pro-independence coefficient, it is the qualifying relational deterrence willed by Taipei's anti-unification determination. A stronger resolution is more likely to evoke the Taiwan-US alliance in support of declaring official independence.

To continue, given that Beijing's ontological security rests upon anti-imperialist territorial sensibilities, let the probability of Beijing resorting to armed unification be p_b:

$$p_b = j\, q$$

where j represents the anti-independence coefficient.

So, Beijing's decision is positively associated with the probability of Taipei declaring official independence, where j denotes the qualifying relational deterrence toward Taipei, with a higher value indicating a more sensitive response to the probability of Taipei declaring independence. To summarize, after further unfolding:

$$p_w = f(M) = 1 - l\,[\,(m_w - m_b)\, /\, m_w]$$

$$q = k / (1 + p_w)$$

$$p_b = j\, q$$

So,

$$p_b = j\, k / (1 + p_w)$$

$$p_b = j\, k / \{2 - l\,[\,(m_w - m_b)\, /\, m_w]\}$$

Adding Taiwan to the scenario reveals the impracticalities of the two-party setup:

1. Given its ontological security and a high-valued k, Taipei's reliance on Washington is perpetual. No realist calculus would induce Taipei to choose a realignment with Beijing to balance the stronger actor Washington. Nor could there be the political morale for Taipei to bandwagon Beijing as the dominant player in the Taiwan Strait region. The only restraint on the determination of independence is the uncertainty about Washington's commitment to the protectorate.

2. For Beijing, Taiwan's independence is a greater threat than Washington's military dominance over Beijing. On the one hand, this is because Washington has been militarily superior to Beijing throughout history. The continuous dominance of Washington alone poses no imminent threat to Beijing's claim to equal sovereignty. On the other hand, Washington's military commitment to Taipei increases the probability of Taipei declaring official independence. This would pose an ontological threat.

3. Washington's military advantage, to be enhanced or maintained, does not necessarily promise stability because Washington's advantage could inspire Taipei to declare independence and, in turn, trigger Beijing's decision to engage in armed unification. Washington could simplify the deterrence consequences by directly deterring Beijing without involving Taipei as a vicarious actor.[70] The South China Sea provides such a scenario.[71] Beijing thus has an incentive to reduce the probability of armed unification to simplify the deterrence condition. Direct deterrence avoids the moral hazard committed by the ally or misperceived concerns of the deterree.[72]

Discussion

The ontological security of the three parties, defined in relational terms, creates an unfamiliar security dilemma. It is not about two powers unintentionally threatening each other physically, nor is it a classic alliance security dilemma, because both the protector and protectorate, instead of just the latter, face the same deterree in their respective security dilemma. Therefore, mutual moral hazards exist between the protector to instigate and the protectorate to entrap; nor does the three-party interaction form a two-level game, given the inconclusive relevance of the material power in pursuing ontological security. The actor's strength is contingent on the felt threat to ontological security in relational terms that it can inflict. All can trigger the spiral. Finally, the situation does not create a strategic triangle since relational settings preclude Taipei or Washington's strategic option to ally with China under the ongoing ontological security circumstances.

A few simulations show three patterns (see table 9.1). The simulations calculate different combinations of the degree of Washington's military advantage over Beijing and the values of the three coefficients. The first pattern is that the less advantaged Washington's military is over Beijing, the less likely it becomes that armed unification will occur.[73] This is primarily because Washington's military dominance does not threaten Beijing's ontological security but affects the felt readiness of Taipei to declare official independence. The second pattern is the irrelevance of Washington's anti-Chinese tendency in determining the probability of armed unification. This is due to the same reason: Washington's military advantage is not critical. Beijing can respond to Washington's anti-Chinese measures and narratives with anti-US measures and narratives without incurring a military demonstration. What may escalate the spiral is Beijing's anti-Taiwan independence and Taipei's anti-unification coefficients. A four-dimensioned diagram combining three coefficients and the military assessment into a continuum indicates the same patterns. In figure 9.3, the greater anti-independence and anti-unification coefficients both contribute to a higher possibility of initiating armed unification. On the contrary, Washington's military advantage or anti-China coefficient does not reduce the possibility. However, a higher anti-China coefficient, combined with Washington's greater military advantage, increases the possibility of resorting to armed unification.

The pair of anti-independence and anti-unification coefficients is universally salient. Although current affairs are not our focus here, several examples may demonstrate what relational deterrence means in practice. One way to escalate Beijing's relational deterrence might be the diplomatic battle of derecognizing Taiwan.[74] Deterrence can also

Table 9.1. Selected Simulated Results for Three-Party Relational Deterrence

Case	Coefficients				Probability of armed reunification (p_b)
	j	*k*	*l*	*m**	
1	0.25	0.50	0.75	0.25	0.09
2	0.25	0.75	0.50	0.25	0.12
3	0.50	0.25	0.75	0.25	0.09
4	0.50	0.75	0.25	0.25	0.21
5	0.75	0.25	0.50	0.25	0.12
6	0.75	0.50	0.25	0.25	0.21
7	0.25	0.50	0.75	0.50	0.08
8	0.25	0.75	0.50	0.50	0.11
9	0.50	0.25	0.75	0.50	0.08
10	0.50	0.75	0.25	0.50	0.20
11	0.75	0.25	0.50	0.50	0.11
12	0.75	0.50	0.25	0.50	0.20
13	0.25	0.50	0.75	0.75	0.07
14	0.25	0.75	0.50	0.75	0.10
15	0.50	0.25	0.75	0.75	0.07
16	0.50	0.75	0.25	0.75	0.19
17	0.75	0.25	0.50	0.75	0.10
18	0.75	0.50	0.25	0.75	0.19
19	0.25	0.50	0.75	1.00	0.06
20	0.25	0.75	0.50	1.00	0.09
21	0.50	0.25	0.75	1.00	0.06
22	0.50	0.75	0.25	1.00	0.19
23	0.75	0.25	0.50	1.00	0.09
24	0.75	0.50	0.25	1.00	0.19

j: anti-independence coefficient; *k*: pro-independence coefficient; *l*: anti-revisionism determination coefficient; *m*: military capability; *b*: Beijing. *: ratio of Chinese versus US military strength. Created by the author and Jason Luo.

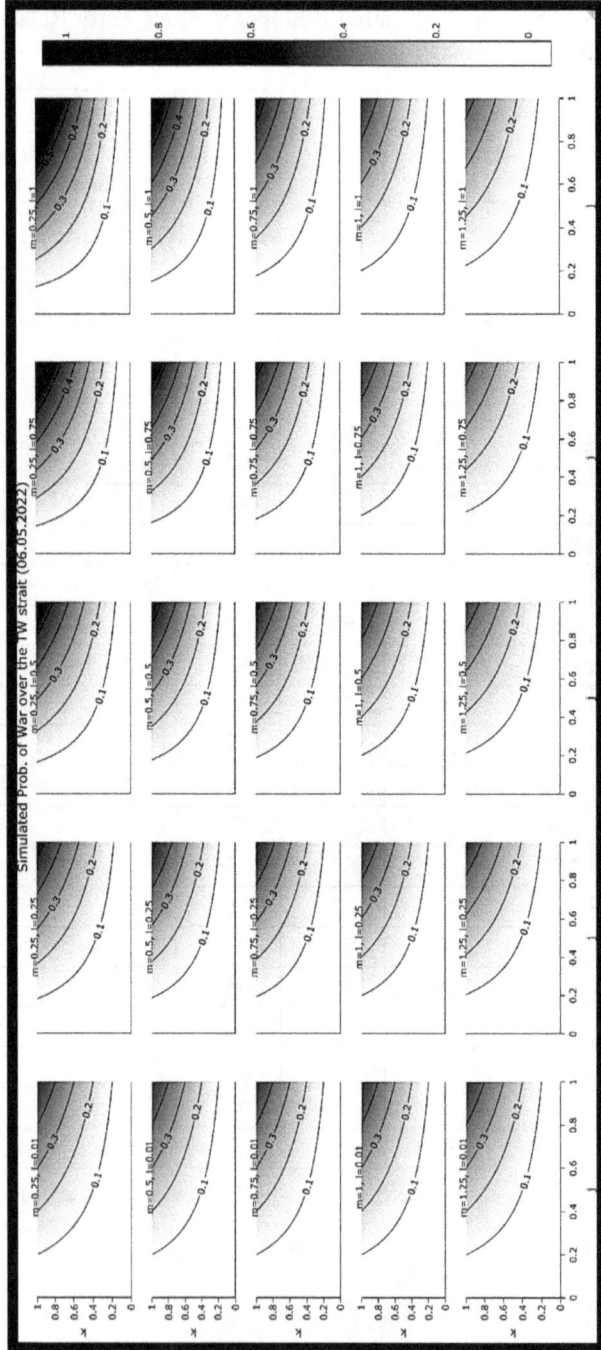

Figure 9.3. A visual representation of the simulated results for three-party relational deterrence, as described in table 9.1. *j*: anti-independence coefficient; *k*: pro-independence coefficient; *l*: anti-revisionism determination coefficient; *m*: military capability. Created by the author.

be indirect, by cyclically granting and withdrawing economic privileges to Taiwan's vulnerable economy,[75] thereby dampening colonial modernity's superiority. Economic leverage also works to sabotage Taiwan's diplomatic recognition.[76] Most noticeable is military demonstration,[77] including exercises in the East China Sea, flights cutting across Taiwan's aviation zone, or simply a mock blockade. Military exercise or demonstration escalation hinges on two relational threats to China's ontological security. One is Washington's display of support for Taiwan's autonomy in the form of diplomatic honoring, military training, and the arranging of a quasi-alliance. The other is Taipei's articulation of its independence intentions, which is primarily discursive in nature and intended to harm unification's legitimacy and prospects. Legally, Taipei may renounce territorial claims over the Senkaku Islands or South China Sea territory made by the previous Civil War regimes to signal Taiwan's increasing non-Chineseness.[78] Politically, pro-independence governmentality ensures that the majority winners in elections display the political correctness of anti-unification.[79]

In sum, deterrence that is intended to incur fear must be relational in nature; otherwise, it either fails or backfires. Washington's military capability does not deter Beijing from entering a spiral because Beijing wishes to deter Taipei from declaring official independence rather than Washington's threat to Beijing. Beijing does not respond to Washington's military activities elsewhere to the same extent. Even over the South China Sea, the Chinese response has been limited to requests to steer away after verifying and identifying passing US warships, rather than seeking to escalate the situation.[80] Likewise, in terms of ontological security, Washington increasingly understands Beijing's anti-Taiwan-independence stance in the double relations of the neoliberal order and hegemonic stability as China becomes the second-strongest military power in the world. Taipei's ontological security concerns both complicate and simplify the mismatched security dilemma between Washington and Beijing. It nullifies Washington's deterrence, because Taipei turns this into its own relational deterrence toward Beijing, which constitutes an ontological issue for Beijing. The Taipei-Beijing pairing constitutes an ontological security dilemma. Their mutual threat reinforces Beijing's One China stance and Taipei's belonging to (non-Chinese) superior modernity. Finally, an implicit security dilemma exists between Washington and Taipei. The inflexibility of Taipei's ontological position incentivizes Washington to transfer the security dilemma to a vicarious dilemma between Beijing and Taipei. Still, Washington risks entrapment in the ontological security dilemma existing between Taipei and Beijing.

There are two caveats here. If Beijing could transcend its historical victim consciousness and begin to accept the anarchical relations alongside national unification, the three-party security dilemma would either involve a degree of the classic security dilemma or evolve into the two-party Thucydides's Trap, constituting the existential security. The possibility of armed unification would be less contingent upon Taipei's independence than on hegemonic transition. The possibility of military confrontation over Taipei may increase, with both greater powers using Taipei as a vicarious site of hegemonic competition. The other caveat is that the value of the three coefficients may also change over time, according to the domestic politics of the relevant parties. If Taipei's anti-unification tendency fails to remain high, Washington's commitment to Taiwan's security will not increase the possibility of armed unification. On the other hand, if the anti-revisionist tendency dropped in the US, revisionism would become less of an issue, and the security dilemma would fall back to become a classic anarchical dilemma.

Conclusion

Adding the notion of ontological security enables an analysis of the dilemma that arises, not from the anarchical structure but from the actor's geo-cultural and historical experiences. To that extent, the anarchical structure is simply another ontological security sensibility. Deterrence aims to preempt the disruption of the relational order that constitutes the collective identity of the subscribers to that order. Uncertainty arises from three sources in our cases: the moral hazard of the protector, Washington, to instigate the protectorate, Taipei, to deter Beijing's revisionism; the moral hazard of the protectorate to entrap the protector to deter Beijing's unification; and Beijing's loss of the unification credit that requires actions to rebuild. If Washington's purpose is to deter revisionism, Taipei's moral hazard will alert Washington to reconsider abandoning Taipei. In other words, given that the goal is hegemonic competition, there would be no space for the protector and protectorate to join forces to engage in Taiwan's independence. To what extent Beijing's internal politics, as opposed to the perceived hegemonic competition or the relational threat of Taiwan's independence, will prompt action to rescue unification credit remains to be seen.

Today, the military simulations of the Taiwan Strait war unanimously treat China's internal politics as the sole reason for Beijing to resort to armed unification. Such a game design poses an ontological threat to Beijing because it also insinuates the Chinese side's lack of legitimacy with regard to unification. Instead, Beijing's relational platforms seek to treat the Taiwanese people as benevolently as possible so that Taiwan and China are portrayed as one family rather than sovereign rivals. The dilemma has no solution, as Taipei considers all such privileges an ontological threat. To deter Beijing's further concession, Taipei could discriminate against all of the Chinese people within Taiwan. No military action is involved in these rounds of exchanges. It is a relational battle of de-Sinicization vs. re-Sinicization. The neoliberal order is almost irrelevant, as granting or abolishing rights and privileges is a resource for engaging in the relational battle rather than rights per se. All three parties claim that their purpose is to maintain the status quo. To give them the benefit of the doubt, a tentative solution to the escalating spiral would be to maintain or even symbolically reduce the level of Washington's military dominance over the Taiwan issue. The likelihood of Taipei declaring independence will be stabilized as a result, and so the probability of armed unification occurring will drop in the long run.

10

Building Post-Western Regionalism

Moral Superiority or Post-*Tianxia*?

Introduction

Confucian relationality and role making, usually reified by improvisation, gift giving, patience, hierarchy, and reciprocal selves, have culminated, probably coincidentally, in the "Community of Shared Future for Human-kind" (CSFH) policy platform. Chinese president Hu Jintao initially introduced it in 2012 under the title of the "Community of Common Destiny for Humankind,"[1] which was widely advocated by his successor, Xi Jinping, and written into the preface of the People's Republic of China (PRC) constitution in 2018.[2] The concept is that everyone in the world belongs to a (future) globally connected "big family." Although the CSFH currently seems more like a myth, the Chinese authorities have used every opportunity to appear serious about transforming this myth into a reality. Xi presented the rationale of China's gargantuan infrastructure project, the Belt and Road Initiative (BRI), as being to "connect . . . the Asian, African, and European continents"[3] and further link the so-called global "big family." It has appeared increasingly relevant amid the spread of mutually estranging national sensibilities during the COVID-19 pandemic and the US-China rivalry.

This chapter concerns why and how this method of publicly framing the purpose of Chinese internationalism made sense to Xi and his colleagues. The prevailing international relations (IR) lenses, pre-dominantly the (neo)realist and (neo)liberal ones, have inadequately defined these atypical discourses and practices as either overly idealistic or threatening due to the fear that Beijing is primarily acting out of a revisionist intent to overtake the United States' hegemonic position and reconstitute the identity of "others"[4] in the network of colonialism—first in the formerly colonized Global South, and ultimately in the colonizers' liberal "core"—due to the all-encompassing nature of CSFH and the BRI. However, such views are self-centered and narrow because they effectively impose upon Chinese actors a worldview that is no different from colonizer states' own past.[5]

A quotation from the *Economist* can serve as an early representative example of such a mentality: the "ultimate aim [of the BRI] is to make Eurasia (dominated by China) an economic and trading area to rival the transatlantic one (dominated by America)."[6] This quotation enlists two competing "regions"—Eurasia versus the transatlantic one—apparently to essentialize the differences between them—China-dominated versus US-dominated, "them" versus "us," and even "enemy" versus "friend"[7]—and therefore not only reconstitutes the monotonous Cold War schema of the world but also entirely silences and thus negates the reification of the alternative provided by the practice of a de-territorialized China-in-the-world, that is, the idea of a globally connected "big family."

Chapter 8 traced the realignment of Confucianism and socialism following the Cultural Revolution. The same process had engulfed Xi far earlier. Xi had survived a peasant life during the Cultural Revolution with two hard-learned lessons:[8] (1) the individual, like himself, is vulnerable to politics; (2) the "mass line" (i.e., learning from and taking care of the interests of the people) is the key to political security. Therefore, the higher the level of his political participation, the deeper and broader the need for the masses to follow him. History and culture enable him to inspire and protect the grandeur of the masses and feel himself intimately related to the masses whereby socialism and Confucianism join forces, with the former attending to the welfare of the masses and the latter to the role integrity of the cadres to adhere to the mass line. His favorite brand of "the Great Rejuvenation of the Chinese Nation," which discursively unites his citizens, reflects the two early lessons combined. Once on the world stage, an international mass line creates a natural course of action to enable the PRC to survive the estranging power politics.

Xi's repetitive references to Confucian values since assuming the presidency give a clue regarding the lens through which he views CSFH and the BRI.[9] At this stage of the book, such a lens may feel familiar already, given its improvisational role in casting Xi's quest for relational security on behalf of, and through, China. Still, Confucianism is intellectually challenging due to its particular take on the quest for modernity, originally introduced to the world by European colonialism. Consequently, a picture of post-Western and post-Chinese regionalism emerges that characterizes CSFH and the BRI as an alignment of intellectual rather than territorial regions where the borders are, at best, undetermined. The trans-border sensibilities can contribute to the discussion of post-Western IR theory in general and the Chinese school of IR in particular, both of which still register territorializing temptations.

This chapter introduces Beijing's developmental model of "directed improvisation" and illustrates this model's strong connection to Confucian thought. The domestic experiences with this "China model" provide a clue about how the BRI proceeds. The chapter then retrieves from the first section of the book the worldview of *tianxia* (all-under-heaven), which undergirds the idea of CSFH. The CSFH discourse legitimizes the BRI, while the BRI is becoming the reification of the CSFH. The inclusive and potentially ever-expanding BRI under Beijing's presumedly (or self-romanticizing) impartial, virtuous leadership constitutes a territorially unfixed form of post-Western regionalism. Once informed by *tianxia*, such regionalism attains the idealistic momentum to expand through multiple exceptional arrangements (see chapter 7), to the effect that no one can be legitimately excluded.

Relations through "Directed Improvisation"

As discussed in chapters 1 and 7, in a Confucian "just" world, the supreme morality is constituted by the ruler's selflessness and ability to practice self-restraint, embodied by their reign without governing (also, nonintervention in the natural flow of things). This makes the ruler's citizens (the "small people" who mainly attend to security-related rather than ethical matters) feel secure and view them as an impartial leader.[10] Therefore, morality constitutes power, rather than vice versa.[11] Moreover, the imagined audience of Confucian morality is not just the nation-state of China. All citizens, in the Confucian state of nature, are bound to be related through metaphorical kinship relationships. The kindred metaphor is, typically, dyadic and hierarchical in nature. Each relationship has attached to it a role obligation to reciprocate benevolence according to the role relationship.[12] The rights and obligations attached to each role ensured that "in this Confucian doctrine there was, therefore, no possibility of naked exploitation,"[13] since this would ruin one's humanity embedded in the role relationship and justify the slaying of them by anyone.

The cosmologically inspired value and institutions from Confucianism thus find no fit in the modern thinking on governance. The consensus among Western policymakers, academics, and international institutions like the World Bank and International Monetary Fund has long been that markets can only grow if one first "gets the governance right" (meaning the implementation of neoliberal governance).[14] The reason for this rests upon the identity of a community of practice that distinguishes an insider-self from an outsider-*alter*: "All prosperous economies share a common set of strong, law-bound governmental institutions."[15] Hence, when "developing" a country, actors who take these ideas for granted first seek to replicate this model of strong institutions and "best practices found in wealthy democracies"[16]—that is, the implementation of a free market, democracy, the rule of law, respect for human rights, social solidarity, antidiscrimination, sustainable development, and good governance—and hope that this will naturally lead to the growth that exists in their own countries, too. In other words, they seek to convert developing nations ("Others") into entities that are like the "self." Unfortunately, such thinking fails to appreciate the social and political cleavages caused by the prior ethnic, religious, productive, and colonial relations that the former colonialism imposed and left behind.[17] In other words, the postcolonial complication at each particular site is to establish regime legitimacy that can never be justified from the former colonizer states' point of view due to these colonially crafted cleavages.

In comparison, according to Yuen Yuen Ang, the successful model that the Beijing authorities implemented to raise 800 million people out of poverty is different. The Chinese authorities rely on "directed improvisation," which means that "central reformers direct," whereas "local state agents improvise."[18] The center does not direct by providing fixed guidelines from which the localities cannot deviate. Instead, the center offers three types of relatively vague guidelines within which the actors at their sites can improvise using the resources they possess within their context. This room for "adaptation" or "experimentation" can be summarized as three steps: (1) "authorizing yet delimiting the boundaries of localization (variation)," (2) "clearly defining and rewarding bureaucratic success (selection)," and (3) "encouraging mutual exchanges between highly unequal regions (niche creation)."[19]

What ensues is a "coevolutionary process" between institutions and markets that provides mutual feedback to each and can be summarized in three steps: "Harness weak institutions to build markets → emerging markets stimulate strong institutions → strong institutions preserve markets."[20] Note that these cycles are not premised upon a prior or staging design.

The process that Ang describes is in line with a Confucian perspective. As such, neither the center nor the locality can have a particular agenda to prioritize, as an actor usually would. Still, all are relationally pressured to craft a proper self-role that fits the mandate of reform, although self-interests are not excluded and can be necessary to incentivize the prioritizing of the collective interests. Self-interests are nevertheless collective, albeit at the local level, and only legitimate to accrue once the collective interest of the higher level has been satisfied. In this model, the center provides the guidelines. Since the center is selfless, the guidelines are deliberately noninterventionist, unspecific, and at times exploratory (e.g., as vague as economic development, social stability, or gender equality and as specific as enhancing the literacy rate or forest cover).

At a level lower in the hierarchy, a person must rely on their own interpretation to derive the subsequent actions (variation). There are no fixed rules about how to achieve them. Also, from the prosperous regions, who act like ethically Confucian good friends (see chapter 6), other regions would be obliged to learn something, a process that attests to the idea of *tianxia*; the center decides (selects) which ones should be used and tries to improve order by connecting the advantages and success stories of different regions (niche creation). Note that the duty of the political center is understood as ensuring the promotion of the national interest at the lower levels. On the one hand, the local variation ensures that no monopoly of the national interest by the center is likely, conceptually or institutionally. On the other hand, all local agents form a national platform from which no local agent can escape. The center fulfills the selfless virtue, while the local agents both contribute to the national interest and protect the local interest.

The individual level is also essential. For example, reform unfolds more easily in those places where a prior relationship between the local and the central elite is strong.[21] On the other front, rent seeking has been rampant in actuality. Officials at different levels have not been selfless. In terms of embezzlement, fake statistics, kickbacks, insider trading, monopolies, and so on, creative gift giving between individuals for personal or collective gain undermines the selfless gift giving (e.g., exemptions, privileges, and subsidies) by the center to the locality and by the locality to the population. One of the most hotly debated topics during the 1990s was whether or not bribery was more conducive or destructive to reform. It was conducive because it familiarized local reformers with the material incentives necessary for reform in a broader scope and at a later stage but destructive of the selfless role-play required for credible leadership of the party in the long run.[22]

Making endless judgments on the proper relationships in the public and the private spheres deconstructs the plausibility of clear boundaries between the center and the locality, the party and the state, the state and society or business, or the cadre and the population. Universal rules hardly apply. Intersubjectivity is necessarily per se a practical combination of selfless, mundane considerations. Such a relational lens has important implications for understanding the BRI and reform anywhere.

The Confucian Attitude

Mencius's classic advice underscores why and how improvisational developmentalism differs fundamentally from rule-based qua "Western" developmentalism. According to him, leaders do not specify how people learn rules and norms. Rather, they should ensure that people have enough to eat first and improve their living conditions so that they may support their nuclear family sufficiently. Provided that this has been achieved, people will spontaneously care about their social roles and learn morally and intellectually proper behavior accordingly.[23] Thus, in Beijing's relating of countries along the BRI, the long-term view, rather than the rapid development of the underdeveloped population, would point to an ultimate capacity for creating reciprocally benevolent roles between actors and populations under different regimes. Underdevelopment jeopardizes the relational security of all because people are incapable of tending to their relational needs and learning their role obligations. Their self-identities and understanding of the world would be reduced to biological needs, which is detrimental to relationship building and the fulfillment of harmonious order. The claim of "best practices found in major democracies" is neither developmental nor relational in nature.

From a Confucian perspective, self-restrained, selfless leadership ought not to speak to populations of a specific scope but to all. China as a national category would otherwise be reduced to self-centrism and jeopardize its very existence by becoming a definable target. If the rise of China has become a popular image, the only sensible approach to ensuring its survival, from the Confucian perspective, is to improvise gift giving everywhere, including in distant lands,[24] so that China can constitute and be constituted by all identities. It is hoped that China will become a relational method or a system of relations where supreme morality belongs to the most selfless. Confucius stated, "To be poor without feeling resentful is difficult; to be rich without feeling arrogant is easy."[25] Therefore, "exemplary persons help out the needy; they do not make the rich richer."[26]

Chinese people who work in Africa or Europe should be perceived in such a light.[27] On the one hand, it is essential to help the needy because poverty encourages negative emotions, whereas prosperity makes it easier to act in a morally upright manner. For those who adopt reciprocal roles who are backed by good living, their relations with Beijing would resemble a greater self. This refers to the mutual constitution of relational selves, ultimately meaning the physical safety of all. On the other hand, it is likewise essential for a self-perceived victimized China to mingle with, and become intrinsic to, a historically imperialist Europe in ways that testify to the overcoming of such a shameful past of a distinctive *alter* China. The rich will not make a distinctive target to be blamed for the poverty of the poor. This is the embryo of the de-territorialized notion of post-Western regionalism.

Therefore, the BRI represents a metaphor of gift giving[28] or exemplifies Beijing's "vague" developmental model of "directed improvisation" to the rest of the world. This places the BRI in the nascent process of becoming a center of Beijing's self-realization. However, its recognized rise is a mixed blessing. It constitutes, on the one hand, a lauded recognition by the world that compensates for the historically felt shame and, on the other, an alarming acquisition of a reputation for constituting a threat to international order. The danger is particularly acute since the territorial disputes between the PRC and its neighbors reproduce self/other binaries, to the detriment of its relational and moral quest. This reduces the PRC to a metaphorical local actor, prioritizing its own interest over the metaphorical national interest. The BRI is thus urgently needed and vital because togetherness with the BRI nations may lift the PRC from its maritime self-centrism and evolve into the classic notion of *tianxia*[29] (see also chapter 2). The National Development and Reform Commission (NDRC) of the PRC provides that its goal is "connecting the Asian, African, and European continents"; "opening-up"; and "integrating" China and the BRI region.[30] The "Silk Road Spirit" presumably encompasses "peace and cooperation, openness and inclusiveness, mutual learning and mutual benefit," representing "a *common aspiration of all countries* along their routes."[31]

The NDRC narrative renders the logic of power almost irrelevant, if not completely illegitimate. The vagueness and level of abstraction make no ready plan or mechanism of control, as realist analysts would have their readers believe. Granted, the identity of China is self-positioned in a kernel, and the actual benefit that the PRC is to accrue is likewise vague until actual negotiations begin at a particular site. Even what constitutes China may prove more complicated than previously thought. Different Chinese local authorities must improvise ways of connecting neighbors and faraway countries alike through the BRI.[32] Such a decentralizing approach renders China an evasive category in practice. Neither her control nor her influences, if any, are centralized. The security of this nascent high position relies on the recognition embodied in each of those negotiations that bring resources to the sites. Without a blueprint for transforming the local conditions or controlling the local resources, the BRI fails realism badly.

No clear method can be found in any official document through which the NDRC goals might be achieved. Hence, there is plenty of space for local adaptation. Note that the simple practices and processes that exhibit Beijing's unprecedented initiative and goodwill at the international level are accompanied by widespread bribery at the national level. Moreover, an extreme rhetorical statement, that the BRI is a "*common aspiration of all countries* along their routes," is a relatively large assumption. From a Confucian perspective, however, a statement such as this constitutes superior moral examples posed by the PRC. In short, the current plan is only the first stage of a developmental process; experimentation will follow along with the local conditions. While lacking clear rules for all to abide by attests to a problematic casualty, from the perspective of Confucian theory, only an attempt to substantiate the processual monopoly by the purportedly ritual center can destroy the improvisational prosperity; the local actors cannot.[33]

However, apologism is insufficiently convincing to external watchers of the BRI. Analyses regarding how China merely needs outlets for its surplus construction materials; squeezes its competitors, such as India, in its expanded sphere of influence undergirded by the BRI projects; and inspires a hegemonic kind of eastern Marshall Plan are becoming increasingly widespread.[34] On the contrary, Xi can convince his Chinese audience. Abundant and award-winning publications in China that aim to promote the selfless image of the BRI indicate how Xi's logic resonates well with the Chinese cultural logic.[35] Given the financial capacity and ambitious conception of the BRI, its host's actual and ulterior purposes in Beijing can only suffer contending views that make sense primarily to the narrators, each embedded in their relational world. No participants need to engage in any "conversion" of themselves into a correct Chinese entity. Rather, joining the BRI indicates mutual acceptance and guarantees exemption from any pressure to conform.

A "Community of Shared Future for Humankind" as Post-Western Regionalism

The notion of *tianxia* has, arguably, defined "Chinese" worldviews over the last three thousand years or so.[36] Due to the failure of the Qing dynasty (1644 to 1912) to fend off imperialist nations, the concept of *tianxia* largely lost its legitimacy.[37] *Tianxia* was discarded in favor of imported Western modernity and its associated concepts of the nation-state and national sovereignty, mainly due to the need to invent and secure a discernable scope of Chinese territory from foreign imperialists. However, with the Chinese nation-state and most of its sovereign territory "secured" after 1949, the need emerged to explain *how* Beijing views the world. This was presumably because of the practical and psychological finding that imported Western theories in various fields—economic, developmental, and international relations—failed to provide the frameworks to explain Chinese contexts and practices or solve local Chinese problems.[38]

The concept of *tianxia*, famously reintroduced into the picture by Zhao Tingyang, refers to the ancient Chinese world order, in which China was the "Middle Kingdom" or "the center of the (known) world" (for its supporters).[39] It is more a symbol of oneness than a piece of land. At the end of the Qing dynasty, Chinese scholars began translating the Western concept of "the world" as *shijie* rather than *tianxia*:[40] "The word *shijie*, formed from *shi* (generation or "this life") and *jie* (a circle or boundary),

[. . .] described the modern world in which the Chinese world ceased to be the central place of *tianxia*."[41] Instead, the "West" became the new (exemplary) center, and China moved to the periphery.[42] However, it is possible that, with the control of contemporary territorial China enabling the rise of legitimacy and power in the world, its leaders and academics will reimagine the PRC as a symbol of oneness that is acceptable to all again, hence (re)making China the center of *tianxia*.[43]

Originally, *tianxia* was given meanings in the diverse activities of those who ventured, intellectually and politically, to make sense of an "*asymmetrical relationship* between earth and heaven."[44] On the one hand, this relationship was asymmetrical because of the clear fact that "the earth is smaller than heaven."[45] On the other hand, however, "in relation to *tianxia* as a polity, this asymmetrical relationship specifically referred to the gap between the *realistic geography* of the territorial coverage of *tianxia* as an actual political system and the *imaginary cosmography* in which *tianxia* was situated. The former is limited, whereas the latter is infinite. *Tianxia*, in other words, was a *world-scape*, built into the larger cosmology that covered earth, heaven, and everything-in-between."[46] Such a distinction between the *realistic geography* of *tianxia* and an *imaginary cosmography* corresponds to Wang Gungwu's distinction between "reality" and "myth."[47] Over the course of Chinese history, the size of the realistic geography of *tianxia* shifted, whereas the imaginary cosmography remained the same. *Tianxia*, as a myth, is an inexpressible system in which all are bound to be related and spontaneously hierarchical.[48] The function of mundane politics is to improvise how to relate in context properly. In practice, all improvised hierarchies can be disputed, however. Recording and assessing the various ways in which *tianxia* was ruled was the primary function of classical Chinese historiography.

This line of historiography highlights how the course of Chinese history is cyclical in nature rather than teleological.[49] Such historiography is keen on the tension between material power (*wei*), as emphasized by legalism, and virtuous humane rule (*de*), as propagated by Confucianism.[50] However, Confucian historians conclude that, in practice, one could not live without the other. Following the successful unification of the Middle Kingdom under the Sui and Tang emperors, an unprecedented consensus emerged among Confucian scholars that "good government manifested itself through the concept of *te* [*de*] (virtue, *vertu*, power)."[51] Moreover, "it was the presence of this *te* [*de*] that persuaded people within and outside the empire to offer submission and accept the leadership of the Son of

Heaven."⁵² Consequently, the strategies of the Tang and Song dynasties became to use *de*, or virtuous leadership, to "persuade the world to submit to Chinese moral superiority."⁵³ However, the Mongols who established the Yuan dynasty (emphasizing the significance of *wei*) overthrew the Song dynasty. The Yuan, in turn, focused mainly on *wei* and ignored *de*. The classical wisdom suggests that, when a dynasty focused too much on *de* and ignored *wei* (such as during the Song dynasty), the dynasty would fall and vice versa, as shown above in the cases of the Qin and Yuan. It thus became logical for Chinese dynasties to seek to create a balance between *de* and *wei* (i.e., individual rulers' virtue in benevolent and hegemonic *tianxia*, respectively, as described in chapter 1). In other words, "the Mongols had reminded the subsequent dynasties [particularly the Han dynasty] of what had been the winning combination in the past, a hard core of *wei* surrounded by a soft pulp of *te*."⁵⁴ In fact, this is something that the Chinese elite reiterated after facing Western and Japanese imperialism in the nineteenth and twentieth centuries.⁵⁵ "Good government manifested itself through the concept of *te* [*de*]"; however, it was not enough to survive. When faced with foreign invaders, material "power" (*wei*) was necessary to defend the Middle Kingdom or vassal states with which it had relationships or punish those who deviated from maintaining harmony within this "familial" system.⁵⁶

Given both the materialist approach during the crisis and the abovementioned tendency to be inclusive and indifferent toward regime type or institutional values, not only could *tianxia* accommodate Marxism, but it could also enable an intellectual twist that reimagines China on the rise in the twenty-first century into a system of *tianxia*. In a nutshell, all are bound to be related, except that they must prepare proper gifts each time according to the context and status of the other party to improvise, oblige, and reproduce mutual role obligations. The other party certainly includes those considered morally higher than China to receive gifts, reflecting China's submissive respect. In such a way, these discourses transcend the boundaries of "inside" and "outside," the "self" and "other," since, by existing, all already belong to *tianxia*. The obvious caveat is that China is simultaneously susceptible to sovereignty and *tianxia*. Given that sovereignty was the role first contrived in the twentieth century for China to oppose imperialism, it defines a proper contemporary relation of *tianxia*. In the twenty-first century, sovereignty is insufficient to guide the dramatically expansive influences of the Chinese people. Different role relations are demanded. Role conflicts emerge between lingering sovereign sensibilities and renegotiation for different role relations.

Nevertheless, the skeleton of a post-Western regionalism framework can be constructed from the above. First of all, while the PRC-as-nation triumphs primarily through economic development, China-as-*tianxia* obliges Beijing to aim at selfless leadership and seek to "help out the needy," as if they share sensibilities of regionalism. Such regionalism can be substantiated by "connectivity," through which localities can enrich themselves and provide one another's "basic means of existence."[57] Second, China-as-*tianxia* is inevitably inclusive. "The Belt and Road Initiative is an economic cooperation initiative, not a geopolitical or military alliance,"[58] Xi commented during the fifth-anniversary celebrations for the BRI. "It is an open and inclusive process and not about creating exclusive circles or a China club." In other words, this regionalism dispenses with a definitive scope but corresponds to the traditional idea of "show nothing left outside" so that "all rulers of foreign lands could benefit."[59] However, under regionalism without borders, the distribution of benevolence is inevitably contextual and judgmental, so some of the more strategically relevant localities (i.e., a hub of potentially extensive new relations or an extant intimate relationship to be rescued) did receive more attention from strategic competitors, and better-related neighbors (Cambodia or Brunei, for instance), much less.[60]

Although not without romanticism, the BRI and CSFH are the material and discursive instruments for Beijing to relate to the rest of the world. They assert a romantic form of regionalism—no borders, no general rules, yet mutually beneficial (i.e., win-win). To establish the PRC as a credible competitive center in *tianxia*, Beijing must yield where the targets of relating show reluctance or regret (e.g., once in Pakistan or Malaysia) and remain patient where disinterests prevail for the time being. Selling the idea and project of the BRI too hard would appear self-centered. Rigidity in enforcing payment schedules indicates a lack of self-restraint. Fluid and expansive regionalism, once aggressively pushed, would undermine the virtue of selflessness under these circumstances. In this light, European countries, for instance, can only become partners of BRI regionalism when they are ready. From a Confucian perspective, they are bound to be related, albeit in different ways at the time.

Below is an example of how a Chinese actor tries to convince the European Union of the win-win benefits of the BRI. Six reasons follow for why the EU should support the BRI, according to Professor Song Xinning:[61]

1. The BRI provides economic opportunities for both China and the EU along the BRI: China provides low- to middle-end technology, and the EU provides high-end technology.

2. The BRI facilitates trade increase between China and the EU, allowing the EU to strengthen the cohesion and legitimacy of the EU and thus lead to the further unification of a "destined community."

3. BRI shifts the "civilizational structure" from a "US—Atlantic—Western EU single core" to a "China—Eurasia hinterland—Western EU double core." Within the latter, Europe's status in the world will be even higher than in the former.

4. The BRI passes through many poor countries (those that have below sixty percent of the global average GDP). The economic development of these countries will limit the pressure from immigrant streams for Europe and the spread of radical Islam over the globe.

5. The BRI represents a new phase of globalization that the EU hopes will eradicate right-wing populism in the US and Europe.

6. The success of the BRI will put pressure on the existing multilateral institution to compete, thereby improving its operation and giving the world new motivation to develop.

The above six points all illustrate how this particular agent imagines the PRC as standing in the shoes of the EU (i.e., thinking from the perspective of the "Other" and hence exhibiting "selfless" behavior). This is done to establish the relationality between the two actors. Numbers 1 and 4 have BRI regionalism offering resources to cope with the problems in Europe. Numbers 3, 5, and 6 present BRI regionalism as an alternative model that Europe can appreciate. Number 2 seeks to relate to the EU through establishing kinship ties. Adherence to such a tie would impose a moral obligation on Europe to act according to the relational rituals to keep the CSFH intact. Note that chapter 1 cites Richard Neustadt—the key is not the belief in Confucianism but persuasion in the interests of the other party.[62]

This makes CSFH a form of post-Western regionalism. It is similar to "Western" regionalism because it pragmatically seeks to connect localities through "modern" means yet transcends Western regionalism, as one is not compelled to convert one's own identity in terms of value and institution in order to join the BRI. On the contrary, one merely needs to (or sincerely pretend to) acknowledge through ritual China qua *tianxia*, in return for which China qua the relational self will ensure the "autonomy" of a locality and confer benefits upon it (mainly through gift giving). Moreover, this post-Western regionalism also calls upon both parties to a bilateral relationship to avoid harming each other's core interests. Finally, there is the spirit of directed improvisation, as regions emerge and evolve only where encounters prove successful. These are where Chinese diplomats and businesspeople can strike deals with the hosting regimes, each with their differing relations, to constitute the mandate of CSFH. Thus, BRI regionalism that abides by no permanent or universal rules can come and go in cycles at any particular site.

In light of the above, a statist scheme to connect China to Central and Eastern European countries (CEEC) through the 16+1 framework and bilateral agreements with Greece, Italy, and Spain can be considered relational gift giving to keep Europe viable in its network, something that the EU itself does not have the will or funding to undertake, particularly after the 2008 economic crisis. An alternative perspective could be to see 16+1 as an effort to reconnect and develop the former communist and socialist countries, showing that *tianxia*'s selfless character is absent in the former Soviet Union. The BRI can also be seen as "shaming" self-centered performances, past as well as present—those of the US (for relinquishing its role as the leader of globalization), the EU leadership in Brussels (for failing to develop its eastern and southern countries), and the former Soviet Union (for its disintegration). Otherwise, these strategies could also be a way of shaming the former colonizers and imperialist nations. After all, the PRC elite now initiating the BRI carries bifurcating messages: either a China that is successfully on top, having emerged from a "century of humiliation," leaving the Allied forces lagging in moral leadership, or another China that is ready to evaporate into formless *tianxia*. That said, the soft power of the BRI members is to withdraw from the initiative to ruin China's credibility as a role player. In fact, Lithuania, Latvia, and Estonia already did, reducing 16+1 to 14+1, after the joining of Greece.

China as *tianxia* needs no definite or fixed agents who come and go depending on the reception of their selfless performance. The PRC as a nation faces serious challenges, however. First and foremost is the communication issue. What happens when such "vague guidelines" (such as those provided by the BRI "Visions and Actions" plan) are provided over national boundaries and cultural contexts in which the actors are unprepared to conceive reciprocal benevolence as a role obligation? Consider the "Western" media, where vagueness leads to severe suspicion. Why should BRI watchers trust Chinese diplomats or investors and their usually authoritarian local allies? Granted that conversion may not be an option for the Chinese authorities anywhere or at any level, the arrangements that either reinforce or revise the idiosyncratic conditions at each site inevitably lead to a charge of new imperialism or colonialism.

Second is the issue that "the world" is accustomed to the situation of theoretically "equal" nation-states. How can *tianxia* ever successfully convince countries that are unaware of its inevitability and alert the world to the moral superiority conveyed by the enactment of self-restraint? Moreover, would not a respected PRC, welcomed by allegedly failing regimes, disrupt the rules and liberalism that undergird the current global order? Ironically, the way to protect the local autonomy from intervention is for Beijing to ensure the capacity of a regime to fulfill its role obligation that reconstitutes its relational self-identity. Such an irony testifies to the conviction that *tianxia* is embedded in the oneness of varieties—all being mutually accepted because all are attracted to a selfless China now as a cosmology rather than a territory. This is how, as the contemporary thinker Zhao Tingyang argues, sovereignty and *tianxia* contribute to each other, but also why this is alarming to critics who regard *tianxia* as no more than a vastly expanded Chinese sovereignty.

Third, the proposal of the BRI and CSFH connotes resistance to (past) Western developmentalism for its problems, mainly initiated by the US and the EU, but also Russia and Japan for their failure to maintain a region (the Soviet Union and Greater East Asia Co-Prosperity Sphere). An all-encompassing claim of China as *tianxia*, which is discursively confused with the PRC as a national agent of *tianxia*, immediately invites suspicion of revisionism, not to mention the lingering territorial disputes between Beijing and its neighbors that plague their relationships. While neither Washington, Tokyo, nor Moscow have officially "joined" the BRI, Tokyo and Moscow prefer to "cooperate" with the

PRC by aligning the BRI with their own developmental projects.[63] For Washington, the reason seems to be more that it is stuck in its "bifocal" neorealist-neoliberal lens.[64]

In short, what is hidden in the name of the BRI is a type of post-Western regionalism facing considerable challenges and legitimacy issues both inside and outside the territorial PRC. This is a communicative issue of understanding. Moreover, in the current global system of theoretically equal nation-states, one country's ritual (i.e., moral) superiority is hard to accept. However, the agents of *tianxia* can adapt to the local situations. Unless the material strength is insufficient, the drive to remain related through gift giving may continue to rise among increasing numbers of subscribers to *tianxia*. The PRC, as a nation, may fare badly in the world due to its intense, competitive self-centrism; China as *tianxia*, without such a label, will continue to inspire people elsewhere.

Conclusion

This chapter has constructed a rough framework of post-Western regionalism based on the "Chinese" practice of directed improvisation in the shape of developmental experiences and philosophy. The BRI should be perceived as a developmental project through which the Chinese authorities seek ex post facto to bridge the gap between the "myth" of a CSFH and the gradually developing, increasingly connected (open-ended) and inclusive BRI "reality." The primary motivation of the Beijing leadership for doing so is the desire to strive and be acknowledged and accepted by others for its "moral superiority," albeit implicitly, due to its "selflessness" and "inclusiveness," particularly when contrasted with former Western attempts at developmentalism, thus enhancing its legitimacy. Moreover, a system of ultimate, permanent security, peace, and harmony, which will presumably ensue upon the yielding of a bordered China to a constant process of practicing oneness, informs a romanticized motivation. By doing so, this book not only further "provincializes" Euro- and West-centric IR theories, such as neorealism and neoliberalism, but also contributes to the research on non- and post-Western IR theories and globalizing IR.

At the same time, however, due to historical experiences of facing foreign invaders (Mongols, Manchus, Western imperialists, the Japanese, etc.), the elite is also acutely aware of the importance of material power (*wei*) to back up its moral power (*de*), as well as the sovereign institution that affirms dignity and equality. The need for defense against future invaders underscores the necessity for the Chinese leaders to make the BRI profitable and strategic. This highlights the main *problematique* of this state-centric post-Western regionalism: it has not yet escaped the binaries of Western IR theory and regionalism or sovereign statehood. The PRC-as-nation continues to stress the protection of national rather than mutual interests, despite *tianxia*, which constantly references relationality as the ultimate base for survival. Consequently, the rising national China humiliates her neighbors while the *tianxia* China placates them. In such a light, the BRI might symbolize, for China, a sort of pluriversal *tianxia* or even post-*tianxia*—consisting of fast-changing or pluralistic moral centers in different regions and with different policy agendas. In the spirit of *tianxia*, the balance of gift giving, such as investments in economic corridors by different national groups with overlapping memberships, substitutes for the balance of power, along with actors practicing gift giving each of their own style.

11

Experimenting with Twin Sovereignty

Implications for the Security Community

Introduction

The discussion in this chapter follows the theoretical chapters, especially chapters 9 and 10, with a whimsical proposal to move beyond the ontological security dilemmas and the obsession with the quest for security community, which have become increasingly apparent in the 2020s. Indeed, two simultaneous topics have become increasingly popular among East Asian security watchers since the situation between Russia and Ukraine began to ignite in March 2022. One is when and how the People's Liberation Army will follow suit by launching a unification war against Taiwan, which might confront and end the US dominance in East Asia.[1] This stream of discussion fills the think tank reports in the Anglosphere. The other is how the White House can allegedly instigate Taipei to enter into an independence war with Beijing to trap China.[2] Presumably Beijing would become the West's (or NATO's, liberal circles', or former colonizer states') enemy, as the war in Ukraine has made Moscow.[3] The second stream has attracted the attention of a huge number of Chinese bloggers. On these topics, Taipei's adamant pro-US and anti-China position ostensibly lacks relevance.[4] After all, Taipei renounces authentic choices, for it sets aside plausible alternatives of bandwagoning Beijing, hedging between Washington, DC, and Beijing, or posing as neutral.

Note that Taiwan and Ukraine differ in terms of their culture, history, and geography, indicating that the imagined parallel between them is based upon realist internationalism in terms of small actors' unrelinquished need to take sides during hegemonic competition. Note also the shared assumption of all of the speculations, conspiracy theories, choices, and plausible alternatives—Taiwan is a territorial identity, bounded yet vulnerable, enabling all sides to strategize or weaponize to enforce the claimed order of each.[5]

This shared assumption reveals the ontological security nature of the Taiwan issue.[6] For Taiwan to become officially independent—that is, a sovereign nation—no immediate change in the balance of power is required. However, it would destroy the regime legitimacy of the Chinese Communist Party, which rests upon a national-revival promise to cleanse all imperialist and colonialist legacies from modern Chinese history.[7] This entails unification with Taiwan. Taiwan's independence would also strengthen Washington's hegemonic leadership, in Graham Allison's terms,[8] embedded in its reputation as the protector of liberal democracy and rules of international relations.[9] Therefore, effective hegemonic leadership would rule out unification. Moreover, Taiwan's independence would affirm its proponents' quest for self-respect, undergirded by a sense of civilizational superiority over China.[10] Colonial modernity from Japan and neoliberal partnership with the United States would enhance such self-respect.[11]

Against this background, which promises no way out,[12] this provocative chapter impractically considers a solution, practically a nonsolution (chapter 5) and exception (chapter 7), intended to prompt outside-the-box thinking, that does not take for granted sovereignty as the conceptual basis for devising a settlement. Instead, the solution targets the population's identity rather than the territory, recognizing that the population is readily fluid.[13] Specifically, the solution is for the Taiwanese population to substitute two concurrent passports, one from the People's Republic of China and the other from the US, for its present Taiwan (i.e., Republic of China) passport. The chapter is divided into three parts. The first part reviews how the literature is consistently tied to national sovereignty. The second shows how a twin-passport arrangement would transcend the sovereignty system, reconfigure ontological security, and turn Taiwan into a pluriversal, as opposed to territorial, identity. The third part extends the critiques of the system of sovereignty to the study of (de)securitization and the security community. The conclusion will mention the caveats.

The Sovereignty-Locked Literature

The literature on the hegemonic transition adopts the dominant inter-national relations approach to the Taiwan issue.[14] In this view, China is allegedly a revisionist state that seeks to overtake the US.[15] Two revisionist dimensions denote the hegemonic transition.[16] One is the all-around rising power of China to engage in world affairs and damage US influence. This dimension is geostrategic and manifested in China's omniscient investment in Africa, emerging networking in Latin America, and assertive stance over the South China Sea. The other is the poten-tial of China's authoritarian model of governance to attract followers in the Global South.[17] As noted in chapter 9, given Taiwan's identity as a liberal democracy and China's unification with Taiwan as the last mile of China's quest for independent statehood, the alert to hegemonic transition cannot afford to leave territorial Taiwan's future unattended.

The discussions of the inevitability of the hegemonic war often pick Taiwan as a potential catalyst. If the narrative deems hegemonic war escapable, the narrators' position on Taiwan is usually inarticulate and ambiguous.[18] On the contrary, in the narrative of an inevitable war, Taiwan would serve as strategic leverage.[19] The war in Ukraine even gives some analysts the impression that Taiwan could fight a vicarious war on behalf of the US.[20] The perspective of hegemonic competition thus focuses only on Taiwan as a strategic resource, regardless of the distinctive issue con-texts of the two sites that complicate and qualify their comparison. On the other hand, the Chinese scholarly opinion tends to refute the inevitability theme.[21] Almost no Chinese literature would question the inevitability of unification, as if unification and the continuation of peace between the US and China contain no contradiction. The implication is that any concession in exchange for Washington's consent to unification is negotiable, from the Chinese standpoint. The Chinese literature thus reproduces Taiwan as a fixed boundary. This is the same epistemological foundation as adopted by Washington when strategizing Taiwan in its China policy.

Another related thread of literature attends to American national interests.[22] The debate focuses on Taiwan's importance to Washington's grand strategy. On one side of the debate, Taiwan is insignificant, represent-ing Beijing's vital interest but only a moderate interest for Washington.[23] According to this view, allowing Taiwan's independence to take priority over other of Washington's agendas makes little sense. The narrators in this stream either believe in the renouncement of Taiwan as a US interest or conservatively consider the value of an indefinite medium term of the status quo, in which Taipei does not officially declare independence and Beijing does not push for unification.[24] Alongside this is the suggestion of Finlandization as a possible approach for Taipei to adopt in the face of a menacing Beijing.[25] The unstated logic of these discussions is entirely territorial in nature. Namely, under the circumstance that Washington could not possibly own Taiwan strategically, Washington could only yield Taiwan to Beijing or keep Taiwan from Beijing, at best.

On the other side of the debate, which has increasingly represented the consensual position in the US in the past decade, is the possibility of adopting an all-society approach to cope with the threat of Chinese revisionism. The need to keep the US ahead of China increases the temptation to ally with Taipei more closely. This temptation treats Taipei's remaining autonomous, if not officially independent, from Beijing as a genuine strategic value.[26] This calls for an overall strategy, with the support of the allies, to enhance Taipei's international stance, including participation in international organizations, diplomatic recognition by a minimal number of states, a security guarantee by the US and its allies, and legitimacy in replacing "Chinese Taipei" with "Taiwan" as its official label wherever enforceable.[27]

The Taiwan-studies literature is a third thread in the literature, which is indirect but essential to reproducing sovereign sensibilities. This literature has a long history. Its origin reflected a discursive renovation, seeking to rescue the United States' reputation in the aftermath of the Vietnam War. The renovation proceeded with the cooking up of four tigers—the newly industrialized countries of South Korea, Singapore, Hong Kong, and Taiwan. This was the first time that Taiwan became a legitimate topic, independent from China studies in the academic world.[28] In addition to reducing Vietnam from its victory to a failing state, Taiwan provided ammunition for her neoliberal colleagues to craft a rebuttal of the dependency theory, which blames the underdevelopment in Latin America on world capitalism.[29] Samuel Huntington's publication of The Third Wave,[30] together with Taiwan's political development in the early 1990s, promoted Taiwan as a model of democratization and an exotic trajectory.[31] Internationally, the officially sanctioned research agenda of the strategic triangle boomed in the same decade, to involve numerous Western and Taiwanese scholars in interrogating how Taiwan could fare in US-China-Taiwan relations, thereby further reinforcing Taiwan as a structurally equal identity in the academic discourse.[32]

Since then, through grants provided by the semiofficial Chiang Ching-kuo Foundation, the promotion of Taiwan studies in the West has been Taiwan's national endeavor and has successfully established Taiwan studies as a named discipline in the field of comparative studies.[33] The topics are broad, but the theme and message are consistent and focused throughout. In short, Taiwan is a dynamic place where the local practices testify to the voice, construction, innovation, and ambivalence of the researched targets, the four terms that characterize the Routledge Research on Taiwan Series.[34] Together, they give rise to the varieties, possibilities, and reinventions of Taiwanese subjectivities. Taiwan can hardly be described in a nutshell, except to state that she is anything but Chinese. Such sovereign cultural consciousness is ostensibly not directly territorial. As Cambridge University's Taiwan Studies series webpage states: "This book series presents a nuanced and close-to-the-ground analysis of Taiwan, a critical node in US-China-Japan competition in the Asia-Pacific region. It studies the island's social complexities and transitions from the geopolitical perspective while also focusing closely on its people's lives and cultural vibrancy."[35]

Even so, the resulting impossibility of calling Taiwan Chinese in this nascent literature continues to privilege territorial sovereignty peculiarly—Taiwan in every sense lies outside China's sovereign territory. The studies of Taiwanese businesspeople and students in China are preoccupied with the finding that their identification with Taiwan remains resilient.[36] From the literature's point of view, Taiwan is full of agency for constant changes and differences to emerge, to the extent that Taiwan is not a substantive label in itself while being, at the same time, increasingly un-Chinese. Arguably, the determined quest for un-Chinese subjectivities necessitates the celebration of undecidability. Sovereignty is the discursive equivalent of subjectivities that are informed by undecidability qua un-Chineseness. The political implications are both that China will lose Taiwan as part of its territory and that the US will lose Taiwan if China forces unification.

An Exit from Sovereignty

Sovereignty is particularly unsuitable for the population in Taiwan as a representative institution or identity. To begin with, sovereignty was initially the result of a host of European practices to transcend the City of God during the European wars of religion.[37] It presumably enabled the princes to choose their way of being Christian. Sovereignty did not apply to colonies in the subsequent centuries, until the decolonization after World War II. Although the definition of sovereignty has evolved and changed, according to the practices of Christian nations, becoming sovereign has always been a triumph for non-white communities or non-Christian worlds[38]—in other words, the formerly colonized sites of the Global South. The regimes in Taiwan, by all means, have likewise yearned for sovereign status, regardless of which national identity they claim during their respective terms.

Still, the postcolonial conditions promise former colonies neither equality nor independence.[39] In practice, they turn sovereignty as a domain question into a people's question. Postcolonial nations cannot command the ready loyalty of their populations, for their artificial borders cut across ethnic and religious identities to inflict domestic social and cross-border cleavages that bar either the emergence of civil society or the planning of good governance. The entitlement to sovereign protection is an unattainable assumption. Sovereignty plagued by these cleavages fails to clarify who belongs or whom to exclude from within. In addition, migration between colonies and former colonizer communities further complicates the people's identification,[40] from a fixed population into a trans-population. From the sovereignty perspective, every Taiwanese person can be a suspect for insufficient normativity; a strategic balancer between birthplace and homes in the US, China, Australia, Southeast Asia, and Europe; and a bridge between incongruent sites in the form of an interpreter or buffer.[41]

The quest for sovereignty by the postcolonial Taiwanese regimes reflects, recreates, and reproduces colonially inflicted civilizational cleavages. All sides remain simultaneously embedded in varying degrees of Chinese, American/Western, and Japanese relations. Taiwan's sovereign sensibilities are registered in several contradictions that suffer politicization and push for taking a side regarding which sovereignty to belong to. At least four pairs of them can be identified.

1. Taiwan's independent sovereignty denotes the self-determination of the population for Taiwan's pro-independence regime but self-denial for the Chinese government.

2. It is defensive from the perspective of maintaining the hegemonic order but offensive from the perspective of Chinese nationalism.

3. It is a statement of owning modernity for the people of Taiwan but a security concern from the United States' grand-strategy perspective.

4. It connotes de-sinicizing, as opposed to a return of the colonial legacy, from Taiwan's internal cleavage perspective.

These four pairs of contradictions guarantee the implausibility of any settlement within the epistemological scope of sovereignty, which stresses a single highest authority in the bounded borders. Not only is the population in Taiwan divided, but it is living across borders and experiencing an internal split whenever a sovereignty-induced interrogation is involved. Many Taiwanese families have second or third homes in China and the US. Some may conveniently invoke different stances at different sites about sovereign belonging.[42] None of these features make the Taiwanese distinctive from other people, but the US-China rivalry compels them to be conscious of them and choose a side. Before, China could challenge the hegemonic order, the US was not alerted to the possibility of China's armed unification, and China could bear with Taiwan's autonomy, short of an official pledge of independent sovereignty. In short, it used to be a nonsolution through which China and Taiwan could bypass the sovereignty issue. This nonsolution is no longer convincing in the twenty-first century, in which China poses a revisionist gesture in the eyes of Washington, with the protection of one party's sovereign status threatening the continuity of another's.[43]

The opposite of this current nonsolution, which rests upon the power asymmetry of the US over China and China over Taiwan, could be another nonsolution, given the fact that the United States' asymmetry over China is becoming obscure in general and on the Taiwan issue in particular.[44] The following nonsolution, impractical but illuminating, is to turn Taiwan's non-sovereignty into a twin sovereignty. What if both China and the US were to issue a passport automatically to any Taiwanese person who chose to have both? All of the strategic resources that the US might lose to China, including the frequently cited world-leading semiconductor sector, could remain in the hands of the Americans after Taiwan and China reunite. The Taiwanese could claim civilizational superiority, as the institutional intimacy between Taiwan and the US would no longer need to be anti-Chinese. Taiwan would not need to declare independence, as the population would legally possess non-Chinese citizenship. However, China's quest for unification would also be realized, not through the territorial occupation and subjugation of the Taiwanese people but by integrating the same-passport holders across the Taiwan Strait. Whatever interpretations of Taiwan's sovereign status might evolve, the Chinese would still own Taiwan's sovereignty through the population's legal nationality.

As a bilingual person need not declare their loyalty to either tongue when translating between two language communities, a twin-passport-holding Taiwanese person could avoid the interrogation of their loyalty that would follow the convention of single sovereignty. An in-between condition can be either a liability or an asset. First, twin sovereignty creates a consensual value for the different sides of the cleavage to ease the mutual aversion caused by the colonial and Civil War legacies. Second, without the need to settle on which sovereignty to claim, the US and China could resolve the hegemonic competition over the future of Taiwan. Third, once the anxiety about the other side colluding with Taiwan to tilt the status quo subsided, the spiral of the security dilemma would lose momentum. In the last case, as long as unification occurs between the populations, it is not equivalent to the conquest of territory. The threat of revisionism would decrease; in fact, on the contrary, unification could breed a pluriversal order.[45]

Pluriversal international relations celebrate the coexistence of various relational configurations that are informed not only by languages, religions, conventions, and the means of production but also, most significantly, by colonial networking. One rising agenda is that of the Global South, defined as the networking to sustain perpetual colonization. A major feature of the Global South is the mingling of populations whose living necessities, social relationships, and political loyalty transcend borders while they are continuously regulated by multiple states. A vast number of migrants hold a dual passports from the colonizer state and the former colony state. Different states regulate and serve them in different ways, and they adapt to the contexts imbued with incompatible values, ways of life, and views of moral correctness. Pluriversalism describes the coexistence of these threads of relationality and their fluid representations. Individual lives and the capacities of the states are similarly constituted by pluriversalism, with only the former capable of strategizing such hybridity. The irony of "a fluid population versus a fixed territory" indicates "realistic people versus unrealistic states." Such irony gives a clue regarding why the states will not adopt the twin-passport solution in practice and why its revelation among academics and think tanks can contribute to a critical reflection on the territorial fixation in the long term.

The twin-sovereignty (non)solution might be deemed more practical were the relevant authorities to acknowledge that the phenomenon of individuals holding two passports is already widespread throughout the world, including among Chinese citizens. Such an arrangement is not even unfamiliar at the group level, as all of the people of Northern Ireland are entitled to both an Irish and a British passport. The history of Northern Ireland is different in the sense that Taiwan has traditionally been ethnically and culturally more Chinese than American yet sought to become legally non-Chinese. In addition, Great Britain and Ireland are not rivals in the form of revisionism versus anti-revisionism concerning the overall order. The international significance of the Northern Irish case is thus limited.

De-territorializing the Security Community

In the Westphalian system, war was legal, legitimate, and even essential to a claim to sovereignty. The balance of power, war, alliance, piracy, colonization, and slave trade together testified to a prior, consensual entitlement of a sovereign state to act without (self-)restraint. With sovereignty the core of the security problem, only the former colonizer states seem to have achieved de-securitization. No longer fighting for territorial expansion in either Europe or the colonial world, a relatively stable security community has emerged in Europe and the Anglosphere,[46] in which the rules-based order constitutes arguably post-Westphalian role identities and de-securitizes their previously mutually exclusive sovereignty. Transcending a brutal history of war and conquest, such a highly self-regarded achievement,[47] or a miracle,[48] furthers the preaching of the role expectation for self-restraint to abide by the commonly subscribed rules as well as the practice of mutually conceding sovereignty.

What is missing is the awareness that, prior to the security community, all these former colonizer states were ostensibly individualized sovereign actors. However, the Global South (GS) states were, in contrast, overlapping communities of various sorts before colonization first forced them into a separable, occupiable territorial sphere, followed by decolonization in the 1960s transforming them into a sovereign state by themselves. In their newly acquired state role, there had not been such a memory of war in the colonized sphere that postcolonial regimes felt a need to overcome the guilt for causing the catastrophes that the past imperial and colonial wars inflicted on humankind. On the contrary, the postcolonial regimes in the GS had witnessed no expansion war, or conquest. Instead, the sovereign status has brought them civil war, informed mainly by those standing disputes colonially crafted and unresolved at the time of decolonization. Their incapacity to enforce the domestic order and international norms as expected reduces their sovereignties to illiberal, rogue, or failing states that are plagued by coups, civil war, authoritarianism, ethnic cleansing, corruption, and refugees, which invites intervention by post-Westphalian states.

The challenge to a postcolonial regime in the GS is about the inability to integrate and win mutual recognition rather than restraining the impulse of expansion.[49] However, a lack of self-restraint consciousness connotes a security threat to the rules-based order that justifies securitization alarm in the circle of former colonizer states. The alliance of autocrats and autocracies is their simplified label,[50] which derides their claims on distinguishable sovereignty. Even so, a rules-based order offers no solution to the governance failures in the GS when cross- and subnational groups are independent of the regimes. In brief, colonialism artificially created the postcolonial regimes in the contemporary GS and the roots of their failure in the networking that sustains colonialism. Their name of being a sovereign, that is, self-responsible state disguises the inhumanity of past colonialism. That is why the European style of the security community is essentially an alliance or a club of colonizers.

Rules-free multilateralism protects the postcolonial regimes in the GS from experiencing anxiety about the inability to resist intervention. The main mission of a postcolonial regime is to ensure the legitimacy of its institution and leadership. This can be best achieved if the regime can stabilize its sovereign borders and monopolize the jurisdiction within them. With ethnic and religious cleavages undermining its role capacity, sovereign integrity cannot be achieved. The alternative is for all the GS members, including colonizers, autocrats, and populations, to opt out of the Westphalian state role by officializing multiple identities to avoid pushing for any definite solution to the existing cleavages. A rules-free gathering can enable the holding of postcolonial regimes to improvise and gradually reciprocate mutual recognition.[51]

In this regard, a GS security community featuring, instead of taking advantage or critical of, the arrangement of double sovereign/passport identities can allow the standing disputes between the members to drag on. There is no pressure on the disputing parties to comply unwillingly and yet remain a member. Given the territorial, cultural, and religious complications under the GS circumstances, the parties to disputes must improvise according to their conditions but can do so only based on the self-confidence and comfort provided by an imagined holding of other members. In a nutshell, a GS security community recognizes sovereign independence, rather than restraining it, to calm and hold regimes that are ready to transcend colonially demarcated cleavages.

Achieving desecuritization through collective holding in the form of double or multiple sovereign identities for any state, group, or community that is suffering cleavages can be an empowering process. Even the difference between democracy and autocracy is irrelevant, through building of capacity and confidence, coordination, experience sharing, crisis management, joint projects, conflict resolution, and so on. What connects the GS population at different sites is the memory of historical victimization by the European colonizers.[52]

In doing without clear rules or values, a GS security community implicitly relies on bilateralism.[53] Since their establishment, the Association of Southeast Asian Nations (ASEAN) and the Shanghai Cooperation Organization (SCO),[54] for two notable examples, have witnessed members interact in a dyadic format to strike up a joint venture, peace approach, or anti-terrorist campaign. No mission exists outside the members' own jurisdiction. However, for the former colonizer states, a multilateral regime is only meaningful when linked with a mission, namely, to preach to nonmembers peace and human rights. In comparison, the ASEAN or the SCO members are supposed to focus only on the security and welfare within the organization's scope and to do so through making multiple bilateral deals on the members' own initiative. The function of a GS security community is thus a community for coexistence, which is, in the first order, regime-based and, in the second and long-term order, development-based. Accordingly, the Confucian advice to enrich the population before expecting their cooperation and modesty rings more contemporary than neoliberalism does.

Conclusion

Conventionally, sovereignty defines territory, which defines the population. In contrast, the fantasy of twin sovereignty redefines the population, who redefine the territory. Note that singular sovereignty is the technical condition that allows the competition over the future of Taiwan to create an agenda of political correctness. Sovereignty has been an obstacle to any solution and an impulse of intense rivalry. A de-territorializing unification through fluid passport-bodies could be socially more genuine and deeper than the institutionally imposed symbolic name change, because monitoring and disciplining any previously perceived incorrectness would be unnecessary for alarmists of either side. The topics and unification processes would cease to allude negatively to security. On the contrary, they would simultaneously facilitate the mingling of the US and China and transform a rival relationship into one of coexistence. An alternative could be a twin passport for China and Taiwan, instead of the US, which would require far less paperwork and emotional adjustment but might cause anxiety about loss among many an American Thucydides.

One caveat of twin sovereignty can, ironically, be a sense of simultaneous alienation from China and the US or the other side of the present internal cleavage, as a Northern Irish person can feel confused about their identity.[55] Another caveat is the extended desire for third passports, such as Japanese, Australian, or Canadian ones. Yet another caveat is the provocation effect on the existing autonomous jurisdiction of minorities everywhere to escalate the politics of identity. A general challenge to the sovereign system may ensue. Where would these caveats lead? A conversation between myself and Professor Hirano Kenichiro in 2005 may provide an appropriate ending here. He asked me what would be an ideal substitute for the sovereign state. I cited the metaphor of a maintenance garage that provides services to all brands of automobiles but charges more for external brands. He approved partially and questioned how such a garage could guarantee the security of its customers. He suggested that a prefectural system that retains the police force would be his ideal substitute.

Conclusion

Unlearning Chinese Relational IR

This book interrogates the irony that the theories of Chinese international relations, which likewise stress both relation and difference,[1] have had limited interaction with the pluriversal literature thus far.[2] Whether "Chinese" or "relational" is more important in the label "Chinese relational IR" is a serious question in the Chinese literature, in which attempts to transcend China-centrism have been emerging in recent years.[3] However, the decentralizing efforts remain embedded in the Newtonian tradition that informs Western realism and liberalism.[4] This tradition underpins the idea of the state of nature and the shared identity of an autonomous actor among all nations. Chinese relational IR fails to connect with substantial relationalities elsewhere that reflect pluriversal cosmologies[5] or multiple worlds.[6]

This book concludes that the challenge facing Chinese relational IR might be less about self-centrism than its unpreparedness to translate other relationalities in their terms critically. Therefore, the mission of relational IR in general, and Chinese relational IR in particular, is to learn and unlearn coexistence through critical translation.

Relations between Relational Systems

The relational turn of international relations has led to dialogues between Western and Chinese relational thinkers.[7] Relational theorists stress process over substance and practice over structure in both the natural and social sciences,[8] making substantive claims of culture and history disputable.[9] Chinese relational theory develops amid the call for a Chinese school of international relations.[10] The latter relies on substantive historical and cultural claims to dispense with the presumably alien Western international theories.[11] This implies substantialism and binaries. Therefore, the Chinese relational theories that adopt the same temperament in their attempts to dispense with Western interpretations[12] risk betraying processual sensibilities.

Such self-conscious China-centrism, once conceived of as a remedy for Eurocentrism,[13] has sparked enthusiasm among those weary of liberal hypocrisy.[14] It has likewise caused alarm ironically regarding the rising Chinese hegemonism in the twenty-first century.[15] Chinese IR represents to alarmists a revisionist version of the world order.[16] One major divide in Chinese IR scholarship exists between those who anticipate contribution to universal knowledge and those who pursue nationally distinctive knowledge.[17] Moreover, there is a tendency to regard the uniqueness argument as normative, and the general pursuit is explanatory.[18]

On the other hand, for Chinese IR to be global, a fundamental challenge is how to connect with relational theories elsewhere for the latter either to appreciate Chinese IR's inspiration regarding their different relationality or to enhance mutual unlearning. Ideally, relational IR everywhere should study how relations can motivate and orient foreign policy, focusing on the practices of national identities that collectively reproduce the consensual norms within their relational systems. As such, relational IR can illustrate how the foreign policies of different relational systems can either succeed or fail to link relational systems together.[19]

The notion of a relational system is critical to the book, defined as *the collective process of reifying the consensual norms that constitute the identities of the interacting members.*[20] Accordingly, consensual norms are consequential to policy behavior, not because relational systems exert an influence over their members as an external force but because the self-identities of the members and consensual norms are mutually constituted through the processes of reification.[21] The mutual constitution of norm and identity ensures that relational IR must be both normative and explanatory—when explaining the purposes and processes of foreign policy, relational IR alludes to the legitimacy of all existing relational systems and the duty of the leaders within these systems to make strangers related, including creating stranger roles so that strangers can stay as familiar strangers—that is, on behalf of and in accordance with the collective identity of their own systems as normative reification.[22]

With all relational systems facing the question of how to become related to strangers, no relational system remains within fixed boundaries.[23] Together with paralleling relational IR elsewhere, Chinese relational IR is obliged to prescribe ways in which strangers can become related to one another for each to remain relationally convincing and sustainable within their own relational system.[24] The existence of a boundary can only cause the demise of a relational system that is surrounded by both external and internal strangers.

Accordingly, relational systems inevitably expand. Still, however, a sustainable strategy does not seek to substitute, synthesize, or convert another's relationality. Substituting mine for yours is power politics rather than relational politics and, at best, reflects the misjudgment that relations ensue after power. In contrast, Chinese IR generally accepts that power ensues after relations, to the extent that a relation calls for moral leadership rather than dominance,[25] enables mobilization through a network,[26] excludes no one,[27] and empowers all relational selves.[28]

Logically, all distinctive relational systems will eventually be related. Although this may sound like Francis Fukuyama's end of history[29] or Alexander Wendt's world government,[30] it is quite different. I agree with Zhao Tingyang's belief that, sooner or later, all will arrive at the consciousness of "all bound to be related."[31] In any case, a relational system can suffer involution at times.[32] Chinese IR must answer how this might happen and end, if at all, to avoid romanticizing any particular relational system.

Expansion and Coexistence of Relational Systems

For all relational systems to become related, their ways of becoming related must be mutual, coexistent, and pluriversal. Still, currently, all relational systems face the challenge of destruction instead of coexisting relationally. This situation is closely linked to the expansion of Westphalia through imperialism and colonialism, which emerged as a result of the misjudgment that relations ensue after power.[33] Presumably, the relationalities of Westphalia were the first platform for bridging the mutually estranged religious systems. They could apply to religious systems everywhere, but, in practice, the relational system of Westphalia has been increasingly receptive to a violent relationality,[34] allowing only one particular form of coexistence—equal sovereignty and ultimately doing harm to everyone. Through imperialism and colonialism, little, if any, pluriversal exchange is considered noteworthy through the expansion of Westphalia.

In a pluriversal world, the populace that subscribes to a different cosmological imagination develops practical ways of coexistence in encountering another, each according to their reinterpretations.[35] On the contrary, the colonial powers engaged in dominance and conversion, reflecting estrangement instead of complexities and bridges.[36] Consequently, the IR research fails to take advantage of the grand scale of mingling under ostensibly decolonized Westphalia to facilitate a pluriversal sensibility. In response, almost all relational IR, including Chinese relationalities, resorts to discursive essentialism and binaries at the national or international level.[37] Nostalgia for certain relational cosmologies, embedded in imagined geo-cultural and religious distinctions, has been thriving since Amitav Acharya and Barry Buzan's special issue entitled "Why Is There No Non-Western International Relations Theory?"[38]

Although these nostalgic threads are geographically and religiously plural, they are self-defeating in the long run due to their faddish quest for substantive uniqueness and difference. This quest is flourishing in the non-Western, postcolonial, and national IR literature. The effort to retrieve these relational cosmologies, which have usually already been half-ruined by colonial Westphalia, is eventually self-defeating if the scholarly posture is to romanticize relational systems and not trace, explain, and critically assess the approaches and practices that are already complicating their widespread encountering.

At the end of the day, however, a relational system is not justifiable if people readily accept its rejection outside their living circles. Once it is realized that relational systems have always survived through successfully relating strangers, the next stage of relational IR will probably witness critical self-reflections that will trace the previously unnoticed practices of foreign policy makers to improvise ways to become related with strangers. These practices necessitate a specific relational agenda that focuses on the theoretical and empirical conditions that are conducive as well as destructive to the coexistence of people belonging to different relational systems. On the one hand, the empirical evidence shows the widespread development of such a seemingly successful coexistence.[39] Such evidence enables the interrogation of the definitions and conditions of successful coexistence. On the other hand, the ideological preparation to acknowledge and make sense of such pluriversal processes is lacking.[40]

Critical Translation

With its mounting influence and policy engagement, Chinese relational IR can further the recognition of pluriversalism by presenting how Chinese international policy has learned and unlearned (self-centric) ways to engage different relational systems.[41] Learning requires "critical cultural translation," referring to *emancipation from self-centrism to enable understanding of the self from the perspective of a different relationality in its terms*. Thus, critical translation facilitates self-transformation.[42] Intellectually, unlearning attests to the realization that all self-understandings are incomplete, insufficient, and inconsistent, hence no sense for one to consider onself an exclusive standard to appraise the varieties of lives in the world. In fact, attempts have emerged to decentralize Chinese *tianxia* and relate it to various universalisms, predominantly liberal governmentality.[43] In a pluriversal world in general, the populace subscribing to a different cosmological imagination develops practical ways of coexistence in encountering another, each according to their own (re)interpretations.[44]

Pluriversalism is not necessarily elegant, however, if a binary consciousness continues and strangers remain discursively segregated. Critical translation is necessary for relational expansion that seeks no substitution of "mine for yours." In theory, critical translation is safe if it can be as shallow as diplomacy.[45] In practice, critical translation may still backfire, resulting in coexistence-and-estrangement cycles.[46]

Given the practical failure of the relationalities of Westphalia to convert other relational systems entirely, alongside the necessity for people subscribing to different relational systems to become related in the long run,[47] it is useful to distinguish between the following three dimensions of relation to analyze how relational systems are prone to expand. The first dimension is between the system and (super)nature qua cosmology;[48] the second, between those who presumably belong to the same system;[49] and the third, between different systems.[50] All relational systems probably have all three, to ensure their eventual expansion and coexistence.

First, regarding the foundational dimension, relational cosmologies almost always comprise in the imagination of (super)natural forces, such as *Dao* or God,[51] that justify the evolution of the relational system. Accordingly, all are bound to be related.

Second, regarding the systemic dimension, there is a minimal degree of consensual resemblance between people, such as kinship or the rights of nature,[52] with discursive, institutional, and psychological self-reproduction, which constitutes all relational selves subscribing to the same system. Even so, estrangement or involution is an inevitable and even recurring cycle everywhere.[53]

Third, regarding the strategic dimension, certain mechanisms to get strangers related, such as a tributary system or market system,[54] can adapt to unfamiliar relationalities and normalize pluriversal practices, realizing that people related at multiple levels may not be consensually or continuously related in the same way.

A failure regarding the last strategic dimension reveals the cosmo-logical hypocrisy that no relational system can survive if its cosmology appears partial or transient rather than foundational or (super)natural. That said, an overcommitment to one's relational cosmology causes self-defeating rigidity, however powerful it may appear materialistically for the time being. The solid but revisable systemic dimension can support the strategic adaptation to pluriversal relationalities. With the sense of belonging and solidarity embedded in a certain consensual resemblance, the systemic dimension provides the necessary relational security to engage in extension, exchange, and integration.[55] That is why a degree of self-centrism can be healthy.

Pluriversal Practices and Chinese Relational IR

Pluriversal exchanges rely on people understanding and appreciating how a relational system other than their own justifies matters. In short, how do we find room in our relational systems to accommodate what is thought to be critical to either achieve or avoid in the encountered system? Cultural translation is the indispensable duty of relational IR. Given that systemic relations proceed and evolve each in their discursive practice, translative communicability enables epistemological journeys between relational systems and a subsequent appreciation of coexistence. Empirically, a populace living between two different systems can readily provide various clues regarding how relational systems coexist and expand both ways in practice.[56]

THE COSMOLOGICAL DIMENSION: CRITICAL TRANSLATION
AND ABSTRACTION

On the cosmological dimension, the responsibility of relational IR is to establish a linguistics prototype for each self-claimed relational system that is so foundational and abstract that the other relationalities can all coexist harmlessly. To illustrate, a provocative attempt the book adopts translates all-under-heaven, or *tianxia*, as "a system where all are bound to be related."[57] Another attempt might be to translate the relationalities of Westphalia into "solidarity embedded in the entitlement to rights of nature."[58] Both translations are experimental in nature, seeking to rid the original value-laden concepts of their cultural or religious sensibilities and approach a prototype.

The two experimental translations are surely insufficient, if not misleading, for understanding these aesthetic beliefs. The experiment aims merely to demonstrate the function of critical translation, however. It can be continuously pushed further. For example, given the above-mentioned abstraction of Westphalia, two Chinese premodern thoughts can be cited to support Westphalia's introduction to Chinese IR after a critical translation of them. It could be a fit for Moism,[59] for one example, whose translation could be "solidarity embedded in the entitlement to peace and love." Daoism, for another example, is arguably a fit, too,[60] with a critical translation, as a stretch from Zhao Tingyang's narrative, being "the necessity of all to preserve all." The two unfamiliar stranger schools are now externally connected with liberal cosmology. Internally, the abstraction compels their claimed disciples to reflect critically on their identities through such a connection.

With these translated Chinese cosmological beliefs, both Moism and Daoism, as well as *tianxia*, can find inspiration in *Ubuntu*, a southern African cosmological belief, which can join the experiment through translating its meaning as "solidarity embedded in the necessity of all to nurture all."[61] These abstractions preach how cosmological strangers can appear inclusive to one another. They provide a vehicle for learning how strangers are unthreateningly inclusive, too. We could then proceed with the abstraction thus achieved, which transcends specific cultural contexts.[62] The exchange of abstract formulations encourages a pluriversal discovery of previously unnoticeable readiness that can explain the practices of coexistence and (un)learning in daily life.

While historically and culturally unfamiliar to nonsubscribers, none of the formulations "all bound to be related," "entitlement to love and peace," or "all to preserve all" necessarily find Westphalia or *Ubuntu* threatening, and vice versa. This explains how, at a cosmological level, a rights appeal can nonetheless achieve intuitive legitimacy among many ordinary Chinese in daily life, at times. On the other hand, the theme of harmony that Confucianism embraces can reveal a harmonious tendency in individuals who are set up in competitively interactive relations.[63]

Each belief is certainly distinctive in imagining the relationships between individuals as prioritizing and pursuing various needs, and uneasy about contrasting approaches espoused by other coexisting beliefs. This kind of uneasiness, which is an unfailing source of confrontation, simultaneously alludes to the window of opportunities to unlearn the naturalness of sticking with a single cosmology. More importantly, after abstraction, it pushes the rediscovery of the hitherto neglected or inexpressible need of the self that can be explained by coexisting cosmologies elsewhere. Chinese IR is destined to answer how unlearning happens empirically in contemporary Chinese internationalism.

SYSTEMIC DIMENSION: METAPHORS AND IN-BETWEENNESS

On the systemic dimension, metaphors can improvise the relationships between relational systems. To illustrate, a revised Christian lens of Chineseness can include the following improvisations: (1) discovering their (possibly imagined) overlapping, such as the Christian heaven likened to the Confucian heaven; (2) preparing proxies in another system, such as painting God in the local image; and (3) accommodating the consensual order of another relationality, such as ancestor worship reconceived of as nonreligious convention.[64] The ritual of gift giving can be another metaphor for mutual acceptance.[65] To that extent, gifts sufficiently reify the cosmology of all who are bound to be related without certain consensual norms or rules to constitute the self-identities of all belonging to the same relational system and enjoying solidarity.

Through the Confucian lens, the ritual of gift giving can represent a metaphor for mutual acceptance.[66] Presumably, all displays of goodwill, nominal as well as materialistic, are some kind of gift to improvise relationships. As gift giving is a universal practice, the practices of inclusiveness abiding by different cosmological beliefs and rituals can form the topic of comparative studies.[67] The questions of who can be legitimate givers and what gifts are legitimate for whom allude to the clashes of incongruent values and institutions. A metaphor under the Confucian theme that has the potential of wider application is that of a father and son, a pair of original strangers at the latter's birth who evolve into a constantly adjusting relationship, defined by ritual and gift rather than universal values or rules. Chinese IR, characterized by gift giving, can contribute to relational IR by invoking a study of gift giving during civilizational encountering in both daily life and official policy.

An agenda for the encountering of various religious systems with the Chinese population offers numerous clues to the flexibility and creativity of the actors mediating between cosmological systems. Although some may have consciously reproduced the binary and a ranking of civilization to the disadvantage of those whom they encounter, a study of how encounters have reconstituted the cosmological imagination is both the lacuna and duty of Chinese IR. Sinicizing attempts always accompany religious and civilizational assimilation. Not only is Buddhism famously an internalized and yet reinterpreted religion of the Chinese, but it has also reconfigured (neo-)Confucianism. The same is applicable to the identity of Muslim Confucians who preached Islamic views through Confucian lenses;[68] Chinese classical scholars who preached Hinduism or weaponized Buddhism;[69] and the Jewish spirit of *tikkun olam*, which has motivated participatory activism in Chinese state building, regardless of the divergent ideological positions;[70] or the missionary Sinologists who left a legacy for multilingual Chineseness informed by Mandarin and the local dialects,[71] just to name a few examples.

Other than the nationalist and decolonial sensibilities that are alert to the suppressive and exploitative aspect of the encounter, there is an additional adaptive aspect in the lives of in-between populations, such as the migrant or ethnic groups on the borders, the comparators or the expatriates, and the bi- or trilingual people. In-betweenness breeds agency for combining and appropriating cultural resources. Exemplifying coexistence physically as well as intellectually, these individuals can be translators to mitigate a misunderstanding but can also misrepresent to distract the rivalry or do nothing in silence to absorb the incongruence bodily. Incongruence is part of normal life for practitioners and a system in itself for in-between communities. Even a conflict in this context rarely affects the hybrid evolution of cuisines, architecture, gaming, and so on, which is worth an aesthetic IR agenda.[72]

STRATEGIC DIMENSION: ROLE, NONSOLUTION, AND CYCLES

Finally, consider the strategic dimension, employing multilateralism to illustrate how relational systems strategize their expansion. The concept used to be unfamiliar to Confucianism, which was institutionally embedded in tributary and kin relationships, each according to their dyadic context. However, multilateralism has now become an everyday concept. The Chinese official line of multilateralism stresses inclusiveness,[73] as opposed to rule-based governance, which informs American multilateralism.[74] Linguistically, each appears comprehensible to the other. Still, it is often philosophically incomprehensible why the other side can appropriate multilateralism in different terms. Relational IR necessarily relies on a knowledge of the cosmological and systemic dimensions.

Therefore, it is the destiny of Chinese relational IR to expound and juxtapose the Confucian cosmology of *tianxia* alongside the tradition of natural rights to demonstrate the origin of the two types of multilateralism, informed by inclusiveness and rules-based governance, respectively.[75] Chinese IR should also analyze how inclusiveness is institutionally reified at the systemic level through applying improvised decentralization (see chapter 10) in context.[76]

The strategic dimension studies how cosmological relations negotiate roles for strangers inside as well as outside to socialize them into patterns of coexistence. This is intersubjective. In practical terms, the improvisation of a nonsolution between actors acting in the name of their religion, nation, or site, to delay a solution to an indefinite future, is a common method of coexistence that is neglected by the international and foreign policy literature.[77] An element of patience, intended to calm the tension of rivalry, can substitute coexistence for self-centered pursuit. After all, no solution or settlement can possibly be permanent from a historical point of view. Chinese IR can interrogate and compare those cases where leaders are not preoccupied with an unsustainable solution at the sacrifice of coexistence.

A study on how and which particular cosmological belief is invoked to inspire an indefinite extension poses an apparent challenge to the literature's obsession with interest calculi. This is because making exceptions, rather than insisting on a standard, may emerge as the empirical common sense so that double standards in themselves are, arguably, the standard for measuring the degree of relational mutuality.[78] The frequency of attempts to explain away or acquiesce to inconsistency by policymakers reflects the degree of their identities that is constituted by in-betweenness. Friendship, despite its variety, is no less important than rules and standards. Confucianism's ambivalence toward friendship as partisanship and trustworthiness has great potential for explaining the inconsistency in foreign policy everywhere.

The agenda of the in-between groups attends particularly to the use of cycles, as opposed to linear temporality, in explaining the underlying drive toward policy changes due to the coexistence of values and institutions originating in different cosmological beliefs. A plausible project concerns emotions that seem to have already inspired a surge in the literature.[79] However, emotion is not inevitably sincere, as the literature assumes, but, sometimes unknowingly, a role played at a particular time,[80] which must alternate along with other role emotions at a different time. If coexistence leads to a nonsolution in the long run and reconciles the clarity and scope of a cosmology, dialectics testify to coexistence. Therefore, Chinese IR can contribute to the understanding of conflict (non)resolution in, for instance, the Mongolia-China, Vietnam-China, Japan-China, and India-China interactions. It can shed light on the coexistence of multiple cosmological strangers who tolerate their occasional conflicts, each in their evolving cosmologies, to live through cycles of peace and conflict.

If we consider that liberal multilateralism links nations through consensual rights of nature, which line up the identities of all nations, Confucian multilateralism does so through mutual benevolence, no matter how incongruent the existing identities qua consensual norms are. Confucianism espouses a policy style of bypassing the rules to ensure mutual acceptance, so that nations being related in some way is more important than which specific norms and rules unify the nations. Coexisting with rule-based governance requires Confucianism to move beyond mere inclusiveness by, for example, adopting the role of rule observers in specific contexts periodically. These rules may concern nonproliferation, property rights, peacekeeping, and the like. For Confucian actors, role taking is a gift to liberal actors, in exchange for mutual acceptance. In return, the liberal relational system develops complex rules of exception and exemption to accommodate improvisations, nuances, and contingency.

Relational Internationalism?

Critical translation enables Chinese IR to contribute to an empirical agenda of pluriversalism. My discussion does not engage substantive schools of thought since my purpose is not to claim the superiority of any of them. Rather, this is more an epistemological and methodological theme on how to facilitate the preaching and receiving of unfamiliar beliefs and provoke a self-critical reflection on the limitation as well as potential of each particular belief. Such multiple and reciprocal provocation complicates, adapts, and enriches the explanations of international relations for all. The relational IR that is embedded in decolonial sensibilities currently struggles between national epistemologies and Westphalia to the effect of decentralizing the latter. With an atmosphere of the rise of China and the emerging Chinese school of IR, the conclusion imposes a special duty on those, willingly and unwillingly, named scholars of Chinese IR to engage consciously in decentralizing cosmological, and subsequently epistemological, relations. By avoiding a centralizing lens, Chinese IR can contribute to an empirical agenda on pluriversal IR, in which the currently dominant Westphalia can plausibly (un)learn, too. By saying that decentralizing is essential to (un)learning and expansion, the allusion is that danger remains in centralizing a particular cosmology to represent a population, to the effect of substituting identity politics for transcendence over binary. This happens when the romantic recognition of a specific cosmology avows its distinction rather than translatability. Once invoked as representative of Chinese IR in practice, Confucianism supersedes and marginalizes multiple other classical cosmological beliefs, for example. Romanticism defeats the purpose of critical translation and aborts the study of expansion through unlearning. Nevertheless, Confucianism constituted by different threads of Buddhism, Daoism, liberalism, fascism, and socialism can nonetheless remain Confucian only after critical translation that accommodates further appropriation and reconstitution. It is the cosmological abstraction, instead of a school, geo-cultural site, or population, that reduces its exoticness or canonicity and permits mutual constitution.

The challenge facing Chinese relational IR is, above all, the unavailability of a linguistic prototype to transcend cultural specificity—that is, a cosmologic pattern intelligible to both Chinese and non-Chinese scholars. Even if one were available, it could not readily communicate since the relational consciousness of the time is registered in asserting and defending differences. Consequently, inclusiveness is reduced to simply another self-centric statement. On the other hand, at the strategic level, the Belt and Road Initiative, presently the poster child for Chinese internationalism, invokes the metaphor of gift giving to oblige the ironic acceptance of China's territorial self. Such a self is indicated primarily by the pretentiously rigid "One China" principle.[81] My conviction is, though, that the coexistence of interconnected, exclusionary kinds of territoriality will ultimately yield, ex post facto, a critical (i.e., emancipative) interrogation of the expansion of relations and pluriversal exchanges of Chinese relational IR, albeit cyclically in recession.

Notes

Introduction

1. Milja Kurki, *International Relations in a Relational Universe* (Oxford: Oxford University Press, 2020); Valerie de Koeijer and Robbie Shilliam, "Forum: International Relations as a Geoculturally Pluralistic Field," *International Politics Reviews* 9 (2021): 272–75, https://doi.org/10.1057/s41312-021-00112-2; Arlene B. Tickner and Karen Smith, eds., *International Relations from the Global South: Worlds of Difference* (London: Routledge, 2020); Kimberly Hutchings, "Decolonizing Global Ethics: Thinking with the Pluriverse," *Ethics & International Affairs* 33, no. 2 (2019): 115–25; Daniel J. Levine and David M. McCourt, "Why Does Pluralism Matter When We Study Politics? A View from Contemporary International Relations," *Perspectives on Politics* 16, no. 1 (2018): 92–109.

2. Amitav Acharya and Barry Buzan, "Why Is There No Non-Western International Relations Theory? An Introduction," *International Relations of the Asia-Pacific* 7, no. 3 (2007): 287–312; Amitav Acharya and Barry Buzan, "Why Is There No Non-Western International Relations Theory? Ten Years On," *International Relations of the Asia-Pacific* 17, no. 3 (2017): 341–70; Arlene B. Tickner and David L. Blaney, eds., *Claiming the International* (London: Routledge, 2013); Catherine Owen, John Heathershaw, and Igor Savin, "How Postcolonial Is Post-Western IR? Mimicry and Mētis in the International Politics of Russia and Central Asia," *Review of International Studies* 44, no. 2 (2018): 279–300.

3. Bonnie Girard, "Racism, a Challenge for an Increasingly Global China: Confronting a Problem the PRC Does Not Know It Has," *Brown Journal of World Affairs* 27, no. 2 (2021): 199–215; Chih-yu Shih, "Role and Relation in Confucian IR: Relating to Strangers in the States of Nature," *Review of International Studies* 48, no. 5 (2022): 910–29, https://doi.org/10.1017/S0260210521000322; Astrid H. M. Nordin et al., "Towards Global Relational Theorizing: A Dialogue between Sinophone and Anglophone Scholarship on Relationalism," *Cambridge Review of International Affairs* 32, no. 5 (2019): 570–81; Emilian Kavalski, *The*

Guanxi of Relational International Theory (London: Routledge, 2018); Emilian Kavalski, "The *Guanxi* of Relational International Affairs," *Chinese Political Science Review* 3 (2018): 233–51; Yongjin Zhang and Teng-chi Chang, eds., *Constructing a Chinese School of International Relations: Ongoing Debates and Sociological Realities* (London: Routledge, 2016).

4. Lily H. M. Ling, *The Dao of World Politics: Towards a Post-Westphalian, Worldist International Relations* (London: Routledge, 2014); Tickner and Blaney, *Claiming the International*; Rosa Vasilaki, "Provincialising IR? Deadlocks and Prospects in Post-Western IR Theory," *Millennium* 41, no. 1 (2012): 3–22; Pinar Bilgin, "Thinking Past 'Western' IR?," *Third World Quarterly* 29, no. 1 (2008): 5–23.

5. Milja Kurki, "Relational Revolution and Relationality in IR: New Conversations," *Review of International Studies* 48, no. 5 (2022): 821–36, https://doi.org/10.1017/S0260210521000127; Tamara A. Trownsell et al., "Differing about Difference: Relational IR from around the World," *International Studies Perspectives* 22, no. 1 (2021): 25–64; Arlene B. Tickner and Amaya Querejazu, "Weaving Worlds: *Cosmopraxis* as Relational Sensibility," *International Studies Review* 23, no. 2 (2021): 391–408; Hutchings, "Decolonizing Global Ethics."

6. Jon D. Carlson and Russell Arben Fox, *The State of Nature in Comparative Political Thought: Western and Non-Western Perspectives* (Lanham, MD: Lexington Books, 2013); Beate Jahn, *The Cultural Construction of International Relations: The Invention of the State of Nature* (New York: Palgrave, 2000).

7. Tao-Wei Hu, "The Chinese Version of the Law of Nature," *Ethics* 38, no. 1 (1927): 27–43; Hu Shih, "The Natural Law in the Chinese Tradition," in *English Writings of Hu Shih: Chinese Philosophy and Intellectual History*, ed. Chih-P'ing Chou, vol. 2 (Heidelberg: Foreign Language Teaching and Research Publishing / Springer, 2013), 217–34.

8. Derk Bodde, "Evidence for 'Laws of Nature' in Chinese Thought," *Harvard Journal of Asiatic Studies* 20, no. 3/4 (1957): 709–27; Joseph Needham, *Science and Civilisation in China*, vol. 2, *History of Scientific Thought* (Cambridge: Cambridge University Press, 1956).

9. Roger T. Ames, "What Ever Happened to 'Wisdom'? Confucian Philosophy of Process and 'Human Becomings,'" *Asia Major*, 3rd ser., 21, no. 1 (2008): 45–68.

10. Yaqing Qin, *A Relational Theory of World Politics* (Cambridge: Cambridge University Press, 2018); Chih-yu Shih et al., *China and International Theory: The Balance of Relationships* (Abingdon, UK: Routledge: 2019); Tingyang Zhao, *Redefining a Philosophy for World Governance*, trans. Liqing Tao (Beijing: Foreign Language Teaching and Research Publishing / Palgrave Macmillan, 2019).

11. Felix Berenskötter, "Deep Theorizing in International Relations," *European Journal of International Relations* 24, no. 4 (2018): 814–40.

12. This can be a parallel to Hannah Arendt's notion of natality as "capacity to begin." See Hannah Arendt, *The Human Condition* (Chicago: University of Chicago Press, 1958), 247.

13. Evan A. Feigenbaum, "Reluctant Stakeholder: Why China's Highly Strategic Brand of Revisionism Is More Challenging Than Washington Thinks," in *China's Economic Arrival: Decoding a Disruptive Rise*, ed. Damien Ma, 113–30 (Singapore: Springer, 2020); Bonnie Glaser, "China as a Selective Revisionist Power in the International Order," compiled by Khairulanwar Zaini, *ISEAS Perspective* 2019, no. 21 (5 April 2019), https://www.iseas.edu.sg/images/pdf/ISEAS_Perspective_2019_21.pdf; Jeffrey W. Legro, "What China Will Want: The Future Intentions of a Rising Power," *Perspectives on Politics* 5, no. 3 (2007): 515–34; Jeanne L. Wilson, "Are Russia and China Revisionist States?," *Asia Dialogue*, June 11, 2019, https://theasiadialogue.com/2019/06/11/are-russia-and-china-revisionist-states/.

14. See cases in Jonathan R. Adelman and Chih-yu Shih, *Symbolic War: The Chinese Use of Force, 1840–1980* (Taipei: Institute of International Relations, 1993).

15. Kenneth N. Waltz, *Theory of International Politics* (Long Grove, IL: Waveland Press, 1979).

16. Samuel P. Huntington, *The Clash of Civilizations and the Remaking of World Order* (New York: Simon and Schuster, 1996).

17. Yun-han Chu and Yongnian Zheng, *The Decline of the Western-Centric World and the Emerging New Global Order: Contending Views* (New York: Routledge, 2020).

18. Hendrik Spruyt, *The World Imagined: Collective Beliefs and Political Order in the Sinocentric, Islamic and Southeast Asian International Societies* (Cambridge: Cambridge University Press, 2020).

19. Daniel A. Bell and Thaddeus Metz, "Confucianism and Ubuntu: Reflections on a Dialogue between Chinese and African Traditions," *Journal of Chinese Philosophy* 38, no. S1 (2011): 78–95.

20. Jan Niklas Rolf, "The State of Nature Analogy in International Relations Theory," *International Relations* 28, no. 2 (2014): 150–82.

21. Kurki, *International Relations*; Joseph MacKay, review of *Social Practices of Rule-Making in World Politics*, by Mark Raymond, *Cambridge Review of International Affairs* 33, no. 3 (2020): 452–57; Bentley B. Allan, *Scientific Cosmology and International Orders* (Cambridge: Cambridge University Press, 2018).

22. Anthony Giddens, *The Constitution of Society: Outline of the Theory of Structuration* (Cambridge: Polity Press, 1984).

23. My definition is indebted to Yuri Pines, "'The One That Pervades the All' in Ancient Chinese Political Thought: The Origins of 'The Great Unity' Paradigm," *T'oung Pao* 86, no. 4/5 (2020): 280–324; Michael Loewe,

230 Notes to Chapter 1

"China's Sense of Unity as Seen in the Early Empire," *T'oung Pao* 80, nos. 1–3 (1994): 6–26; Yih-Jye Hwang, "Reappraising the Chinese School of International Relations: A Postcolonial Perspective," *Review of International Studies* 47, no. 3 (2021): 311–30, https://doi.org/10.1017/S0260210521000152.

Chapter 1

1. See Asit K. Biswas and Kris Hartley, "China's Soft Power Struggle," *Policy Forum*, Asia & the Pacific Policy Society, November 9, 2017, https://www.policyforum.net/chinas-soft-power-struggles/; Jing Sun, *Japan and China as Charm Rivals: Soft Power in Regional Diplomacy* (Ann Arbor: University of Michigan Press, 2013); Hongyi Lai and Yiyi Lu, eds., *China's Soft Power and International Relations* (Abingdon, UK: Routledge, 2013); Mingjiang Li, ed., *Soft Power: China's Emerging Strategy in International Politics* (Lanham, MD: Lexington Books, 2011); Joshua Kurlantzick, *Charm Offensive: How China's Soft Power Is Transforming the World* (New Haven, CT: Yale University Press, 2007).

2. See William A. Callahan and Elena Barabantseva, eds., *China Orders the World: Normative Soft Power and Foreign Policy* (Baltimore: Johns Hopkins University Press, 2011); Bonnie S. Glaser and Melissa E. Murphy, "Soft Power with Chinese Characteristics: The Ongoing Debate," in *Chinese Soft Power and Its Implications for the United States: Competition and Cooperation in the Developing World*, ed. Carola McGiffert, 10–26 (Washington, DC: Center for Strategic and International Studies, 2009).

3. See B. M. Jain, *China's Soft Power Diplomacy in South Asia: Myth or Reality?* (Lanham, MD: Lexington Books, 2017).

4. William Callahan, "Identity and Security in China: The Negative Soft Power of the China Dream," *Politics* 35, nos. 3–4 (2015): 216–29.

5. Trefor Moss, "Soft Power? China Has Plenty," *Diplomat*, June 4, 2013, https://thediplomat.com/2013/06/soft-power-china-has-plenty/.

6. See Suisheng Zhao, "Rethinking the Chinese World Order: The Imperial Cycle and the Rise of China," *Journal of Contemporary China* 24, no. 96 (2015): 961–82; Kelvin Cheung Chi Kin, "China's Rise and the International Politics of East Asia: The Development of Chinese IR Theory," *China: An International Journal* 12, no. 2 (2014): 31–45; Wang Mingming, "All under Heaven (*Tianxia*): Cosmological Perspectives and Political Ontologies in Pre-modern China," *HAU: Journal of Ethnographic Theory* 2, no. 1 (2012): 337–83; Elena Barabantseva, "Change vs. Order: *Shijie* Meets *Tianxia* in China's Interactions with the World," *Alternatives* 34, no. 2 (2009): 129–55.

7. See Le Hong Hiep, "Vietnam's Hedging Strategy against China since Normalization," *Contemporary Southeast Asia* 35, no. 3 (2013): 333–68.

8. See Ban Wang, ed., *Chinese Visions of World Order: Tianxia, Culture, and World Politics* (Durham, NC: Duke University Press, 2017).

9. See Marc Andre Matten, *Imagining a Postnational World: Hegemony and Space in Modern China* (Leiden: Brill, 2016); Allen Carlson, "Moving beyond Sovereignty? A Brief Consideration of Recent Changes in China's Approach to International Order and the Emergence of the *Tianxia* Concept," *Journal of Contemporary China* 20, no. 68 (2011): 89–102.

10. See Feng Zhang, *Chinese Hegemony: Grand Strategy and International Institutions in East Asian History* (Stanford, CA: Stanford University Press, 2015); Yang Shih-Yueh, *Benevolent Strategic Culture and Chinese Strategic Decision Making, 1745–1860* (Saarbrücken, Germany: Golden Light Academic Publishing, 2017); Bettina Hückel, "Theory of International Relations with Chinese Characteristics: The Tian-Xia System from a Metatheoretical Perspective," *Journal for Interventions in the Social Sciences and Humanities* (February 2012): 34–64; Yaqing Qin, "A Relational Theory of World Politics," *International Studies Review* 18, no. 1 (2016): 33–47; Zhao Tingyang, "A Political World Philosophy in Terms of All-under-Heaven (Tian-xia)," *Diogenes* 56, no. 1 (2009): 5–18.

11. See Fei-Ling Wang, *The China Order: Centralia, World Empire, and the Nature of Chinese Power* (Albany: State University of New York Press, 2017); Astrid H. M. Nordin, *China's International Relations and Harmonious World: Time, Space, and Multiplicity in World Politics* (London: Routledge, 2016); Christopher Ford, *The Mind of Empire: China's History and Modern Foreign Relations* (Lexington: University Press of Kentucky, 2010); Chishen Chang, "*Tianxia* System on a Snail's Horns," *Inter-Asia Cultural Studies* 12, no. 1 (2011): 28–42; William Callahan, "Chinese Visions of World Order: Post-Hegemonic or a New Hegemony," *International Studies Review* 10, no. 4 (2008): 749–61.

12. See Howard W. French, *Everything under the Heavens: How the Past Helps Shape China's Push for Global Power* (New York: Knopf, 2017).

13. See Niv Horesh, Hyun Jin Kim, and Peter Mauch, *Superpower, China? Historicizing Beijing's New Narratives of Leadership and East Asia's Response Thereto* (Singapore: World Scientific, 2015); Evelyn Goh, *The Struggle for Order: Hegemony, Hierarchy, and Transition in Post-Cold War East Asia* (Oxford: Oxford University Press, 2013).

14. See Nordin, *China's International Relations.*

15. See Salvatore Babones, *American Tianxia: Chinese Money, American Power and the End of History* (Bristol, UK: Policy Press, 2017); Sun, *Japan and China as Charm Rivals.*

16. See Yong Deng, "The Power and Politics of Recognition: Status in China's Foreign Relations," in *Major Powers and the Quest for Status in International Politics*, ed. Thomas J. Volgy et al., 77–95 (New York: Palgrave Macmillan, 2011).

17. See Alexis P. I. Goh and Peirchyi Lii, "Examining Leader-Follower Interactions through the Lens of Chinese Politeness," *China Report* 53, no. 3 (2017): 331–53.

18. B. Wang, *Chinese Visions of World Order*; Shan Chun, "On Chinese Cosmopolitanism (*Tian Xia*)," *Culture Mandala: Bulletin of the Centre for East-West*

Cultural & Economic Studies 8, no. 2 (December 2009): 20–29; Yan Xuetong, "Xun Zi's Thoughts on International Politics and Their Implications," *Chinese Journal of International Politics* 2, no. 1 (2008): 135–65.

19. See Philip J. Ivanhoe, "Filial Piety as a Virtue," in *Filial Piety in Chinese Thought and History*, ed. Alan K. L. Chan, 189–202 (London: Routledge Curzon Press, 2004).

20. Bijun Xu, "Is Zhao's Tianxia System Misunderstood?" *Tsinghua China Law Review* 6 (2013): 95–108.

21. See Ji-young Lee, *China's Hegemony: Four Hundred Years of East Asian Domination* (New York: Columbia University Press, 2016).

22. See Nadège Rolland, *China's Eurasian Century? Political and Strategic Implications of the Belt and Road Initiative* (Washington, DC: National Bureau of Asian Research, 2017); Wang Yiwei, *China Connects the World: What behind the Belt and Road Initiative* (Beijing: China Intercontinental Press, 2017).

23. James Der Derian, "The Value of Security: Hobbes, Marx, Nietzsche, and Baudrillard," in *On Security*, ed. Ronnie D. Lipschutz (New York: Columbia University Press, 1995), 34.

24. See F.-L. Wang, *The China Order*.

25. See Alan Shiu Cheung Kwan, "Hierarchy, Status and International Society: China, and the Steppe Nomads," *European Journal of International Relations* 22, no. 2 (2016): 362–83.

26. See Emanuel Adler, "The Spread of Security Communities: Communities of Practice, Self-Restraint, and NATO's Post–Cold War Transformation," *European Journal of International Relations* 14, no. 2 (2008): 195–230; Morten Skumsrud Andersen and Iver B. Neumann, "Practices as Models: A Methodology with an Illustration concerning Wampum Diplomacy," *Millennium* 40, no. 3 (2012): 457–81.

27. See Zhou Fangyin, "Equilibrium Analysis of the Tributary System," *Chinese Journal of International Politics* 4, no. 2 (2011): 147–78.

28. See Salvatore Babones, "Taking China Seriously: Relationality, *Tianxia*, and the 'Chinese School' of International Relations," in *Oxford Research Encyclopedia of Politics*, ed. William R. Thompson (Oxford: Oxford University Press, 2017), https://doi.org/10.1093/acrefore/9780190228637.013.602.

29. Richard Neustadt, *Presidential Power and the Modern Presidents: The Politics of Leadership from Roosevelt to Reagan* (New York: Free Press, 1991).

30. See Peter C. Perdue, "The Tenacious Tributary System," *Journal of Contemporary China* 24, no. 96 (2015): 1002–14; Mark Mancall, "The Ch'ing Tribute System: An Interpretive Essay," in *The Chinese World Order: Traditional China's Foreign Relations*, ed. John King Fairbank (Cambridge, MA: Harvard University Press, 1968), 65.

31. See Burak Oc and Michael R. Bashshur, "Followership, Leadership and Social Influence," *Leadership Quarterly* 24, no. 6 (2013): 919–34.

32. See Yonghong Yang, *Sovereignty in China's Perspective* (Frankfurt: Peter Lang, 2017).

33. See Sun, *Japan and China as Charm Rivals*.

34. See John M. Friend and Bradley A. Thayer, "China's Use of Multilateral Institutions and the US Response: The Need for American Primacy 2.0," in *China's Challenges and International Order Transition: Beyond "Thucydides's Trap,"* ed. Huiyun Feng and Kai He, 259–79 (Ann Arbor: University of Michigan Press, 2020).

35. See Oliver Stuenkel, *Post-Western World: How Emerging Powers Are Remaking Global Order* (Cambridge: Polity Press, 2016).

36. See Yiwei Wang, "Public Diplomacy and the Rise of Chinese Soft Power," *Annals of the American Academy of Political and Social Science* 616, no. 1 (2008): 257–73.

37. See Scott D. DeRue and Susan J. Ashford, "Who Will Lead and Who Will Follow? A Social Process of Leadership Identity Construction in Organizations," *Academy of Management Review* 35, no. 4 (2010): 627–47.

38. Thucydides, *History of the Peloponnesian War*, trans. William Smith (London: Jones, 1831), 5.89.1.

39. See Brantly Womack, *Asymmetry and International Relations* (Cambridge: Cambridge University Press, 2016).

40. See Emmet McElhatton and Brad Jackson, "Paradox in Harmony: Formulating a Chinese Model of Leadership," *Leadership* 8, no. 4 (2012): 441–61.

41. Suisheng Zhao, "A Time of Test for the China Model of Economic Growth," *East Asia Forum*, January 29, 2017, http://www.eastasiaforum.org/2017/01/29/a-time-of-test-for-the-china-model-of-economic-growth/.

42. Kenneth King, *China's Aid and Soft Power in Africa: The Case of Education and Training* (Suffolk, UK: James Curry, 2013); R. Evan Ellis, "Chinese Soft Power in Latin America: A Case Study," *Joint Force Quarterly* 60, no. 1 (2011): 85–91.

43. Tuong Vu, *Vietnam's Communist Revolution: The Power and Limits of Ideology* (Cambridge: Cambridge University Press, 2016).

Chapter 2

I would like to thank Chiung-chiu Huang for consenting to the inclusion in this chapter of a revised version of the coauthored paper "Competing for a Better Role Relation: International Relations, Sino-US Rivalry as Game of Weiqi," first presented at the Conference on Emerging Powers at Bath University on June 10–11, 2018.

1. Henry Kissinger, On China (New York: Penguin, 2011).

2. Alexander Wendt, Social Theory of International Politics (Cambridge: Cambridge University Press, 1999).

3. Steve Chan, "More Than One Trap: Problematic Interpretations and Overlooked Lessons from Thucydides," Journal of Chinese Political Science 24, no. 1 (2019): 11–24.

4. Kai He and Stephen Walker, "Role Bargaining Strategies for China's Peaceful Rise," Chinese Journal of International Politics 8, no. 4 (2015): 371–88.

5. Karin M. Fierke, "Contraria sunt Complementa: Global Entanglement and the Constitution of Difference," International Studies Review 21, no. 1 (2019): 146–69; Lily H. M. Ling, The Dao of World Politics: Towards a Post-Westphalian, Worldist International Relations (London: Routledge, 2014).

6. David Lai, Learning from the Stones: A Go Approach to Mastering China's Strategic Concept, Shi (Carlisle, PA: Strategic Studies Institute, 2004); Elisabeth Papineau, "The Game of Go: A Chinese Way of Seeing the World," 2001, https://vdocuments.mx/a-chinese-way-to-see-the-world.html.

7. Scott Boorman, The Protracted Game: A Wei-ch'i Interpretation of Maoist Revolutionary Strategy (Oxford: Oxford University Press, 1969); Zhongqi Pan, "Guanxi, Weiqi and Chinese Strategic Thinking," Chinese Political Science Review 1, no. 2 (June 2016): 303–21; Michael Posner, "Weiqi: The Game That Holds China's Key to World Domination," Globe and Mail, March 26, 2017, https://www.theglobeandmail.com/globe-debate/munk-debates/weiqi-the-game-that-holds-chinas-key-to-world-domination/article598664/.

8. Marc L. Moskowitz, Go Nation: Chinese Masculinities and the Game of Weiqi in China (Berkeley: University of California Press, 2013), xvii, 3.

9. Boorman, Protracted Game.

10. Sam Bateman, "Increasing Competition in the South China Sea: Need for a New Game Plan" in The South China Sea Disputes, ed. Yang Razali Kassim (Singapore: World Scientific Press, 2017), 55–58.

11. Pan, "Guanxi."

12. Lai, Learning from the Stones; Timothy L. Thomas, "China's Concept of Military Strategy," Parameters 44, no. 4 (2014): 39–48.

13. Ray Jovana, "Go: For a Winning Anarchist Strategy," Ideas & Action, March 8, 2012, http://ideasandaction.info/2012/03/go-for-a-winning-anarchist-strategy/.

14. Kwang-kuo Hwang, "Face and Favor: The Chinese Power Game," American Journal of Sociology 92, no. 4 (1987): 945–74; Mayfair Mei-hui Yang, Gifts, Favors, and Banquets: The Art of Social Relationships in China (Ithaca, NY: Cornell University Press, 1994).

15. Moskowitz, Go Nation, 8–9.

16. Andrew J. Nathan, "What China Wants: Bargaining with Beijing," Foreign Affairs 90, no. 4 (2011): 153.

17. Meiyao Wu, "The Process of Self-Cultivation and the Mandala Model of the Self," Frontiers in Psychology 8 (2017): 9–19; Kwang-Kuo Hwang, "The Mandala Model of Self," Psychological Studies 56, no. 4 (2011): 329–34.

18. William Bain, "Rival Traditions of Natural Law: Martin Wight and the Theory of International Society," International History Review 36, no. 5 (2014): 943–60; Aurélie Lacassagne, "Cultures of Anarchy as Figurations: Reflections on Wendt, Elias and the English School," Human Figuration 1, no. 2 (2012), https://quod.lib.umich.edu/h/humfig/11217607.0001.207?view=text;rgn=main.

19. Wendt, Social Theory of International Politics, 283.

20. Barry Buzan, "The English School: A Neglected Approach to International Security Studies," Security Dialogue 46, no. 2 (2015): 126–43; Barry Buzan, "Not Hanging Separately: Responses to Dunne and Adler," Millennium 34, no. 1 (2005): 183–94; Barry Buzan, From International to World Society? English School Theory and the Social Structure of Globalisation (Cambridge: Cambridge University Press, 2004).

21. Fareed Zakaria, "The Self-Destruction of American Power: Washington Squandered the Unipolar Moment," Foreign Affairs, July/August 2019, https://www.foreignaffairs.com/articles/2019-06-11/self-destruction-american-power.

22. Wendt, Social Theory of International Politics; Cristian Cantir and Juliet Kaarbo, eds. Domestic Role Contestation, Foreign Policy, and International Relations (London: Routledge, 2016); Sebastian Harnisch, "Conceptualizing in the Minefield: Role Theory and Foreign Policy Learning," Foreign Policy Analysis 8, no. 1 (2012): 47–69.

23. Karl Baker, The Way to Go (New York: American Go Association, 2008).

24. Martin Shubik, "It Is Not Just a Game!," Simulation & Gaming 40, no. 5 (2009): 587–601.

25. "No Go," The Economist, May 19, 2011, https://www.economist.com/node/18709581.

26. Robert G. Sutter, US-China Relations: Perilous Past, Uncertain Present, 3rd ed. (Lanham, MD: Rowman & Littlefield, 2018).

27. Boorman, Protracted Game.

28. Xuetong Yan, "China Values vs. Liberalism: What Ideology Will Shape the International Normative Order?" Chinese Journal of International Politics 11, no. 1 (2018): 1–22; G. John Ikenberry, "The Rise of China and the Future of the West: Can the Liberal System Survive?," Foreign Affairs 87, no. 1 (2008): 23–37; G. John Ikenberry, "The Future of Liberal Order in East Asia," in The Future of East Asia, ed. Peter Hays and Chung-In Moon, 81–101 (New York: Springer, 2018); Kevin Rudd, "What the West Doesn't Get about Xi Jinping," New York Times, March 20, 2018, https://www.nytimes.com/2018/03/20/opinion/xi-jinping-china-west.html.

29. Brandon K. Yoder, "Uncertainty, Shifting Power and Credible Signals in US-China Relations: Why the 'Thucydides Trap,' Is Real, but Limited," Journal of Chinese Political Science 24, no. 1 (2019): 87–104; Biao Zhang, "The Perils

of Hubris? A Tragic Reading of 'Thucydides' Trap' and China-US Relations," Journal of Chinese Political Science 24, no. 1 (2019): 129–44.

30. Jude Webber and John Paul Rathbone, "Tillerson Extols 19th-Century US Foreign Policy in Latin America," Financial Times, February 2, 2018, https://www.ft.com/content/bdaee8d2-07c3-11e8-9650-9c0ad2d7c5b5.

31. He and Walker, "Role Bargaining Strategies."

32. Jinghan Zeng, "Constructing a 'New Type of Great Power Relations': The State of Debate in China (1998–2014)," British Journal of Politics and International Relations 18, no. 2 (2016): 422–42.

33. Roy D. Kamphausen, "China's Belt and Road Initiative (Testimony)," June 12, 2019, National Bureau of Asian Research, https://www.nbr.org/publication/chinas-belt-and-road-initiative-testimony/.

34. Michael Pillsbury, Hundred-Year Marathon: China's Secret Strategy to Replace America as the Global Superpower (New York: Henry Holt, 2015.)

35. Chas W. Freeman Jr., "On the Souring of Sino-American Relations," May 5, 2018, http://chasfreeman.net/on-the-souring-of-sino-american-relations/.

36. Chinese foreign minister Wang Yi told reporters at the US State Department that Beijing's military moves have been justified by provocative military actions by others in the region. Guy Taylor, "China Bent on 'Hegemony in East Asia,' Navy Adm. Harry Harris Jr. Warns," Washington Times, February 23, 2016, https://www.washingtontimes.com/news/2016/feb/23/china-bent-on-hegemony-in-east-asia-navy-adm-harry/.

37. Howard W. French, "China's Quest to End Its Century of Shame," New York Times, July 13, 2017, https://www.nytimes.com/2017/07/13/opinion/chinas-quest-to-end-its-century-of-shame.html.

38. Kishore Mahbubani, "Beijing in the South China Sea—Belligerent or Assertive?," The Exchange, Financial Times, March 15, 2016, https://www.ft.com/content/58c676ed-f3f4-32ac-b3c9-69efd0ae07fd.

39. Kamphausen, "China's Belt and Road Initiative."

40. PACOM stands for the United States Pacific Command. Keith Griffith, "Navy Admiral Nominated as Next Ambassador to Australia Warns Congress That the US Must Be Prepared for War with China," DailyMail.com, February 16, 2018, http://www.dailymail.co.uk/news/article-5401881/Harry-Harris-says-prepared-war-China.html.

41. Peter Symonds, "Former US Ambassador Advocates American Military Bases on Taiwan," World Socialist Web Site, January 19, 2017, https://www.wsws.org/en/articles/2017/01/19/taiw-j19.html.

42. "Clinton Warns against 'New Colonialism' in Africa," Reuters, June 11, 2011.

43. Flavia Krause-Jackson, "Clinton Chastises China on Internet, African 'New Colonialism,'" Bloomberg, June 12, 2011, http://www.bloomberg.com/news/articles/2011-06-11/clinton-chastises-china-on-internet-african-new-colonialism-.

44. Jude Webber and John Paul Rathbone, "Tillerson Extols 19th-Century US Foreign Policy in Latin America," Financial Times, February 2, 2018, https://www.ft.com/content/bdaee8d2-07c3-11e8-9650-9c0ad2d7c5b5.

45. Ricardo Neeb and Fernando Menéndez, "The Dragon and the Condor: Beyond China's Economic Influence in the Americas," Global Dispatch 6 (2018), http://www.securefreesociety.org/wp-content/uploads/2018/02/SFS-Global-Dispatch-Issue-6.pdf.

46. Fergus Hodgson, "The Rise of Chinese Imperialism in Latin America: China's Soft and Hard Power Initiatives Are Threatening US Influence," Epoch Times, April 5, 2018, https://www.theepochtimes.com/the-rise-of-chinese-imperialism-in-latin-america-2_2480449.html.

47. Jeffrey Reeves, "Imperialism and the Middle Kingdom: The Xi Jinping Administration's Peripheral Diplomacy with Developing States," Third World Quarterly 39, no. 5 (2018): 976–98.

48. Ashley J. Tellis, "New Bipolarity between the United States and China Poses Challenges for India," Carnegie Endowment for International Peace, April 19, 2017, https://carnegieendowment.org/2017/04/19/new-bipolarity-between-united-states-and-china-poses-challenges-for-india-pub-69904.

Chapter 3

1. David Yau-fai Ho and Rainbow Tin Hung Ho, "Knowledge Is a Dangerous Thing: Authority Relations, Ideological Conservatism, and Creativity in Confucian-Heritage Cultures," Journal for the Theory of Social Behavior 38, no. 1 (2008): 67–86; David Yau-fai Ho, Si-qing Peng, and Fiona Shui-fun Chan, "Authority and Learning in Confucian-Heritage Education: A Relational Methodological Analysis," in Multiple Competencies and Self-Regulated Learning: Implications for Multicultural Education, ed. Chi-yue Chiu, Farideh Salili, and Ying-yi Hong (Greenwich, CT: Information Age Publishing, 2001): 29–47.

2. Maria Adele Carrai, "Adaptive Governance along Chinese-Financed BRI Railroad Megaprojects in East Africa," World Development 141 (2021), https://doi.org/10.1016/j.worlddev.2020.105388.

3. For example, gifts can range from engaging in a joint sanction, arranging zero-interest-rate loans, lowering tariffs, abstaining from boycotting, sending a goodwill ambassador, extending an invitation to a gathering, awarding a medal, sending condolences, sharing pandemic information, conceding in a dispute, praising an action, and many other improvised offerings, both symbolic and material in nature.

4. Confucius, Analects (chapter on Wei Ling Gong), Chinese Text Project, https://ctext.org/analects/wei-ling-gong.

5. Confucianism is particularly sensitive to the stranger component of every self; see Thomas Metzger, Escape from Predicament (New York: Columbia University Press, 1986).

6. Anisha Datta, "The 'Other' in Sociological Canons: Reading the Trinity through a Critical Post-colonial Lens," *Journal of Intercultural Studies* 33, no. 6 (2012): 657–73.

7. Lucy Jackson, Catherine Harris, and Gill Valentine, "Rethinking Concepts of the Strange and the Stranger," *Social & Cultural Geography* 18, no. 1 (2017): 1–15.

8. Frederick D. Weil, "The Stranger, Prudence, and Trust in Hobbes's Theory," *Theory and Society* 15, no. 5 (1986): 759–88.

9. See James Der Derian, *On Diplomacy: A Genealogy of Western Estrangement* (Oxford: Blackwell, 1992).

10. Sharon A. Lloyd and Susanne Sreedhar, "Hobbes's Moral and Political Philosophy," Stanford Encyclopedia of Philosophy, spring 2019 ed., ed. Edward N. Zalta, https://plato.stanford.edu/archives/spr2019/entries/hobbes-moral/.

11. Lloyd and Sreedhar, "Hobbes's Moral and Political Philosophy."

12. Martin Weber, "The Concept of Solidarity in the Study of World Politics: Towards a Critical Theoretical Understanding," *Review of International Studies* 33, no. 4 (2007): 693–713; Nicolas J. Wheeler, *Saving Strangers: Humanitarian Intervention in International Society* (Oxford: Oxford University Press, 2003).

13. Lloyd and Sreedhar, "Hobbes's Moral and Political Philosophy."

14. James Glass, *Psychosis and Power: Threat to Democracy in the Self and the Group* (Ithaca, NY: Cornell University Press, 1995).

15. For a critical reflection, see Jana S. Rošker, *The Rebirth of the Moral Self: The Second Generation of Modern Confucians and Their Modernization Discourses* (Hong Kong: Chinese University Press, 2016).

16. Confucius himself combined the two: "My way is oneness." Zengzi explained that his teacher meant forgiveness and faithfulness. See the chapter on Li Ren in the *Analects*, https://ctext.org/analects/li-ren.

17. I rely on the interpretations of scholars of Song-Ming Confucianism. For further discussion, please refer to William Theodore de Bary, *The Trouble with Confucianism* (Cambridge, MA: Harvard University Press, 1991); Justin Tiwald, "Song-Ming Confucianism," *Stanford Encyclopedia of Philosophy*, March 19, 2020, https://plato.stanford.edu/entries/song-ming-confucianism/; Robert Neville, "Wang Yang-Ming's 'Inquiry on the Great Learning,'" *Process Studies* 7, no. 4 (1977): 214–37.

18. See Tingyang Zhao, *Redefining a Philosophy for World Governance*, trans. Liqing Tao (Singapore: Palgrave Macmillan, 2019).

19. See Xi Jinping's remark on ecological protection on May 18, 2018, at the National Conference on Ecological and Environmental Protection, *China News*, May 23, 2018, http://www.chinanews.com/gn/2018/05-23/8520332.shtml.

20. Astrid Nordin and Graham M. Smith, "Relating Self and Other in Chinese and Western Thought," *Cambridge Review of International Affairs* 32, no. 5 (2019): 636–53.

21. Cameron G. Thies, "The US and China: Altercast Roles and Changing Power in the 20th Century," in *China's International Roles: Challenging or Supporting International Order*, ed. Sebastian Harnisch, Sebastian Bersick, and Jörn-Carsten Gottwald (New York: Routledge, 2016), 98–100; Susann Gjerde and Gro Ladegård, "Leader Role Crafting and the Functions of Leader Role Identities," *Journal of Leadership and Organizational Studies* 26, no. 1 (2018): 44–59.

22. Ryan K. Beasley and Juliet Kaarbo, "Casting for a Sovereign Role: Socialising an Aspirant State in the Scottish Independence Referendum," *European Journal of International Relations* 24, no. 1 (2018): 8–32.

23. Astrid Nordin et al., "Towards Global Relational Theorizing: A Dialogue between Sinophone and Anglophone Scholarship on Relationalism," *Cambridge Review of International Affairs* 32, no. 5 (2019): 570–81; Yaqing Qin and Astrid Nordin, "Relationality and Rationality in Chinese and Western Traditions of Thought," *Cambridge Review of International Affairs* 32, no. 5 (2019): 601–14.

24. Cameron G. Thies, *The United States, Israel, and the Search for International Order: Socializing States* (New York: Routledge, 2013).

25. Sin Liang, Sibin Wu, and Shujuan Zhang, "From Friendship to Family: Jiangyiqi and Strong Interpersonal Relationship Development in Chinese Organizations," *Management and Organization Review* 14, no. 2 (2018): 75–303; Hak Yin Li and Seanon Wong, "The Evolution of Chinese Public Diplomacy and the Rise of Think Tanks," *Place Branding and Public Diplomacy* 14, no. 1 (2018): 36–46; Chuka Enuka, "Aid in Sino-African Relations: An Analysis of the Promptings, Pluses and Problems of China's Aid to Africa," *IUP Journal of International Relations* 5, no. 2 (2011): 41–53.

26. Examples of relational configurations include linguistic (e.g., Portuguese), religious (e.g., Catholic), racial (e.g., Caucasian), productive (e.g., capitalist), ideological (e.g., socialist), historical (e.g., postcolonial), cultural (e.g., Confucian), civilizational (e.g., nomadic), and geographical (e.g., Eurasian).

27. Roles are derived from "others' expectations and one's own conceptions"; see Stephen Walker, "Symbolic Interactionism and International Politics: Role Theory's Contribution to International Organization," in *A Cognitive Approach to International Organizations*, ed. Martha Cottam and Chih-yu Shih, 19–38 (New York: Praeger, 1992), 23. Also see Leslie Wehner, "Role Expectations as Foreign Policy: South American Secondary Powers' Expectations of Brazil as a Regional Power," *Foreign Policy Analysis* 11, no. 4 (2015): 435–55.

28. I mainly use George Herbert Mead, *Mind, Self, and Society*, ed. Charles W. Morris (Chicago: University of Chicago, 1934).

29. Patrick Jackson and Daniel Nexon, "Relations before States: Substance, Process, and the Study of World Politics," *European Journal of International Relations* 5, no. 3 (1999): 291–332; Zhao Tingyang, "A Political World Philosophy in Terms of All-under-Heaven (Tian-xia)," *Diogenes* 56, no. 1 (2009): 5–18; Chengxin Pan, "Toward a New Relational Ontology in Global Politics: China's

Rise as Holographic Transition," *International Relations of the Asia-Pacific* 18, no. 3 (2019): 229–67.

30. Cameron G. Thies, "Role Theory and Foreign Policy," May 2009, 3–4, https://myweb.uiowa.edu/bhlai/workshop/role.pdf; Cameron G. Thies, "China's Rise and the Socialisation of Rising Powers," *Chinese Journal of International Politics* 8, no. 3 (2015): 281–300.

31. Peter Jackson, "Pierre Bourdieu, the 'Cultural Turn' and the Practice of International History," *Review of International Studies* 34, no. 1 (2008): 155–81.

32. Iver Neumann, "Entry into International Society Reconceptualized: The Case of Russia," *Review of International Studies* 37, no. 2 (2011): 463–84; Chih-yu Shih and Chihyun Chang, "The Rise of China Between Cultural and Civilizational Relationalities: Lessons from Four Qing Cases," *International Journal of Asian Studies* 14, no. 1 (2017): 1–25.

33. Leslie Wehner, "The Narration of Roles in Foreign Policy Analysis," *Journal of International Relations and Development* 23, no. 2 (2020): 359–84.

34. For the domestic turn of role theory, see Cristian Cantir and Juliet Kaarbo, eds., *Domestic Role Contestation, Foreign Policy, and International Relations* (New York: Routledge, 2016); Leslie Wehner and Cameron G. Thies, "Role Theory, Narratives, and Interpretation: The Domestic Contestation of Roles," *International Studies Review* 16, no. 3 (2014): 411–36.

35. Chih-yu Shih and Yinji Wu, "Between Core National Interest and a Harmonious World: Reconciling Self-Role Conceptions in Chinese Foreign Policy," *Chinese Journal of International Politics* 6, no. 1 (2013): 59–84.

36. Yaqing Qin, *A Relational Theory of World Politics* (Cambridge: Cambridge University Press, 2018), xii.

37. Sebastian Harnisch, "Conceptualizing in the Minefield: Role Theory and Foreign Policy Learning," *Foreign Policy Analysis* 8, no. 1 (2012): 47–69.

38. "The individual must select a role that is appropriate to the situation. This is accomplished by locating both the position of the self and other." Thies, "Role Theory and Foreign Policy," 11; see also Cameron G. Thies, "Role Theory and Foreign Policy Analysis in Latin America," *Foreign Policy Analysis* 13, no. 3 (2017): 663.

39. Chiung-Chiu Huang, "Interpreting Vietnam's China Policy from the Perspective of Role Theory: Independent Role versus Interactive Role," *International Relations* 34, no. 4 (2020): 524–43.

40. Samuel Kim, *China, the United Nations and World Order* (Princeton, NJ: Princeton University Press, 2016); Allen Carlson, *Unifying China, Integrating with the World: Securing Chinese Sovereignty in the Reform Era* (Stanford, CA: Stanford University Press, 2005); Iain Johnston, *Social States: China in International Institutions, 1980–2000* (Princeton, NJ: Princeton University Press, 2008).

41. Noel Malcolm, "Thomas Hobbes: Liberal Illiberal," *Journal of the British Academy* 4 (2016): 113–36.

42. Jack Donnelly, "Human Rights: A New Standard of Civilization?," *International Affairs* 74, no. 1 (1998): 1–21.

43. Thies, *The United States, Israel, and the Search for International Order*; Chih-yu Shih, "Assigning Role Characteristics to China: The Role State versus the Ego State," *Foreign Policy Analysis* 8, no. 1 (2012): 71–91.

44. Laura Zhou, "China May Take Bigger Role as 'Guarantor and Mediator' after Trump-Kim Talks," *South China Morning Post*, June 10, 2018, https://www. politico.com/story/2018/06/10/china-mediator-trump-korea-talks-635361; Larry A. Niksch, *North Korea's Nuclear Weapons Program*, CRS issue brief for Congress IB91141 (Congressional Research Service, February 21, 2006), https://sgp.fas. org/crs/nuke/IB91141.pdf; Hakan Mehmetcik and Ferit Belder, "China's Role in the Regional and International Management of Korean Conflict: An Arbiter or Catalyst?," *Third World Quarterly* 39, no. 12 (2019): 2255–71.

45. Feng Zhu, "Flawed Mediation and a Compelling Mission: Chinese Diplomacy in the Six-Party Talks to Denuclearise North Korea," *East Asia* 28, no. 3 (2011): 191–218.

46. Hochul Lee, "China in the North Korean Nuclear Crises: 'Interest' and 'Identity' in Foreign Behavior," *Journal of Contemporary China* 22, no. 80 (2013): 312–31.

47. Sebastian Harnisch, "The Military Alliance between North Korea and China," World International Studies Committee (WISC) conference, Taipei, Taiwan, June 22, 2017, https://www.uni-heidelberg.de/md/politik/harnisch/person/ publikationen/harnisch_sino_dprk_military_alliance_2017.pdf.

48. Nele Noesselt, "China's Contradictory Role(s) in World Politics: Decrypting China's North Korean Strategy," *Third World Quarterly* 35, no. 7 (2014): 1307–25.

49. Leon V. Sigal, "What Have Twenty-Five Years of Nuclear Diplomacy Achieved?," in *Pathways to a Peaceful Korean Peninsula: Denuclearization, Reconciliation and Cooperation*, ed. Kyung-ok Do, Jeong-Ho Roh, and Henri Féron, 29–53 (Seoul: Korea Institute for National Unification / Columbia Law School Center for Korean Legal Studies, 2016).

50. For a timeline, see "Timeline: How the Trump-Kim Summit Came Together," *AP News*, June 10, 2018, https://apnews.com/ a36832b15604498a927257ddebc73647.

51. Andrei Lankov, "North Korea Doesn't Seem to Care about Its International Relations," *Radio Free Asia*, August 11, 2015, https://www.rfa.org/english/ commentaries/parallel-thoughts/korea-international-08112015134739.html; Shine Choi, *Re-imaging North Korea in International Politics: Problems and Alternatives* (London: Routledge, 2011); Seongji Woo, "Pyongyang and the World: North Korean Perspectives on International Relations under Kim Jong-il," *Pacific Focus* 26, no. 2 (2011): 188–205.

52. Details are available in Sigal, "Twenty-Five Years."

53. Caisová discovers a new role—that of the "powerful state"—having emerged in Pyongyang's discourse since 2015. Lenka Caisová, "Role Theoretic Approach and North Korean Foreign Policy Analysis," *Journal of International Relations* 15, no. 1 (2017): 22.

54. Peter Hays, "Trump and the Interregnum of American Nuclear Hegemony," *Journal for Peace and Nuclear Disarmament* 1, no. 2 (2018): 219–37; Matthew Green, "A Brief History of North Korea and How It Became One of America's Biggest Threats (with Lesson Plan)," *KQED*, April 25, 2017, https://www.kqed.org/lowdown/26701/how-north-korea-became-a-rogue-state-a-brief-history-with-lesson-plan; Narushige Michishita, "Coercing to Reconcile: North Korea's Response to US 'Hegemony,'" *Journal of Strategic Studies* 29, no. 6 (2006): 1015–40. Concerning the "rogue state," see Alexandra Homolar, "Rebels without a Conscience: The Evolution of the Rogue States Narrative in US Security Policy," *European Journal of International Relations* 17, no. 4 (2010): 710.

55. Lionel Babicz, "Shadows of the Past Haunt Japan–North Korea Relations," *East Asia Forum*, November 18, 2017, https://www.eastasiaforum.org/2017/11/18/shadows-of-the-past-haunt-japan-north-korea-relations/; Adrien Carbonnet, "Imperialist vs Rogue: Japan, North Korea and the Colonial Issue since 1945," *Cipango* 4 (2015).

56. Linus Hagström and Marie Söderberg, "Taking Japan–North Korea Relations Seriously: Rationale and Background," *Pacific Affairs* 79, no. 3 (2006): 373–85.

57. Derek Bolton, *Nuclear Negotiations with North Korea: Why Negotiators Should Consider North Korean Narratives* (American Security Project, May 2018), https://www.researchgate.net/profile/Derek_Bolton3/publication/324918695_Nuclear_Negotiations_with_North_Korea_Why_Negotiators_Should_Consider_North_Korean_Narratives/links/5aeb17cca6fdcc03cd9103d0/Nuclear-Negotiations-with-North-Korea-Why-Negotiators-Should-Consider-North-Korean-Narratives.pdf; Jae-Jung Suh, ed., *Origins of North Korea's Juche: Colonialism, War, and Development* (Lanham, MD: Lexington Books, 2014); Charles K. Armstrong, *Tyranny of the Weak: North Korea and the World, 1950–1992* (Ithaca, NY: Cornell University Press, 2013).

58. Inyeop Lee, "Can North Korea Follow China's Path? A Comparative Study of the Nexus between National Security and Economic Reforms," *Pacific Focus* 34, no. 1 (2019): 102–26; Justin V. Hastings, *A Most Enterprising Country: North Korea in the Global Economy* (Ithaca, NY: Cornell University Press, 2016); Nicholas Eberstadt, *A New International Engagement Framework for North Korea* (Seoul: Korean Economic Institute, 2004). Caisová traces this "internal developer" role to as early as 2011; see Caisová, "Role Theoretic Approach," 15.

59. Seo-Hyun Park, "Dueling Nationalism in North and South Korea," *Palgrave Communications* 5, no. 40 (2019), https://doi.org/10.1057/s41599-019-

0248-3; Jin Woong Kang, "Historical Changes in North Korean Nationalism," *North Korean Review* 3, no. 1 (Spring 2007): 86–104.

60. Carla Freeman, ed., *China and North Korea: Strategic and Policy Perspectives from a Changing China* (New York: Palgrave Macmillan, 2015); Noesselt, "China's Contradictory Role(s)."

61. Hongseo Park and Jae Jeok Park, "How Not to Be Abandoned by China: North Korea's Nuclear Brinkmanship Revisited," *Korean Journal of Defense Analysis* 29, no. 3 (2017): 371–87.

62. Weiqi Zhang, "Neither Friend nor Big Brother: China's Role in North Korean Foreign Policy Strategy," *Palgrave Communications* 4, no. 16 (2018), https://doi.org/10.1057/s41599-018-0071-2.

63. Caisová, "Role Theoretic Approach," 22.

64. Chung-in Moon, "A Miracle in a Day: The Moon-Kim Summit and Prospects for Peace in Korea," *Global Asia* 13, no. 2 (June 2018): 52.

65. The previous two were between North Korean leader Kim Jong-il and South Korean leaders Kim Dae-jung, in 2000, and Roh Moo-hyun, in 2007.

66. Moon, "Miracle in a Day," 51.

67. Sang-sook Lee, "Assessment of the Third Inter-Korean Summit and Reasons for Change in North Korea's Policy Stance—Focused on 'New Strategic Line,'" *IFANS Focus*, May 11, 2018, 2.

68. C.-i. Moon, "Miracle in a Day," 54.

69. Eleanor Albert, "The China–North Korea Relationship," *Council on Foreign Relations*, March 13, 2019, https://www.cfr.org/backgrounder/china-north-korea-relationship.

70. Mehmetcik and Belder, "China's Role"; Sebastian Harnisch, "The Life and Near-Death of an Alliance: China, North Korea and Autocratic Military Cooperation," WISC conference, Taipei, Taiwan, April 2017.

71. Zhou, "China May Take Bigger Role."

72. Bonnie S. Glaser, "For China, One of the Greatest Risks of Trump-Kim Talks Is Being Sidelined," *Parallels* (blog), NPR, March 12, 2018, https://www.npr.org/sections/parallels/2018/03/12/592859517/for-china-one-of-the-greatest-risks-of-trump-kim-talks-is-being-sidelined.

73. Jane Perlez, "China, Feeling Left Out, Has Plenty to Worry about in North Korea-U.S. Talks," *New York Times*, April 22, 2018, https://www.nytimes.com/2018/04/22/world/asia/china-north-korea-nuclear-talks.html.

74. Huang, "Interpreting Vietnam's China Policy"; see also Chiung-Chiu Huang, "Embedded Relationality and Role: History and Hierarchy in Vietnam's China Policy," *Korean Political Science Review* 51, no. 6 (December 2017): 129–45.

75. Christopher Bodeen, "US Diplomat: China Tightened Border Controls with N. Korea," *AP News*, May 26, 2017, https://www.apnews.com/4bf8f9e0fe334dcbacd1345bf92063cb.

76. Raymond Lee, A *Trump-Kim Summit: Hyper Rapprochement or Marginalization of China?* (Al Jazeera Centre for Studies, May 1, 2018), 7.

77. "Xi Jinping Met with Kim Jong Un," *Xinhua*, March 28, 2018, http://www.xinhuanet.com/politics/2018-03/28/c_1122600292.htm.

78. J. Berkshire Miller, "China's Trump Card on North Korea," editorial, *Al Jazeera*, March 30, 2018, https://www.aljazeera.com/indepth/opinion/china-trump-card-north-korea-180330072706375.html.

79. Lee, *Trump-Kim Summit*, 10.

80. Min Hong, "Evaluation of 2018 Inter-Korean Summit and Future Prospect: Meaning and Implementation Measures of Complete Denuclearization," *Online Series*, CO 18, no. 12, Korea Institute for National Unification (May 2, 2018): 4.

81. Jong Chul Park, "How to Promote Peace on the Korean Peninsula after the PyeongChang Winter Olympics," *Online Series*, CO 18, no. 5 (February 8, 2018): 3.

82. Choe Sang-Hun, "North Korea, Seeking 'an Equal Footing,' Rejects Preconditions for U.S. Talks," *New York Times*, March 4, 2018, p. A11.

83. Choe Sang-Hun, "Koreans Think Trump Has Earned Nobel Peace Prize," *New York Times*, May 1, 2018, p. A11.

84. Kuyoun Chung, "Three North-South Summits and Singapore: Moon Jae-in's High-Stakes Diplomacy," *Global Asia* 13, no. 4 (December 2018): 34.

85. Ki-Young Sung, "Evaluation of 2018 Inter-Korean Summit and Future Prospects," *Online Series* CO 18, no. 11 (April 29, 2018): 2.

86. In retrospect, this inter-Korean platform provided a far safer channel for communication than the bilateral summitry between Pyongyang and Washington, the two strangers. The fact that Trump walked out of his second meeting with Kim in Hanoi attests to the value of Seoul as a go-between.

Chapter 4

I would like to thank Jason Kuo for consenting to the inclusion in this chapter of a revised version of the coauthored paper "Theorizing Anger in East Asia," presented at the International Conference on Political Psychology in East Asia on July 27, 2018, at National Taiwan University.

1. Andrew Ross, "Coming in from the Cold: Constructivism and Emotions," *European Journal of International Relations* 12, no. 2 (2006): 213.

2. This is true in a general sense. See Jonathan Turner, "The Sociology of Emotions: Basic Theoretical Arguments," *Emotion Review* 1, no. 4 (2009): 340–54. Specifically on anger, see Thomas Dixon, "What Is the History of Anger a History of?," *Emotions: History, Culture, Society* 4, no. 1 (2020): 1–34; Charles D. Spielberger and Eric C. Reheiser, "The Nature and Measurement of

Anger," in *International Handbook of Anger: Constituent and Concomitant Biological, Psychological, and Social Processes*, ed. Michael Potegal, Gerhard Stemmler, and Charles Spielberger, 403–12 (Heidelberg: Springer, 2010).

3. For example, Jo-Ansie Van Wyk, "Anger in International Relations," *Politeia* 40, no. 1 (2021); Regina Heller, "More Rigor to Emotions! A Comparative, Qualitative Content Analysis of Anger in Russian Foreign Policy," in *Researching Emotions in International Relations: Methodological Perspectives on the Emotional Turn*, ed. Maéva Clément and Eric Sangar, 75–99 (London: Palgrave, 2018); Janice Bially Mattern, "On Being Convinced: An Emotional Epistemology of International Relations," *International Theory* 6, no. 3 (2014): 589–94; Jonathan Mercer, "Feeling Like a State: Social Emotion and Identity," *International Theory* 6, no. 3 (2014): 515–35.

4. Katie Barclay, "State of the Field: The History of Emotions," *History* 106, no. 371 (2021): 456–66.

5. For a general discussion of dispositional negativity, see Lisa Feldman Barrett, *How Emotions Are Made: The Secret Life of the Brain* (Boston: Houghton Mifflin Harcourt, 2017).

6. Laura Silva, "Anger and Its Desires," *European Journal of Philosophy* 29, no. 4 (2021): 1115–35; see also Laura Silva, "The Efficacy of Anger: Recognition and Retribution," in *The Politics of Emotional Shockwaves*, ed. Ana Falcato and Sara Graça da Silva, 27–56 (Cham, Switzerland: Springer Nature, 2021).

7. Aaron Sell, John Tooby, and Leda Cosmides, "Formidability and the Logic of Human Anger," *Proceedings of the National Academy of Sciences of the United States of America* 106, no. 35 (2009): 15073–78.

8. Özlem Terzi, "Norms of Belonging: Emotion Discourse as Factor in Determining Future 'Europeans,'" *Global Affairs* 7, no. 2 (2021):139–55; Diana Carolina Pelaez Rodriguez, "Emotional Communities: An Understanding of Collective Situated Knowledge and Action," *Emotions: History, Culture, Society* 5, no. 2 (2021): 303–30; Diane M. Mackie, Angela T. Maitner, and Eliot R. Smith, "Intergroup Emotions Theory," in *Handbook of Prejudice, Stereotyping, and Discrimination*, ed. Todd D. Nelson, 149–74 (New York: Psychology Press, 2016).

9. Individuals do not necessarily feel their anger. See, for example, Jean L. Briggs, *Never in Anger: Portrait of an Eskimo Family* (Cambridge, MA: Harvard University Press).

10. For earlier, but not too early, examples, see Stephen Côté, Ivona Hideg, and Gerben Alexander Van Kleef, "The Consequences of Faking Anger in Negotiations," *Journal of Experimental Social Psychology* 49, no. 3 (2013): 453–63; Shirli Kopelman, Ashleigh Shelby Rosette, and Leigh Thompson, "The Three Faces of Eve: Strategic Displays of Positive, Negative, and Neutral Emotions in Negotiations," *Organizational Behavior and Human Decision Processes* 99, no. 1 (2006): 81–101.

11. Alexander Wendt, "The State as Person in International Theory," *Review of International Studies* 30, no. 2 (2004): 304.

246 | Notes to Chapter 4

12. Janice Gross Stein, "Psychological Explanations of International Decision Making and Collective Behavior," in *Handbook of International Relations*, ed. Walter Carlsnaes, Thomas Risse, and Beth A. Simmons, 195–219 (London: Sage, 2013), 206.

13. Brian Parkinson, Agneta H. Fischer, and Antony S. R. Manstead, *Emotions in Social Relations: Cultural, Group, and Interpersonal Processes* (London: Routledge, 2005).

14. Robert C. Solomon, "Getting Angry: The Jamesian Theory of Emotion in Anthropology," in *Culture Theory: Essay on Mind, Self, and Emotion*, ed. Richard A. Shweder and Robert A. LeVine, 238–54 (Cambridge: Cambridge University Press), 250.

15. Todd H. Hall, "We Will Not Swallow This Bitter Fruit: Theorizing a Diplomacy of Anger," *Security Studies* 20, no. 4 (2011): 521–55; for a case study, see Benjamin R. Young, "Before 'Fire and Fury': The Role of Anger and Fear in U.S.–North Korea Relations, 1968–1994," *Korean Journal of Defense Analysis* 32, no. 2 (2020): 207–29, https://scholar.dsu.edu/anspapers/22.

16. Agnes Callard, "The Reason to Be Angry Forever," in *The Moral Psychology of Anger*, ed. Myisha Cherry and Owen Flanagan, 123–38 (New York: Rowman & Littlefield, 2018).

17. Todd H. Hall and Karen Yarhi-Milo, "The Personal Touch: Leaders' Impressions, Costly Signaling, and Assessments of Sincerity in International Affairs," *International Studies Quarterly* 56, no. 3 (2012): 560–73; Jay Wallace, "Trust, Anger, Resentment, Forgiveness: On Blame and Its Reasons," *European Journal of Philosophy* 27, no. 3 (2019): 537–52.

18. Jonathan J. Pierce, "Emotions and the Policy Process: Enthusiasm, Anger, and Fear," *Policy & Politics* 49, no. 4 (2021): 600–601.

19. Pierce, "Emotions and the Policy Process."

20. David Matsumoto, Seung Hee Yoo, and Joanne Chung, "The Expression of Anger across Cultures," in Potegal, Stemmler, and Spielberger, *International Handbook of Anger*, 125–37.

21. Robert C. Solomon, "On Emotions as Judgments," *American Philosophical Quarterly* 25, no. 2 (1988): 186.

22. Hyisung C. Hwang and David Matsumoto, "Emotional Expression," in *The Expression of Emotion: Philosophical, Psychological and Legal Perspectives*, ed. Catharine Abell and Joel Smith, 137–56 (Cambridge: Cambridge University Press, 2018), 130.

23. Hajo Adam, Aiwa Shirako, and William W. Maddux, "Cultural Variance in the Interpersonal Effects of Anger in Negotiations," *Psychological Science* 21, no. 6 (2010): 882–89; Michael Eid and Ed Diener, "Norms for Experiencing Emotions in Different Cultures: Inter- and Intranational Differences," *Journal of Personality and Social Psychology* 81, no. 5 (2001): 869–85.

24. Arlie Russell Hochschild, "Emotion Work, Feeling Rules, and Social Structure," *American Journal of Sociology* 85, no. 3 (1979): 551–75.

25. This applies to positive as well as negative emotions. See Lucile Eznack, "Crises as Signals of Strength: The Significance of Affect in Close Allies' Relationships," *Security Studies* 20, no. 2 (2011): 238–65.

26. John King Fairbank, *The United States and China* (Cambridge, MA: Harvard University Press, 1967).

27. David Kang, *China Rising: Peace, Power, and Order in East Asia* (New York: Columbia University Press, 2008).

28. The national and the personal are mutually constituted. See, for example, Shogo Suzuki, "Japanese Revisionists and the 'Korea Threat': Insights from Ontological Security," *Cambridge Review of International Affairs* 32, no. 3 (2019): 303–21; Oded Löwenheim and Gadi Heimann, "Revenge in International Politics," *Security Studies* 17, no. 4 (2008): 691–92.

29. Karen E. Smith, "Emotions and EU Foreign Policy," *International Affairs* 97, no. 2 (2021): 287–304; Maria Mälksoo, "The Normative Threat of Subtle Subversion: The Return of 'Eastern Europe' as an Ontological Insecurity Trope," *Cambridge Review of International Affairs* 32, no. 3 (2019): 365–83; Anthony Burke, "Security Cosmopolitanism," *Critical Studies on Security* 1, no. 1 (2013): 13–28; Ingrid Creppell, "The Concept of Normative Threat," *International Theory* 3, no. 3 (2011): 450–87.

30. See Marijke Breuning and Anna Pechenina, "Role Dissonance in Foreign Policy: Russia, Power and Intercountry Adoption," *Foreign Policy Analysis* 16, no. 1 (2020): 21–40; Ryan Beasley and Juliet Kaarbo, "Casting for a Sovereign Role: Socialising an Aspirant State in the Scottish Independence Referendum," *European Journal of International Relations* 24, no. 1 (2018): 18–32; Cameron G. Thies, *The United States, Israel, and the Search for International Order: Socializing States* (New York: Routledge, 2013).

31. See Leslie E. Wehner and Cameron G. Thies, "Leader Influence in Role Selection Choices: Fulfilling Role Theory's Potential for Foreign Policy Analysis," *International Studies Review* 23 no. 4 (2021): 1424–41.

32. Alisher Faizullaev, "Diplomacy and Self," *Diplomacy and Statecraft* 17, no. 3 (2006): 497–522.

33. This reciprocal state informs what Eznack calls affective dispositions. See Lucile Eznack, "The Mood Was Grave: Affective Disposition and States' Anger-Related Behaviour," *Contemporary Security Policy* 34, no. 3 (2013): 552–80.

34. Jungmin Seo, "Diagnosing Korea–Japan Relations through Thick Description: Revisiting the National Identity Formation Process," *Third World Quarterly* (2021).

35. Ronald Burke, "Emotional Diplomacy and Human Rights at the United Nations," *Human Rights Quarterly* 39, no. 2 (2017): 273–95.

36. Smith, "Emotions and EU Foreign Policy."

37. Arjun Clair, "Reason, Emotion and Solidarity in Humanitarian Advocacy," *Journal of Humanitarian Affairs* 3, no. 1 (2021): 51–50; Emma Hutchison, "Humanitarian Emotions through History: Imaging Suffering and Performing Aid," in *Emotional Bodies: The Historical Performativity of Emotions*, ed. Dolores Martín-Moruno and Beatriz Pichel, 219–41 (Urbana: University of Illinois Press, 2019).

38. Astrid H. M. Nordin et al., "Towards Global Relational Theorizing: A Dialogue between Sinophone and Anglophone Scholarship on Relationalism," *Cambridge Review of International Affairs* 32, no. 5 (2019): 570–81.

39. Brian Parkinson, "Interpersonal Emotion Transfer: Contagion and Social Appraisal," *Social and Personality Psychology Compass* 5, no. 7 (2011): 428–39.

40. Job van der Schalk et al., "Convergent and Divergent Responses to Emotional Displays of Ingroup and Outgroup," *Emotion* 11 (2011): 286–98.

41. A typical example is anti-racism. See Myisha Cherry, *The Case for Rage: Why Anger Is Essential to Anti-Racist Struggle* (Oxford: Oxford University Press, 2021).

42. Lisa J. Carlson and Raymond Dacey, "The Use of Fear and Anger to Alter Crisis Initiation," *Conflict Management and Peace Science* 31, no. 2 (2014): 168–92; Seanon S. Wong, "Stoics and Hotheads: Leaders' Temperament, Anger, and the Expression of Resolve in Face-to-Face Diplomacy," *Journal of Global Security Studies* 4, no. 2 (2019): 190–208.

43. A canonical reading of Confucianism is being keen to express anger as a ritual. See Zhaokun Xin, "A Fatal Encounter: Anger, Ritual, and Righteousness in *The Romance of the Three Kingdoms*," *Chinese Literature: Essays, Articles, Reviews* 41 (2019): 1–24. Alternatively, anger at out-group members reproduces the group identity. See Mehr Latif et al., "How Emotional Dynamics Maintain and Destroy White Supremacist Groups," *Humanity & Society* 42, no. 4 (2018): 480–501.

44. Limin Zhang, Shulin Yu, and Lianjiang Jiang, "Chinese Preschool Teachers' Emotional Labor and Regulation Strategies," *Teaching and Teacher Education* 92 (2020), https://www.sciencedirect.com/science/article/abs/pii/S0742051X19310972.

45. Neta C. Crawford, "Institutionalizing Passion in World Politics: Fear and Empathy," *International Theory* 6, no. 3 (2014): 535–57.

46. Vladimir I. Ozyumenko and Tatiana V. Larina, "Threat and Fear: Pragmatic Purposes of Emotionalisation in Media Discourse," *Russian Journal of Linguistics* 25, no. 3 (2021): 746–66.

47. Mabel Berezin, "Emotions and Political Identity: Mobilizing Affection for the Polity," in *Passionate Politics: Emotions and Social Movements*, ed. Jeff Goodwin, James M. Jasper, and Francesca Poletta, 83–98 (Chicago: University of Chicago Press, 2001); James M. Jasper, "Constructing Indignation: Anger Dynamics in Protest Movements," *Emotion Review* 6, no. 3 (2014): 208–13.

48. Catarina Kinnvall, "Ontological Insecurities and Postcolonial Imaginaries: The Emotional Appeal of Populism," *Humanity & Society* 42, no. 4 (2018): 523–43.

49. Céline Leboeuf, "Anger as a Political Emotion: A Phenomenological Perspective," in Cherry and Flanagan, *Moral Psychology of Anger*, 15–30; Antti Kauppinen, "Valuing Anger," in Cherry and Flanagan, *Moral Psychology of Anger*, 31–48.

50. Barrett, *How Emotions Are Made*; Batja Mesquita and Janxin Leu, "The Cultural Psychology of Emotions," in *The Handbook of Cultural Psychology*, ed. Shinobu Kitayama and Dov Cohen, 734–59 (New York: Guilford Press, 2008).

51. For example, Myisha Cherry, "Gendered Failures in Extrinsic Emotional Regulation; Or, Why Telling a Woman to 'Relax' or a Young Boy to 'Stop Crying Like a Girl' Is Not a Good Idea," *Philosophical Topics* 47, no. 2 (2019): 95–111; also Cherry, *Case for Rage*.

52. For example, see Benno Gammerl, Philipp Nielsen, and Margrit Pernau, eds., *Encounters with Emotions: Negotiating Cultural Differences since Early Modernity* (New York: Berghahn, 2019).

53. For a pioneering work, see Chiung-Chiu Huang, "Emotions and Relations: The Group Resentment in Vietnam and Mongolia's China Policy," International Studies Association Annual Convention, webinar, April 2021.

54. Martha C. Nussbaum, *Anger and Forgiveness: Resentment, Generosity, Justice* (Oxford: Oxford University Press, 2018); Andrew Linklater, "Anger and World Politics: How Collective Emotions Shift over Time," *International Theory* 6, no. 3 (2014): 574–78.

55. Taryn Shepperd, *Sino-US Relations and the Role of Emotion in State Action: Understanding Post–Cold War Crisis Interactions* (New York: Palgrave Macmillan, 2013).

56. Jessica Chen Weiss, "How Hawkish Is the Chinese Public? Another Look at 'Rising Nationalism' and Chinese Foreign Policy," *Journal of Contemporary China* 28, no. 119 (2019): 679–95.

57. Peter Gries and Richard Turcsányi, "Chinese Pride and European Prejudice: How Growing Resentment of China Cools Feelings toward Chinese in Europe," *Asian Survey* 61, no. 5 (2021): 742–66.

58. Wendt, "The State as Person in International Theory."

59. See "Angry China," the cover story of the May 3, 2008, issue of *The Economist*; also see Oxford Analytica, "Taipei Will Bear the Brunt of Beijing's Anger," *Expert Briefings*, January 11, 2017, https://doi.org/10.1108/OXAN-ES217216.

60. See, for example, Andrew Chubb, "Assessing Public Opinion's Influence on Foreign Policy: The Case of China's Assertive Maritime Behavior," *Asian Security* 15, no. 2 (2019): 159–79; Heller, "More Rigor to Emotions!"

61. Lena Masch, *Politicians' Expressions of Anger and Leadership Evaluations: Empirical Evidence from Germany* (Baden-Baden: Nomos, 2020).

62. Ming Dong Gu, "The Theory of the Dao and Taiji: A Chinese Model of the Mind," *Journal of Chinese Philosophy* 36, no. 1 (2009):157–75; Jiansheng Hu, *Big Tradition and Chinese Mythological Studies* (Singapore: Springer, 2020).

63. On the bilateral necessity of the relationship culture, see Jan B. Heide, "Interorganizational Governance in Marketing Channels," *Journal of Marketing* 58, no. 1 (1994): 71–85.

64. Min Wang, Yulan Han, and Yiyi Su, "Social Contagion or Strategic Choice? The Interpersonal Effects of Emotions during Chinese Negotiations," *Chinese Management Studies* 11, no. 3 (2017): 463–78.

Chapter 5

I would like to thank Hung-Jen Wang for consenting to the inclusion in this chapter of a revised version of the coauthored paper "Hanging On without a Solution," presented at the Second International Forum on China and World Order on September 28–29, 2019, at Renmin University.

1. The idea that disputes require resolution is considered common sense in IR studies, and conflict resolution occupies a central position in the IR curricula of almost all universities.

2. Burak Kadercan, "Making Sense of Survival: Refining the Treatment of State Preferences in Neorealist Theory," *Review of International Studies* 39, no. 4 (2013): 1015–37.

3. David M. Edelstein, *Over the Horizon: Time, Uncertainty, and the Rise of Great Powers* (Ithaca, NY: Cornell University Press, 2017).

4. Tamara A. Trownsell et al., "Differing about Difference: Relational IR from around the World," *International Studies Perspectives* 22, no. 1 (2021): 25–64; Daniel Fischlin, Ajay Heble, and George Lipsitz, *The Fierce Urgency of Now: Improvisation, Rights, and the Ethics of Cocreation* (Durham, NC: Duke University Press, 2013).

5. Myisha Cherry and Owen Flanagan, eds., *The Moral Psychology of Anger* (London: Rowman & Littlefield, 2018).

6. Gülden Gökçen, Coskun Arslan, and Zeliha Tras, "Examining the Relationship between Patience, Emotion Regulation Difficulty and Cognitive Flexibility," *European Journal of Educational Studies* 7, no. 7 (2020): 131–52.

7. Sarah A. Schnitker, "An Examination of Patience and Well-Being," *Journal of Positive Psychology* 7, no. 4 (2012): 263–80

8. Peter J. Jankowski et al., "The Influence of Experiential Avoidance, Humility and Patience on the Association between Religious/Spiritual Exploration and Well-Being," *Journal of Happiness Studies* 23, no. 5 (2022): 2137–56.

9. Jennifer Shubert et al., "Disentangling Character Strengths from Developmental Competencies: The Virtue of Patience and Self-Regulatory Competencies," *Journal of Positive Psychology* 17, no. 2 (2022): 203–9.

10. Yeşim Aksan and Mustafa Aksan, "Armed with *Patience, Suffering* an Emotion: Conceptualization of Life, Morality, and Emotion in Turkish," in *Metaphor in Use: Context, Culture, and Communication*, ed. Fiona MacArthur et al., 285–308 (Amsterdam: John Benjamins, 2012).

11. Owen Flanagan, introduction to Cherry and Flanagan, *Moral Psychology of Anger*, xxi.

12. Bryce Huebner, "Anger and Patience," in Cherry and Flanagan, *Moral Psychology of Anger*, 93, 99, 101.

13. Simine Vazire and David C. Funder, "Impulsivity and the Self-Defeating Behaviour of Narcissists," *Personality and Social Psychology Review* 10, no. 2 (2006): 154–65.

14. Salman Akhtar, "Patience," *Psychoanalytic Review* 102, no. 1 (2015): 93–122.

15. Leanne E. Bishara, "Anger Regulation, Parenting Characteristics and Adolescent Patience" (PhD diss., Fuller Theological Seminary, 2020), 135, https://www.proquest.com/openview/3879636d67ac0a707767e5c95af8d281/1.

16. Sarah A. Schnitker and Robert A. Emmons, "Patience as a Virtue: Religious and Psychological Perspectives," in *Research in the Social Scientific Study of Religion*, vol. 18, ed. Ralph L. Piedmont, 177–207 (Leiden: Brill, 2007); Sarah A. Schnitker et al., "The Virtue of Patience, Spirituality, and Suffering: Integrating Lessons from Positive Psychology, Psychology of Religion, and Christian Theology," *Psychology of Religion and Spirituality* 9, no. 3 (2017): 264–75.

17. N. Ibn Rasoul Sanaati, F. Hossein Sabet, and A. Motamedi, "Role of Patience with Mediating Self-Differentiation in Emotional Regulation and Perceived Stress among Nurses," *Islamic Life Style Centered on Health* 2, no. 4 (2018): 211–16.

18. I. William Zartman, "Ripeness: The Hurting Stalemate and Beyond," in *International Conflict Resolution after the Cold War*, ed. Paul C. Stern and Daniel Druckman, 225–50 (Washington, DC: National Academy Press, 2000).

19. James W. McAuley, Catherine McGlynn, and Jon Tonge, "Conflict Resolution in Asymmetric and Symmetric Situations: Northern Ireland as a Case Study," *Dynamics of Asymmetric Conflict* 1, no. 1 (2008): 88–102.

20. Hedley Bull, *The Anarchical Society: A Study of Order in World Politics* (London: Macmillan, 1977).

21. Emannuel Adler, "The Spread of Security Communities: Communities of Practice, Self-Restraint, and NATO's Post-Cold War Transformation," *European Journal of International Relations* 14, no. 2 (2008): 195–230

22. Stephen Krasnes, *Sovereignty: Organized Hypocrisy* (Princeton, NJ: Princeton University Press, 1999).

23. Ian Manners, "The Normative Ethics of the European Union," *International Affairs* 84, no. 1 (2008): 46–60.

24. Emilian Kavalski, "*Guanxi* or What Is the Chinese for Relational Theory of World Politics," *International Relations of the Asia-Pacific* 18, no. 3 (2018):

397–420; Chih-yu Shih, "Engendering International Relations of Shanghai: The Metaphor of Cheongsam and the Construction of Post-Western Identities," *International Politics* 58 (2021): 661–78.

25. Henry Kissinger, *World Order* (New York: Penguin Press, 2014); Hans Morgenthau, *Politics among Nations: The Struggle for Power and Peace*, 4th ed. (New York: Knopf, 1967).

26. Alexander Wendt, "Anarchy Is What States Make of It: The Social Construction of Power Politics," *International Organization* 46, no. 2 (1992): 405.

27. Wendt, "Anarchy," 407.

28. David L. Hall and Roger T. Ames, *The Democracy of the Dead: Dewey, Confucius, and the Hope for Democracy in China* (Chicago: Open Court, 1999).

29. Yaqing Qin, "A Relational Theory of World Politics," *International Studies Review* 18, no. 1 (2016): 33–47.

30. Karen Danna Lynch, "Modeling Role Enactment: Linking Role Theory and Social Cognition," *Journal for the Theory of Social Behavior* 37, no. 4 (2007): 379–99; John R. Rizzo, Robert J. House, and Sidney I. Lirtzman, "Role Conflict and Ambiguity in Complex Organizations," *Administrative Science Quarterly* 15, no. 2 (1970): 150–63; William Goode, "A Theory of Role Strain," *American Sociological Review* 25, no. 4 (1960): 483–96.

31. Nele Noesselt, "Revisiting the Debate on Constructing a Theory of International Relations with Chinese Characteristics," *China Quarterly* 222 (2015): 430–48; Chiung-chiu Huang and Chih-yu Shih, *Harmonious Intervention: China's Quest for International Security* (New York: Ashgate, 2015); Chih-yu Shih et al., *China and International Theory: The Balance of Relationships* (Abingdon, UK: Routledge, 2019).

32. Aaron M. Hoffman, "A Conceptualization of Trust in International Relations," *European Journal of International Relations* 8 (September 2002): 375–401.

33. Morton Deutsch, "Trust and Suspicion," *Journal of Conflict Resolution* 2, no. 4 (1958): 265–79; Morton Deutsch, "The Effect of Motivational Orientation upon Trust and Suspicion," *Human Relations* 13, no. 2 (1960): 123–39; Glen D. Mellinger, "Interpersonal Trust as a Factor in Communication," *Journal of Abnormal Social Psychology* 52, no. 3 (1956): 304–9.

34. Ken Booth and Nicholas Wheeler, *The Security Dilemma: Fear, Cooperation and Trust in World Politics* (New York: Palgrave MacMillan, 2007).

35. For example, see Bill McEvily, Akbar Zaheer, and Darcy K. Fudge Kamal, "Mutual and Exclusive: Dyadic Sources of Trust in Interorganizational Exchange," *Organization Science* 28, no. 1 (2017): 74–92; Stephen T. La Macchia et al., "In Small We Trust: Lay Theories about Small and Large Groups," *Personality and Social Psychology Bulletin* 42, no. 10 (2016): 1321–34.

36. For example, see Pengfei Rong, Chengyan Li, and Jiaqi Xie, "Learning, Trust, and Creativity in Top Management Teams: Team Reflexivity as a Moderator," *Social Behavior and Personality* 47, no. 5 (2019): 1–14, https://doi.

org/10.2224/sbp.8096; A. Phill Pearce, David N. Naumann, and David O'Reilly, "Mission Command: Applying Principles of Military Leadership to the SARS-CoV-2 (COVID-19) Crisis," *BMJ Military Health* 167, no. 1 (2020): 3–4, https://doi.org/10.1136/bmjmilitary-2020-001485.

37. For example, see Melissa E. Graebner, Fabrice Lumineau, and Darcy Fudge Kamal, "Unrequited: Asymmetry in Interorganizational Trust," *Strategic Organization* 18, no. 2 (2018): 362–74; Marek Michalski, Jose Luis Montes, and Ram Narasimhan, "Relational Asymmetry, Trust, and Innovation in Supply Chain Management: A Non-Linear Approach," *International Journal of Logistic Management* 30, no. 4 (2019): 303–28.

38. For example, see Carolina Ramirez and Carol Chan, "Making Community under Shared Conditions of Insecurity: The Negotiation of Ethnic Borders in a Multicultural Commercial Neighbourhood in Santiago, Chile," *Journal of Ethnic and Migration Studies* 46, no. 13 (2020): 2764–81; Jermaine S. Ma and Paul R. Hoard, "A Tale of Two Fears: Negotiating Trust and Neighborly Relations in Urbanizing Turkey," *Journal of Contemporary European Studies* 28, no. 3 (2020): 322–34.

39. For example, see Tessa Haesevoets et al., "Understanding the Positive Effect of Financial Compensation on Trust after Norm Violations: Evidence from fMRI in Favor of Forgiveness," *Journal of Applied Psychology* 103, no. 5 (2018): 578–90; Yubao Cui et al., "How to Use Apology and Compensation to Repair Competence—versus Integrity-Based Trust Violations in E-Commerce," *Electronic Commerce Research and Applications* 32 (November/December 2018): 37–48.

40. See David Kang, "Hierarchy and Stability in Asian International Relations," in *International Relations Theory and the Asia-Pacific*, ed. G. John Ikenberry and Michael Mastanduno, 163–190 (New York: Columbia University Press, 2003); Dong Ryul Lee, "China's Policy and Influence on the North Korea Nuclear Issue: Denuclearization and/or Stabilization of the Korean Peninsula?," *Korean Journal of Defense Analysis* 22, no. 2 (2010): 163–81; Junsheng Wang, *Chaohe wenti yu zhongguo yuese: Duoyuan beijingxia de gongtong guanli* [The North Korean nuclear crisis and the role of China: Common management under the multi-factor background] (Beijing: Beijing Zhishi Publisher, 2012).

41. Jane Perlez, "China and South Korea Affirm Antinuclear Goals," *New York Times*, July 3, 2014, https://www.nytimes.com/2014/07/04/world/asia/presidents-of-china-and-south-korea-reaffirm-push-for-north-korean-denuclearization.html.

42. When commenting on the statement's level of uncertainty about denuclearizing the Korean Peninsula, *New York Times* reporter Jane Perlez also cited the opinion of Moon Chung-in, special national security adviser to then South Korean president Moon Jae-in, who argued that China will never make reference to North Korea in its official public statement regarding the Korean Peninsula crisis.

43. Alexander Smith, "North Korea Launched No Missiles in 2018, but That Isn't Necessarily Due to Trump," *NBC News*, December 31, 2018, https://www.nbcnews.com/news/world/north-korea-launched-no-missiles-2018-isn-t-necessarily-due-n949971.

44. "Sheping: Zhongguo zhenxi zhongchao youhao, chaoxian yexu zhenxi" [Editorial comment: China cherishes Sino–North Korea friendship, North Korea should do so as well], *Huanqiu News*, February 6, 2013, http://opinion.huanqiu.com/editorial/2013-02/3622838.html.

45. "Waijiaobu fayanren qin gang jiu anlihui tongguo chaoxian heshiyan wenti jueyi da jizhe wen" [Ministry of Foreign Affairs spokesman Qin Gang answers reporters' questions on UN Security Council's resolution on North Korea nuclear test], Ministry of Foreign Affairs of the People's Republic of China (website), March 7, 2013, http://mo.ocmfa.gov.cn/chn/jbwzlm/fyrth_1/201303/t20130307_7647147.htm.

46. Yan Liang, Bao Er-wen, and Zhao Yue, "Guoji guancha: Zhongguo zancheng duichao xinjueyi de sanda yinsu" [International observation: Three major factors for why China agrees to new resolution on North Korea], *Xinhua News*, March 2, 2016, http://www.gov.cn/xinwen/2016-03/03/content_5048431.htm.

47. Ministry of Commerce of the People's Republic of China, General Administration of Customs announcement no. 11, April 5, 2016, http://www.mofcom.gov.cn/article/b/c/201604/20160401289770.shtml.

48. "Sheping: Zhongchao guanxi huo geng zaogao, zhongguo yingyou zhunbei" [Editorial comment: Sino–North Korea relations may worsen, China should prepare], *Huanqiu News*, April 28, 2017, http://opinion.huanqiu.com/editorial/2017-04/10555325.html.

49. See Ministry of Commerce of the People's Republic of China, General Administration of Customs announcement no. 52, September 22, 2017, http://www.mofcom.gov.cn/article/b/c/201709/20170902648729.shtml.

50. "Engagement," in this case, refers to the normalization of diplomatic/political relations, especially in terms of the dialogue between top Chinese and North Korean leaders during periods of economic limitations and UN sanctions. See Ba Gao, *China's Economic Engagement in North Korea* (Singapore: Palgrave Macmillan, 2019).

51. Xinhua News Agency, "Xijinping tong jinzhengen juxing huitan" [Xi Jinping holds meeting with Kim Jong-un], *Chinese Communist Party News*, March 28, 2018, http://cpc.people.com.cn/n1/2018/0328/c64094-29892765.html. Regarding the military links between the two countries, see Xinhua News Agency, "Guofangbu: Chuancheng zhongchao youyi, fazhan liangjun guanxi" [Defense department: To inherit Sino–North Korea friendship, to develop mutual military relationship], *People's Daily Online*, June 27, 2019, http://military.people.com.cn/BIG5/n1/2019/0627/c1011-31199766.html. Despite the international sanctions, China and North Korea opened a new border checkpoint connecting

the Chinese city of Jian with Manpo in North Korea. See Jon Herskovitz and Dandan Li, "China, North Korea Open New Border Crossing Despite Sanctions," *Bloomberg*, April 8, 2019, https://www.bloomberg.com/news/articles/2019-04-08/china-north-korea-open-new-border-crossing-despite-sanctions.

52. Xinhua News Agency, "Zhongguo daibiao: Dui chaoxian zhicai buying yingxiang rendao jiuyuan" [Chinese representative: Sanction on North Korea should not affect humanitarian aid], *Sohu*, April 11, 2019, http://www.sohu.com/a/307265627_267106.

53. "China Suggests Sanctions Relief for North Korea after Trump-Kim Summit," June 12, 2018, *CNBC*, https://www.cnbc.com/2018/06/12/china-suggests-sanctions-relief-for-north-korea-after-trump-kim-summit.html. The Chinese government made the same recommendation for sanctions relief in April 2018 and June 2019. See "Zhongguoo jiang guli anli hui fangsong dui chaoxian zhicai: zhongguo huiying" [Will China Encourage the Security Council to Relax Sanctions on North Korea? Ministry of Foreign Affairs Response], *Baidu*, April 23, 2018, http://baijiahao.baidu.com/s?id=1598538822264167526; "Zhong e zai anli hui lianshou gezhi meiguo yaoqiu tingzhi dui chao chukou shiyou tian" [China and Russia Join Forces at the Security Council to Shelve the U.S. Proposal to Halt Oil Exports to North Korea], *Sina News*, June 20, 2019, http://news.sina.com.cn/o/2019-06-20/doc-ihytcitk6434265.shtml.

54. Yan Xuetong, "Dui zhongmei guanxi buwendingxin fenxi" [The instability of China-US relations], *Shijie Jingji yu Zhengzhi* [World economics and politics] 12 (2010): 4–30.

55. Michael C. Desch, "America's Liberal Illiberalism: The Ideological Origins of Overreaction in U.S. Foreign Policy," *International Security* 32, no. 3 (2007/8): 7–43.

56. "Jiangou zhongmei xinxing daguo guanxi" [Constructing a new type of Sino-US great power relations], *People's Daily Online*, June 7, 2013, http://cpc.people.com.cn/xuexi/n/2015/0721/c397563-27337996.html.

57. Six months prior to the September 2016 G20 meeting, Beijing used the idea of reciprocity to address what Chinese scholar Shi Yinhong describes as "the lowest point of the two countries' relations in 15 years." He was quoted by a *New York Times* reporter as speculating that "Mr. Xi could pledge not to go any further in militarizing disputed islands . . . [and] the Americans could agree to stop sending their warships and aircraft on 'freedom of navigation' patrols in territory claimed by China." Jane Perlez, "Obama Faces a Tough Balancing Act over South China Sea," *New York Times*, March 30, 2016, https://www.nytimes.com/2016/03/30/world/asia/obama-xi-jinping-meeting-washington.html.

58. For details on Chinese views regarding US willingness to build a constructive relationship, see Ding Jian-ting, "You aobama guoqing ziwen panduan zhongmei guanxi" [Judging Sino-US relations from Obama's State of Union address], *Chinese Communist Party News*, January 23, 2015, http://cpc.people.

com.cn/n/2015/0123/c87228-26434983.html. See also "Xijinping tong meiguo zongtong aobama gongtong huijian jizhe" [Xi Jinping and US president Obama meet news reporters together], *Xinhua News*, September 26, 2015, http://www.xinhuanet.com/politics/2015-09/26/c_1116685447.htm; "Zongjie zhongmei guanxi fazhan jingyan" [To sum up the experiences of Sino-US relations development], *People's Daily*, overseas edition, November 21, 2016, http://paper.people.com.cn/rmrbhwb/html/2016-11/21/content_1729086.htm.

59. "Meiguo huanying zhongguo jiechu meiguo niurou jinling" [US welcomes China's lifting of ban on US beef exports], *Huanqiu News*, September 23, 2016, http://world.huanqiu.com/hot/2016-09/9479022.html.

60. "'Xiaohui' chengguo churen yilia, dacheng duoxiang zhongda xieyi" [Achievements of 'Xi-Obama meeting' exceed expectations, reaching many important agreements], *Huanqiu News*, November 14, 2014, http://world.huanqiu.com/exclusive/2014-11/5202135.html.

61. Mark Landler, "U.S. and China Reach Climate Accord after Months of Talks," *New York Times*, November 11, 2014, https://www.nytimes.com/2014/11/12/world/asia/china-us-xi-obama-apec.html.

62. An anecdote concerning the Taiwan Relations Act of that same year illustrates the challenges related to the Sino-US negotiations. According to a 2014 congressional research report on the evolution of the One China policy, Senator Jacob Javits commented on the ambiguity of the Chinese word for "acknowledge" (*cheng ren*, also interpreted as "recognize") when arguing that the US should not subscribe to the Chinese version of "One China." However, deputy secretary of state Warren Christopher eventually announced, "We regard the word 'acknowledge' as being the word that is determinative for the US." Shirley A. Kan, *China/Taiwan: Evolution of the "One China" Policy—Key Statements from Washington, Beijing, and Taipei* (Washington, DC: Congressional Research Service, 2014), 39n90.

63. Jon Sharman, "China Flies Nuclear Bomber over South China Sea as a 'Message' to Donald Trump," *Independent*, December 11, 2016, https://www.independent.co.uk/news/world/asia/china-bomber-flight-send-message-donald-trump-taiwan-a7468021.html.

64. "Zhongfan duncu mei xinyijie zhengfu hanlingdaoren shenzhong tuoshan chuli taiwan wenti" [Chinese side urges new US government and leader to handle Taiwan issue seriously], *Xinhua News*, December 12, 2016, http://www.xinhuanet.com/world/2016-12/12/c_1120103304.htm.

65. National Defense Authorization Act for Fiscal Year 2019, H.R. 5515, 115th Cong. (2018), pp. 422–23, https://www.congress.gov/115/bills/hr5515/BILLS-115hr5515enr.pdf.

66. "Jiefangjun taihai junyan jinggao taimei: Guojia tongyi dizian burong tiaozhan" [The People's Liberation Army's military exercise in Taiwan Strait warns Taiwan and the United States: The bottom line of national unification

cannot be challenged], *Sina News*, April 14, 2018, http://mil.news.sina.com.cn/china/2018-04-14/doc-ifzcyxmu3997262.shtml.

67. Kristin Huang, "China Flexes Its Military Might with Series of Naval Exercises in Local Waters," *South China Morning Post*, August 13, 2018, https://www.scmp.com/news/china/diplomacy-defence/article/2159532/china-flexes-its-military-might-series-naval-exercises.

68. "China Demands U.S. Cancel Potential Arms Sale to Taiwan," *Reuters*, July 19, 2019, updated July 18, 2022, https://www.reuters.com/business/aerospace-defense/china-demands-us-cancel-potential-arms-sale-taiwan-2022-07-18/.

69. Laurie Chen, "China to Conduct Military Exercises near Taiwan after US Agrees US$2.2 Billion Arms Deal," *South China Morning Post*, July 14, 2019, https://www.scmp.com/news/china/military/article/3018551/china-conduct-military-exercises-near-taiwan-after-us-agrees.

Chapter 6

1. Andrea Oelsner and Simon Koschut, "A Framework for the Study of International Friendship," in *Friendship and International Relations*, ed. Simon Koschut and Andrea Oelsner, 3–31 (London: Palgrave Macmillan, 2014).

2. Todd H. Hall, *Emotional Diplomacy: Official Emotion on the International Stage* (Ithaca, NY: Cornell University Press, 2015); Simon Keller, "Against Friendship between Countries," *Journal of International Political Theory* 5, no. 1 (2009): 59–74.

3. Felix Berenskötter, "Friends, There Are No Friends? An Intimate Reframing of the International," *Millennium* 35, no. 3 (2007): 647–76.

4. Ramon Aron, *Peace and War: A Theory of International Relations* (New Brunswick, NJ: Transaction, 2003); Zeev Maoz et al., "What Is the Enemy of My Enemy? Causes and Consequences of Imbalanced International Relations, 1816–2001," *Journal of Politics* 69, no. 1 (2007): 100–115.

5. Astrid H. M. Nordin and Graham M. Smith, "Relating Self and Other in Chinese and Western Thought," *Cambridge Review of International Affairs* 32, no. 5 (2019): 636–53, https://doi.org/10.1080/09557571.2019.1576160.

6. Astrid H. M. Nordin and Graham M. Smith, "Reintroducing Friendship to International Relations: Relational Ontologies from China to the West," *International Relations of the Asia-Pacific* 18, no. 3 (2018): 369–96.

7. Alexander Wendt, *Social Theory of International Politics* (Cambridge: Cambridge University Press, 1999); Ruth Craggs, "Hospitality in Geopolitics and the Making of Commonwealth International Relations," *Geoforum* 52 (2014): 43.

8. P. E. Digeser, *Friendship Reconsidered: What It Means and How It Matters to Politics* (New York: Columbia University Press, 2016); Caroline Patsias and Sylvie Patsias, "Social Forums and Friendship: A New Way of Contemplating

the Notion of Friendship in International Relations," in Koschut and Oelsner, *Friendship and International Relations*, 167; Jussi M. Hanhimäki, *Scandinavia and the United States: An Insecure Friendship* (London: Prentice-Hall International, 1997).

9. Graham M. Smith, "Friendship, State, and Nation," in Koschut and Oelsner, *Friendship and International Relations*, 51–71.

10. Thomas Risse-Kappen, "Democratic Peace—Warlike Democracies? A Social Constructivist Interpretation of the Liberal Argument," *European Journal of International Relations* 1, no. 4 (1995): 491–517.

11. William K. Rawlins, *Friendship Matters: Communication, Dialectics, and the Life Course* (London: Routledge, 2017), 17–20; Kristin Davies and Arthur Aron, "Friendship Development and Intergroup Attitudes: The Role of Interpersonal and Intergroup Friendship Processes," *Journal of Social Issues* 71, no. 3 (2016): 489–510; Dali Ma, "Social Belonging and Economic Action: Affection-Based Social Circles in the Creation of Private Entrepreneurship," *Social Forces* 94, no. 1 (2015): 87–114; Rosemary Blieszner, "The Worth of Friendship: Can Friends Keep Us Happy and Healthy?" *Generations* 38, no. 1 (2014): 24–30.

12. Yunxiang Yan, *The Flow of Gifts: Reciprocity and Social Networks in a Chinese Village* (Stanford, CA: Stanford University Press, 1996); Mayfair Mei-hui Yang, *Gifts, Favors, and Banquets: The Art of Social Relationships in China* (Ithaca, NY: Cornell University Press, 1994).

13. Sin Liang, Sibin Wu, and Shujuan Zhang, "From Friendship to Family: *Jiangyiqi* and Strong Interpersonal Relationship Development in Chinese Organizations," *Management and Organization Review* 14, no. 2 (2018): 275–303; Hak Yin Li and Seanon Wong, "The Evolution of Chinese Public Diplomacy and the Rise of Think Tanks," *Place Branding and Public Diplomacy* 14, no. 1 (2018): 36–46; Chuka Enuka, "Aid in Sino-African Relations: An Analysis of the Promptings, Pluses and Problems of China's Aid to Africa," *IUP Journal of International Relations* 5, no. 2 (2011): 41–53.

14. Mencius said, "Friends exhibit trustworthiness" (*Mencius*, Tengwengong 1). Zengzi reflected on himself everyday: "Do my friends not benefit from my trustworthiness?" (Tengwengong 1).

15. Confucius advised that the prince and his officials should not meet other princes or their officials outside the capacity authorized by the son of heaven (*Analects*, Guliangzhuan).

16. Heather Devere, "Friendship in International Treaties," in Koschut and Oelsner, *Friendship and International Relations*, 182–98; Andrea Oelsner, "Friendship, Mutual Trust and the Evolution of Regional Peace in the International System," *Critical Review of International Social and Political Philosophy* 10, no. 2 (2007): 257–79.

17. William C. Kirby, "China's Internationalization in the Early People's Republic: Dreams of a Socialist World Economy," *China Quarterly* 188 (2006): 870–90.

18. Rachel Applebaum, "The Friendship Project: Socialist Internationalism in the Soviet Union and Czechoslovakia in the 1950s and 1960s," *Slavic Review* 74, no. 3 (2015): 484–507; Benjamin Tromly, "Brother or Other? East European Students in Soviet Higher Education Establishments, 1948–1956," *European History Quarterly* 44, no. 1 (2014): 80–102; Cristofer Scarboro, "The Brother-City Project and Socialist Humanism: Haskovo, Tashkent and 'Sblizhenie,'" *Slavonic and East European Review* 85, no. 3 (2007): 522–42.

19. Nicolai Volland, "Translating the Socialist State: Cultural Exchange, National Identity, and the Socialist World in the Early PRC," *Twentieth-Century China* 33, no. 2 (2008): 51–72.

20. Yan Li, "Building Friendship: Soviet Influence, Socialist Modernity, and Chinese Cityscape in the 1950s," *Quarterly Journal of Chinese Studies* 1, no. 4 (2012): 50.

21. Yan Li, "Building Friendship," 50.

22. Jing-he Luan and Fu-sheng Li, "A Comparison between the Sino-Soviet Treaty of Friendship and Alliance and the Sino-Soviet Treaty of Friendship, Alliance and Mutual Assistance," *Contemporary China History Studies* 11, no. 2 (2004): 94–103.

23. Greg Guldin, "Anthropology by Other Names: The Impact of Sino-Soviet Friendship on the Anthropological Sciences," *Australian Journal of Chinese Affairs* 27 (January 1992): 133–49.

24. Shaun Breslin, "China and the Global Order: Signalling Threat or Friendship?," *International Affairs* 89, no. 3 (2013): 615–34; Chih-yu Shih and Jiwu Yin, "Between Core National Interest and a Harmonious World: Reconciling Self-Role Conceptions in Chinese Foreign Policy," *Chinese Journal of International Politics* 6, no. 1 (2013): 59–84.

25. Robert Albro, "The Disjunction of Image and World in US and Chinese Soft Power Projection," *International Journal of Cultural Policy* 21, no. 4 (2015): 381–99; Gary D. Rawnsley and Ming-yeh Rawnsley, *Routledge Handbook of Chinese Media* (Abingdon, UK: Routledge, 2015), 468.

26. Fei-Ling Wang, *The China Order: Centralia, World Empire, and the Nature of Chinese Power* (Albany: State University of New York Press, 2017).

27. Austin Jersild, *The Sino-Soviet Alliance: An International History* (Chapel Hill: University of North Carolina Press, 2014).

28. Fei-Ling Wang, *The China Order*, 8.

29. Yafeng Xia, *Negotiating with the Enemy: U.S.-China Talks during the Cold War, 1949–1972* (Bloomington: Indiana University Press, 2006), 25, 153.

30. James Beatti and Richard Bullen, "Embracing Friendship through Gift and Exchange: Rewi Alley and the Art of Museum Diplomacy in Cold War China and New Zealand," *Australian and New Zealand Journal of Art* 16, no. 2 (2016): 149–66; Casper Wits, "The Japan Group: Managing China's People's Diplomacy toward Japan in the 1950s," *East Asia* 33, no. 2 (2016): 91–110.

31. Franziska Seraphim, "People's Diplomacy: The Japan-China Friendship Association and Critical War Memory in the 1950s," *Asia-Pacific Journal* 5, no. 8 (2007): 1–19.

32. Huanxin Zhao, "Everyday People Crucial to Sino-US Friendship," *China Daily*, November 1, 2018, http://www.chinadaily.com.cn/a/201811/01/WS5bda38d9a310eff303285c9a.html; Falk Hartig, "Communicating China to the World: Confucius Institutes and China's Strategic Narratives," *Politics* 35, nos. 3–4 (2015): 245–58; Hong Fang and Xiaozheng Xiong, "Communist China: Sport, Politics and Diplomacy," *International Journal of the History of Sport* 19, nos. 2–3 (2010): 319–42; Guanhua Wang, " 'Friendship First': China's Sports Diplomacy during the Cold War," *Journal of American-East Asian Relations* 12, nos. 3–4 (2003): 133–53.

33. Pak Nung Wong, *Destined Statecraft: Eurasian Small Power Politics and Strategic Cultures in Geopolitical Shifts* (Singapore: Springer, 2018), 149–79.

34. Austin Jersild, "The Dilemmas of Cultural Collaboration in Sino-Soviet Relations: The Failure of Suzhong Youhao, 1958–1960," *Modern China Studies* 22, no. 1 (2015): 169–90.

35. Mikio Oishi and Nguyen Minh Quang, "Brothers in Trouble: China-Vietnam Territorial Disputes and Their Bilateral Approach to Conflict Management," *International Journal of China Studies* 8, no. 3 (2017): 287–319.

36. Solomon Tai Okajare, "Sino-Western Rivalry as a New Trajectory of Neo-imperialism," *Social Transformations* 3, no. 1 (2015): 27–55.

37. Sunny Ifeanyi Odinye, "China-Africa Relationship and Friendship," *Interdisciplinary Journal of African & Asian Studies* 2, no. 1 (2016), https://www.nigerianjournalsonline.com/index.php/published_Articles/article/view/496; Reynaldo C. Ileto, "Independence and Friendship: Shared Histories in the China–Philippines Sea Crisis," in *Southeast Asia and China: A Contest in Mutual Socialization*, ed. Lowell Dittmer and Ngeow Chow Bing, 71–92 (Singapore: World Scientific, 2017).

38. Evgeny Roshchin, "The Concept of Friendship: From Princes to States," *European Journal of International Relations* 12, no. 4 (2006): 599–624.

39. Melissa Leftkowitz, "Revolutionary Friendship: Representing Africa during the Mao Era," in *China-Africa Relations: Building Images through Cultural Cooperation, Media Representation, and Communication* (Abingdon, UK: Routledge, 2017); Martin Bailey, "China and Tanzania: A Friendship between Most Unequal Equals," *Millennium* 2, no. 1 (1973): 17–31.

40. Krishna Prakash Gupta, "China's Theory and Practice of Intervention," *China Report* 7, no. 6 (1971): 21.

41. Kuisong Yang, "The Initial Clashes of National Interests and National Sentiments between China and the Soviet Union—On the Negotiation and Signing of the Treaty of Friendship, Alliance and Mutual Assistance," *Historical Research* 6 (2001): 103–19.

42. Ariel Cohen, "The Russia-China Friendship and Cooperation Treaty: A Strategic Shift in Eurasia?" Heritage Foundation (website), last modified July 18, 2001, https://www.heritage.org/europe/report/the-russia-china-friendship-and-cooperation-treaty-strategic-shift-eurasia.

43. Huiyun Feng, *Will China and Russia form an Alliance against the United States? The New Geostrategic Game*, DIIS report 2015:07 (Copenhagen: Danish Institute for International Studies, 2015), https://www.econstor.eu/handle/10419/120393.

44. Alexander Korolev, "Beyond the Putin-Xi Relationship: China, Russia, and Great Power Politics," *The Diplomat*, February 1, 2023, https://magazine.thediplomat.com/#/issues/-NMXxJxnFrdSSLJ9iQlX/preview/-NMXxKRvMSpxQNdTfKaL.

45. Benjamin Self, "China and Japan: A Façade of Friendship," *Washington Quarterly* 26, no. 1 (2002): 77–88.

46. Jae Ho Chung, "The Rise of China and East Asia: A New Regional Order on the Horizon?" *Chinese Political Science Review* 1, no. 1 (2016): 47–59; Jin Qiu, "The Politics of History and Historical Memory in China-Japan Relations," *Journal of Chinese Political Science* 11, no. 1 (2006): 25–53.

47. Self, "China and Japan."

48. Breslin, "China and the Global Order."

49. James Rice, "China-US Friendship Goes Deeper Than Fights over Trade, Pollution," *Caixin*, September 12, 2018, https://www.caixinglobal.com/2018-09-12/opinion-us-china-relations-have-always-been-mutually-beneficial-101325096.html.

50. Cheng Li and Lucy Xu, "Chinese Enthusiasm and American Cynicism: The 'New Type of Great Power Relations,'" *China-US Focus*, last modified December 4, 2014, https://www.chinausfocus.com/foreign-policy/chinese-enthusiasm-and-american-cynicism-over-the-new-type-of-great-power-relations/.

51. Quanyu Shang, "Sino-Indian Friendship in the Nehru Era: A Chinese Perspective," *China Report* 41, no. 3 (2005): 237–52.

52. Manoj Kumar, "China's a Factor in India's Regional Approach," *Asian Times*, January 17, 2020, https://asiatimes.com/2020/01/china-as-a-factor-in-indias-regional-approach/.

53. Weiqi Zhang, "Neither Friend nor Big Brother: China's Role in North Korean Foreign Policy Strategy," *Palgrave Communications* 4 (2018), https://doi.org/10.1057/s41599-018-0071-2.

54. Alexander L. Vuving, "Strategy and Evolution of Vietnam's China Policy: A Changing Mixture of Pathways," *Asian Survey* 46, no. 6 (2006): 805–24.

55. Inayat Kalim, "China Pakistan Economic Corridor—A Geo-economic Masterstroke of China," *South Asian Studies* 32, no. 2 (2017): 461–75.

56. Chi-shad Liang, "Burma's Relations with the People's Republic of China: From Delicate Friendship to Genuine Co-operation," in *Burma: The*

Challenge of Change in a Divided Society, ed. Peter Carey, 71–93 (London: Palgrave Macmillan, 1997).

57. Chih-yu Shih, "Identities in Sino-Pakistani 'Iron Brotherhood': Theoretical Implications beyond the Economic Corridor," *Chinese Journal of International Politics* 11, no. 2 (2018): 1–22.

58. Michael R. Pompeo, "Secretary Michael R. Pompeo at a Press Availability," U.S. Embassy & Consulates in Italy (website), May 6, 2020, https://it.usembassy.gov/secretary-michael-r-pompeo-at-a-press-availability/.

59. Christopher Wray, "Confronting the China Threat: Director Wray Says Whole-of-Society Response Is Needed to Protect U.S. Economic and National Security," Federal Bureau of Investigation (website), February 6, 2020, https://www.fbi.gov/news/stories/wray-addresses-china-threat-at-doj-conference-020620.

60. Henry M. Paulson Jr., "The United States and China at a Crossroads: Speech at Asia Society by Henry M. Paulson, Jr.," Asia Society Policy Institute (website), last modified November 13, 2018, https://asiasociety.org/policy-institute/united-states-and-china-crossroads.

Chapter 7

1. Heather Exner-Pirot and Robert W. Murray, "Regional Order in the Arctic: Negotiated Exceptionalism," *Politik* 20, no. 3 (2017): 47–64; Leif Hoffmann, "Becoming Exceptional? American and European Exceptionalism and Their Critics: A Review," *L'Europe en formation* 359, no. 1 (2011): 83–106.

2. Fred Block, "The End of American Exceptionalism" The Social Question in the United States," in *The Social Question in the Twenty-First Century: A Global View*, ed. Jan Breman et al. (Oakland: University of California Press, 2019), 56.

3. Rebecca Strating, "Enabling Authoritarianism in the Indo-Pacific: Australian Exemptionalism," *Australian Journal of International Affairs* 74, no. 3 (2020): 301–21; Christian Kaunert, Sarah Léonard, and Alex MacKenzie, "'They Need Us More Than We Need Them': British Exceptionalism, Brexit, and Justice and Home Affairs," *European Foreign Affairs Review* 25, no. 4 (2020): 573–88; Emilia Nolan and Maverick Kennedy, "Explaining the American Exceptionalism," *INOSR Arts and Humanities* 3, no. 1 (2017): 1–8.

4. Aliénor Ballangé, "The Exemplarity of Europe: European Identity beyond Exceptionalism and Universalism," *Raisons politiques* 80, no. 4 (2020): 43–57.

5. Kate Sullivan de Estrada, "IR's Recourse to Area Studies: Siloisation Anxiety and the Disruptive Promise of Exceptionalism," *St Antony's International Review* 16, no. 1 (2020): 207–14.

6. Nicola Nymalm and Johannes Plagemann, "Comparative Exceptionalism: Universality and Particularity in Foreign Policy Discourses," *Review of International Studies* 21, no. 1 (2019): 12–37

7. Matt Killingsworth, "America's Exceptionalist Tradition: From the Law of Nations to the International Criminal Court," *Global Society* 33, no. 2 (2019): 285–304.

8. Angela Zhang, *Chinese Antitrust Exceptionalism: How the Rise of China Challenges Global Regulation* (Oxford: Oxford University Press, 2021); Asselin Charles, "Haitian Exceptionalism and Caribbean Consciousness," *Journal of Caribbean Literatures* 3, no. 2 (2002): 115–30.

9. Elizabeth Economy, "China's Inconvenient Truth: Official Triumphalism Conceals Societal Fragmentation," *Foreign Affairs*, May 28, 2021, https://www.foreignaffairs.com/articles/china/2021-05-28/chinas-inconvenient-truth; William Callahan, "Sino-Speak: Chinese Exceptionalism and the Politics of History," *Journal of Asian Studies* 71, no. 1 (2012): 33–55; Yuan-kang Wang, "The Myth of Chinese Exceptionalism: A Historical Perspective on China's Rise," in *Responding to China's Rise: US and EU Strategies*, ed. Vinod K. Aggarwal and Sara A. Newland, 51–74 (Berlin: Springer, 2015).

10. Simona R. Soare, "Biden's Security Policy: Democratic Security or Democratic Exceptionalism?" *Intereconomics* 56, no. 1 (2021): 14–20; Sally Weintrobe, *Psychological Roots of the Climate Crisis: Neoliberal Exceptionalism and the Culture of Uncare* (New York: Bloomsbury, 2021).

11. Courtney Fung, *China and Intervention at the UN Security Council: Reconciling Status* (Oxford: Oxford University Press, 2019); Feng Zhang, "The Rise of Chinese Exceptionalism in International Relations," *European Journal of International Relations* 19, no. 2 (2011): 305–28; Benjamin Ho, "Understanding Chinese Exceptionalism: China's Rise, Its Goodness, and Greatness," *Alternatives: Global, Local, Political* 39, no. 3 (2014): 164–76.

12. Iulian Chifu and Teodor Frunzeti, "Trump Doctrine: The 'Principled Realism,'" *Strategic Impact* 68, nos. 3–4 (2018): 7–17.

13. Xuetung Yan, "Political Leadership and Power Redistribution," *Chinese Journal of International Politics* 9, no. 1 (2016): 1–26.

14. Dennis R. Hoover, ed., *Religion and American Exceptionalism* (London: Routledge, 2018); Andreas Bøje Forsby, *The Non-Western Challenger? The Rise of a Sino-Centric China*, DIIS report 2011:16 (Copenhagen: Danish Institute for International Studies, 2011); William Callahan, *China: The Pessoptimist Nation* (Oxford: Oxford University Press, 2009).

15. John Gerard Ruggie, "American Exceptionalism, Exemptionalism, and Global Governance," in *American Exceptionalism and Human Rights*, ed. Michael Ignatieff, 304–38 (Princeton, NJ: Princeton University Press, 2009).

16. S. Jonathon O'Donnell, "Unipolar Dispensations: Exceptionalism, Empire, and the End of One America," *Political Theology* 20, no. 1 (2019): 66–84; Jeffrey Sachs, *A New Foreign Policy: Beyond American Exceptionalism* (New York: Columbia University Press, 2018); Sven H. Steinmo, "American Exceptionalism Reconsidered: Culture or Institutions?," in *The Dynamics of American Politics:*

Approaches and Interpretations, ed. Lawrence C. Dodd and Calvin Jillson, 106–31 (London: Routledge).

17. Anu Bradford and Eric A. Posner, "Universal Exceptionalism in International Law," *Harvard International Law Journal* 52, no. 1 (2011): 1–54.

18. Sullivan de Estrada, "IR's Recourse to Area Studies"; Robert R. Geyer, "Globalization, Europeanization, Complexity, and the Future of Scandinavian Exceptionalism," *Governance* 16, no. 4 (2003): 559–76.

19. Miles M. Evers, "Just the Facts: Why Norms Remain Relevant in an Age of Practice," *International Theory* 12, no. 2 (2020): 220–30; Simon Frankel Pratt, "From Norms to Normative Configurations: A Pragmatist and Relational Approach to Theorizing Normativity in IR," *International Theory* 12, no. 1 (2019): 59–82.

20. Thomas P. Narins and John Agnew, "Missing from the Map: Chinese Exceptionalism, Sovereignty Regimes and the Belt Road Initiative," *Geopolitics* 25, no. 4 (2020): 809–37; Chih Yuan Woon, "China's Contingencies: Critical Geopolitics, Chinese Exceptionalism and the Uses of History," *Geopolitics* 23, no. 1 (2018): 67–95.

21. Hugh De Santis, *The Right to Rule: American Exceptionalism and the Coming Multipolar World Order* (Lanham, MD: Lexington Books, 2021); Abram C. Van Engen, *City on a Hill: A History of American Exceptionalism* (New Haven, CT: Yale University Press, 2020); David P. Fields, *Foreign Friends: Syngman Rhee, American Exceptionalism, and the Division of Korea* (Lexington: University Press of Kentucky, 2019).

22. Lily H. M. Ling, "Three-ness: Healing World Politics with Epistemic Compassion," *Politics* 39, no. 1 (2019): 35–49; Priya Chacko, "A New 'Special Relationship'?: Power Transitions, Ontological Security, and India–US Relations," *International Studies Perspectives* 15, no. 3 (2014): 329–46.

23. Chih-yu Shih, *Eros of International Relations: Self-Feminization and the Claiming of Postcolonial Chineseness* (Hong Kong: Hong Kong University Press, 2022); Chih-yu Shih, "Knowledge as Civilizational Role Play: China Watching by Its Southern Neighbours," *Third World Quarterly* 40, no. 12 (2019): 2170–89; Chih-yu Shih and Chiung-chiu Huang, "Bridging Civilizations through Nothingness: Manchuria as Nishida Kitaro's 'Place,'" *Comparative Civilizations Review* 65 (Fall 2011): 4–17.

24. Peter Van Ness, "Collapse of Moral Authority and the End of the Civilizer State: Comparing Two Cases—Mao's China and George W. Bush's United States," EAI Fellows Program Working Paper Series no. 37 (Seoul: East Asia Institute, 2012); Kevork K. Oskanian, "A Very Ambiguous Empire: Russia's Hybrid Exceptionalism," *Europe-Asia Studies* 70, no. 1 (2018): 26–52.

25. Alastair Iain Johnston, "Is Chinese Exceptionalism Undermining China's Foreign Policy Interests?" in *The China Questions: Critical Insights into a Rising Power*, ed. Jennifer Rudolph, 90–98 (Cambridge, MA: Harvard University Press,

2018); Willian V. Spanos, *American Exceptionalism in the Age of Globalization: The Specter of Vietnam* (Albany: State University of New York Press, 2008); David Hastings Dunn, "Isolationism Revisited: Seven Persistent Myths in the Contemporary American Foreign Policy Debate," *Review of International Studies* 31, no. 2 (2005): 237–61.

26. Xiaoting Li, "Saving National IR from Exceptionalism: The Dialogic Spirit and Self-Reflection in Chinese IR Theory," *International Studies Review* 23, no. 4 (2021): 1399–423; Amitav Acharya, "Global International Relations (IR) and Regional Worlds: A New Agenda for International Studies," *International Studies Quarterly* 58, no. 4 (2014): 647–59; Peter Katzenstein, ed., *Sinicization and the Rise of China: Civilizational Processes beyond East and West* (New York: Routledge, 2012).

27. Amaya Querejazu, "Cosmopraxis: Relational Method for a Pluriversal IR," *Review of International Studies* 48, no. 5 (2022): 875–90; Milja Kurki, "Relational Revolution and Relationality in IR: New Conversations," *Review of International Studies* 48, no. 5 (2022): 821–36.

28. Narins and Agnew, "Missing from the Map."

29. Alexander Wendt, *Social Theory of International Politics* (Cambridge: Cambridge University Press, 1999).

30. Naeem Inayatullah and David Blaney, *International Relations and the Problem of Difference* (New York: Routledge, 2003).

31. Lucian Pye, *Asian Power and Politics: The Cultural Dimensions of Authority* (Cambridge, MA: Harvard University Press, 1985).

32. Louis Hartz, *The Liberal Tradition in America: An Interpretation of American Political Thought since the Revolution* (New York: Harcourt Brace, 1955); Monica Prasad, *The Land of Too Much* (Cambridge, MA: Harvard University Press, 2012); Alexis de Tocqueville, *Democracy in America*, trans. Henry Reeve (New York: Vintage, 1945).

33. Lindsay DiCuirci, ed., *Millennial Aspirations and Providentialism*, vol. 3 of *American Exceptionalism*, Timothy Roberts and Lindsay DiCuirci, general editors (London: Routledge, 2013); Arthur M. Schlesinger Jr., *The Cycles of American History* (New York: Houghton Mifflin, 1986).

34. Henry Kissinger, *On China* (New York: Penguin Press, 2011).

35. Evan S. Medeiro and Ashley J. Tellis, "Regime Change Is Not an Option in China: Focus on Beijing's Behavior, Not Its Leadership," *Foreign Affairs*, July 8, 2021, https://www.foreignaffairs.com/articles/asia/2021-07-08/regime-change-not-option-china; Jason Gilmore, "Translating American Exceptionalism: Comparing Presidential Discourse about the United States at Home and Abroad," *International Journal of Communication* 8, no. 1 (2014): 2416–37; Deborah L. Madsen, *American Exceptionalism* (Edinburgh: Edinburgh University Press, 1998).

36. See Joshua Rosenfield, "Debate: Are the U.S. and China Long-Term Enemies?," Asia Society (blog), October 15, 2015, https://asiasociety.org/blog/

asia/debate-are-us-and-china-long-term-enemies; Anonymous, *The Longer Tele-gram: Toward a New American China Strategy*, Atlantic Council Strategy Papers (Washington, DC: Scowcroft Center for Strategy and Security, 2021), https://www.atlanticcouncil.org/wp-content/uploads/2021/01/The-Longer-Telegram-To-ward-A-New-American-China-Strategy.pdf.

37. Prasad, *Land of Too Much*; Schlesinger, *Cycles of American History*.

38. Congyan Cai, *The Rise of China and International Law: Taking Chinese Exceptionalism Seriously* (Oxford: Oxford University Press, 2019); Johnston, "Chinese Exceptionalism"; Ho, "Understanding Chinese Exceptionalism"; Benjamin Tze Ern Ho, *China's Political Worldview and Chinese Exceptionalism: International Order and Global Leadership* (Amsterdam: Amsterdam University Press, 2021).

39. Katarína Sárvári, "Modern Constructions of China's Exceptionalism in International Relations," *Köz-gazdaság* 14, no. 4 (2019): 282–92.

40. Alastair Iain Johnston, "China in a World of Orders: Rethinking Compliance and Challenge in Beijing's International Relations," *International Security* 44, no. 2 (2019): 9–60; Astrid H. M. Nordin and Graham M. Smith, "Reintroducing Friendship to International Relations: Relational Ontologies from China to the West," *International Relations of Asia-Pacific* 18, no. 3 (2018): 369–96; Chih-yu Shih, "Assigning Role Characteristics to China: The Role State versus the Ego State," *Foreign Policy Analysis* 8, no. 1 (2012): 71–91; Allen Carlson, *Unifying China, Integrating with the World: Securing Chinese Sovereignty in the Reform Era* (Stanford, CA: Stanford University Press, 2005).

41. Matthieu Burnay, *Chinese Perspectives on the International Rule of Law: Law and Politics in the One-Party State* (Cheltenham, UK: Edward Elgar, 2018); Chih-yu Shih and Chiung-chiu Huang, "Preaching *Self-Responsibility*: The Chinese Style of *Global Governance*," *Journal of Contemporary China* 22, no. 79 (2013): 351–65.

42. Jorg Kustermans, "Gift-Giving as a Source of International Author-ity," *Chinese Journal of International Politics* 12, no. 3 (2019): 395–426; Dominik Niezejewski and Bartosz Kowalski, *China's Selective Identities: State, Ideology and Culture* (Berlin: Springer, 2018); Lina Benabdallah, "Power or Influence? Making Sense of China's Evolving Party-to-Party Diplomacy in Africa," *African Studies Quarterly* 19, nos. 3–4 (2020): 95–119.

43. Lauren Johnston and Marina Rudyak, "China's 'Innovative and Pragmatic' Foreign Aid: How China's Aid Program Is Shaped by and Shaping Globalisation," *Policy Forum*, September 5, 2017, https://www.policyforum.net/chinas-innova-tive-pragmatic-foreign-aid; Allan Chan, L. Trey Denton, and Alex S. L. Tsang, "The Art of Gift Giving in China," *Business Horizons* 46, no. 4 (2003): 47–52.

44. Jana S. Rošker, "Modernization of Chinese Philosophical Methodol-ogy," *Asian Studies* 9, no. 2 (2021): 121–41; Rachel Fedock, Michael Kuhler, and Raja Rosenhagen, eds., *Love, Justice, and Autonomy: Philosophical Perspectives* (London: Routledge, 2020).

45. Mencius specifically likened famine to leaders "leading on beasts to devour men." See *Mencius*, Tengwengong 2.

46. Astrid H. M. Nordin, *China's International Relations and Harmonious World: Time, Space and Multiplicity in World Politics* (London: Routledge, 2016); Callahan, "Sino-Speak."

47. Chih-yu Shih, "Role and Relation in Confucian IR: Relating to Strangers in the State of Nature," *Review of International Studies* 48, no. 5 (2022): 910–29, https://doi.org/10.1017/S0260210521000322; Shih, "Assigning Role Characteristics to China."

48. Burnay, *Chinese Perspectives*.

49. Anna L. Ahlers, "Political Inclusion in Contemporary China," *Journal of Chinese Governance* 4, no. 3 (2019): 201–6.

50. Raoul Bunskoek and Chih-yu Shih, " 'Community of Common Destiny' as Post-Western Regionalism: Rethinking China's Belt and Road Initiative from a Confucian Perspective," *Uluslararası İlişkiler / International Relations* 18, no. 70 (2021): 85–101; Yuen Yuen Ang, *How China Escaped the Poverty Trap* (Ithaca, NY: Cornell University Press, 2016); Tianbiao Zhu, "Compressed Development, Flexible Practices, and Multiple Traditions in China's Rise," in *Sinicization and the Rise of China: Civilizational Processes beyond East and West*, ed. Peter Katzenstein, 99–119 (New York: Routledge, 2012).

51. Xi Jingping, "Pulling Together through Adversity and toward a Shared Future for All," keynote speech transcript, Boao Forum for Asia Annual Conference, April 20, 2021, https://www.fmprc.gov.cn/mfa_eng/wjdt_665385/zyjh_665391/202104/t20210421_9170540.html.

52. "Wang Yi: 'Four Adherences' and 'Three Oppositions' Are Needed for Genuine Multilateralism," January 13, 2021, Embassy of the People's Republic of China in Nepal (website), http://np.china-embassy.gov.cn/eng/zgwj/202101/t20210114_1633074.htm.

53. Lena Benabdallah, "Spanning Thousands of Miles and Years: Political Nostalgia and China's Revival of the Silk Road," *International Studies Quarterly* 65, no. 2 (2021): 294–305, https://doi.org/10.1093/isq/sqaa080.

54. See *Analects*, Tai Bo.

55. *Book of Rites*, Tan Gong 2. Xunzi referred to overthrowing in a metaphor of water overthrowing the boat in *Xunzi*, Duke Ai.

56. Sungmoon Kim, "Mencius on International Relations and the Morality of War: From the Perspective of Confucian *Moralpolitik*," *History of Political Thought* 31, no. 1 (2010): 33–56.

57. According to Mencius, executing Zhou, the last king of the Shang dynasty, was about the "slaying of a despot, never any regicide." See *Mencius*, King Hui of Liang 2.

58. Killing the last emperor of Shang dynasty, Zhou, was "perfectly beautiful but not perfectly good." *Analects*, Ba Yi.

59. Confucius: "Why do you rely on killing to govern? Striving for what is good, you make the people good." *Analects*, Yan Yuan.

60. ". . . being benevolent, as such, being sufficiently benevolent, as such." *Analects*, Xian Wen.

61. *Mencius*, Duke Hui of Liang 1.

62. Adam William Chalmers and Susanna Theresia Mocker, "The End of Exceptionalism? Explaining Chinese National Oil Companies' Overseas Investment," *Review of International Political Economy* 24, no. 1 (2017): 119–43.

63. Narins and Agnew, "Missing from the Map."

64. Narins and Agnew.

65. *Analects*, Xian Wen.

66. *Analects*, Wei Ling Gong. Both chapter Zi Han and chapter Zi Lu mentioned living with the alien.

67. Confucius inquired into every detail in the temple of heavenly worship, where he would sacrifice precious sheep to honor the system of propriety. *Analects*, Ba Yi.

68. Therefore, according to Zi Xia, one who has received no schooling is nonetheless a learned person if faithful to their parents, the prince, and their friends. See Zi Xia's remarks in *Analects*, Xue Er. However, Confucius himself denies any knowledge of the ritual of heavenly worship because this ought to be knowledge that is exclusive to the prince. See Confucius's remark in *Analects*, Ba Yi. Jana S. Rošker, "Traditional Chinese Epistemology: The Structural Compatibility of Mind and External World," *Zheng da Zhong Wen Xue Bao* 17 (2012): 1–16.

69. Confucius felt "less worried if people's (self-)identities were not known to others than if they did not know each other." He felt concerned that "people are incapable of being benevolent." *Analects*, Xue Er and Xian Wen.

70. Zhao Tingyang, "All-under-Heaven and Methodological Relationism: An Old Story and New World Peace," in *Contemporary Chinese Political Thought*, ed. Fred Dallmayr and Zhao Tingyang, 46–66 (Lexington: University Press of Kentucky, 2012); Daniel Bell, preface to *Confucian Political Ethics*, ed. Daniel Bell, ix–xiv (Princeton, NJ: Princeton University Press, 2008); Daniel Bell, "The Making and Unmaking of Boundaries: A Contemporary Confucian Perspective," in *States, Nations, and Borders: The Ethics of Making Boundaries*, ed. Allen Buchanan and Margaret Moore, 57–85 (Cambridge: Cambridge University Press, 2003); Chih-yu Shih, "Role and Relation in Confucian IR."

71. William A. Callahan, "Dreaming as a Critical Discourse of National Belonging: China Dream, American Dream and World Dream," *Nations and Nationalism* 23, no. 3 (2017): 248–70.

72. Tingyang Zhao, *Redefining a Philosophy for World Governance*, trans. Liqing Tao (London: Palgrave Macmillan, 2019); Lily H. M. Ling, *The Dao of World Politics: Towards a Post-Westphalian, Worldist International Relations* (London: Routledge, 2014).

73. "Between the ten thousand different and scattering things, the rituals operate" (*Book of Rites*, Yue Ji); "Rituals set the ten thousand things in peace" (*Book of Rites*, Jiao Te Shen).

74. Qiyog Guo and Tao Cui, "The Values of Confucian Benevolence and the Universality of the Confucian Way of Extending Love," *Frontiers of Philosophy in China* 7, no. 1 (2012): 20–54; also see Chih-yu Shih, *Confucian Governmentality and Socialist Autocracy in Contemporary China* (Bristol: Bristol University Press, 2024).

75. Lena Benabdallah, *Shaping the Future of Power: Knowledge Production and Network-Building in China-Africa Relations* (University of Michigan Press, 2020); Yan Xuetong, *Leadership and the Rise of Great Powers* (Princeton, NJ: Princeton University Press, 2019).

76. Pye, *Asian Power and Politics*.

77. Bruce Dickson, *The Party and the People: Chinese Politics in the 21st Century* (Princeton, NJ: Princeton University Press, 2012); Yan, *Leadership and the Rise of Great Powers*.

78. Ian Johnson, "A Most Adaptable Party," *New York Review*, July 1, 2021, https://www.nybooks.com/articles/2021/07/01/chinese-communist-party-most-adaptable/

79. The New Atlantic Charter, issued by the White House on June 10, 2021, is available at https://www.whitehouse.gov/briefing-room/statements-releases/2021/06/10/the-new-atlantic-charter/.

80. Zhao Tingyang, "Ontology of Coexistence: Relations and Hearts," *Philosophical Researches* 8 (2009): 22–30; Zhao Tingyang, "An Interpretation of Harmony in Terms of Confucian Improvement," *Fudan Journal of the Humanities and Social Sciences* 2, no. 1 (2009): 113–26; Lily H. M. Ling, "Borders of Our Minds: Territories, Boundaries, and Power in the Confucian Tradition," in Buchanan and Moore, *States, Nations, and Borders*, 86–100.

81. Kim Tallbear and Angela Willey, "Critical Relationality: Queer, Indigenous, and Multispecies Belonging beyond Settler Sex and Nature," *Imaginations* 10, no. 1 (2019): 10–15; Anthony Burke et al., "Planet Politics: A Manifesto from the End of IR," *Millennium* 44, no. 3 (2016): 495–523.

82. For a recent example, see the Strategic Competition Act of 2021 at https://www.foreign.senate.gov/imo/media/doc/DAV21598%20-%20Strategic%20Competition%20Act%20of%202021.pdf

83. Michael J. Mazarr, Timothy R. Heath, and Astrid Stuth Cevallos, *China and the International Order* (Santa Monica, CA: Rand, 2018).

84. Xuetong Yan, "Chinese Values vs. Liberalism: What Ideology Will Shape the International Normative Order?" *Chinese Journal of International Politics* 11, no. 1 (2018): 1–22.

85. Petros C. Mavroidis and André Sapir, *China and the WTO: Why Multilateralism Still Matters* (Princeton, NJ: Princeton University Press, 2021); Yeling Tan, "How the WTO Changed China: The Mixed Legacy of Economic

Engagement," *Foreign Affairs*, March/April 2021, https://www.foreignaffairs.com/articles/china/2021-02-16/how-wto-changed-china; Narins and Agnew, "Missing from the Map."

86. Robert G. Patman and Laura Southgate, "Globalization, the Obama Administration and the Refashioning of US Exceptionalism," *International Politics* 53, no. 2 (2016): 220–38; Dick Cheney and Liz Cheney, *Exceptional: Why the World Needs a Powerful America* (New York: Simon & Schuster, 2015).

87. Anne F. Thurston, ed., *Engaging China: Fifty Years of Sino-American Relations* (New York: Columbia University Press, 2021).

88. Johnston, "Chinese Exceptionalism."

Chapter 8

1. See, for example, Peter Van Ness, *Revolution and Chinese Foreign Policy: Peking's Support for Wars of National Liberation* (Berkeley: University of California Press, 1971); Julia Lovell, "The Cultural Revolution and Its Legacies in International Perspective," *China Quarterly* 227 (2016): 632–52; Fei-Ling Wang, *The China Order: Centralia, World Empire, and the Nature of Chinese Power* (Albany: State University of New York Press, 2017).

2. Michael Pillsbury, *The Hundred-Year Marathon: China's Secret Strategy to Replace America as the Global Superpower* (New York: St. Martin's Griffin, 2015).

3. Hans J. Morgenthau, *Politics among Nations: The Struggle for Power and Peace* (New York: McGraw-Hill, 2005), 102–3. Also see Jason W. Davidson, *The Origins of Revisionist and Status-Quo States* (New York: Palgrave Macmillan, 2006).

4. John J. Mearsheimer, *The Tragedy of Great Power Politics* (New York: W. W. Norton, 2001), 2.

5. Chih-yu Shih, "A Markov Model of Diplomatic Change and Continuity in Mainland China," *Issues and Studies* 28, no. 6 (1992): 1–15.

6. See Robert B. Zoellick, "Whither China: From Membership to Responsibility?," speech to the National Committee on U.S.-China Relations, September 21, 2005, U.S. Department of State Archive (website), http://www.state.gov/s/s/rem/53682.htm. For more discussion, see also Julia Bowie, "China: A Responsible Stakeholder?," *National Interest*, May 10, 2016, https://nationalinterest.org/blog/the-buzz/china-responsible-stakeholder-16131.

7. David Shambaugh, "Coping with a Conflicted China," *Washington Quarterly* 34, no. 1 (Winter 2011): 23–24; John Pomfret, "China's Strident Tone Raises Concerns among Western Governments, Analysts," *Washington Post*, January 31, 2010, https://www.washingtonpost.com/wp-dyn/content/article/2010/01/30/AR2010013002443.html.

8. G. John Ikenberry, "The Rise of China and the Future of the West: Can the Liberal System Survive?," *Foreign Affairs* 87, no. 1 (2008): 32.

9. Ikenberry, "Rise of China," 30, 32.

10. For example, see James Mann, *The China Fantasy: How Our Leaders Explain Away Chinese Repression* (London: Viking, 2007).

11. Larry Diamond and Orville Schell, eds., *Chinese Influence & American Interests: Promoting Constructive Vigilance*, report of the Working Group on Chinese Influence Activities in the United States (Stanford, CA: Hoover Institute, 2018); Orville Schell and Susan L. Shirk, chairs, *Course Correction: Toward an Effective and Sustainable China Policy*, Asia Society Center on U.S.-China Relations Task Force report, February 2019, https://asiasociety.org/sites/default/files/inline-files/CourseCorrection_FINAL_2.7.19_1.pdf.

12. *National Security Strategy of the United States of America* (Washington, DC: White House, December 2017), https://www.whitehouse.gov/wp-content/uploads/2017/12/NSS-Final-12-18-2017-0905.pdf.

13. Jim Mattis, *Summary of the 2018 National Defense Strategy of the United States of America. Department of Defense Washington United States: Sharpening the American Military's Competitive Edge* (Washington, DC: U.S. Department of Defense, 2018), https://dod.defense.gov/Portals/1/Documents/pubs/2018-National-Defense-Strategy-Summary.pdf.

14. Schell and Shirk, *Course Correction*.

15. Richard Haass, *A World in Disarray: American Foreign Policy and the Crisis of the Old Order* (New York: Penguin, 2017).

16. Allen Carlson, *Unifying China, Integrating with the World: Securing Chinese Sovereignty in the Reform Era* (Stanford, CA: Stanford University Press, 2005); Alastair Iain Johnston, *Social States: China in International Institutions, 1980–2000* (Princeton, NJ: Princeton University Press, 2007).

17. Alexander Cooley, Daniel Nexon, and Steven Ward, "Revising Order or Challenging the Balance of Military Power? An Alternative Typology of Revisionist and Status-Quo States," *Review of International Studies* 45, no. 4 (2019): 689–708, https://www.cambridge.org/core/journals/review-of-international-studies/article/revising-order-or-challenging-the-balance-of-military-power-an-alternative-typology-of-revisionist-and-statusquo-statesFA5C1C5932F13DFED94C4B1068CDD203/core-reader.

18. For example, Dingding Chen, Xiaoyu Pu, and Alastair Iain Johnston, "Debating China's Assertiveness," *International Security* 38, no. 3 (Winter 2013/14): 176–83; Jean-Pierre Cabestan, "What Kind of International Order Does China Want? Between Reformism and Revisionism," *China Perspectives* 2 (2016): 3–35; Alastair Iain Johnston, "China in a World of Orders: Rethinking Compliance and Challenge in Beijing's International Relations," *International Security* 44, no. 2 (2019): 9–20.

19. Bonnie Glaser, "China as a Selective Revisionist Power in the International Order," compiled by Khairulanwar Zaini, *ISEAS Perspective*, no. 21 (2019), https://www.iseas.edu.sg/images/pdf/ISEAS_Perspective_2019_21.pdf.

20. Jeanne L. Wilson, "Are Russia and China Revisionist States?," *Asia Dialogue*, June 11, 2019, https://theasiadialogue.com/2019/06/11/are-russia-and-china-revisionist-states/.

21. Nadège Rolland, *China's Vision for a New World Order*, NBR special report no. 83 (Seattle, WA: National Bureau of Asian Research, 2020).

22. One leading institute in setting up the agenda is the Hudson Institute. For example, see John Lee, *Ambition and Overreach: Countering One Belt One Road and Beijing's Plans to Dominate Global Innovation* (Washington, DC: Hudson Institute, 2020).

23. For further references, see Hung-chao Tai, ed., *Confucianism and Economic Development: An Oriental Alternative?* (Washington, DC: Washington Institute Press, 1989); Geert Hofstede and Michael Harris Bond, "The Confucius Connection: From Cultural Roots to Economic Growth," *Organizational Dynamics* 16, no. 4 (Spring 1988): 5–21; Wei-bin Zhang, *On Adam Smith and Confucius: The Theory of Moral Sentiments and the Analects* (Hauppauge, NY: Nova Publishers, 2000); Shigeto Sonoda, "Confucianism and Modernization: A Tentative Analysis (1)," *International Review of Sociology* 2, no. 3 (1991): 175–96.

24. Mark P. Petracca and Mong Xiong, "The Concept of Chinese Neo-Authoritarianism: An Exploration and Democratic Critique," *Asian Survey* 30, no. 11 (1990): 1099–117.

25. Steven N. S. Cheung, *Will China Go "Capitalist"? An Economic Analysis of Property Rights and Institutional Change*, Hobart paper 94 (London: Institute of Economic Affairs, 1982).

26. Victor Nee, "A Theory of Market Transition: From Redistribution to Market in State Socialism," *American Sociological Review* 54, no. 5 (1989): 663–81.

27. Andrew Walder, *Communist Neo-traditionalism: Work and Authority in Chinese Industry* (Berkeley: University of California Press, 1986); Jean Oi, *State and Peasant in Contemporary China: The Political Economy of Village Government* (Berkeley: University of California Press, 1989).

28. Vivienne Shue, *The Reach of the State: Sketches of the Chinese Body Politic* (Stanford, CA: Stanford University Press, 1988).

29. Keun Lee, *Chinese Firms and the State in Transition: Property Rights and Agency Problems in the Reform Era* (Armonk, NY: M. E. Sharpe, 1991).

30. Andrew J. Nathan, *Chinese Democracy* (New York: Alfred A. Knopf, 1985); Gordon White, "The Impact of Economic Reforms in the Chinese Countryside: Towards the Politics of Social Capitalism," *Modern China* 13, no. 4 (1987): 411–40.

31. Susan Solinger, "Capitalist Measures with Chinese Characteristics," *Problems of Communism* 38, no. 1 (1989):19–33; Susan Shirk, *The Political Logic of Economic Reform in China* (Berkeley: University of California Press, 1992).

32. Shilian Shan, "Hui dao qimeng: Li shenzhi sixiang de lishi mailuo" [Back to enlightenment: The trajectory of Li Shenzhi's thoughts], *21st Century*

Bimonthly 111 (February 2009): 92–96. For additional links to Republican liberalism, see Weiping Cui, "Con wu si zai chufa: Balingniandai Liu Xiaopo de sixiang qidian" [Embark upon the May Fourth again: The beginning of Liu Xiaobo's thought in the 1980s], *Reflection* 38 (October 4, 2019): 114–34; Xu Youyu, "Wu si yundong luanshengzi: Ziqiang he qimeng" [The twin sons of the May Fourth Movement—Self-strengthening and enlightenment], *Time Weekly*, April 30, 2009, http://book.sina.com.cn/news/c/2009-04-30/1152255606.shtml.

33. Keping Yu, "Minzhu shi ge hao dongxi" [Democracy is a good thing], *Study Times*, December 26, 2006, http://www.china.com.cn/xxsb/txt/2006-12/26/content_7562036.htm.

34. The Central Compilation and Translation Press (Beijing) has published several series on democratic governance and political reform; see, for example, Xuelian Chen, *Zhongguo de minzhu zhili, lilun, shijian: Xiaolv zhengfu* [China's democratic governance, theory and practice: The efficient government] (Beijing: Central Compilation and Translation Bureau, 2013); Keping Yu, *Jingwei min yi: Zhongguo de minzhu zhili yu zhengzhi gaige* [In awe of the public opinion: China's democratic governance and political reform] (Beijing: Central Compilation and Translation Bureau, 2012).

35. Li Chung-chien and Tsai Wu-yan, "Cong wenge chuangjiang dao gong-gong zhishifenzi" [From a Cultural Revolution radical to a public intellectual], *Storm Media*, July 9, 2018, https://www.storm.mg/article/460031.

36. Ming-chin Tsai, *Huiyi wen ge: Zai chaoyue yu zaixian jian de xuanze shiye* [Memorizing the Cultural Revolution: The spectrum of choices between transcendence and re-presentation] (Taipei: Political Science, National Taiwan University, 2009).

37. Xiaokang Su and Ruxiang Wang, *He Shang* [River elegy] (Beijing: Modern Press, 1988).

38. Jean Oi, "The Role of the Local State in China's Transitional Economy," *China Quarterly* 144 (1995): 1132–49; Andrew G. Walder, "The Decline of Communist Power: A Theory of Institutional Change," *Theory and Society* 23 (April 1994): 297–323; Gordon White, "Democratization and Economic Reform in China," *Australian Journal of Chinese Affairs* 31 (January 1994): 73–92.

39. Chih-yu Shih, *Collective Democracy: Political and Legal Reform in China* (Hong Kong: Chinese University Press of Hong Kong, 1999).

40. Shaoguang Wang, "The Construction of State Extractive Capacity," *Modern China* 27, no. 2 (2001): 229–61; Angang Hu, "Background to Writing the Report on State Capacity," *Chinese Economy* 31, no. 4 (1998): 4–29.

41. Yongnian Zheng and Sow Keat Tok, *"Harmonious Society" and "Harmonious World": China's Policy Discourse under Hu Jintao*, Briefing Series no. 26 (Nottingham, UK: China House, University of Nottingham, October 2007).

42. See "China's Charter 08," trans. Perry Link, *New York Review of Books* 56, no. 1 (January 15, 2009).

43. Chih-yu Shih, "Breeding a Reluctant Dragon: Can China Rise into Partnership and Away from Antagonism?" *Review of International Studies* 31, no. 4 (2005): 755–74.

44. For example, Yu Xilai and Chengzi Wu, "Shijie zhixu yu xin xing da guo de lishi jueze" [The world order and the historical choice of the rising great power], *Zhanlue yu guanli* [Strategy and management] 27 (February 1998): 1–13; Zhongyun Zi, "Zhongguo ying ruhe kandai guoji xingshi he ruhe zi chu?" [How should China view the international conditions and position itself?], *China Review*, December 1999, 20–25.

45. Zheng Bijian, "China's 'Peaceful Rise' to Great-Power Status," *Foreign Affairs* 84, no. 5 (September/October 2005): 18–24.

46. Bonnie S. Glaser and Evan S. Medeiros, "The Changing Ecology of Foreign Policy-Making in China: The Ascension and Demise of the Theory of 'Peaceful Rise,'" *China Quarterly* 190 (2007): 291–310.

47. Yaqing Qin, *A Relational Theory of World Politics* (Cambridge: Cambridge University Press, 2018).

48. Ronald Keith, "China as a Rising World Power and Its Response to 'Globalization,'" *Review of International Affairs* 3, no. 4 (2004): 507–23; Christopher Hughes, "Nationalism and Multilateralism in Chinese Foreign Policy: Implications for Southeast Asia," *Pacific Review* 18, no. 1 (2006): 119–35.

49. Frank N. Pieke, *Knowing China: A Twenty-First Century Guide* (Cambridge: Cambridge University Press, 2016).

50. William A. Callahan, "Chinese Visions of World Order: Post-hegemonic or a New Hegemony?," *International Studies Review* 10, no. 4 (2008): 749–61.

51. David Kang, *East Asia before the West: Five Centuries of Trade and Tribute* (New York: Columbia University Press, 2012); also his *China Rising: Peace, Power, and Order in East Asia* (New York: Columbia University Press, 2009).

52. Lucian Pye, "China: Erratic State, Frustrated Society," *Foreign Affairs* 69, no. 4 (Fall 1990): 56–74.

53. Martin Jacques, *When China Rules the World: The End of the Western World and the Birth of a New Global Order* (New York: Penguin Press, 2009).

54. Martin Jacques, "When China Rules the World: From 2009: The Dire Consequences of the Coming Shift in Global Power," interview by Charlie Gillis, *Maclean's*, July 13, 2009, https://www.macleans.ca/news/world/macleans-interview-martin-jacques/.

55. Lucian Pye, *The Mandarin and the Cadre: China's Political Culture* (Ann Arbor: Center for Chinese Studies, University of Michigan, 1988).

56. Richard Madsen, *Morality and Power in a Chinese Village* (Berkeley: University of California Press, 1984).

57. Wang Gungwu, *Renewal: The Chinese State and the New Global History* (Hong Kong: Chinese University Press, 2013).

58. Fei-Ling Wang, *The China Order*.

59. Yeling Tan, "How the WTO Changed China: The Mixed Legacy of Economic Engagement," *Foreign Affairs*, February 16, 2021, https://www.foreignaffairs.com/articles/china/2021-02-16/how-wto-changed-china.

60. Liuzi Shi, ed., *Beijing dixia wan yan shu* [The Ten-Thousand-Word and other underground writings in Beijing] (Hong Kong: Mirror Books, 1997).

61. Shitao Li, ed., *Zhishifenzi lichang: Ziyouzhuyi zhi zheng yu zhongguo sixiang jie de fenhua* [Positions of intellectuals: Debates on liberalism and the division of Chinese intellectual circles] (Changchun, China: Shidai Yishu, 2000).

62. For example, Licheng Ma and Zhijun Ling, *Jiaofeng: Dangdai zhongguo sanci sixiang jiefang shi lu* [Crossfires: A real record of the three thought-liberations in contemporary China] (Beijing: Jinri zhongguo, 1998); Licheng Ma, *Dangdai zhongguo bazhong shehui sichao* [Eight social thoughts in contemporary China] (Beijing: Social Science Literature Press, 2012).

63. He Li, "The Chinese Discourse on Good Governance: Content and Implications," *Journal of Contemporary China* 29, no. 126 (2020): 824–37, https://doi.org/10.1080/10670564.2020.1744376.

64. Yuan Yang, "Inside China's Crackdown on Young Marxists," *Financial Times Magazine*, February 14, 2019, https://www.ft.com/content/fd087484-2f23-11e9-8744-e7016697f225.

65. Qi Zhi, ed., *Essays by Chinese Scholars on the Cultural Revolution*, vol. 4 (Austin, TX: Remembering Publishing), 379.

66. See the special issue *The Adolescence of Mainland New Confucianism* in the journal *Contemporary Chinese Thought* 49, no. 2 (2018).

67. Li Minghui, "Wo burentong 'dalu xin rujia'" [I disapprove of the phrase "Mainland New Confucianism"], *Contemporary Chinese Thought* 49, no. 2 (2018): 100–112.

68. See Gan Yang, *Zhongguo daolu: Sanshi nian yu liushi nian*[The Chinese way: Thirty years and sixty years], *Du Shu* (June 2007): 3–13; also see Gan Yang et al., *Ruxue yu shehuizhuyi* [Confucianism and socialism], *Open Epoch* 1 (March/April 2016): 9–80.

69. Jiang Qing, *A Confucian Constitutional Order: How China's Ancient Past Can Shape Its Political Future* (Princeton, NJ: Princeton University Press, 2013).

70. Liselotte Odgaard, *Double-Edged Aid: China's Strategy to Gain Influence through Regional Assistance* (Washington, DC: Hudson Institute, 2020).

71. Daniel A. Bell, "Exchanges: Reconciling Confucianism and Socialism?," January 14, 2010, *China Beat Blog: Archive 2008–2012*, http://digitalcommons.unl.edu/chinabeatarchive/687.

72. Wang Gungwu, "How Political Heritage and Future Progress Shape the China Challenge," Harvard Fairbank Center for Chinese Studies, October 21, 2020, p. 5, https://pdfgoes.com/downloads/The%20China%20Challenge%20Shaping%20The%20Choices%20Of%20A%20Rising%20Power.

73. Yuhai Han, *Wu bian nian lai shei zhu shi: yiqianwubai nian yilai de zhongguo yu shijie* [Who have been writing history: China and the world since 1500 AD] (Beijing: Jiuzhou, 2009).

74. Gan Yang et al., "Bei da de xiang gang hua gaige shi weixiande" [Abiding by the Hong Kong Model engenders the PKU], *Guangcha*, January 16, 2015, https://m.hswh.org.cn/wzzx/llyd/jy/2015-01-17/29794.html.

75. For remarks in a workshop, see Tingyang Zhao, Jiaying Chen, and Lian Zhou, *Zhongguo·xiandaixing duitan* [A dialogue on Chinese·modernity], 34th Youth Forum of the Institute of Marxism, March 14, 2015, https://www.aisixiang.com/data/87627.html.

76. Fei-Ling Wang, *The China Order*, 221.

77. Liu Shaoqi, *How to Be a Good Communist* (New York: Prism Key Press, 2011); for rule by virtue, see Zheng Yongnian, "Globalisation and the Chineseness of the Chinese State," in *Chineseness and Modernity in a Changing China: Essays in Honour of Professor Wang Gungwu*, ed. Zheng Yongnian and Zhao Litao (Singapore: World Scientific, 2020), 79–83.

78. Xuetong Yan, "From Keeping a Low Profile to Striving for Achievement," *Chinese Journal of International Politics* 7, no. 2 (2014): 153–84.

79. Xi Jinping's remarks at the International Conference on Commemorating the 2,565th Anniversary of Confucius's Birthday and the Opening Session of the Fifth Plenary Meeting of the International Confucian Association, September 2014.

80. Jiang Qing et al., *Zhongguo bixu zai ruhua: Dalu xin rujia xin zhuzhang* [China must be re-Confucianized: New platforms of mainland Chinese New Confucianism] (Singapore: World Scientific, 2016).

81. Maximilian Mayer and Xin Zhang, "Theorizing China-World Integration: Sociospatial Reconfigurations and the Modern Silk Roads," Review of International Political Economy 28, no. 4 (2020): 974–1003.

82. Michael D. Swaine, "Perceptions of an Assertive China," China Leadership Monitor no. 32 (May 3, 2010).

83. National Security Strategy; Mattis, Summary.

84. Benjamin Smith, "Explaining Bipartisan Support for the US Innovation and Competition Act," *E-International Relations*, September 17, 2021, https://www.e-ir.info/2021/09/17/explaining-bipartisan-support-for-the-us-innovation-and-competition-act/.

Chapter 9

1. Hoo Tiang Boon and Hannah Elyse Sworn, "Strategic Ambiguity and the Trumpian Approach to China–Taiwan Relations," *International Affairs* 96, no. 6 (2020): 1487–508; Zuo Xiying, "Unbalanced Deterrence: Coercive Threat,

Reassurance and the US-China Rivalry in Taiwan Strait," *Pacific Review* 3, no. 4 (2021): 547–76; Dean P. Chen, "The End of Liberal Engagement with China and the New US-Taiwan Focus," *Pacific Focus* 35, no. 3 (2020): 397–435; Dean P. Chen, "The Trump Administration's One-China Policy: Tilting toward Taiwan in an Era of U.S.-PRC Rivalry?," *Asian Politics & Policy* 11, no. 2 (2019): 250–78; Andrew Scobell, "China and Taiwan: Balance of Rivalry with Weapons of Mass Democratization," *Political Science Quarterly* 129, no. 3 (2014): 449–68.

2. Oriana Skylar Mastro, "The Taiwan Temptation: Why Beijing Might Resort to Force," *Foreign Affairs* 100, no. 4 (2021): 58–67.

3. Larry Diamond and Orville Schell, eds., *Chinese Influence and American Interests: Promoting Constructive Vigilance* (Stanford, CA: Hoover Institute, 2018); Orville Schell and Susan L. Shirk, *Course Correction: Toward an Effective and Sustainable China Policy*, Asia Society Center on U.S.-China Relations Task Force report, February 2019, https://asiasociety.org/sites/default/files/inline-files/CourseCorrection_FINAL_2.7.19_1.pdf.

4. Hal Brands, "The Emerging Biden Doctrine: Democracy, Autocracy, and the Defining Clash of Our Time," *Foreign Affairs*, June 29, 2021, https://www.foreignaffairs.com/articles/united-states/2021-06-29/emerging-biden-doctrine; Jared M. McKinney and Peter Harris, "Broken Nest: Deterring China from Invading Taiwan," *Parameters* 51, no. 4 (2021): 23–36.

5. Glenn H. Snyder, "The Security Dilemma in Alliance Politics," *World Politics* 36, no. 4 (1984): 461–95.

6. Laurel Stewart, "What Do Taiwan Residents Really Think about Independence?," *The China Project*, April 8, 2022, https://supchina.com/2022/04/08/what-do-taiwan-residents-really-think-about-independence/; Anson Au, "The Sunflower Movement and the Taiwanese National Identity: Building an Anti-Sinoist Civic Nationalism," *Berkeley Journal of Sociology*, April 27, 2017, https://berkeleyjournal.org/2017/04/27/the-sunflower-movement-and-the-taiwanese-national-identity-building-an-anti-sinoist-civic-nationalism/.

7. Robert S. Ross, "Navigating the Taiwan Strait: Deterrence, Escalation Dominance, and U.S.-China Relations," *International Security* 27, no. 2 (2002): 48–85.

8. Robert S. Ross, "Explaining Taiwan's Revisionist Diplomacy," *Journal of Contemporary China* 15, no. 48 (2011): 443–58.

9. Richard Haass and David Sacks, "The Growing Danger of U.S. Ambiguity on Taiwan: Biden Must Make America's Commitment Clear to China—and the World," *Foreign Affairs*, December 13, 2021, https://www.foreignaffairs.com/articles/china/2021-12-13/growing-danger-us-ambiguity-taiwan; Patrick Porter and Michael Mazarr, *Countering China's Adventurism over Taiwan: A Third Way* (Sydney: Lowy Institute, May 20, 2021), http://www.jstor.org/stable/resrep33506; Elbridge Colby and Jim Mitre, "Why the Pentagon Should Focus on Taiwan," *War on the Rocks*, October 7, 2020, https://warontherocks.com/2020/10/why-the-

278 | Notes to Chapter 9

pentagon-should-focus-on-taiwan/; Jennifer Lind, "Life in China's Asia: What Regional Hegemony Would Look Like," *Foreign Affairs* 97, no. 2 (2018): 71–82.

10. Michèle Flournoy and Michael Brown, "Time Is Running Out to Defend Taiwan: Why the Pentagon Must Focus on Near-Term Deterrence," *Foreign Affairs*, September 14, 2022, https://www.foreignaffairs.com/china/time-running-out-defend-taiwan; Richard Haass and David Sacks, "American Support for Taiwan Must Be Unambiguous: To Keep the Peace, Make Clear to China That Force Won't Stand," *Foreign Affairs*, September 2, 2020, https://www.foreign affairs.com/articles/united-states/american-support-taiwan-must-be-unambiguous; Ross, "Navigating the Taiwan Strait."

11. Joel Wuthnow, "U.S. 'Minilateralism' in Asia and China's Responses: A New Security Dilemma?," *Journal of Contemporary China* 28, no. 115 (2018): 133–50; David C. Kang and Xinru Ma, "Power Transitions: Thucydides Didn't Live in East Asia," *Washington Quarterly* 41, no. 1 (2018): 137–54; Andrew Scobell, "Learning to Rise Peacefully? China and the Security Dilemma," *Journal of Contemporary China* 21, no. 76 (2012): 713–21.

12. David J. Bulman, "The Economic Security Dilemma in US-China Relations," *Asian Perspective* 45, no. 1 (2020): 49–73; Erik Lin-Greenberg, "Non-traditional Security Dilemmas: Can Military Operations Other Than War Intensify Security Competition in Asia?" *Asian Security* 14, no. 3 (2017): 282–302; Adam P. Liff and G. John Ikenberry, "Racing toward Tragedy? China's Rise, Military Competition in the Asia Pacific, and the Security Dilemma," *International Security* 39, no. 2 (2014): 52–91; Baohui Zhang, "The Security Dilemma in the U.S.-China Military Space Relationship: The Prospects for Arms Control," *Asian Survey* 51, no. 2 (2011): 311–32; Thomas J. Christensen, "China, the U.S.-Japan Alliance, and the Security Dilemma in East Asia," *International Security* 23, no. 4 (1999): 49–80.

13. Shiping Tang, "The Security Dilemma: A Conceptual Analysis," *Security Studies* 18, no. 3 (2009): 587–623; Charles L. Glaser, "The Security Dilemma Revisited," *World Politics* 50, no. 1 (1997): 171–201; Snyder, "Security Dilemma in Alliance Politics"; Robert Jervis, "Cooperation under the Security Dilemma," *World Politics* 30, no. 2 (1978): 167–214; John H. Herz, "Idealist Internationalism and the Security Dilemma," *World Politics* 2, no. 2 (1950): 157–80.

14. James Samuel Johnson, "Chinese Evolving Approaches to Nuclear 'War-Fighting': An Emerging Intense US-China Security Dilemma and Threats to Crisis Stability in the Asia Pacific," *Asian Security* 15, no. 3 (2018): 215–32; Viljar Veebel, "NATO Options and Dilemmas for Deterring Russia in the Baltics States," *Defence Studies* 18, no. 2 (2018): 229–51; Liff and Ikenberry, "Racing toward Tragedy?"; Thomas J. Christensen, "The Contemporary Security Dilemma: Deterring a Taiwan Conflict," *Washington Quarterly* 25, no. 4 (2002): 5–21.

15. Liff and Ikenberry, "Racing toward Tragedy?"; Glaser, "Security Dilemma Revisited."

16. Ted Hopf, "The Promise of Constructivism in International Relations Theory," *International Security* 23, no. 1 (1998): 171–200.

17. Malte Riemann and Norma Rossi, "Remote Warfare as 'Security of Being': Reading Security Force Assistance as an Ontological Security Routine," *Defence Studies* 21, no. 4 (2022): 489–507.

18. Alan Collins, "State-Induced Security Dilemma: Maintaining the Tragedy," *Cooperation and Conflict* 39, no. 1 (2004): 27–44.

19. Patricia Shamai, "What's in a Name? Deterrence and the Stigmatisation of WMD," in *Deterrence: Concepts and Approaches for Current and Emerging Threats*, ed. Anastasia Filippidou, 77–96 (Cham, Switzerland: Springer, 2020); Adam Breuer and Alastair Iain Johnston, "Memes, Narratives and the Emergent US-China Security Dilemma," *Cambridge Review of International Affairs* 32, no. 4 (2019): 429–55; Maysam Behravesh, "State Revisionism and Ontological (In)security in International Politics: The Complicated Case of Iran and Its Nuclear Behavior," *Journal of International Relations and Development* 21 (2018): 836–57; Ross, "Explaining Taiwan's Revisionist Diplomacy"; Amir Lupovici, "The Emerging Fourth Wave of Deterrence Theory: Toward a New Research Agenda," *International Studies Quarterly* 54, no. 3 (2010): 705–32; Stefano Guzzini, "The Cold War Is What We Make of It: When Peace Research Meets Constructivism in International Relations," in *Contemporary Security Analysis and Copenhagen Peace Research*, ed. Stefano Guzzini and Dietrich Jung, 40–53 (New York: Routledge, 2004).

20. Iver Neumann, "Entry into International Society Reconceptualized: The Case of Russia," *Review of International Studies* 37, no. 2 (2011): 463–84; Alexander Wendt, *Social Theory of International Politics* (Cambridge: Cambridge University Press, 1999); Hopf, "Promise of Constructivism."

21. Kang and Ma, "Power Transitions"; Ronan Tse-min Fu et al., "Looking for Asia's Security Dilemma," *International Security* 40, no. 2 (2015): 181–86; David C. Kang, "Getting Asia Wrong: The Need for New Analytical Frameworks," *International Security* 27, no. 4 (2003): 57–85.

22. John J. Mearsheimer, *The Tragedy of Great Power Politics* (New York: W. W. Norton, 2001), 2.

23. Zhiqun Zhu, "'One China' in the Beijing-Washing-Taipei Trilateral Relationship," *Asia-Pacific Journal: Japan Focus* 20, no. 2 (2022), https://apjjf.org/2022/2/Zhu.html; Steve Chan et al., *Contesting Revisionism: China, the United States, and the Transformation of International Order* (Oxford: Oxford University Press, 2021).

24. Amir Lupovici, *The Power of Deterrence: Emotions, Identity and American and Israeli Wars of Resolve* (Cambridge: Cambridge University Press, 2016).

25. R. D. Laing, *The Divided Self: An Existential Study in Sanity and Madness* (London: Penguin Books, 1960); Karl Gustafsson and Nina C. Krickel-Choi, "Returning to the Roots of Ontological Security: Insights from Existentialist

Anxiety Literature," *European Journal of International Relations* 26, no. 3 (2020): 875–95.

26. Ayşe Zarakol, "Ontological (In)security and State Denial of Historical Crimes: Turkey and Japan," *International Relations* 24, no. 1 (2010): 3–23; Jennifer Mitzen, "Ontological Security in World Politics: State Identity and the Security Dilemma," *European Journal of International Relations* 12, no. 3 (2006): 341–70; Catarina Kinnvall, "Globalization and Religious Nationalism: Self, Identity, and the Search for Ontological Security," *Political Psychology* 25, no. 5 (2004): 741–67.

27. Emanuel Adler and Michael Barnett, "Security Communities in Theoretical Perspective," in *Security Communities*, ed. Emanuel Adler and Michael Barnett, 3–28 (Cambridge: Cambridge University Press, 1998).

28. Janis Grzybowski, "Separatists, State Subjectivity, and Fundamental Ontological (In)security in International Relations," *International Relations* 36, no. 3 (2022): 504–22.

29. M. L. deRaismes Combes, "Encountering the Stranger: Ontological Security and the Boston Marathon Bombing," *Cooperation and Conflict* 52, no. 1 (2017): 126–43; Jef Huysmans, "Security! What Do You Mean? From Concept to Thick Signifier," *European Journal of International Relations* 4, no. 2 (1998): 226–55.

30. Tanya Narozhna, "Misrecognition, Ontological Security and State Foreign Policy: The Case of Post-Soviet Russia," *Australian Journal of International Affairs* 76, no. 1 (2022): 76–97; Sara Bjerg Moller, "Domestic Politics, Threat Perceptions, and the Alliance Security Dilemma: The Case of South Korea," *Asian Security* 18, no. 2 (2022): 119–37; Alanna Krolikowski, "Shaking Up and Making Up China: How the Party-State Compromises and Creates Ontological Security for Its Subjects," *Journal of International Relations and Development* 21, no. 4 (2018): 909–33; Brent J. Steele and Alexandra Homolar, "Ontological Insecurities and the Politics of Contemporary Populism," *Cambridge Review of International Affairs* 32, no. 3 (2019): 214–21; Priya Chacko, "A New 'Special Relationship'? Power Transitions, Ontological Security, and India–US Relations," *International Studies Perspective* 15, no. 3 (2014): 329–46.

31. Chih-yu Shih et al., *China and International Theory: The Balance of Relationships* (London: Routledge, 2019); Brantly Womack, *Asymmetry and International Relationships* (Cambridge: Cambridge University Press, 2015).

32. Paul Cornish, "The Deterrence and Prevention of Cyber Conflict," in *The Oxford Handbook of Cyber Security*, ed. Paul Cornish, 273–94 (Oxford: Oxford University Press, 2021).

33. Womack, *Asymmetry and International Relationships*; Chiung-chiu Huang and Cong Tung Nguyen, "Dancing between Beijing and Taipei: Vietnam in the Shadow of the Belt and Road Initiative," *China Review* 22, no. 2 (2022): 315–39.

34. Behravesh, "State Revisionism."

35. Karl Gustafsson, "International Reconciliation on the Internet? Ontological Security, Attribution and the Construction of War Memory Narratives in Wikipedia," *International Relations* 34, no. 1 (2020): 3–24; Alexandra Homolar and Ronny Scholz, "The Power of Trump-speak: Populist Crisis Narratives and Ontological Security," *Cambridge Review of International Affairs* 32, no. 3 (2019): 344–54; Amir Lupovici, "Toward a Securitization Theory of Deterrence," *International Studies Quarterly* 63, no. 1 (2019): 177–86; Breuer and Johnston, "Memes"; George Dimitriu and Beatrice de Graaf, "Fighting the War at Home: Strategic Narratives, Elite Responsiveness, and the Dutch Mission in Afghanistan, 2006–2010," *Foreign Policy Analysis* 12, no. 1 (2016): 2–23; Juha A. Vuori, "Deterring Things with Words: Deterrence as a Speech Act," *New Perspectives* 24, no. 2 (2016): 23–50.

36. Badredine Arfi, "Security *qua* Existential Surviving (while Becoming Otherwise) through Performative Leaps of Faith," *International Theory* 12, no. 2 (2020): 291–305; Felix Berenskoetter, "Parameters of a National Biography," *European Journal of International Relations*, 20, no. 1 (2014): 262–88.

37. Catarina Kinnvall and Jennifer Mitzen, "Ontological Security and Conflict: The Dynamics of Crisis and the Constitution of Community," *Journal of International Relations and Development* 21, no. 4 (2018): 825–35.

38. Molly Krasnodębska, "Confrontation as Ontological Security Russia's Reactions to the EU-Ukraine Association Agreement," in *European-Russian Power Relations in Turbulent Times*, ed. Mai'a Cross and Ireneusz Pawel Karolewski, 135–59 (Ann Arbor: University of Michigan Press, 2021); Constance Duncombe, *Representation, Recognition, and Respect in World Politics: The Case of Iran–US Relations* (Manchester: Manchester University Press, 2019); Flemming Splidsboel Hansen, "Russia's Relations with the West: Ontological Security through Conflict," *Contemporary Politics* 22, no. 3 (2016): 359–75; Robbie Shilliam, "In Recognition of the Abyssinian General," in *Recognition and Global Politics: Critical Encounters between State and World*, ed. Patrick Hayden and Kate Schick, 121–38 (Manchester: Manchester University Press, 2016); Mitzen, "Ontological Security in World Politics."

39. Yoo Hyon Joo, "Reluctant Flexibility Caused by Abandonment Fears: A Theoretical Analysis of South Korea's Approach toward China in the 1970s and the Early 1980s," *Korean Journal of Defense Analysis* 26, no. 2 (2014): 225–42; Galia Press-Barnathan, "Managing the Hegemon: NATO under Unipolarity," *Security Studies* 15, no. 2 (2006): 271–309; Snyder, "Security Dilemma in Alliance Politics."

40. For example, Bruce Klingner, *The U.S.–Japan Security Alliance Must Act Now to Deter China from Attacking Taiwan* (Washington, DC: Heritage Foundation, April 29, 2022), https://www.heritage.org/asia/report/the-us-japan-security-alliance-must-act-now-deter-china-attacking-taiwan; Melanie W.

Sisson, *Taiwan and the Dangerous Illogic of Deterrence by Denial* (Washington, DC: Brookings Foreign Policy, May 2022), https://www.brookings.edu/wp-content/uploads/2022/05/FP_20220505_taiwan_strategy_sisson.pdf; Mastro, "Taiwan Temptation"; Justin Feng, "Maintaining Deterrence in the Taiwan Strait: Strategic Ambiguity versus Strategic Clarity," *Southern California International Review* 11, no. 1 (2021): 44–53.

41. For example, Joseph Trevithick, "Massive Drone Swarm over Strait Decisive in Taiwan Conflict Wargames," *War Zone*, May 19, 2022, https://www.thedrive.com/the-war-zone/massive-drone-swarm-over-strait-decisive-in-taiwan-conflict-wargames; Jeremy Sepinsky and Sebastian J. Bae, "War-Gaming Taiwan: When Losing to China Is Winning," *Foreign Policy*, April 3, 2022, https://foreignpolicy.com/2022/04/03/taiwan-china-war-game-military-planning-strategy/; Chris Dougherty, Jennie Matuschak, and Ripley Hunter, *The Poison Frog Strategy: Preventing a Chinese Fait Accompli against Taiwanese Islands* (Washington, DC: Center for a New American Security, October 2021), https://www.cnas.org/publications/reports/the-poison-frog-strategy; David Axe, "How to Lose a War over Taiwan–Get Hacked, Panic," *Forbes*, July 6, 2021, https://www.forbes.com/sites/davidaxe/2021/07/06/how-to-lose-a-war-with-china-over-taiwan-get-hacked-panic/.

42. For example, Asle Toje, ed., *Will China's Rise be Peaceful? Security, Stability, and Legitimacy* (Oxford: University of Oxford Press, 2018).

43. Viktoria Akchurina and Vincent Della Sala, "Russia, Europe and the Ontological Security Dilemma: Narrating the Emerging Eurasian Space," *Europe-Asia Studies* 70, no. 10 (2018): 1638.

44. Cornish, "Deterrence and Prevention of Cyber Conflict," 274.

45. Colin S. Gray, "The Definitions and Assumptions of Deterrence: Questions of Theory and Practice," *Journal of Strategic Studies* 13, no. 4 (1990): 4.

46. Chacko, "New 'Special Relationship'?"

47. Tanya Narozhna, "Revisiting the Causes of Russian Foreign Policy Changes: Incoherent Biographical Narrative, Recognition and Russia's Ontological Security-Seeking," *Central European Journal of International & Security Studies* 15, no. 2 (2021): 56–81.

48. Lowell Dittmer, "Taiwan as a Factor in China's Quest for National Identity," *Journal of Contemporary China* 15, no. 49 (2006): 671–86.

49. Victor Louzon, "From Japanese Soldiers to Chinese Rebels: Colonial Hegemony, War Experience, and Spontaneous Remobilization during the 1947 Taiwanese Rebellion," *Journal of Asian Studies* 77, no. 1 (2017): 161–79; Wan-yao Chou, "The Kominka Movement" (PhD diss., Yale University, 1991).

50. George Watson Barclay, *Colonial Development and Population in Taiwan* (Princeton, NJ: Princeton University Press, 2016); Stéphane Corcuff, "The Liminality of Taiwan: A Case-Study in Geopolitics," *Taiwan in Comparative Perspective* 4 (2012): 34–64.

51. J. Bruce Jacobs, "Taiwan's Colonial Experiences and the Development of Ethnic Identities: Some Hypotheses," *Taiwan in Comparative Perspective* 5 (2014): 47–59.

52. Bruce Jacobs and Peter Kang, *Changing Taiwanese Identities* (London: Routledge, 2018); Wolfgang Gerhard Thiele, "Decolonization and the Question of Exclusion in Taiwanese Nationalism since 1945," *Global Histories* 3, no. 1 (2017): 62–84.

53. Yih-jye Hwang and Edmund Frettingham, "Sovereignty and Identity: Taiwan's Claims in the South China Sea," in *Maritime and Territorial Disputes in the South China Sea: Faces of Power and Law in the Age of China's Rise*, ed. Yih-jye Hwang and Edmund Frettingham, 69–90 (Abingdon, UK: Routledge, 2021).

54. Stéphane Corcuff, "Liminality and Taiwan Tropism in a Postcolonial Context—Schemes of National Identification among Taiwan's 'Mainlanders' on the Eve of the Kuomintang's Return to Power," in *Politics of Difference in Taiwan*, ed. Tak-Wing Ngo and Hong-zen Wang, 34–62 (London: Routledge, 2011).

55. Hans Stockton, "National Identity, International Image, and a Security Dilemma: The Case of Taiwan," in *The 'One China' Dilemma*, ed. Peter C. Y. Chow, 99–115 (New York: Palgrave Macmillan, 2008); Christensen, "Contemporary Security Dilemma."

56. Wendt, *Social Theory of International Politics*.

57. Graham Allison, "The Thucydides Trap: Are the U.S. and China Headed for War?," *The Atlantic*, September 24, 2015, https://www.theatlantic.com/international/archive/2015/09/united-states-china-war-thucydides-trap/406756/; Graham Allison, "Thucydides's Trap Has Been Sprung in the Pacific," *Financial Times*, August 21, 2012, https://www.ft.com/content/5d695b5a-ead3-11e1-984b-00144feab49a.

58. Nadège Rolland, *China's Vision for a New World Order*, NBR special report no. 83 (Seattle, WA: National Bureau of Asian Research, 2020); John Lee, *Ambition and Overreach: Countering One Belt One Road and Beijing's Plans to Dominate Global Innovation* (Washington, DC: Hudson Institute, 2020); Jeanne L. Wilson, "Are Russia and China Revisionist States?" *Asia Dialogue*, June 11, 2019, https://theasiadialogue.com/2019/06/11/are-russia-and-china-revisionist-states/.

59. For example, Huiyun Feng and Kai He, eds., *China's Challenges and International Order Transition: Beyond "Thucydides's Trap"* (Ann Arbor: University of Michigan Press, 2020).

60. Diamond and Schell, *Chinese Influence and American Interests*; Schell and Shirk, *Course Correction*.

61. Anonymous, *The Longer Telegram: Toward a New American China Strategy*, Atlantic Council Strategic Papers (Washington, DC: Scowcroft Center for Strategy and Security, 2021), https://www.atlanticcouncil.org/wp-content/uploads/2021/01/The-Longer-Telegram-Toward-A-New-American-China-Strategy.

pdf; Lindsay DiCuirci, ed., *Millennial Aspirations and Providentialism*, vol. 3 of *American Exceptionalism*, Timothy Roberts and Lindsay DiCuirci, general editors (London: Routledge, 2013); Monica Prasad, *The Land of Too Much* (Cambridge, MA: Harvard University Press, 2012); G. John Ikenberry, *Liberal Leviathan: The Origins, Crisis, and Transformation of the American World Order* (Princeton, NJ: Princeton University Press, 2011).

62. Robert G. Patman and Laura Southgate, "Globalization, the Obama Administration and the Refashioning of US Exceptionalism," *International Politics* 53, no. 2 (2016): 220–38; Dick Cheney and Liz Cheney, *Exceptional: Why the World Needs a Powerful America* (New York: Simon & Schuster, 2015).

63. Karl Gustafsson, "Memory Politics and Ontological Security in Sino-Japanese Relations," *Asian Studies Review* 38, no. 1 (2014): 71–86; Shogo Suzuki, "The Importance of 'Othering' in China's National Identity: Sino-Japanese Relations as a Stage of Identity Conflicts," *Pacific Review* 20, no. 1 (2007): 23–47.

64. Siavash Chavoshi and Mohammad Reza Saeidabadi, "The Struggle for Recognition, Ontological Security and the Case of China as a Rising Power," *International Politics Reviews* 9, no. 2 (2021): 390–411; Michelle Murray, *The Struggle for Recognition in International Relations: Status, Revisionism, and Rising Powers* (Oxford: Oxford University Press, 2018); Steven Ward, *Status and the Challenge of Rising Powers* (Cambridge: Cambridge University Press, 2017).

65. Robert Weatherley and Qiang Zhang, *History and Nationalist Legitimacy in Contemporary China* (London: Macmillan, 2017); Orville Schell and John Delury, *China's Long March to the Twenty-First Century* (New York: Random House, 2013); William Callahan, *China: The Pessoptimist Nation* (Oxford: Oxford University Press, 2009).

66. Xuefeng Sun, "United States Leadership in East Asia and China's State-by-State Approach to Regional Security," *Chinese Political Science Review* 3, no. 2 (2017): 100–114.

67. Xiaojun Ke, "South Korea's Intangible Cultural Heritage Claims and China's Ontological Security," *International Journal of Cultural Policy* 28, no. 4 (2022): 476–98; Derek Bolton, "Balancing Identity: The Sino-Soviet Split, Ontological Security, and North Korean Foreign Policy," *Security Studies* 30, no. 2 (2021): 271–301; Womack, *Asymmetry and International Relationships.*

68. Muhsin Puthan Purayil and Mufsin Puthan Purayil, "The Ladakh Crisis and India's Ontological Security," *Global Changes, Peace & Security* 33, no. 1 (2021): 85–91; Deborah Welch Larson, "An Equal Partnership of Unequals: China's and Russia's Status Relationship," *International Politics* 57, no. 5 (2020): 790–808; Gustafsson, "Memory Politics."

69. Anisa Heritage and Pak K. Lee, *Order, Contestation and Ontological Security-Seeking in the South China Sea* (New York: Palgrave Macmillan, 2020); Henry Curtis, "Constructing Cooperation: Chinese Ontological Security Seeking in the South China Sea Dispute," *Journal of Borderlands Studies* 31, no. 4 (2016): 537–49.

70. Baohui Zhang, "U.S.-China Military Space Relationship."

71. Axel Berkofsky, "US Freedom of Navigation Operations (FONOPs) in the South China Sea—Able to Keep Chinese Territorial Expansionism in Check?," in *US Foreign Policy in a Challenging World: Building Order on Shifting Foundations*, ed. Marco Clementi, Matteo Dian, and Barbara Pisciotta, 339–56 (Cham, Switzerland: Springer Nature, 2018).

72. James Morrow, "How Do Defensive Alliances Provoke Rather than Deter?," *Journal of Politics* 79, no. 1 (2017): 341–45; Brett V. Benson, Adam Meirowitz, and Kristopher W. Ramsay, "Inducing Deterrence through Moral Hazard in Alliance Contracts," *Journal of Conflict Resolution* 58, no. 2 (2014): 307–35.

73. The result echoes Beijing's first peaceful-unification initiative in 1979, upon Washington's consent to withdraw troops from Taiwan, diplomatic recognition of the PRC, and acknowledgment of the One China policy.

74. Thomas J. Shattuck, "Options for Taiwan to Better Compete with China," *Divergent Options*, October 14, 2020, https://divergentoptions.org/2020/10/14/options-for-taiwan-to-compete-with-china/.

75. Christina Lai, "Power of the Weak: Taiwan's Strategy in Countering China's Economic Coercion," *China Brief* 21, no. 21 (2021): 5–10; Xin Qiang, "Selective Engagement: Mainland China's Dual-Track Taiwan Policy," *Journal of Contemporary China* 29, no. 124 (2020): 535–52; Shu Keng, Jean Yu-Chen Tseng, and Qiang Yu, "The Strengths of China's Charm Offensive: Changes in the Political Landscape of a Southern Taiwan Town under Attack from Chinese Economic Power," *China Quarterly* 232 (2017): 956–81.

76. Šárka Cabadová Waisová, "China's Strategy vis-à-vis Taiwan's Diplomatic Friends: Is Beijing Using Dollar Diplomacy?," *Journal of Comparative Politics* 13, no. 1 (2020): 76–101.

77. Klingner, "U.S.-Japan Security Alliance."

78. Ching-hsin Yu, "Taiwan in 2020: Beyond the Pandemic," *Asian Survey* 61, no. 1 (2021): 83–89; Au, "Sunflower Movement."

79. Kharis Templeman, "How Taiwan Stands Up to China," *Journal of Democracy* 31, no. 3 (2020): 85–99.

80. Liu Xiaobo, "How China Can Resolve the FONOP Deadlock in the South China Sea," Asia Maritime Transparency Initiative (website), March 1, 2019, https://amti.csis.org/how-china-can-resolve-fonop-deadlock/.

Chapter 10

The original version of this chapter was published as a research article in *Uluslararası İlişkiler / International Relations* in 2021. I would like to thank the editorial board of *Uluslararası İlişkiler* for their contributions and cooperation. For the full version of the article, please see Raoul Bunskoek and Chih-yu Shih, "'Community of Common Destiny' as Post-Western Regionalism: Rethinking

China's Belt and Road Initiative from a Confucian Perspective," *Uluslararası İlişkiler* 18, no. 70 (2021): 85–101, https://doi.org/10.33458/uidergisi.954744.

1. Hu Jintao, "Full Text of Hu Jintao's Report at the 18th Party Congress" [in Chinese], Ministry of Foreign Affairs of the People's Republic of China (website), November 8, 2012, https://www.mfa.gov.cn/web/zyxw/201211/t20121108_321115.shtml.

2. *"Zhonghua Renmin Gongheguo Xianfa Xiuzheng An"* [People's Republic of China Constitutional Amendment], *Xinhua*, March 11, 2018, http://www.xinhuanet.com/politics/2018lh/2018-03/11/c_1122521235.htm.

3. National Development and Reform Commission (NDRC) of the People's Republic of China, "Visions and Actions on Jointly Building Silk Road Economic Belt and 21st-Century Maritime Silk Road," Ministry of Foreign Affairs of the PRC, March 28, 2015, https://www.fmprc.gov.cn/eng/topics_665678/2015zt/xjpcxbayzlt2015nnh/201503/t20150328_705553.html.

4. Chengxin Pan, *Knowledge, Desire, and Power in Global Politics: Western Representations of China's Rise* (Cheltenham, UK: Edward Elgar Publishing, 2012); Nadège Rolland, *China's Vision for a New World Order*, NBR Special Report no. 83 (National Bureau of Asian Research, January 27, 2020), https://www.nbr.org/publication/chinas-vision-for-a-new-world-order/; *United States Strategic Approach to the People's Republic of China*, White House Archives, May 20, 2020, https://trumpwhitehouse.archives.gov/wp-content/uploads/2020/05/U.S.-Strategic-Approach-to-The-Peoples-Republic-of-China-Report-5.24v1.pdf.

5. Dipesh Chakrabarty, *Provincializing Europe: Postcolonial Thought and Historical Difference* (Princeton, NJ: Princeton University Press, 2000); Stephen Chan, *The Morality of China in Africa: The Middle Kingdom and the Dark Continent* (London: Zed Books, 2013).

6. J. P., "What is China's Belt and Road Initiative?," *The Economist*, May 15, 2017, https://www.economist.com/the-economist-explains/2017/05/14/what-is-chinas-belt-and-road-initiative.

7. Chantal Mouffe, *The Democratic Paradox* (London: Verso, 2005), 550.

8. Swaran Singh, "Cultural Revolution and the Making of Xi Jinping," *Micro Intellectual History through De-central Lenses*, ed. Chih-yu Shih, Mariko Tanigaki, and Tina S. Clement, vol. 2 of *Studies of China and Chineseness since the Cultural Revolution*, 153–180 (Singapore: World Scientific, 2023).

9. See Xi's first speech at the United Nations, "Xi Jinping zai di qishi jie lianheguo dahui yibanxing bianlun shi de jianghua (quanwen)" [Xi Jinping's full statement at the General Debate of the seventieth session of the UN General Assembly], *Xinhua*, September 29, 2015, http://www.xinhuanet.com//world/2015-09/29/c_1116703645.htm, in which he stated, "When the great way prevails, the world is equally shared by all," which is a direct quote from the Confucian classic the *Book of Rites*, ch. 9; and Xi Jinping, "Communique of the 4th Plenary Session of the 18th Central Committee of CPC," October 23,

2014, trans. Compilatin and Translation Bureau of the Central Committee of the CPC, December 2, 2014, http://www.china.org.cn/china/fourth_plenary_session/2014-12/02/content_34208801.htm, during which Xi directed that "we must [. . .] combine the rule of law with the rule of virtue."

10. Chih-yu Shih, *China's Just World: The Morality of Chinese Foreign Policy* (London: Lynne Rienner Publishers, 1993).

11. Lucian W. Pye and Mary W. Pye, *Asian Power and Politics: The Cultural Dimensions of Authority* (Cambridge, MA: Belknap Press, 1985).

12. Henry Rosemont Jr. and Roger T. Ames, *The Chinese Classic of Family Reverence: A Philosophical Translation of the "Xiaojing"* (Honolulu: University of Hawai'i Press, 2009).

13. Chan, *Morality of China in Africa*, 16. Lily Ling, conversely, bases her view on the BRI mostly on a combination of Daoism and Buddhism, which is useful for illustrating the inherent interrelatedness of selves and others (plus the existence of the self in every other, and vice versa), but says less about how relationships are practiced and the role obligations inherent in Confucianism. L. H. M. Ling, "Squaring the Circle: China's 'Belt and Road Initiative' (BRI) and the Ancient Silk Roads," *Critical Reflections on China's Belt & Road Initiative*, ed. Alan Chong and Quang Minh Pham, 23–40 (Singapore: Palgrave Macmillan, 2020).

14. Yuen Yuen Ang, *How China Escaped the Poverty Trap* (Ithaca, NY: Cornell University Press, 2016); Justin Yifu Lin, *New Structural Economics: A Framework for Rethinking Development and Policy* (Washington, DC: World Bank, 2012); Justin Yifu Lin, *Demystifying the Chinese Economy* (Cambridge: Cambridge University Press, 2012).

15. Ang, *How China Escaped the Poverty Trap*, 2.

16. Ang, 2.

17. Lawrence E. Harrison and Samuel Huntington, eds., *Culture Matters: How Values Shape Human Progress* (New York: Basic Books, 2000).

18. Ang, *How China Escaped the Poverty Trap*, 17.

19. Ang, 17.

20. Ang, 14.

21. Also, as Tsai and Dean point out, in localities where the relationship (*guanxi*) between the provincial secretaries and general secretaries is closer. Wen-Hsuan Tsai and Nicola Dean, "Experimentation under Hierarchy in Local Conditions: Cases of Political Reform in Guangdong and Sichuan, China," *China Quarterly* 218 (2014): 339–58.

22. One ardent supporter of the conducive argument is Steven N. S. Cheung, "A Simplistic General Equilibrium Theory of Corruption," *Contemporary Economic Policy* 13, no. 3 (1996): 1–5; on the destructive side, the strongest voice is probably Qinglian He, *Xiandaihua de Xianjing* [The pitfall of modernization] (Guangzhou: Today's China Press, 1998).

23. *Mencius* 1A7 (see also 3A3), quoted in Daniel A. Bell, *The China Model: Political Meritocracy and the Limits of Democracy* (Princeton, NJ: Princeton University Press, 2015), 143.

24. The Zuo Commentary to the *Spring and Autumn Annals*, Xiang Year 31.

25. *Analects*, Xianwen.

26. *Analects*, Yongye.

27. Yaqing Qin, "Continuity through Change: Background Knowledge and China's International Strategy," *Chinese Journal of International Politics* 7, no. 3 (2014): 285–314.

28. For the importance of gift giving in Confucian culture, see Yunxiang Yan, *The Flow of Gifts: Reciprocity and Social Networks in a Chinese Village* (Stanford, CA: Stanford University Press, 1996).

29. Tingyang Zhao, *Redefining a Philosophy for World Governance*, trans. Liqing Tao (Singapore: Palgrave, 2019).

30. NDRC, "Visions and Actions."

31. NDRC; emphasis added.

32. Chen Zhimin and Jian Junbo, *Chinese Provinces as Foreign Policy Actors in Africa*, China in Africa Project Occasional Paper no. 22 (South African Institute of International Affairs, January 2009), https://saiia.org.za/wp-content/uploads/2009/02/Occasional-Paper-22.pdf.

33. For instance, after the new Malaysian prime minister Mahathir Mohamad canceled a China-backed high-speed-rail project on August 20, 2018, Chinese premier Li Keqiang said that China's "friendly approach" toward Malaysia would not change. Catherine Wong, "Malaysia Big Part of Beijing's Belt and Road Vision for Future, Says Xi Jinping," *South China Morning Post*, August 20, 2018, https://www.scmp.com/news/china/diplomacy-defence/article/2160469/debt-laden-malaysia-wants-fair-and-free-trade-china.

34. Srikanth Kondapalli and Hu Xiaowen, eds., *One Belt, One Road: China's Global Outreach* (New Delhi: Pentagon Press, 2017).

35. Wang Yiwei, *The Belt and Road Initiative: What Will China Offer the World in Its Rise* (Beijing: New World Press, 2016).

36. Mingming Wang, *The West as the Other: A Genealogy of Chinese Occidentalism* (Hong Kong: Chinese University Press, 2014); Tingyang Zhao, *Tianxia de Dangdaixing: Shijie Zhixu de Shijian yu Xiangxiang* [A possible world of all-under-heaven system: The world order in the past and for the future] (Beijing: China Citic Press, 2016).

37. Wang Gungwu, *Renewal: The Chinese State and the New Global History* (Hong Kong: Chinese University Press, 2013).

38. Lin, *Demystifying the Chinese Economy*.

39. Tingyang Zhao, *Tianxia Tixi: Shijie Zhidu Zhexue Daolun* [The *tianxia* system: An introduction to the philosophy of a world institution] (Nanjing: Jiangsu Jiaoyu Chubanshe, 2005); Tingyang Zhao, "Rethinking Empire from

a Chinese Concept 'All-under-Heaven' (Tian-xia)," *Social Identities* 12, no. 1 (2006): 29–41; Tingyang Zhao, "A Political World Philosophy in Terms of All-under-Heaven (Tian-xia)," *Diogenes* 56, no. 1 (2009): 5–18.

40. Wang Mingming, "All under Heaven (*Tianxia*): Cosmological Perspectives and Political Ontologies in Pre-modern China," *Hau: Journal of Ethnographic Theory* 2, no 1 (2012): 337–83.

41. Wang Mingming, "All under Heaven," 339.

42. Chih-yu Shih, "The West That Is Not in the West: Identifying the Self in Oriental Modernity," *Cambridge Review of International Affairs* 23, no. 4 (2011): 537–60.

43. Shih, "West That Is Not the West."

44. Wang Mingming, "All under Heaven," 338.

45. Wang Mingming, 338.

46. Wang Mingming, 338.

47. Wang Gungwu, "Early Ming Relations with Southeast Asia: A Background Essay," *The Chinese World Order*, ed. John King Fairbank (Cambridge, MA: Harvard University Press, 1968), 62.

48. Chih-yu Shih, "Bound to Relate: Retheorizing International Order through the Chinese Culture of Power," in *China's Challenges and International Order Transition: Beyond "Thucydides's Trap,"* ed. Huiyun Feng and Kai He, 182–201 (Ann Arbor: University of Michigan Press, 2020).

49. Mingming Wang, *The West as the Other*.

50. Wang Gungwu, "Early Ming Relations."

51. Wang Gungwu, 43.

52. Wang Gungwu, 43.

53. Wang Gungwu, 49.

54. Wang Gungwu, 49.

55. Kai Wang, "Scientific Gentry and Socialisation of Western Science in China's Modernisation during 'Self-Strengthening' Movement (1860–1895)," *Almagest* 9, no. 1 (2018): 69–95; Zhuran You, A. G. Rud, and Yingzi Hu, *The Philosophy of Chinese Moral Education: A History* (New York: Palgrave Macmillan, 2018).

56. Suisheng Zhao, *Power Competition in East Asia: From the Old Chinese World Order to Post-Cold War Regional Multipolarity* (New York: St. Martin's Press, 1997).

57. Catherine Wong, "Xi Jinping Says Belt and Road Plan Isn't about Creating a 'China Club,'" *South China Morning Post*, August 27, 2018, https://www.scmp.com/news/china/diplomacy-defence/article/2161580/xi-jinping-says-belt-and-road-plan-isnt-about-creating.

58. Xi Jinping, quoted in Wong, "Xi Jinping."

59. Brantly Womack, "Dongfang yu Xifang de 'Tianxia' ('Tianxia' East and West)," *Jilin Daxue Shehui Kexue Xuebao* [Jilin University Journal of Social Sciences] 51, no. 2 (2011): 85–91.

60. Wang Gungwu, "Early Ming Relations," 58.

61. Song Luzheng, "Guandian: Ouzhou yinggai zhichi 'Yidai, Yilu' de liu da liyou" [Opinion: Six reasons why the EU should support the Belt and Road Initiative], *BBC News*, May 8, 2018, https://www.bbc.com/zhongwen/trad/world-39847203.

62. Richard Neustadt, *Presidential Power and the Modern Presidents: The Politics of Leadership from Roosevelt to Reagan* (New York: Free Press, 1991).

63. Kumakura Jun, "China's Influence in Central Asia and Sino-Russian Relations," lecture at the Institute of Political Science, Academia Sinica, Taipei, Taiwan, September 4, 2018.

64. Pan, *Knowledge, Desire, and Power in Global Politics*.

Chapter 11

1. In addition to the abundant debate in the Chinese literature in China and Taiwan, these topics attract widespread attention elsewhere also. See Bruce Klingner, *The U.S.–Japan Security Alliance Must Act Now to Deter China from Attacking Taiwan* (Washington, DC: Heritage Foundation, April 29, 2022); David J. Keegan and Kyle Churchman, "Taiwan and China Seek Lessons from Ukraine as Taiwan's International Position Strengthens," *Comparative Connections* 24, no. 1 (May 2022): 93–94; Ramsha Faisal and Talal Maqbool, "China-Taiwan Dispute and the Role of United States: War Risks and Conflict," *Pakistan Journal of International Affairs* 5, no. 2 (2022): 391–401; Drew Thompson, "'Ukraine Today, Taiwan Tomorrow': Should Southeast Asia Worry?," *ISEAS Perspective* no. 39 (2022): 3–4; Yamaguchi Noboru, "Japan's New Security Posture and Its Implications for Taiwan," *Asan Forum*, September 24, 2021, https://theasan-forum.org/japans-new-security-posture-and-its-implications-for-taiwan/; Oxford Analytica, "Washington Shows Support for Taiwan during Ukraine War," *Expert Briefings*, May 16, 2022, https://doi.org/10.1108/OXAN-DB270223.

2. Tyler O'Neil, "Ukraine War Upended China's Plan to Invade Taiwan, Alleged FSB Whistleblower Says," *Fox News*, March 16, 2022, https://www.foxnews.com/world/ukraine-war-upended-chinas-plan-to-invade-taiwan-alleged-fsb-whistleblower-says.

3. More attention is paid to the arrangements to encircle China by neighboring countries and NATO involvement, in addition to Taiwan's street-war capabilities. Nathaniel Sher, "The Real Lesson of the War in Ukraine for Taiwan," *Responsible Statecraft*, May 4, 2022, https://responsiblestatecraft.org/2022/05/04/the-real-lesson-of-the-war-in-ukraine-for-taiwan/.

4. For example, see Graham Allison, "The Russia–Ukraine War, the US–China Rivalry and Thucydides's Trap," hosted by Benjamin Rhode, April 19, 2022, International Institute for Strategic Studies, London, https://www.iiss.org/

events/2022/04/the-russia-ukraine-war-the-us-china-rivalry-and-thucydidess-trap; "How the Ukraine Crisis Affects China's View on Taiwan—*Intelligence Matters*," CBS News, March 16, 2022, https://www.cbsnews.com/news/russia-china-chris-johnson-intelligence-matters/; José Pardo de Santayana, *From Ukraine to Taiwan: Learning to Live in a Worse World*, IEEE Analysis Paper 28/2022 (Madrid: Instituto Espanol de Estudios Estrategicos, 2022), https://www.ieee.es/Galerias/fichero/docs_analisis/2022/DIEEEA28_2022_JOSPAR_Ucrania_ENG.pdf.

5. For example, see Chris Horton, "The Lessons Taiwan Is Learning from Ukraine," *The Atlantic*, May 7, 2022, https://www.theatlantic.com/international/archive/2022/05/defend-taiwan-democracy-china-threat/629782/; Andrew Scobell and Lucy Stevenson-Yang, "China Is Not Russia. Taiwan Is Not Ukraine.," United States Institute of Peace, March 4, 2022, https://www.usip.org/publications/2022/03/china-not-russia-taiwan-not-ukraine.

6. Martin Boyle, "*Huadu*: A Realist Constructivist Account of Taiwan's Anomalous Status," in *The Social Construction of State Power: Applying Realist Constructivism*, ed. J. Samuel Barkin, 73–100 (Cambridge: Cambridge University Press, 2021); Ching-chang Chen and Kosuke Shimizu, "International Relations from the Margins: The Westphalian Meta-narratives and Counter-narratives in Okinawa–Taiwan Relations," *Cambridge Review of International Affairs* 32, 4 (2019): 521–40.

7. Linus Hagstrom, "Great Power Narcissism and Ontological (In) Security: The Narrative Mediation of Greatness and Weakness in International Politics," *International Studies Quarterly* 65, no. 2 (2021): 339; Siavash Chavoshi and Mohammad reza Saeidabadi, "The Struggle for Recognition, Ontological Security and the Case of China as a Rising Power," *International Politics Reviews* 9, no. 2 (2021): 390–411.

8. Graham Allison, *Destined for War: Can America and China Escape Thucydides's Trap?* (Boston: Houghton Mifflin Harcourt, 2017).

9. Anisa Heritage and Pak K. Lee, *Order, Contestation and Ontological Security-Seeking in the South China Sea* (Cham, Switzerland: Palgrave Macmillan), 207–10.

10. Adam Chen-Dedman, "Seeing China Differently: National Contestation in Taiwan's LGBTQ (*tongzhi*) Movement," *Nations and Nationalism* 25, no. 4 (2022): 1212–29; Ketty W. Chen, "Island Sunrise: The Sunflower Movement and Taiwan's Democracy in Transition," in *Dynamic Transition: Nation Building and Democratization*, ed. Ryan Dunch and Ashley Esarey, 121–39 (Seattle: University of Washington Press, 2020).

11. Shelly Rigger, *The Tiger Leading the Dragon: How Taiwan Propelled China's Economic Rise* (Lanham, MD: Rowman & Littlefield, 2021); Wen Liu, "From Independence to Interdependence: Taiwan Independence as Critique, Strategy, and Method toward Decoloniality," *American Quarterly* 73, no. 2 (2021): 371–77; Raoul Bunskoek, "Colonial Relationality and Its Post-Chinese

Consequences: Japanese Legacies in Contemporary Taiwan's Views on China," in *Colonial Legacies and Contemporary Studies of China and Chineseness: Unlearning Boundaries, Strategizing Self*, ed. Chih-yu Shih et al. (Singapore: World Scientific, 2020), 232–36.

12. A typical proposal reproduces great-power bargaining and minor-power irrelevance, thus failing to soothe ontological security concerns. See Heritage and Lee, *Order, Contestation and Ontological Security-Seeking*, 219–23; Yana Zuo, "The U.S. Global Strategy and Its Taiwan Policy," *China Review* 18, no. 3 (2018): 169; Feng Zhang and Richard Ned Lebow, *Taming Sino-American Rivalry* (Oxford: Oxford University Press, 2020); Charles L. Glaser, "A U.S.-China Grand Bargain? The Hard Choice between Military Competition and Accommodation," *International Security* 39, no. 4 (2015): 49–90.

13. Chen and Shimizu, "International Relations from the Margins."

14. This is true even among scholars from the East Asian region. For example, see Nien-chung Chang-Liao and Chi Fang, "The Case for Maintaining Strategic Ambiguity in the Taiwan Strait," *Washington Quarterly* 44, no. 2 (2021): 45–60; Huang Jaw-Nian, "Between American and Chinese Hegemonies: Economic Dependence, Norm Diffusion and Taiwan's Press Freedom," *China: An International Journal* 17, no. 2 (2019): 82–105; Zuo Xiying, "Unbalanced Deterrence: Coercive Threat, Reassurance and the US-China Rivalry in Taiwan Strait," *Pacific Review* 34, no. 4 (2021): 547–76; Pan Zhongqi, "US Taiwan Policy of Strategic Ambiguity: A Dilemma of Deterrence," *Journal of Contemporary China* 12, no. 35 (2003): 387–407.

15. For example, see Ryan Hass, "How China Is Responding to Escalating Strategic Competition with the US," Brookings (website), March 1, 2021; Michael Pillsbury, *The Hundred-Year Marathon: China's Secret Strategy to Replace America as the Global Superpower* (New York: St. Martin's Press, 2015); John J. Mearsheimer, "Taiwan's Dire Straits," *National Interest*, no. 130 (March/April 2014): 29–39; Aaron L. Friedberg, *A Contest for Supremacy: China, America, and the Struggle for Mastery in Asia* (New York: W. W. Norton, 2011); Thomas J. Christensen, "The Contemporary Security Dilemma: Deterring a Taiwan Conflict," *Washington Quarterly* 25, no. 4 (2002): 5–21.

16. Nadège Rolland, *China's Vision for a New World Order*, NBR Special Report no. 83 (Seattle, WA: National Bureau of Asian Research, 2020); *National Security Strategy of the United States of America* (Washington, DC: White House, December 2017), https://trumpwhitehouse.archives.gov/wp-content/uploads/2017/12/NSS-Final-12-18-2017-0905.pdf; Jim Mattis, *Summary of the 2018 National Defense Strategy of the United States of America: Sharpening the American Military's Competitive Edge* (Washington, DC: U.S. Department of Defense, 2018), https://dod.defense.gov/Portals/1/Documents/pubs/2018-National-Defense-Strategy-Summary.pdf.

17. Sheena Chestnut Greitens, *Dealing with Demand for China's Global Surveillance Exports* (Washington, DC: Brookings Institution, April 2020), https://www.brookings.edu/wp-content/uploads/2020/04/FP_20200428_china_surveillance_greitens_v3.pdf; Larry Diamond and Orville Schell, eds., *Chinese Influence and American Interests: Promoting Constructive Vigilance* (Stanford, CA: Hoover Institute, 2018).

18. For example, Richard Haass, "The Taiwan Triangle," *Project Syndicate*, October 18, 2021, https://www.project-syndicate.org/commentary/us-policy-to-prevent-chinese-invasion-of-taiwan-by-richard-haass-2021-10; Shelly Rigger, "Testimony for the U.S.-China Economic and Security Review Commission, Hearing on Cross-Strait Deterrence," February 18, 2021, https://www.uscc.gov/sites/default/files/2021-02/Shelley_Rigger_Statement_for_the_Record.pdf; Richard C. Bush, "Cross-Strait Relations: Not a One-Way Street," Brookings (website), April 22, 2016, https://www.brookings.edu/blog/order-from-chaos/2016/04/22/cross-strait-relations-not-a-one-way-street/.

19. Bonny Lin, "U.S. Allied and Partner Support for Taiwan: Responses to a Chinese Attack on Taiwan and Potential U.S. Taiwan Policy Changes," testimony presented before the U.S.-China Economic and Security Review Commission, February 18, 2021, https://www.uscc.gov/sites/default/files/2021-02/Bonny_Lin_Testimony.pdf. Also see the discussion on the Baltic states as a model for Taiwan by Michael A. Hunzeker and Dennis L. Weng, "The Painful, but Necessary, Next Steps in the U.S.-Taiwanese Relationship," *War on the Rocks*, September 24, 2020, https://warontherocks.com/2020/09/the-painful-but-necessary-next-steps-in-the-u-s-taiwanese-relationship/.

20. Lara Seligman, " 'Deadly Serious': U.S. Quietly Urging Taiwan to Follow Ukraine Playbook for Countering China," *Politico*, May 19, 2022, https://www.politico.com/news/2022/05/19/deadly-serious-u-s-quietly-urging-taiwan-to-follow-ukraine-playbook-for-countering-china-00033792.

21. Wang Wen, "Hypocrisy and Malevolence of US Policy toward China," *Global Times*, June 6, 2022; Wang Jisi, "The Plot against China? How Beijing Sees the New Washington Consensus," *Foreign Affairs* 100, no. 4 (July/August 2021): 48–57.

22. For a good summary, see Orville Schell and Susan L. Shirk, chairs, *Course Correction: Toward an Effective and Sustainable China Policy*, Asia Society Center on U.S.-China Relations Task Force report, February 2019, https://asiasociety.org/sites/default/files/inline-files/CourseCorrection_FINAL_2.7.19_1.pdf; Mark Stokes, "The United States and Future Policy Options in the Taiwan Strait," Project 2049 Institute (website), January 17, 2017, https://project2049.net/2017/01/17/the-united-states-and-future-policy-options-in-the-taiwan-strait-2/; Harry Harding, "Has U.S. China Policy Failed?" *Washington Quarterly* 38, no. 3 (2015): 95–122.

23. The representative voice is Mearsheimer, "Taiwan's Dire Straits"; also see Bruce Gilly, "Not So Dire Straits: How the Finlandization of Taiwan Benefits U.S. Security," *Foreign Affairs* 89, no. 1 (January/February 2010): 44–56, 58–60.

24. For a summary of this perspective, see Gang Lin and Wenxing Zhou, "Does Taiwan Matter to the United States? Policy Debates on Taiwan Abandonment and Beyond," *China Review* 18, no. 3 (2018): 177–206; also see the US rationale for supporting the status quo by Nancy Bernkopf Tucker and Bonnie Glaser, "Should the United States Abandon Taiwan?," *Washington Quarterly* 34, no. 4 (2011): 35–36.

25. Gilly, "Not So Dire Straits."

26. Yuan-kang Wang, "Rethinking US Security Commitment to Taiwan," in *Taiwan's Political Re-Alignment and Diplomatic Challenges*, ed. Wei-chin Lee, 245–70 (Palgrave Macmillan, 2018).

27. Lin, "U.S. Allied and Partner Support for Taiwan."

28. Chih-yu Shih, "Constituting Taiwanese Statehood: The World Timing of Un-Chinese Consciousness," *Journal of Contemporary China* 16, no. 53 (2007): 699–716.

29. For example, see Thomas B. Gold, *State and Society in the Taiwan Miracle* (London: Routledge, 1986), 122–34.

30. For example, see Yun-han Chu, "China and East Asian Democracy: The Taiwan Factor," *Journal of Democracy* 23, no. 1 (2012): 42–56; Hung-mao Tien, ed., *Taiwan's Electoral Politics and Democratic Transition: Riding the Third Wave* (Armonk, NY: M. E. Sharpe, 1996).

31. Murray A. Rubinstein, ed., *The Other Taiwan, 1945–1992* (New York: Routledge, 2016).

32. For a few examples, see Cal Clark, ed., *The Changing Dynamics of the Relations among China, Taiwan, and the United States* (Newcastle upon Tyne, UK: Cambridge Scholars Publishing, 2011); Jacques deLisle, "Soft Power in a Hard Place: China, Taiwan, Cross-Strait Relations and U.S. Policy," *Orbis* 54, no. 4 (2010): 493–524; Lowell Dittmer, "Bush, China, Taiwan: A Triangular Analysis," *Journal of Chinese Political Science* 10, no. 1 (2005): 21–42; Yu-Shan Wu, "From Romantic Triangle to Marriage? Washington-Beijing-Taipei Relations in Historical Comparison," *Issues & Studies* 41, no. 1 (2005): 113–61; Bruce J. Dickson, "New Presidents Adjust Old Policies: US-Taiwan Relations under Chen and Bush," *Journal of Contemporary China* 11, no. 33 (2002): 645–56; William M. Carpenter, "The Taiwan Strait Triangle," *Comparative Strategy* 19, no. 4 (2000): 329–40.

33. Every call for applications on its website (http://www.cckf.org/en/programs) specifically states that "projects on Taiwan Studies are especially encouraged." These include funding for Taiwanese research centers.

34. The series includes Dafydd Fell, *Taiwan's Green Parties: Alternative Politics in Taiwan* (2021); Kuang-hao Hou, *The Social Construction of the Ocean*

and Modern Taiwan (2023); Mei-Fang Fan, *Deliberative Democracy in Taiwan: A Deliberative Systems Perspective* (2021); and Phyllis Yu-ting Huang, *Literary Representations of "Mainlanders" in Taiwan: Becoming Sinophone* (2021). All come from Routledge in Abingdon, UK.

35. See https://www.cambridge.org/core/series/taiwan-studies/03CFE4A E52D0E497ADDA27660C4C1B7A.

36. Lara Momesso and Chun-yi Lee, "Nation, Migration, Identity: Learning from the Cross-Strait Context," *International Migration* 57, no. 4 (2019): 218–31; Pei-chia Lan and Yi-Fan Wu, "Exceptional Membership and Liminal Space of Identity: Student Migration from Taiwan to China," *International Sociology* 31, no. 6 (2016): 742–63; Yen-Fen Tseng, "How Do Identities Matter? Taiwanese Cultural Workers in China," in *Border Crossing in Greater China: Production, Community and Identity*, ed. Jenn-hwan Wang (London: Routledge, 2015), 196–200.

37. Andreas Osiander, "Sovereignty, International Relations, and the Westphalian Myth," *International Organization* 55, no. 2 (2001): 251–87.

38. Christopher Clapham, "Sovereignty and the Third World State," *Political Studies* 47, no. 3 (1999): 522–37.

39. Navid Pourmokhtari, "A Postcolonial Critique of State Sovereignty in IR: The Contradictory Legacy of a 'West-Centric' Discipline," *Third World Quarterly* 34, no. 10 (2013): 1767–93.

40. Nicholas De Genova, "Migration and Race in Europe: The Trans-atlantic Metastases of a Post-colonial Cancer," *European Journal of Social Theory* 13, no. 3 (2010): 405–19.

41. Bunskoek, "Colonial Relationality."

42. Yen-Fen Tseng, "How Do Identities Matter?"

43. Oriana Skylar Mastro, "The Precarious State of Cross-Strait Deterrence," testimony presented before the U.S.-China Economic and Security Review Commission, February 18, 2021, https://www.uscc.gov/sites/default/files/2021-02/Oriana_Skylar_Mastro_Testimony.pdf; Liu Zhen, "Xi Jinping Orders China's Military to Be Ready for War 'at Any Second,'" *South China Morning Post*, January 5, 2021, https://www.scmp.com/news/china/military/article/3116436/xi-jinping-orders-chinas-military-be-ready-war-any-second.

44. For an earlier attempt in this direction, see Lily H. M. Ling, Ching-chane Hwang, and Boyu Chen, "Subaltern Straits: 'Exit,' 'Voice,' and 'Loyalty' in the United States–China–Taiwan Relations," *International Relations of the Asia-Pacific* 10, no. 1 (2010): 33–59.

45. See the discussion on thin normativity by Hartmut Behr and Giorgio Shani, "Rethinking Emancipation in a Critical IR: Normativity, Cosmology, and Pluriversal Dialogue," *Millennium* 49, no. 2 (2022): 375.

46. Lynn Miller, "The Prospects for Regional Order through Regional Security," in *The Future of the International Legal Order: Trends and Patterns*, ed. Cyril E. Black, vol. 1, 556–96 (Princeton, NJ: Princeton University Press, 1969).

47. Andrew Linklater, *The Idea of Civilization and the Making of the Global Order* (Bristol: Bristol University Press, 2020); Norbert Elias, *The Civilizing Process: Sociogenetic and Psychogenetic Investigations* (Oxford: Blackwell, 2000).

48. Mark Beeson, "The Regional Path to Peaceful Change: What the Asian and European Experiences Tell Us," *Ethics & International Affairs* 34, no. 4 (2020): 536.

49. Nina C. Krickel-Choi, "Ontological Security and the Emotional Significance of Sovereignty," in *Variations on Sovereignty: Contestations and Transformations from around the World*, ed. Hannes Černy and Janis Grzybowski, 68–86 (London: Routledge, 2023); Sorpong Peou, "Toward a Security Community in Asia? The Limits of Constructivism, Developmental Statism, Liberalism, and Realism," *International Relations and Diplomacy* 10, no. 1 (2022): 1–24.

50. Hal Brands, "The Battle for Eurasia," *Foreign Policy*, June 4, 2023, https://foreignpolicy.com/2023/06/04/russia-china-us-geopolitics-eurasia-strategy/; Roland Benedikter, "The New Global Direction: From 'One Globalization' to 'Two Globalizations'? Russia's War in Ukraine in Global Perspective," *New Global Studies* 17, no. 1 (2023): 71–104.

51. Tangguh Chairil, Ratu Ayu Asih Kusuma Putri, and Sukmawani Bela Pertiwi, "Road to ASEAN Political Security Community Vision 2025: Understanding Convergence and Divergence in ASEAN Voting Behaviors in the UNGA," *Journal of ASEAN Studies* 10, no. 2 (2022): 275–76.

52. John J. Hogan, "Shame, Exasperation and Institutional Design: The African Union as an Emotional Security Community," *African and Asian Studies* 22, nos. 1–2 (2023): 88–112; Chih-yu Shih, "From 'Asia's East' to 'East Asia': Aborted Decolonization of Taiwan in the Cold-War Discourse," *Asian Perspectives* 44, no. 2 (2020): 279–302.

53. Karin Costa Vazques, "Brazil and Brics Multilateralism à la Carte: From Bilateralism to Community Interest," *Global Policy* 12, no. 4 (2021): 534–38.

54. James MacHaffie, *The Shanghai Cooperation Organization and Conflict De-escalation: Trust Building and Interstate Rivalries* (London: Routledge, 2023); Rafael Duarte Villa, Fabrício H. Chagas-Bastos, and Camila De Macedo Braga, "Going beyond Security Community and Balance of Power: South America's Hybrid Regional Security Governance," *Global Studies Quarterly* 1, no. 4 (2021): 1–10; Amitav Acharya, *ASEAN and Regional Order: Revisiting Security Community in Southeast Asia* (Abingdon, UK: Routledge, 2021); Stéphanie Martel, *Enacting the Security Community: ASEAN's Never-Ending Story* (Stanford, CA: Stanford University Press, 2022).

55. Katie Liston and Elizabeth Moreland, "Hockey and Habitus: Sport and National Identity in Northern Ireland," *New Hibernia Review* 13, no. 4 (2009): 127; John Coakley, "National Identity in Northern Ireland: Stability or Change?," *Nations and Nationalism* 13, no. 4 (2007): 573–93.

Conclusion

1. Xiao Ren, "Grown from Within: Building a Chinese School of International Relations," *Pacific Review* 33, nos. 3–4 (2020): 386–412; Chengxin Pan and Emilian Kavalski, "Theorizing China's Rise in and beyond International Relations," *International Relations of the Asia Pacific* 18, no. 3 (2018): 289–311; Yaqing Qin, "Recent Developments toward a Chinese School of IR Theory," *E-International Relations*, April 26, 2016, https://www.e-ir.info/2016/04/26/recent-developments-toward-a-chinese-school-of-ir-theory/; Tingyang Zhao, "Rethinking Empire from a Chinese Concept 'All-under-Heaven (Tian-xia, 天下),'" *Social Identities* 12, no. 1 (2006): 29–41.

2. For example, Bonnie Girard, "Racism, a Challenge for an Increasingly Global China: Confronting a Problem the PRC Does Not Know It Has," *Brown Journal of World Affairs* 27, no. 2 (2021): 199–215; Astrid H. M. Nordin et al., "Towards Global Relational Theorizing: A Dialogue between Sinophone and Anglophone Scholarship on Relationalism," *Cambridge Review of International Affairs* 32, no. 5 (2019): 570–81; Emilian Kavalski, *The Guanxi of Relational International Theory* (London: Routledge, 2018); Emilian Kavalski, "The Guanxi of Relational International Affairs," *Chinese Political Science Review* 3, no. 3 (2018): 233–51; Yongjin Zhang and Teng-chi Chang, eds., *Constructing a Chinese School of International Relations: Ongoing Debates and Sociological Realities* (London: Routledge, 2016).

3. I would mention Zhao Tingyang, Xu Jilin, Liu Qin, Bai Tongdong, and Zhao He. For further details, see a good review by He Zhao, "Xin tianxia zhuyi: Yizhong shijie zhixu gouxiang de lunzheng yu qinshi" [The principles of neo-*tianxia*: A world-order perspective debated and interpreted], *Forum of World Economics & Politics*, no. 2 (2021): 38–54.

4. Chengxin Pan, "Toward a New Relational Ontology in Global Politics: China's Rise as Holographic Transition," *International Relations of the Asia-Pacific* 18, no. 3 (2018): 355–57; Emanuel Adler, "The Spread of Security Communities: Communities of Practice, Self-Restraint, and NATO's Post–Cold War Transformation," *European Journal of International Relations* 14, no. 2 (2008): 195–230; Alexander Wendt, *Social Theory of International Relations* (Cambridge: Cambridge University Press, 1999).

5. Milja Kurki, "Relational Revolution and Relationality in IR: New Conversations," *Review of International Studies* 48, no. 5 (2021): 1–16; Tamara A. Trownsell et al., "Differing about Difference: Relational IR from around the World," *International Studies Perspectives* 22, no. 1 (2021): 25–64; Tamara Trownsell et al., "Recrafting International Relations through Relationality," *E-International Relations*, January 8, 2019, https://www.e-ir.info/2019/01/08/recrafting-international-relations-through-relationality/.

6. David Blaney and Arlene Tickner, "Worlding, Ontological Politics and the Possibility of a Decolonial IR," *Millennium: Journal of International Studies* 45, no. 3 (2017): 293–311; Arlene B. Tickner and David L. Blaney, eds., *Claiming the International* (London: Routledge, 2013).

7. Nordin et al., "Towards Global Relational Theorizing"; Kavalski, *Guanxi*; Nele Noesselt, "Revisiting the Debate of Constructing a Theory of International Relations with Chinese Characteristics," *China Quarterly* 222 (2015): 430–48.

8. Kurki, "Relational Revolution"; Chengxin Pan, "Enfolding Wholes in Parts: Quantum Holography and International Relations," *European Journal of International Relations* 26, no. 1 (2020): 14–38; Chengxin Pan, "Enfolding Wholes in Parts: Quantum Holography and International Relations," *European Journal of International Relations* 26, no. 1 (2020): 14–38.

9. Kosuke Shimizu and Sei Noro, "Political Healing and Mahāyāna Buddhist Medicine: A Critical Engagement with Contemporary International Relations," *Third World Quarterly* (2021), https://doi.org/10.1080/01436597.2021.1891878; Lily H. M. Ling, *The Dao of World Politics: Towards a Post-Westphalian, Worldist International Relations* (London: Routledge, 2014).

10. Hung-jen Wang, "Chinese IR Scholarship as a Relational Epistemology in the Study of China's Rise," *China Quarterly* 245 (2021): 262–75; Zhang and Chang, *Chinese School*; Pan and Kavalski, "Theorizing China's Rise."

11. Ren, "Grown from Within."

12. Qin, "Recent Developments."

13. Yih-Jye Hwang, "Reappraising the Chinese School of International Relations: A Postcolonial Perspective," *Review of International Studies* 47, no. 3 (2021): 311–30; Yuzo Mizoguchi, *China as Method* (Tokyo: University of Tokyo Press, 1989); Paul Cohen, *Discovering History in China: American Historical Writing on the Recent Chinese Past* (New York: Columbia University Press, 1984).

14. Martin Jacques, *When China Ruled the World: The Rise of the Middle Kingdom and the End of the Western World* (London: Penguin Books, 2009).

15. William A. Callahan, "Chinese Visions of World Order: Post-hegemonic or a New Hegemony?," *International Studies Review* 10, no. 4 (2008): 749–61.

16. Fei-Ling Wang, *The China Order* (Albany: State University of New York Press, 2017); Michael Pillsbury, *The Hundred-Year Marathon: China's Secret Strategy to Replace America as the Global Superpower* (New York: St. Martin's Griffin, 2016).

17. Sinan Chu, "Whither Chinese IR? The Sinocentric Subject and the Paradox of Tianxia-ism," *International Theory* 14, no. 1 (2020): 57–87, https://doi.org/10.1017/S1752971920000214; Yan Xuetong, "Why Is There No Chinese School of International Relations Theory?," in *Ancient Chinese Thought, Modern Chinese Power*, ed. Yan Xuetong, 252–60 (Princeton, NJ: Princeton University, 2011); Tingyang Zhao, "A Political World Philosophy in Terms of All-under-Heaven," *Diogenes* 56, no. 1 (2009): 4–25; Tingyang Zhao, "Rethinking Empire."

18. Xuetong Yan, "Chinese Values vs. Liberalism: What Ideology Will Shape the International Normative Order?" *Chinese Journal of International Politics* 11, no. 1 (2018): 1–22; Salvatore Babones, "Taking China Seriously: Relationality, *Tianxia*, and the 'Chinese School' of International Relations," in *Oxford Research Encyclopedia of Politics* (Oxford University Press, 2017), https://doi.org/10.1093/acrefore/9780190228637.013.602.

19. For a glimpse of its range, see Trownsell et al., "Differing about Difference"; or Kavalski, "*Guanxi.*"

20. Miles M. Evers, "Just the Facts: Why Norms Remain Relevant in an Age of Practice," *International Theory* 12, no. 2 (2020): 220–30; Simon Frankel Pratt, "From Norms to Normative Configurations: A Pragmatist and Relational Approach to Theorizing Normativity in IR," *International Theory* 12, no. 1 (2019): 59–82.

21. Peeter Selg and Andreas Ventsel, *Introducing Relational Political Analysis: Political Semiotics as a Theory and Method* (Berlin: Springer, 2020), 15–40.

22. Emilian Kavalski, "*Guanxi* or What Is the Chinese for Relational Theory of World Politics," *International Relations of the Asia-Pacific* 18, no. 3 (2018): 397–420; Yong Wook Lee, "Relational Ontology and the Politics of Boundary-Making: East Asian Financial Regionalism," *Politics* 39, no. 1 (2019): 18–34.

23. Arlene B. Tickner and Amaya Querejazu, "Weaving Worlds: *Cosmopraxis* as Relational Sensibility," *International Studies Review* 23, no. 2 (2021): 391–408; Milja Kurki, *International Relations in a Relational Universe* (Oxford: Oxford University Press, 2020); Deepshikha Shahi, "Introducing Sufism to International Relations Theory: A Preliminary Inquiry into Epistemological, Ontological, and Methodological Pathways," *European Journal of International Relations* 25, no. 1 (2019): 250–75; Tod D. Swanson and Jarrad Reddekop, "Looking Like the Land: Beauty and Aesthetics in Amazonian Quichua Philosophy and Practice," *Journal of the American Academy of Religion* 85, no. 3 (2017): 682–708.

24. Marcos S. Scauso, "Intersectional Decoloniality: Listening to the Other 'Others,'" *E-International Relations*, June 4, 2021, https://www.e-ir.info/2021/06/04/intersectional-decoloniality-listening-to-the-other-others/.

25. Yan Xuetong, *Leadership and the Rise of Great Powers* (Princeton, NJ: Princeton University Press, 2019).

26. Xiao Ren, "China as an Institution-Builder: The Case of the AIIB," *Pacific Review* 29, no. 3 (2016): 435–42.

27. Tingyang Zhao, *Redefining a Philosophy for World Governance*, trans. Liqing Tao (New York: Palgrave Macmillan, 2019).

28. Yaqing Qin, "A Relational Theory of World Politics," *International Studies Review* 18, no. 1 (2016): 33–47.

29. Francis Fukuyama, "The End of History?" *National Interest*, no. 16 (Summer 1989): 3–18.

30. Alexander Wendt, "Why a World State Is Inevitable," *European Journal of International Relations* 9, no. 4 (2003): 491–542.

31. Tingyang Zhao, *Redefining a Philosophy*; Tingyang Zhao, "Political World Philosophy."

32. Callahan, "Chinese Visions of World Order."

33. Marcos S. Scauso, *Intersectional Decoloniality: Reimagining IR and the Problem of Difference* (New York: Routledge, 2021).

34. Norbert Elias, *On the Process of Civilisation: Sociogenetic and Psychogenetic Investigations* (Dublin: University College Dublin Press, 2012).

35. Charles W. Mills, "Dialogues in Black and White," *Journal of World Philosophies* 2, no. 1 (2017): 160–63; Linda M. G. Zerilli, "Doing without Knowing: Feminism's Politics of the Ordinary," in *The Grammar of Politics: Wittgenstein and Political Philosophy*, ed. Cressida J. Heyes, 129–48 (Ithaca, NY: Cornell University Press, 2003); Walter D. Mignolo, "The Many Faces of Cosmo-polis: Border Thinking and Critical Cosmopolitanism," *Public Culture* 12, no. 3 (2000): 721–48.

36. Jeffrey Sachs, *A New Foreign Policy: Beyond American Exceptionalism* (New York: Columbia University Press, 2018).

37. Gayatri Chakravorty Spivak, *Other Asias* (Malden, MA: Blackwell, 2008).

38. Amitav Acharya and Barry Buzan, "Why Is There No Non-Western International Relations Theory? An Introduction," *International Relations of the Asia-Pacific* 7, no. 3 (2007): 287–312.

39. Reena Marwah, "Colonial Connections through Commerce and Culture: Revisiting China Studies in India," in *Colonial Legacies and Contemporary Studies of China and Chineseness: Unlearning Binaries, Strategizing Self*, ed. Chih-yu Shih et al., 3–24 (Singapore: World Scientific, 2020); Carmelea Ang See, "Examining the Challenges and Possibilities in Tsinoy Studies," in *China Studies in the Philippines: Intellectual Paths and the Formation of a Field*, ed. Tina S. Clemente and Chih-yu Shih, 57–80 (Abingdon, UK: Routledge, 2019); Nordin et al., "Towards Global Relational Theorizing"; Peter J. Katzenstein, ed., *Sinicization and the Rise of China: Civilizational Processes beyond East and West* (London: Routledge, 2012).

40. Kimberly Hutchings, "Decolonizing Global Ethics: Thinking with the Pluriverse," *Ethics & International Affairs* 33, no. 2 (2019):115–25; Pan, "Toward a New Relational Ontology in Global Politics"; Lily H. M. Ling, "World Politics in Color," *Millenium* 45, no. 3 (2017): 473–91.

41. Lu Peng, "Chinese IR Sino-centrism Tradition and Its Influence on the Chinese School Movement," *Pacific Review* 32, no. 2 (2018): 150–67.

42. Zeynep Gulsah Capan, Filipe dos Reis, and Maj Grasten, eds., *The Politics of Translation in International Relations* (Cham, Switzerland: Palgrave Macmillan, 2021).

43. He Zhao, "Xin tianxia zhuyi: Yizhong shijie zhixu gouxiang de lunzheng yu qinshi" [The principles of neo-*tianxia*: A world-order perspective debated and interpreted], *Forum of World Economics & Politics*, no. 2 (2021): 38–54.

44. Mills, "Dialogues in Black and White," 160–63; Zerilli, "Doing without Knowing"; Mignolo, "Many Faces of Cosmo-polis."

45. Costas M. Constantinou and James Der Derian, "Sustaining Global Hope: Sovereignty, Power and the Transformation of Diplomacy," in *Sustainable Diplomacies*, ed. Costas M. Constantinou and James Der Derian, 1–22 (New York: Palgrave Macmillan, 2010).

46. Sabelo J. Ndlovu-Gatsheni, "A World without Others? Specter of Difference and Toxic Identitarian Politics," *International Journal of Critical Diversity Studies* 1, no. 1 (2018): 80–96.

47. Andrew Linklater, *The Idea of Civilization and the Making of Global Order* (Bristol, UK: Bristol University Press, 2020); Shogo Suzuki, "Seeking 'Legitimate' Great Power Status in Post-Cold War International Society: China's and Japan's Participation in UNPKO," *International Relations* 22, no. 1 (2008): 45–63; Christopher Hobson, "Democracy as Civilization," *Global Society* 22, no. 1 (2008): 75–95.

48. Kosuke Shimizu, "Buddhism and the Question of Relationality in International Relations," *Uluslararası İlişkiler* 18, no. 70 (2021): 29–44, https://dx.doi.org/10.33458/uidergisi.954738; Kurki, "Relational Revolution"; Bentley B. Allan, *Scientific Cosmology and International Orders* (Cambridge: Cambridge University Press, 2018); Ling, *The Dao of World Politics*; Kenneth Waltz, *Man, the State, and War: A Theoretical Analysis* (New York: Columbia University Press, 1959).

49. Elias, *On the Process of Civilisation*; David Kang, *East Asia before the West: Five Centuries of Trade and Tribute* (New York: Columbia University Press, 2010); Takeshi Hamashita, *China, East Asia and the Global Economy: Regional and Historical Perspectives*, ed. Linda Grove and Mark Selden (London: Routledge, 2008); Wendt, *Social Theory*; Hedley Bull, *The Anarchical Society: A Study of Order in World Politics* (London: Macmillan, 1997).

50. Katzenstein, *Sinicization*; Jacques, *When China Ruled the World*; Suzuki, "Seeking 'Legitimate' Great Power Status"; John H. Berthrong, *All under Heaven: Transforming Paradigms in Confucian-Christian Dialogue* (Albany: State University of New York Press, 1994).

51. Ling, *The Dao of World Politics*.

52. Kristin Haugevik and Iver B. Neumann, eds., *Kinship in International Relations* (London: Routledge, 2018).

53. John Lowe and Stephan Ortmann, "Unmasking Nativism in Asia's World City: Graffiti and Identity Boundary Un/making in Hong Kong," *Continuum* 34, no. 3 (2020): 398–416; Ellie Vasta, "The Migrant 'Stranger' at Home: 'Australian' Shared Values and the National Imaginary," in *Reimagining Home*

in the 21st Century, ed. Justine Lloyd and Ellie Vasta, 36–53 (Cheltenham, UK: Edward Elgar, 2017).

54. Hamashita, *China East Asia and the Global Economy*.

55. Evers, "Just the Facts."

56. Garrett FitzGerald and Justin de Leon, "Moving Beyond Inclusivity," *International History and Politics Newsletter* 6, no. 2 (2020): 19–22; Marisol De La Cadena, "Indigenous Cosmopolitics in the Andes: Conceptual Reflections beyond 'Politics,'" *Cultural Anthropology* 25, no. 2 (2010): 334–70.

57. Chih-yu Shih et al., *China and International Theory: The Balance of Relationships* (London: Routledge, 2019).

58. I am indebted to the notion of the rights of nature in both a Hobbesian and Lockean sense. A third possibility is to translate the southern African idea of *Ubuntu* as "the necessity of all to nurture all."

59. Chaehyun Chong, "Moism: Despotic or Democratic?," *Journal of Chinese Philosophy* 35, no. 3 (2008): 511–21.

60. David E. Cooper, "Daoism, Nature and Humanity," *Royal Institute of Philosophy Supplements* 74 (2014): 95–108.

61. Fainos Mangena, "*Hunhu/Ubuntu* in the Traditional Thought of Southern Africa," *Internet Encyclopedia of Philosophy*, accessed September 30, 2020, https://iep.utm.edu/hunhu/.

62. Chenyang Li, "In Defense of a Conception of Confucian Harmony," *Philosophy East and West* 67, no. 1 (2017): 256–66.

63. Chenyang Li, "Confucian Harmony, Greek Harmony, and Liberal Harmony," *Dao* 15, no. 3 (2016): 427–35; Stephen C. Angle, "Human Rights and Harmony," *Human Rights Quarterly* 30, no. 1 (2008): 76–94.

64. Berthrong, *All under Heaven*.

65. Lina Benabdallah, *Shaping the Future of Power: Knowledge Production and Network-Building in China-Africa Relations* (Ann Arbor: University of Michigan Press, 2020).

66. Chih-yu Shih, "Friendship in Chinese International Relations: The Confucian Theme of Distance in Practice," *Communist and Post-Communist Studies* 53, no. 4 (2020): 177–99.

67. Jorg Kustermans, "Diplomatic Gifts: An Introduction to the Forum," *The Hague Journal of Diplomacy* 16, no. 1 (2021): 105–9.

68. Ertuğrul Ceylan, "A Review on the Huiru Movement and Key Terms of Traditional Chinese Thought Used in Wang Daiyu's Work," *International Journal of China Studies* 11, no. 2 (2020): 371–92.

69. Shin Kawashima, "The Propagation of Japanese Buddhism in China, 1910–40s: Japan as the Guardian of East Asian 'Traditions,'" *International Journal of China Studies* 11, no. 2 (2020): 213–30.

70. Yitzhak Shichor, "Combining Contradictions: Jewish Contribution to the Chinese Revolution," *International Journal of China Studies* 11, no. 2 (2020): 183–212.

71. Luisa M. Paternicò, "Sinitic Languages in the English Periodical Press of 19th Century China: Focus on *The Chinese Repository* and *The China Review*," *International Journal of China Studies* 11, no. 2 (2020): 347–70; Alexei D. Voskressenski, "The Russian Ecclesiastical Missions (1715–1864) to Peking and Their Influence on China Studies in Russia," *International Journal of China Studies* 11, no. 2 (2020): 231–56.

72. William A. Callahan, "Diasporic Tycoons, Outlaw States, and Beijing Bastards: The Contingent Politics of Greater China," *East Asia* 21, no. 1 (2004): 65–75.

73. For a representative statement, see H. E. Wang Yi, "Working as Cooperation Partners for True Multilateralism," Ministry of Foreign Affairs of the PRC, July 10, 2022, https://www.fmprc.gov.cn/mfa_eng/wjdt_665385/zyjh_665391/202207/t20220710_10718093.html.

74. See the New Atlantic Charter, issued by the White House on June 10, 2021, https://www.whitehouse.gov/briefing-room/statements-releases/2021/06/10/the-new-atlantic-charter/.

75. Zhao Xiaochun, "In Pursuit of a Community of Shared Future: China's Global Activism in Perspective," *China Quarterly of International Strategic Studies* 4, no. 1 (2018): 23–37.

76. Yuen Yuen Ang, *How China Escaped the Poverty Trap* (Ithaca, NY: Cornell University Press, 2016); Raoul Bunskoek, "'Community of Common Destiny' as Post-Western Regionalism: Rethinking China's Belt and Road Initiative from a Confucian Perspective," *Uluslararası İlişkiler* 18, no. 70 (2021): 85–101, https://doi.org/10.33458/uidergisi.954744; Tianbiao Zhu, "Compressed Development, Flexible Practices, and Multiple Traditions in China's Rise," in Katzenstein, *Sinicization*, 99–119.

77. Kavalski, "*Guanxi.*"

78. Chiung-chiu Huang and Tung Cong Nguyen, "Dancing between Beijing and Taipei: Vietnam in the Shadow of the Belt and Road Initiative," *China Review* 22, no. 2 (2022): 315–39.

79. Maéva Clément and Eric Sangar, eds., *Researching Emotions in International Relations* (London: Palgrave, 2018); Janice Bially Mattern, "On Being Convinced: An Emotional Epistemology of International Relations," *International Theory* 6, no. 3 (2014): 589–94; Jonathan Mercer, "Feeling Like a State: Social Emotion and Identity," *International Theory* 6, no. 3 (2014): 515–35.

80. Stéphane Côté, Ivona Hideg, and Gerben A. van Kleef, "The Consequences of Faking Anger in Negotiations," *Journal of Experimental Social Psychology* 49, no. 3 (2013): 453–63.

81. The One China principle mainly refers to the territorial claims concerning Tibet, Xinjiang, Hong Kong, and Taiwan, alongside their concomitant belonging to the domain of China's internal affairs.

Index

www.ingramcontent.com/pod-product-compliance
Lightning Source LLC
Chambersburg PA
CBHW020336270326
41926CB00007B/209